Palgrave Studies in Cultural and Intellectual History

Series Editors

Anthony J. La Vopa, North Carolina State University.
Suzanne Marchand, Louisiana State University.
Javed Majeed, Queen Mary, University of London.

The Palgrave Studies in Cultural and Intellectual History series has three primary aims: to close divides between intellectual and cultural approaches, thus bringing them into mutually enriching interactions; to encourage interdisciplinarity in intellectual and cultural history; and to globalize the field, both in geographical scope and in subjects and methods. This series is open to work on a range of modes of intellectual inquiry, including social theory and the social sciences; the natural sciences; economic thought; literature; religion; gender and sexuality; philosophy; political and legal thought; psychology; and music and the arts. It encompasses not just North America but Africa, Asia, Eurasia, Europe, Latin America, and the Middle East. It includes both nationally focused studies and studies of intellectual and cultural exchanges between different nations and regions of the world, and encompasses research monographs, synthetic studies, edited collections, and broad works of reinterpretation. Regardless of methodology or geography, all books in the series are historical in the fundamental sense of undertaking rigorous contextual analysis.

Published by Palgrave Macmillan:

Indian Mobilities in the West, 1900–1947: Gender, Performance, Embodiment
By Shompa Lahiri

The Shelley-Byron Circle and the Idea of Europe
By Paul Stock

Culture and Hegemony in the Colonial Middle East
By Yaseen Noorani

Recovering Bishop Berkeley: Virtue and Society in the Anglo-Irish Context
By Scott Breuninger

The Reading of Russian Literature in China: A Moral Example and Manual of Practice
By Mark Gamsa

Rammohun Roy and the Making of Victorian Britain
By Lynn Zastoupil

Carl Gustav Jung: Avant-Garde Conservative
By Jay Sherry

Law and Politics in British Colonial Thought: Transpositions of Empire
By Shaunnagh Dorsett and Ian Hunter, eds.

Sir John Malcolm and the Creation of British India (forthcoming)
By Jack Harrington

The American Bourgeoisie: Distinction and Identity in the Nineteenth Century (forthcoming)
By Sven Beckert and Julia Rosenbaum, eds.

Benjamin Constant and the Birth of French Liberalism (forthcoming)
By K. Steven Vincent

Character, Self, and Sociability in the Scottish Enlightenment (forthcoming)
By Thomas Ahnert and Susan Manning, eds.

Nature Engaged: Science in Practice from the Renaissance to the Present (forthcoming)
By Jessica Riskin and Mario Biagioli, eds.

Law and Politics in British Colonial Thought

Transpositions of Empire

Edited by

Shaunnagh Dorsett

and

Ian Hunter

palgrave
macmillan

LAW AND POLITICS IN BRITISH COLONIAL THOUGHT

First published in 2010 by
PALGRAVE MACMILLAN®
in the United States—a division of St. Martin's Press LLC,
175 Fifth Avenue, New York, NY 10010.

Where this book is distributed in the UK, Europe and the rest of the world, this is by Palgrave Macmillan, a division of Macmillan Publishers Limited, registered in England, company number 785998, of Houndmills, Basingstoke, Hampshire RG21 6XS.

Palgrave Macmillan is the global academic imprint of the above companies and has companies and representatives throughout the world.

ISBN: 978–0–230–10455–6

Library of Congress Cataloging-in-Publication Data is available from the Library of Congress.

A catalogue record of the book is available from the British Library.

Design by Newgen Imaging Systems (P) Ltd., Chennai, India.

First edition: November 2010

10 9 8 7 6 5 4 3 2 1

Printed in the United States of America.

Contents

A Note on the Cover Image

The cover image displays the coat of arms of Baron de Thierry (1793–1864) dating from c. 1825 or 1840 (Armes du Baron de Thierry, Charles Ier, roi de Nouvelle Zelande, Warner sc., London or Cambridge?, c. 1825 or 1840, A-320–026, Alexander Turnbull Library, Wellington). Based in Paris, Thierry purchased land at Hokianga, New Zealand, proclaimed himself sovereign chief of the country, and moved there in 1837. He then sought to press his claim to sovereignty on the basis of the alleged agreement of Maori chiefs and the supposed support of the French government, only to find his land purchases repudiated. His bid was finally quashed by the Treaty of Waitangi in 1840.

Acknowledgments

The contributions to this volume were first trialed at a symposium—Transpositions of Empire—held at the Monash Centre, Prato, on April 20–22, 2009. The editors are grateful to the Centre for the History of European Discourses (University of Queensland) and Victoria University of Wellington, for their joint sponsorship of this event. We are also grateful to the Monash Centre's staff for their courteous and efficient organization, to Sarah Collins for her scrupulous editorial work, and to Averil Condren for the index.

Contributors

Shaunnagh Dorsett is Associate Professor in the Faculty of Law at the University of Technology, Sydney. She researches at the intersections of legal history, history of political thought, and jurisprudence. She has written extensively on colonial governance, including on sovereignty, jurisdiction, and the legal settlement of Australia and New Zealand. Her publications include "'Sworn on the Dirt of Graves': Sovereignty, Jurisdiction and the Judicial Abrogation of Barbarous Customs in New Zealand in the 1840s," *The Journal of Legal History*, 30 (2009), 175–197; "The *Persona* Of The Jurist In Salmond's *Jurisprudence*: On The Exposition of 'What Law Is…,'" 38 (2007) *VUWLR* 771–796 (with Shaun McVeigh); and "'Since Time Immemorial': A Story of Common Law Jurisdiction, Native Title and the *Case of Tanistry*," *Melbourne University Law Review*, 26 (2002), 32–59.

Mark Finnane is Professor of History and an ARC Australian Professorial Fellow at Griffith University, where he is a Chief Investigator in the ARC Centre of Excellence in Policy and Security. Professor Finnane has written for many years at the intersections of colonial history, crime, and policing in Australia. His major works include *JV Barry: A Life* (UNSW Press, 2007); *Punishment in Australian Society* (Oxford University Press, 1997); *Police and Government: Histories of Policing in Australia* (Oxford University Press, 1994), and *Insanity and the Insane in Post-Famine Ireland* (Croom Helm, 1981).

Andrew Fitzmaurice is Associate Professor in the Department of History at the University of Sydney. He has published widely in the areas of Early Modern British, European and Atlantic history, the history of political thought, and the history of colonization. Dr Fitzmaurice's publications include *Humanism and America: An Intellectual History of English Colonisation*, 1500–1625 (Cambridge University Press, 2003); "The Commercial Ideology of Colonisation in Jacobean England: Robert Johnson, Giovanni Botero and the Pursuit of Greatness," *William and Mary Quarterly*, October 2007; "A Genealogy of Terra Nullius," *Australian Historical Studies*, April 2007.

Lisa Ford is a Lecturer in the Department of History and Philosophy at the University of New South Wales. Dr. Ford's research centers on ideas and practices of sovereignty in nineteenth-century settler polities. These are explored in depth in her book *Settler Sovereignty* (Cambridge, MA: Harvard University Press, 2010). Her other recent publications include "Empire and Order on the Colonial Frontiers of Georgia and New South Wales," *Itinerario: Geographies of Empire* 3 (2006): 95–113; and "From Pluralism to Territorial Sovereignty: The 1816 Trial of Mow-watty in the Superior Court of New South Wales," *Indigenous Law Journal* (Toronto) 7.1 (2008) (with Brent Salter).

Mark Hickford is Crown Counsel at Crown Law Wellington, New Zealand and the 2008 New Zealand Law Foundation International Research Fellow. Dr. Hickford researches in British imperial history and the history of political thought and has published widely in the area of Maori proprietary rights. His publications include "'Decidedly the Most Interesting Savages on the Globe': An Approach to the Intellectual History of Māori Property Rights, 1837–1853," *History of Political Thought*, 27 (2006), 122–167; "John Salmond and Native Title in New Zealand: Developing a Crown Theory on the Treaty of Waitangi, 1910–1920," *Victoria University of Wellington Law Review*, 38 (2007) 853–924; and "Strands from the Afterlife of Confiscation: Property Rights, Constitutional Histories and the Political Incorporation of Maori, 1920s," in *Raupatu: The Confiscation of Maori Land*, ed. by Richard Boast and Richard Hill (Victoria University Press, Wellington, 2009).

Ian Hunter is an Australian Professorial Fellow in the Centre for the History of European Discourses at the University of Queensland and is a leading scholar in the history of early modern political, religious, and philosophical thought. His major publications include *Rival Enlightenments: Civil and Metaphysical Philosophy in Early Modern Germany* (Cambridge University Press, 2001); *Natural Law and Civil Sovereignty: Moral Right and State Authority in Early Modern Political Thought* (Palgrave, 2002) (coedited with David Saunders); and *The Secularisation of the Confessional State: The Political Thought of Christian Thomasius* (Cambridge University Press, 2007).

Duncan Ivison is Professor of Political Philosophy in the Department of Philosophy at the University of Sydney. He has published extensively in the areas of political theory, history of political thought, theories of justice, and the rights of indigenous peoples. Among his many publications are *The Self at Liberty: Political Argument and the Arts of Government* (Cornell University Press, 1997); *Postcolonial Liberalism* (Cambridge University

Press, 2002); *Rights* (Acumen and McGill Queens Press, 2008); *Political Theory and the Rights of Indigenous Peoples* (Cambridge University Press, 2000; reprinted 2002) (coedited with Paul Patton and Will Sanders); and most recently, as editor, *The Ashgate Research Companion to Multiculturalism* (Ashgate Press, 2010).

P.G. McHugh is Reader in Law at the Department of Land Economy at Cambridge University and a Fellow of Sidney Sussex College. He has published extensively in the areas of aboriginal law and legal historiography. Dr. McHugh's major works include *Aboriginal Societies and the Common Law: A History of Sovereignty, Status and Self-determination* (Oxford University Press, 2005) and *The Maori Magna Carta. New Zealand Law and the Treaty of Waitangi* (Oxford University Press, 1991). He is editor (with Andrew Sharp) of *Histories, Power and Loss: Uses of the Past—A New Zealand Commentary* (Bridget Williams Books, 2001).

John McLaren is Emeritus Professor of Law at the University of Victoria in Canada. He is one of Canada's foremost legal historians. Professor McLaren has published on numerous topics in legal history and has been the recipient of a number of awards for his work. He is currently finishing a monograph entitled *"Dewigged, Bothered and Bewildered": British Colonial Judges on Trial, 1800–1900*. His many earlier publications include *Religious Conscience, the State and the Law: Historical Contexts and Contemporary Significance* (State University New York Press, 1998) (ed. with Harold Coward) and *Despotic Dominion: Law and the History of Property Rights in British Settler Societies* (UBC Press, 2005) (ed. with Andrew Buck and Nancy Wright).

Andrew Sharp is an Emeritus Professor in Political Studies at the University of Auckland, New Zealand. His main intellectual interest is in the development, application of, and opposition to liberal-democratic thinking and philosophizing, with special reference to seventeenth-century England, contemporary New Zealand, and multicultural societies generally. His major works include *The English Levellers* (as editor) (Cambridge University Press, 1998 and 2001); *Political Ideas of the English Civil Wars, 1640–49* (Longmans, 1983 and 1988); and *Justice and the Maori: Philosophy and the Practice of Maori Claims in New Zealand Political Argument since the 1970s* (Oxford University Press, 1990, 1991, and 1997). He has edited (with Paul McHugh) *Histories, Power and Loss: Uses of the Past—A New Zealand Commentary* (Bridget Williams Books, 2001). He is currently writing a book on Samuel Marsden.

Christopher Tomlins is Chancellor's Professor of Law at the University of California, Irvine and formerly Research Professor at the American

Bar Foundation. He is one of the leading legal historians in the United States. He has published on a wide range of topics in legal history, from the beginning of the sixteenth century into the later twentieth century, including the use of law as both a discourse and a technique for the implementation of colonizing activities and practices. Professor Tomlins is editor (with Michael Grossberg) of the multi-volume *Cambridge History of Law in America* (2008) and author of *Freedom Bound: Law, Labor, and Civic Identity in Colonizing English America, 1580–1865* (Cambridge University Press, 2010). He has published numerous other books, and over one hundred articles and chapters.

Mark D. Walters is Professor in the Faculty of Law, Queens University (Canada). He has published widely in the areas of constitutional law, legal history, and legal theory and is well-known for his work on the status of Aboriginal customary laws and government in colonial Canada. His publications include "Legal Humanism and Law as Integrity," *Cambridge Law Journal*, 67 (2008), 352–375; "Histories of Colonialism, Legality and Aboriginality," *University of Toronto Law Journal, 57 (2007)*, 819–832; "The Extension of Colonial Criminal Jurisdiction over the Aboriginal Peoples of Upper Canada: Reconsidering the *Shawanakiskie* Case (1822–26)," *University of Toronto Law Journal*, 46 (1996), 273–310.

Damen Ward is Crown Counsel at Crown Law, Wellington, New Zealand. He researches on colonial governance, settler politics, and aboriginal status in nineteenth-century colonies. Dr. Ward's publications include "Constructing British Authority in Australasia: Charles Cooper and the Legal Status of Aborigines in the South Australian Supreme Court, c. 1840–1860," *Journal of Imperial and Commonwealth History* 34 (2006), 483–504; "A Means and Measure of Civilisation: Colonial Authorities and Indigenous Law in Australasia," *History Compass* 1 (2003), AU 049, 001–024; and "Civil Jurisdiction, Settler Politics and the Colonial Constitution c. 1840–1858," *Victoria University of Wellington Law Review*, 39 (2008), 497–532.

Introduction

Ian Hunter and Shaunnagh Dorsett

The chapters in this volume were generated from a gathering of scholars working on the role of law in colonial societies. All participants in a series of discussions that were held in Prato, Italy, in April 2009 were asked to reflect on the forms in which metropolitan legal doctrines and practices were transposed in colonial settings as part of processes of appropriating territory, subduing indigenous populations, and establishing European governance. Thus discussions concentrated on the relation between law and politics in transpositions of empire or rule in colonial enterprises. In order to sharpen the focus, concrete examples were drawn principally from British colonies. In keeping with the "historical turn" in studies of imperialism and international law, and in an effort to combine legal history and the history of political thought, scholars representing this array of expertise were asked to join forces.[1] As a result, legal historians of empire, social historians of colonization, historians and philosophers of political thought, all found themselves in the same space sharing their research and arguments. The chapters in this book thus have as their substantive focus the relations between law and politics in British colonial settings, and they find their methodological convergence in the (sometimes difficult) nexus between legal history, social history, and the history and philosophy of political thought.

In the event, discussion of the substantive relation between law and politics turns out to be multiplex and contested. This is as a result of the fact that it is overdetermined by the superimposition of two quite different approaches to the relationship. In accordance with the first approach—formed by the nexus of legal history and contextualist history of political thought—relations between law and politics are shaped by the interaction of two counterpoised historical moments: the historical role of judicial systems in ordering the exercise of government in accordance with the "rule of law"; and the historical fact of the governmental use of law as an instrument of rule or empire. This sometimes fraught interaction is typically managed via the instrumentality of public law, which includes inter alia fundamental laws for the establishment of colonies; imperial acts and local ordinances establishing basic institutions; statutes legitimating the appropriation and distribution of land; and treaties between colonizing sovereigns and indigenous "nations." *Jus gentium* doctrines and common law determinations also feed into this process. Public law manages this interaction immanently rather than transcendentally and thus itself manifests the unstable interaction between the role of law as a normative means of ordering government (where it is known as constitutional law) and as the instrumental means of exercising it (where it is known as public law).

In British colonial thought and practice the public law management of the interaction between law and politics was epitomized by the juridical construct of the "Crown." As a public law construction, and depending on concrete historical circumstances, the Crown could function as both the juridically constrained legal personality of the British sovereign and as the legal cipher through which an unconstrained British sovereignty was exercised through the imposed rule of its law. As the principal colonies discussed in the following chapters were British "Crown colonies," they present us with a series of examples in which attempts to transpose the formal legal personality of the British sovereign in colonial jurisdictions had to be undertaken in circumstances where British sovereignty and the rule of its law had yet to be established as a political or governmental fact. In such frontier circumstances—where advocates of settler liberties sought to re-contest the prerogative rights of the Crown; where state authority lacked the disciplinary instruments to control both them and its own soldiery; and where the rule of law was to be imposed on indigenous peoples whose political and cultural amenability to it was radically contested—it was impossible for the settled judicial attributes of the metropolitan Crown to be simply imposed in the colonies, for better or worse. Rather, as several of the following chapters show in detail, what we find is that the juridical attributes of the Crown were subject to a whole series of political improvisations and innovations, as this highly contextual public law construct was continuously adapted to the governance of settlers whose British subjecthood had blurred at the frontier, and of indigenous peoples whose British subjecthood was a matter of governmental aspiration rather than legal proclamation.

Despite the fact that they are typically found together, the second approach to the relation between law and politics differs fundamentally from this first one. Rather than focusing on public law as the historical nexus for the legal ordering of politics and the political utilization of law, the second approach treats law itself as only a proxy for a higher normative principle—variously justice, right, or the good—whose actualization in history is commanded by reason or nature. Methodologically, this approach is grounded in the nexus between legal history and philosophy or philosophical history, and, in treating law as the exponent of justice, right, or the good, it establishes a normative rather than historical relation between law and politics. In the peculiar mytho-history of the English common law, this normative relation is carried in the story of timeless common law tradition whose "time immemorial" rights and liberties lie beyond the reach of any merely historical sovereign powers and function as a permanent check on the latter.[2] Of more importance for our current concerns, however, is the normative relation between law and politics established by certain constructions of natural law: first, the Thomistic Catholic construction, according to which justice is the preeminent virtue derived from the imperative that man must complete or perfect his nascent ("rational and sociable") nature or essence; and second, the Kantian Protestant construction, according to which law is grounded in a higher "principle of right," understood in terms of the harmonization of potentially conflicting wills in a community of rational beings.[3] On either construal, law as the exponent of a higher justice or right obtains normative preeminence over politics, which in exercising power on grounds other than those of justice or right (typically in exercising "Hobbesian" sovereignty on the grounds of territorial security) is regarded as contravening the justice embedded in man's nature or the right embedded in his reason, and so too the merely "positive" or historical law that allows itself to function as a mere instrument of such politics.

When this philosophico-legal or philosophico-historical approach to the relation between law and politics is applied to the deployment of law in colonial settings, it constitutes a means of formulating retrospective normative regret for the historical existence of colonialism and imperialism. From this viewpoint, the European exercise of sovereignty and governance over indigenous peoples in a manner that contravenes justice or right—to whose norms it is presumed such peoples have subscribed through their nature or reason—represents a regrettable deviation from the true historical unfolding of these norms, brought about by an unjust politics and the law it has suborned. This view contrasts starkly with the public law view of the law-politics relation, which, since the seventeenth century, has treated the exercise of sovereignty—including its exercise over conquered nations—as an untranscendable historical-political fact: something that public law seeks to order in accordance with fundamental enactments or treaties, but to which it remains immanent as the exponent not of a higher justice or right but only of these historical enactments and treaties.[4] The philosophico-historical approach has commended itself to postcolonial scholars in particular. They have been drawn to the recovery of natural law in order to effect the normative condemnation of a "positive" law rendered complicit in colonialism and imperialism through its political corruption. Although they continue to maintain a historical view of this process, theirs is a history oriented to what should have happened rather than what happened to happen.

In current research these two approaches to the relation between law and politics in colonial settings do not function as strict alternatives. They operate rather as the opposed poles of a single research field, their counterpoised forces establishing a wide spectrum of positions, characterized not by sharp demarcations but by gradual transitions. All of the contributions to the present volume find their place in this spectrum between the public law historiography of colonial legal governance as a historical fact, and the philosophical history of it as a normative political deviation; most of the chapters contain both perspectives, often shaping their perspectives in the torsion between the two.

It is appropriate then that Part I should contain two chapters that come as close as possible to the two poles that define the field. In his contribution Ian Hunter makes an uncompromising case for an immanent public law historiography of the colonial uses of the law of nature and nations. Explicitly targeting the "critical" philosophical historiography of postcolonial studies, Hunter argues that the natural law perspectives underlying this historiography—neo-Thomist, neo-Kantian, and deconstructionist—constitute "regional" European metaphysical subcultures. Rather than supplying a global normative justice capable of registering the normative deviation of colonialist uses of European law, Hunter argues that such perspectives are themselves ineluctably Eurocentric, indicating that colonial encounters could not be mediated by philosophical reason, only managed in a fumbling manner through law and politics. Rejecting the kind of case made by Hunter, Duncan Ivison argues that philosophical rationality can still bring colonialism and imperialism before the normative bench of a universal justice, albeit a justice that is itself mediated by history and practice. Drawing on a version of natural law that he argues escapes the problems of Eurocentrism—namely, Kant's conception of right or justice as the harmonized willing of a community of rational beings—Ivison nonetheless qualifies Kant's moral cosmopolitanism by insisting on the role of historical institutions (such as the state) in mediating justice, and by arguing for the bottom-up generation of a non-imperialist and non-cosmopolitan justice that is still global.

In the four chapters that comprise Part II of the collection, both approaches to the colonial uses of law—as a public law fact and as normative deviation induced by politics—are strongly present, although it is perhaps the latter approach that provides these chapters with their underlying orientation. Christopher Tomlins searches for the sources of British colonialist thought in the writings of an array of Elizabethan humanists, finding it in their use of a *jus naturae et gentium* suited to the dispossession of "savage" peoples, and in their projection of ideal civil utopias to fill the void of the "uncivilized." Tomlins shows how these two sources combined in the instrument of the colonial "charter" through which the British colonists materialized their European vision of a legally ordered ideal city in the "waste lands" that their politics had depopulated. In a discussion of the colonialist uses of British legal thought, John McLaren's chapter focuses squarely on the language of the "rule of law," here expressed in the English common law idiom of the "Ancient constitution" as a constraint on the exercise of executive government. In discussing various uses of this language in colonial Canada and the British West Indies, McLaren demonstrates its political ambivalence: its political valency shifting radically depending on whether it was used by the Colonial Office as a break on local democratic politics, or by local assemblies in defense of the rights and liberties of "free-born Englishmen" against colonial governors, and sometimes by such assemblies against the rights of local slave populations. Focusing directly on the difficult issue of the commensurability of British and indigenous legal cultures in colonial Canada, Mark Walters' chapter provides a subtle enthno-historical account of a potentially shared political and juridical language, centered in a common characterization of the sovereign and paramount chief as a "great father" charged with the care and protection of his peoples. Walters then charts the political betrayal of this potentially common normative legal culture, with the British colonizers progressively substituting a paternalist conception of the great father's rule in which the indigenous peoples would be reduced to the status of wards and minors. Perhaps the most striking treatment of colonialist law as political betrayal, though, is given in Andrew Fitzmaurice's discussion of Sir Travers Twiss's international-juristic work on behalf of King Leopold's project to establish the Belgian Congo as a "private" state. Fitzmaurice argues that Twiss reversed his own earlier view—that only "public" national states can exercise political sovereignty—following his social disgrace and as a result of the redemption promised through appointment as Leopold's hired juristic gun, providing a vivid case of the corruption of law through a venal politics.

With the transition to Part III of the collection, the focus of discussion shifts away from ideals of justice and their political suborning, turning instead to the concrete institutions of justice, and the contingencies of establishing and maintaining them in threadbare colonial polities containing restive settlers and unassimilated indigenous populations. In his bracingly revisionist discussion of Samuel Marsden—the "flogging parson" and poster-boy of English colonial repression—Andrew Sharp reminds us that it was not principally in doctrines that empire was transposed to the colonies, but in the specific personae that had evolved to occupy judicial and political office. As an Anglican clergyman occupying the magistrate's office, Marsden personified in colonial New South Wales the same combination of spiritual and civil authority that had been established in the form of parochial juridical authority in the (metropolitan) Anglican confessional state. Adapting this authority to impose civility in the marginal conditions of a convict society under ill-disciplined military rule, Marsden's infamous floggings turn out not to be idiosyncratic symptoms of his religious or political sympathies, but standard punishments within norms that now appear brutal to our historically refined eyes. Mark Finnane's discussion of the recognition of "customary law" also focuses on the concrete conditions for establishing the rule of law in the Australian colonies. Calling into question the legalist view that the jurisdictional amenability of the Australian Aborigines was established through declaration in the 1836 case of *R v Murrell*, Finnane discusses a whole series of subsequent cases and administrative decisions in which it was held that Aborigines were not amenable to British legal jurisdiction, and in which their governance was dealt with through "infra-legal" or extra-legal regimes of internal exile, sequestration on reserves, and imaginal pedagogical transformation into self-governing citizens. Lisa Ford is also concerned with the contingencies of establishing legal governance—here the "King's Peace"—under the exigencies of frontier society in New South Wales. In focusing on rival constructions of the King's Peace—as a matter of military honor by the New South Wales, and as a condition of commercial freedom by entrepreneurial settlers—Ford's chapter demonstrates the degree to which the transposition of empire was contingent on local political contestation. Finally, distinguishing itself from the chapters that precede it, no less than from those that follow it, Paul McHugh's essay focuses on the transposition of empire not in legal doctrine or personae, but via the disguised political projections contained in utopian political fictions. Lured into the genre of utopian political fiction by the success of Edward Bellamy's *Looking Backward* (1888), the New Zealand politicians Julius Vogel and William Pember Reeves both produced imaginal political blueprints for a future (entirely Anglo or Pākehā) New Zealand polity: the former projecting a paradisial capitalist federal British Empire, and the latter a statist socialist New Zealand.

Finally, with the chapters that comprise Part IV of the collection—and for which colonial New Zealand provides something approaching an extended case study—the discussion shifts decisively toward the pole of public-law historiography. Here the focus is not law's betrayal of a higher justice, but its role in the ordering of a sovereign jurisdiction whose justice is immanent to its exercise. In her discussion of the New Zealand colonial jurist Henry Samuel Chapman and of George Cornewall Lewis,

Shaunnagh Dorsett focuses on the plurality of legal instruments through which Crown sovereignty and jurisdiction might be asserted—via the doctrine of discovery and occupation, by proclamation, or through the (public law) Treaty of Waitangi (1840)—arguing that the use of these instruments varied with the interests and purposes of particular political factions and authorities. In his writing in the engaged persona of the colonial lobbyist (on behalf of the New Zealand Company) and then that of the Crown jurist (as Supreme Court judge), Chapman's view of the foundations of sovereignty shifted from discovery and occupation to formal treaty and cession. For his part, writing as a master of Austinian academic jurisprudence, Cornewall Lewis championed the formal "absolute" sovereignty ascribed to the institution of the "King-in-parliament," making the imperial parliament definitionally sovereign over New Zealand and its settler and indigenous populations. In his subtle historical analysis of colonial debates around the admissibility of indigenous testimony in colonial courts, Damen Ward's chapter denies that any single legal doctrine—"whether property, territory, jurisdiction, or sovereignty"—provides the key to understanding British colonial government. While formal declarations of sovereignty might establish jurisdiction at the level of parliaments and supreme courts in South Australia, New South Wales, and New Zealand, the actual procedures used in lower courts—including the protocols regarding the evidentiary capacities of indigenous witnesses—were determined by lower-level administrative ordinances, whose juridical orientation and force were informed by specific configurations of political interest, without simply being determined by them. Finally, arguing in a similar vein, Mark Hickford focuses on colonial common law and public law not as points of smooth transposition of metropolitan legal doctrine, but as institutional sites for continuous local political negotiation of rights and entitlements. In the crucial case of Māori property rights, this meant that although such concepts as "occupation" were predefined by the magisterial discourse of European *jus gentium*, their actual juridical importance in New Zealand courts was determined by ongoing negotiations and provisional solutions to political problems posed by Māori land claims, "rather than substantive intellectual consensus or closure."

Notes

1. For discussions of the historical turn, see Duncan Bell, ed., *Victorian Visions of Global Order: Empire and International Relations in Nineteenth-Century*

Political Thought (Cambridge: Cambridge University Press, 2007); and David Armitage, *The Ideological Origins of the British Empire* (Cambridge: Cambridge University Press, 2000).

2. J.G.A. Pocock, *The Ancient Constitution and the Feudal Law: A Study of English Historical Thought in the Seventeenth Century* (Cambridge: Cambridge University Press, 1957).
3. Michael Stolleis, "The Legitimation of Law through God, Tradition, Will, Nature and Constitution," in *Natural Law and Laws of Nature in Early Modern Europe: Jurisprudence, Theology, Moral and Natural Philosophy*, ed. Lorraine Daston and Michael Stolleis (Farnham: Ashgate, 2008), pp. 45–56.
4. For a classic formulation of this view of public law, see Johann Jacob Moser, *Neues teutsches Staatsrecht, Vol. 1: Von Teutschland und dessen Staats-Verfassung überhaupt* (Stuttgart: Mezler, 1766). For modern commentaries, see Michael Stolleis, *Geschichte des öffentlichen Rechts in Deutschland. Erster Band: Reichspublizistik und Policeywissenschaft 1600–1800* (Munich: C.H. Beck, 1988); and Martin Loughlin, *Foundations of Public Law* (Oxford: Oxford University Press, 2010).

Part I

European Law and Global Justice

Chapter 1

Global Justice and Regional Metaphysics

On the Critical History of the Law of Nature and Nations

Ian Hunter

A good deal of the recent historiography of the early modern law of nature and nations—*jus naturae et gentium*—has been critical.[1] This applies in particular to the literature that ties its history to the emergence of European colonialism and imperialism. By "critical" I do not mean pejorative or condemnatory—although much of the scholarship has been this too—but critical in the philosophico-historical sense of positing norms that project a history of what *jus naturae et gentium* should have been or could have become, as opposed to a history of what it contingently happened to be. Antony Anghie thus criticizes the imperialist complicity of early modern *jus gentium* by projecting a global international justice whose "promise" it might have realized but did not.[2] Yet defenders of *jus gentium* in relation to colonialism rely on the same kind of critical or philosophical historiography as its critics. Their central claim is that at least some versions of *jus gentium* did indeed embody norms of global justice, which made it possible to condemn European colonialism as unjust.[3] The many postcolonial critics of early modern *jus gentium* and its occasional philosophical defenders thus share a fundamental philosophico-historical platform: namely, that there is a global principle of justice capable of including European and non-European peoples within the "universal history" of its unfolding. They differ only over whether, or to what degree, *jus gentium* succeeded in realizing this principle and thus stands condemned or vindicated by this history.

In what follows I develop some arguments skeptical of this critical or philosophico-historical approach to the early modern law of nature and nations and sketch the broad lines of an alternative approach, drawing on an array of contextual-historical studies. I argue that the early modern uses of *jus naturae et gentium* were indeed particularistic or Eurocentric—in the dual sense of being regional *to* and *within* Europe—but more profoundly so than either its modern critics or defenders have grasped. That is because these uses—including those justifying the intrusion of European missionaries, traders, and states into New World countries and cultures—could not have been understood by their exponents as failing to realize a truly global normative order or "international justice" and cannot be understood by modern historians in this way either. Against its modern critics and defenders, I argue that the "regional"—geointellectual and geoethical—character of European *jus gentium* discourses cannot be comprehended in relation to a transcendent global justice or universal history that these discourses failed to realize. Instead, their regional character can be grasped only by situating them in the immanent conflicts among the rival intellectual cultures on which they were based, and the clashing religious and political programs in which these discourses were anchored. To the extent that the particularistic limits of European *jus gentium* have become intelligible, then this has occurred neither through a universal reason's philosophical recovery of global norms, nor through a universal history's sociological globalization of such norms over time. Rather, these limits became visible only when the universalistic claims of *jus gentium* were fractured from within by the multiplication of rival forms during the European Reformation, and relativized from without during the encounter with New World cultures.

If this is so then we cannot approach the history of *jus naturae et gentium* as if it were governed by a global principle of justice. Rather we must approach this history at the convergence of two lines of historiographic inquiry: first, into the disparate intellectual sources—the metaphysical anthropologies and cosmologies, the political philosophies and juridical cultures—from which rival *jus gentium* discourses were fashioned; and, second, into the conflicting religious, juridical, and political programs in whose interests such discourses were fashioned, and to whose historical fate they were tied. This history of *jus naturae et gentium* is thus not that of the revelation of its particularism in the course of a universal history of reason, at the center of which sits the colonialist detour from which it might yet recover. Rather it is a history tied to a protracted series of conflicts among the cultural and political programs in which particular *jus gentium* discourses were anchored—including inter alia colonizing programs—whose unforeseeable and uncontrollable outcomes constitute the "present" occupied by today's historians.

I

In treating early modern *jus naturae et gentium* as the ideological origin of modern—state-centered, imperialist—international law, critical historiography grounds its critique of *jus gentium* particularism or regionality on social-theoretic and philosophical premises tacitly assumed to be universal. It is highly likely, though, that the theoretical and philosophical premises of this critique are themselves European-specific—that is, accessible only to those iteratively trained in an array of regional university-based European intellectual cultures. If so, then we will have to give up the idea that the particularism or regionality of *jus gentium* discourses can be comprehended and condemned on the philosophical or theoretical basis of its failure to be universal.

In order to argue this case in the space available, we can construct a composite of the critical historiography of *jus gentium*, acknowledging a degree of over-unification in doing so. Centrally, this historiography claims that early modern *jus naturae et gentium* originated as the ideological justification for the European colonization of the New World, and that a state-centered and imperialistic modern international law is its direct descendant.[4] The core intellectual components of *jus naturae et gentium* are thus supposed to have been ideas or doctrines declaring the intellectual and moral superiority of European culture over non-European ones, as a means of disguising, hence facilitating, the cultural and political domination of the former over the latter.[5] Preeminent and continuous among these ideas were several key European political and cultural concepts—state sovereignty,[6] the rule of law,[7] agricultural and commercial society[8]—that *jus naturae et gentium* represented as universally grounded in man's moral nature, or as indicative of the perfection of human civilization. In allowing non-European cultures to be viewed as particular in relation to European universality, or as uncivilized in relation to the process of European civilization, it was early modern *jus gentium* that supplied the ideological theory for the practice of European colonialism and imperialism, now understood in terms of the coercive imposition of particularistic European norms and concepts on non-European peoples.

The tacitly universalist presumption sustaining this account—that is, the presumption that relations between European and New World peoples should and could have been rendered fair and just on the basis of a common global normative order—draws on three powerful intellectual cultures. First, based ultimately in the Thomist-Catholic natural-law anthropology of man as the bearer of a self-realizing essence or "rational and sociable nature," is the doctrine that all "nations" are corporate moral personalities—"nation-persons"—destined for self-realization or "self-determination" through political autonomy.[9] Second, modern critical historiography also draws on a quite different conception of universal justice, as "cosmopolitan right." This is grounded in the (de facto Protestant) Kantian anthropology and cosmology of men as rational (*noumenal*) beings destined by reason for harmonious sharing of the corporeal globe.[10] Finally, basing itself on Heideggerian metaphysics and "deconstruction," postcolonial critique of "European law" has developed an elaborate metaphorics of colonization as the imposition of a European "self" on a colonized "other." Colonization is thus treated as if it were the project of constructing a repressive yet anxious European identity—"The colonizer constructs himself as he constructs the colony"[11]—that is destined to be undone through the self-manifesting "Being" of the colonized "other."[12]

There are thus good prima facie reasons for suggesting that when the universalist critique of *jus gentium* presumes a norm of global justice—when it is tacitly or explicitly asserted that all nations have a right to self-determination, or that all states should harmonize their interests in accordance with a principle of "cosmopolitan right," or that all colonizers construct their identity through "anxious" occlusion of the colonized—this amounts to neither more nor less than the iteration of a series of regional European metaphysical cultures, each claiming to constitute a universal norm of "international justice." It is quite implausible to imagine that the anthropological and cosmological underpinnings of such European political metaphysics will harmonize with those of non-European political metaphysics: for example, political mythographies teaching that the tribe has been chosen by god, or that its members are the cyclical incarnations of divine beings; or cosmographies teaching that the world is organized around a privileged "middle kingdom"—center of civilization—or is divided into regions of the "abode of Islam" (*dar al-Islam*) and the "abode of war" (*dar al-harb*). Given their reliance on rival philosophical anthropologies and modes of acceding to truth, however, it is equally implausible to imagine that the three European forms of "global justice" can be reconciled with each other. It is thus reasonable to suggest that the main ways of measuring the European particularity of *jus gentium* against a global justice—hence of criticizing it as Eurocentric—are themselves embedded in intellectual cultures that are regional not only *to* Europe but also *within* Europe.

We are thus raising the prospect that the postcolonial critique of a Eurocentric *jus gentium* is not only deeply enmeshed in European academic philosophy, but also that the global philosophical history through which it seeks to localize *jus gentium* is itself local to those geo-intellectual regions in which European academic philosophy has been planted. In arguing that the philosophico-historical critique of *jus gentium* Eurocentrism is itself Eurocentric, however, our aim is not to engage in some kind of "meta-critique"—as if Eurocentrism could be determined in relation to some truly universal norm or history that this critique has yet to realize—but to head in a different direction altogether. Our concern rather is to acknowledge—indeed to insist on—the particularist or regional European character of *jus gentium* intellectual cultures, and to argue that this regionality is indefeasible on purely intellectual grounds—that is, on the grounds of a "global principle of justice" or a "universal history" of the kind presumed by its critical historiography, which turn out themselves to be regional to and within Europe.

In fact, there are compelling historical reasons for thinking that the regionality of European *jus gentium* "universalism" becames comprehensible and contestable not through rational philosophical reflection or universal history, but as a result of two highly contingent sets of historical developments taking place in the a-rational domain of cultural and politico-military conflict. First, the universalism of natural law and *jus gentium* was forcibly fractured from within Europe when, during the multiple Christian "Reformations" of the sixteenth and seventeenth centuries, there emerged rival natural-law universalisms backed by warring religious and political orders.[13] Second, the regional character of *jus gentium* universalism became intelligible when it was forcibly confronted by extra-European cultures characterized by radically different political anthropologies and cosmographies, as in the case of the Chinese containment of the Jesuit mission during the sixteenth century.

From these momentous periods of cultural-political conflict emerged two intellectual genres or disciplinary traditions that make it possible to comprehend the particularistic character of European *jus naturae et gentium* without treating it as a derogation from a global normative order or universal history. The clash between rival armed metaphysical cultures during the European Reformations gave rise to a new kind of (contextualist) historiographic method, at the center of which lay a strategy for suspending the truth-claims of the competing metaphysical systems by treating them all as historical activities from the viewpoint of their impact on civil society.[14] For its part, the building of linguistic and intellectual bridgeheads between otherwise discrepant European and New World cultures gave rise to the disciplines of ethnography and historical ethnology.[15]

These made it possible to grasp the particularism of European *jus gentium* not in terms of a global justice unfolding in a universal history, but in terms of more or less uncontrollable clashes between the emissaries of dispersed cultural-political archipelagos. The powerful relativizing effects of these convergent historiographic and ethnological perspectives can be seen in Onuma Yasuaki's salutary observation with regard to the history of international law:

> What is critical is the question of the scope of a society in which a certain normative system is valid and applied. Whether "ancient international law," the Islamocentric *siyar*, the Sinocentric tribute system or Eurocentric law of nations, they are nothing other than regional normative systems which were applied in only a limited area of the earth and lasted for a limited period of time.[16]

We can thus call into question whether the cultural and political relations in which *jus gentium* discourses were enmeshed—not just the relations between European and non-European peoples but also the relations among Europe's warring moral communities—could have been brought within a single compass of intelligibility and moral or legal judgment, and hence whether they can be today.

II

The juridical legitimation of European religious and commercial intrusions into the New World was indeed one of the contextual uses to which the genre of *jus naturae et gentium* was put, as has been shown in an array of important studies.[17] It needs to be carefully observed though that extra-European colonialist uses did not provide a unifying ideological essence for natural law and *jus gentium*. In fact, the crucial uses of the genre, especially during the seventeenth and eighteenth centuries, were principally dedicated to supplying the intellectual architecture for intra-European state-building and diplomacy.[18] Conversely, European colonialism could be, and was, justified on grounds—of Christian proselytizing, dynastic ambition, military competition, commercial enterprise—quite independent of the quasi-juridical ones offered by natural law and *jus gentium*.

With this sense of the contextual parameters of *jus naturae and gentium* in place, we can turn to its radical internal diversity. Drawing on both Christian theology and the heritage of Roman law—and initially tied to the twin institutions of the papacy and the Holy Roman German Empire—the first iterations of *jus naturae et gentium* were fundamentally theologico-juridical.[19] This theological inheritance remained signposted in the name "natural law" itself, which refers to a law that is supposed to be natural in a twofold sense: first, in being inscribed in and as man's nature as a "rational and sociable" creature; and, second, in being acceded to through man's "natural" reason, as opposed to through revelation or positive statute. Despite its Christian metaphysical basis, theological natural law was deemed to be universally accessible to all men on the basis of their shared rational and sociable nature, and thus to form the basis of a *jus gentium* or law of nations common to all "civilized" peoples.

Following the fracturing of the "universal church" during the sixteenth century, however, the notion of a single universal natural law was increasingly mocked by the diversity of its conflicting constructions. These varied radically and fundamentally, as rival ways of construing man's moral nature—and the manner in which natural law was inscribed within it—were elaborated in the service of conflicting religious and political agendas. From among the diversity of forms of *jus naturae et gentium* that emerged under these circumstances, we can make brief mention of three broad types that are of particular significance for our present concerns. First, the high point of confessional conflict during the late sixteenth and early seventeenth century marked the dominance of scholastic theological constructions of natural law. Drawing on Christian-Aristotelian and Christian-Platonic doctrines of the perfectible intellectual nature through which man accedes to the divine *lex aeterna*, scholastic natural law was designed to provide a theocratic reception-context for positive (Romano-canon) law in confessional states. It could thus justify the use of civil power for such religious ends as the prosecution of heretics and the conversion of infidels, including those found in Spanish South America.[20] Second, emerging in direct competition with this "Christian natural law" was the anti-scholastic or "secular" Protestant natural law of the mid- to late seventeenth century, exemplified in the works of Grotius, Hobbes, Pufendorf, and Thomasius. Symptomatic of a shift in natural law's institutional center of gravity from the theology to the law faculty, this secular construction derived natural law from the worldly end of social peace and viewed the civil law commands of the territorial sovereign as the ultimate arbiter of how natural law is manifest in civil society and positive law.[21] Finally, drawing on the rationalistic scholasticism of Christian Wolff—which continued to treat the nation as a self-perfecting corporate person—but combining this with an epitome of treaty-based war- and peace-making, Vattel produced yet another version of the law of nations: this time conceived as a body of casuistical rules for regulating the conduct of war and peace between equally "just" European sovereigns.[22]

Set against this dispersed array of contextually specific constructions, the modern critical historiography of *jus gentium* begins to unravel. In the first place, in light of this variety, it becomes impossible to sustain the view that nineteenth-century imperialism found its ideological origins in Vitoria's *jus gentium*—that is, as a means of imposing European state sovereignty and law on non-European peoples.[23] Rather than being a "secular" ideology intended to found an international order of states, Vitoria's natural law and *jus gentium* belonged to the first, scholastic-theological form of natural law mentioned above. Under this dispensation natural law is embedded in divine law, and civil states are themselves embedded in the higher community of the universal (Catholic) church headed by Christ.[24] Far from constructing a conception of secular sovereignty as a means of erasing the "cultural difference" of the South American Indians, Vitoria's central concern was to maintain the subordination of civil sovereignty to natural law norms accessible only to the "wise clergy" authorized by the apostolic succession. In *De Indis* this enabled Vitoria to assert a Catholic theocratic construction of civil authority both against the Protestant heretics who were proposing to ground authority in a purely worldly covenant, and against the Indians, should they attempt to resist their conversion to Christianity.[25] It is striking that the moral anthropology lying at the heart of Vitoria's construction—the Christian-Aristotelian conception of man's self-perfecting rational and sociable essence—is subject to rival interpretations by his critics and defenders: the former arguing that this universal anthropology was used to suppress the indigenous culture of the Indians,[26] and the latter insisting that it was used to recognize their universal humanity.[27] Once again, by presuming the existence of a universal norm of justice—disagreeing only over whether Vitoria had discovered it or not—critics and defenders both ignore the possibility that the immensely destructive imposition of this European moral anthropology on indigenous cultures was the uncontrollable consequence of a clash between disparate civilizational cultures.

Second, the notion that European imperialism found its initial justification in a *jus gentium* dedicated to the extra-European imposition of secular state sovereignty fares no better in relation to the second form of natural law mentioned above, which was indeed dedicated to this conception of sovereignty. The most important early modern secular natural law construction of state sovereignty—Pufendorf's *De jure naturae et gentium* of 1672—treats such sovereignty neither as a moral universal nor as a symptom of European civilizational supremacy that might legitimate the subordination of the South Americans within a statist international law. In fact, Pufendorf's text was dedicated to destroying the notion that civil authority could be founded on any kind of universal morality, especially the kind of Christian-Aristotelian moral order championed by Vitoria and the scholastics.[28] Against scholastic political metaphysics, Pufendorf elaborated a secular Hobbesian conception of natural law—derived from the minimalist norm of maintaining civil peace—and thereby elevated the civil law commands of the territorial sovereign into the sole effectual determinant of natural law.[29] Far from being governed by extra-European colonial imperialism, this reconstruction of natural law was driven by Pufendorf's intra-European, anti-imperial campaign to displace the "universal" political order of the Catholic church and the German Empire with a secular-territorial form of political authority, leading him to argue that there could be no positive law between nations.[30] As a result, rather than reinforcing Vitoria's defense of Spain's *jus gentium* rights to convert the South American Indians, Pufendorf argues against Vitoria that if justice is internal to the political order of the territorial state and there are no positive international rights—such as the rights to hospitality, trade, and proselytizing defended by Vitoria—then the question of whether the Spanish can engage in the relevant activities should be wholly at the disposition of the South American peoples themselves.[31]

Finally, similar remarks apply to claims that eighteenth-century public law *jus gentium*—especially that of Emer de Vattel—also originated in the ideological imperative to impose European conceptions of sovereignty, agriculture, and commerce on New World peoples. Unlike Pufendorf, in his *Droit des gens* of 1758 Vattel continued to invoke the universalist scholastic principle of natural law—in terms of the virtues required to perfect man's rational and sociable essence—but transformed its role by insisting that each territorial nation is responsible for perfecting its own corporate essence, and hence for determining what counts as just.[32] Vattel thus suspended the universal principle of natural law by acknowledging that warring sovereigns might be "equally just," turning instead to a voluntaristic law of nations consisting of a myriad of casuistical juristic and diplomatic conventions for regulating the conduct of war and negotiation of peace. In fact, Vattel's central objective in constructing a public law of nations was not to justify New World colonization but to consolidate the civilizing effect of the intra-European regulation of warfare.[33] As a result, despite the evident Eurocentrism of his thinking and program—or perhaps because of it—Vattel located barbarism and savagery not in New World nations but in an array of peoples who had engaged in unregulated atrocious warfare: the European religious zealots of the recent wars of religion; the ancient booty-seeking Germans and Goths; sundry bandit groups; and the "Tartar" pirates.[34] If we consider the one place where Vattel does argue for the impairment of New World rights—in his passing comments on curtailing the property rights of nonagricultural nomadic peoples[35]—then this cannot be understood as symptomatic of his implicit failure to rise to a truly universal conception of justice.[36] On the contrary, this position was the result of Vattel's entirely explicit Protestant moral-republican argument that political rights are grounded in the cultivation of civic virtues—including agricultural, commercial, and military virtues—in a national "country."[37] Vattel thus did not hesitate to apply the same argument in order to diminish the rights of certain European groups: namely, those of the (Catholic) religious orders who also refused to cultivate the agricultural, commercial, and military virtues required for the perfection of the moral republic.[38]

There are thus comprehensive reasons for questioning the entire critical historiographic approach to early modern *jus gentium*, in its both attack and defense modes. There is no evidence to suggest that *jus gentium* originated as the colonialist imposition of a European ideology of secular sovereignty, even if some of its (scholastic) forms were undoubtedly used to justify the religious and political domination of colonized peoples. Neither is there any reason to think that its various regional or contextual forms could or should have realized a universal form of international justice to which "we" (critical moderns) imagine ourselves having acceded. The conception of state sovereignty that critical historiography makes central to its account of the ideological origins of European imperialism—that is, the conception that identifies sovereignty with the progress of European civilization in order to police the admittance of uncivilized peoples to the "community of states"—was simply not present in early modern *jus gentium*. According to Martti Koskenneimi's remarkable study of the rise and fall of international law, this transformation of sovereignty into a universal moral imperative only emerged with the appearance of modern international law in the late nineteenth century and was, in fact, symptomatic of the eclipsing of the European order of sovereign states by emerging hemispheric imperial hegemonies.[39] It is this late nineteenth-century use of state sovereignty as an instrument of trans-territorial imperial hegemony that critical historiography anachronistically projects backward onto early modern *jus gentium*.

III

In light of the preceding discussion, we are now in a position to argue that whatever historical effects might or might not have arisen at the nexus of various *jus gentium* discourses and particular religious, juridical, and political programs, this is not something that can be read-off from the putative signs of their ideological particularism or, conversely, their rational universalism. Rather, this is something that can be determined only through historical investigation of how such discourses were received and used within contexts defined by the relations between concrete cultural and political forces. It is the contingent and often unfinished interactions between these forces that constitute the inherently unstable "present" from which the history of early modern *jus naturae et gentium* must be written.

In order to provide some sense of the use of *jus gentium* discourses within an appropriately concrete colonial context, I will draw on a body of recent investigations into the uses of English law in colonial New Zealand and Australia.[40] These studies are distinguished by the fact that they do not treat *jus gentium* concepts of sovereignty and property as ideological occlusions of true forms that were supposedly already possessed by colonized peoples in the form of indigenous sovereignty and native title.[41] Rather, they treat these concepts as performatives involved in historical struggles over the ordering of political and juridical authority. This means that the ascription (or denial) of sovereignty and property is always the contingent outcome of some contested historical ordering or settlement, whether this be the Anglican Settlement of 1688 or the Treaty of Waitangi of 1840.[42]

This points toward a significant revision of the "critical" historical understanding of the English armed expeditionary intrusions into, and subsequent colonizations of, New Zealand and Australia. In the picture that emerges, colonizing acts were not rendered effectual through false (hence potentially true) concepts—whether of sovereignty and property, or of discovery, conquest, cession, and *terra nullius*—contained in European *jus gentium*. Rather, these acts were the outcome of the concrete play of cultural and political forces in which *jus gentium* discourses provided instrumental forms of juridical and political intelligibility for colonizing programs whose accomplishment depended on neither the falsity nor truth of these discourses. As a result, these colonizing acts and programs cannot be understood today as if they were effected through the ideological distortion of truly universal principles of justice that could have included the European intruders and the indigenous inhabitants within a single global normative order.[43] Several observations are required to clarify the character of this changed approach to the colonialist use of *jus gentium* discourses in the New Zealand and Australian contexts.

First, at the most general level, it is important not to overestimate the significance and effects of *jus gentium* discourses—and indeed of positive legal discourses—as if their ideas of sovereignty and property actually motivated the colonizing acts of intruding soldiers, traders, and missionaries. Rather, colonization was driven by a diversity of sometimes-conflicting logics and interests, including rival interstate military expansionism; public policy initiatives (the penal colony of New South Wales); private economic undertakings (the New Zealand Company and the South Australian Company); and Christian proselytizing (the Anglican Church Missionary

Society and the Wesleyan Missionary Society). If *jus gentium* discourses were present in some of these colonizing projects—for example, supplying concepts of discovery, conquest, and cession to military "voyages of discovery"—then they were absent in others. Christian missionary enterprises thus had no need of such quasi-juridical justification, being driven instead by evangelization, proselytizing, and the logic of "saving souls," and sometimes expressing hostility toward secular law and *jus gentium*. Similarly, if Eurocentric civilizational supremacy informed some of these agendas, then so too did Christian universalist conceptions of human equality—even if the latter turned out to be no less Eurocentric than the former, and equally toxic for non-Christian cultures. Colonialist programs emerged from these crosscutting drivers not as the "practice" from *jus gentium* "theory," but as the contingent outcome of a ramifying series of concrete conflicts, compromises, and circumstantial policies. The juridical and political significance of *jus gentium* concepts depended on their (contested) use within such highly contextual circumstances, which was also true for public and common law concepts, as Damen Ward shows in his discussion of ordinances regulating indigenous testimonial capacity in the present volume.

Second, if *jus gentium* concepts obtained their significance through the ways in which they were put to work in particular colonial programs, then only those *jus gentium* discourses that lent themselves to such uses became effective in colonial New Zealand and Australia. The significant use of Vattel's work in these contexts is almost certainly a result of the fact that—unlike Wolff's and Kant's—his *jus gentium* had combined natural law political philosophy with a historical conspectus of the treaty-based conventions governing war, peace, commerce, and communications between European states. This made it usable as a source of quasi-juridical norms in a variety of positive legal and political circumstances: from European diplomacy and public law, to colonial juridical and political constructions of a law "*inter gentes*." The version of Vattel's *Law of Nations* that found its way into New Zealand (and to a lesser extent Australian) colonial contexts, however, was one that had been significantly transformed by its assimilation into English juridical and political culture in Joseph Chitty's edition of 1834, which was the edition used by British colonial officials and jurists. By suspending Vattel's text in a dense mesh of comments, authorities, and case law, Chitty's edition adapted Vattel's *jus gentium* to British constitutional thought and English common law culture. Chitty's notes thus ignore Vattel's republican political metaphysics and focus solely on the "voluntary law of nations"—particularly the customs and conventions embodied in European treaties regulating maritime commerce with respect to such issues as neutrality, immunity, contraband, confiscation, and reparation—which Chitty anglicized through a web of case-law citations taken from the Courts of Admiralty and the King's Bench.[44]

Chitty's assimilation of Vattel to British politics and English law thus produced a *jus gentium* that was suited to use in British colonial contexts. On the one hand, Chitty's Vattel transmitted the supra-municipal vocabulary of the law of nations—dealing with nation, sovereignty, treaty, occupation, property—thereby activating the longstanding use of *jus gentium* as a reception matrix for positive public law in a conquered or ceded territory. On the other hand, by sidelining Vattel's political metaphysics and tying his European treaty-based diplomatic casuistry to English case law, Chitty reoriented Vattel's *jus gentium* toward English domestic or municipal law. Chitty's Vattel was thus not really a source of ideological justifications for the exercise of British sovereignty over colonial territories—Chitty treated this as a "political" fait accompli beyond the reach of municipal law—but rather a means for receiving English law in colonial territories whose British sovereignty was treated as a military-political presupposition of legal order.

Third, we are now in a position to observe that the historical significance and effects of *jus gentium* concepts of sovereignty and property in colonial contexts were determined not by their falsity or truth—their particularism or their universality—but by the play of concrete forces that determined their use to shape particular orderings of political and legal authority. Mark Hickford has thus argued that Chitty's Vattel, operating in tandem with a Scottish stadial theory of civilizational development, provided a vocabulary through which the British Colonial Office and the New Zealand Company could formulate Māori land-holding as a form of "native title."[45] Through this hybrid vocabulary, Māori could be granted a form of common law title based on "occupation"—understood as grounded in their form of life as "primitive agriculturalists" practicing horticulture on small village land-holdings—hence a title that could be alienated to the New Zealand Company. At the same time, it allowed all "unoccupied" land to be treated as unowned, hence as belonging to the Crown via the doctrine of "eminent domain" and the acquisition of sovereignty that would be formalized with the Treaty of Waitangi in 1840.

This set the scene for an intense struggle between the representatives of the New Zealand Company—who used stadial theory and *jus gentium* to preemptively declare most of New Zealand to be land that the Crown could grant to its settlers—and representatives of the Colonial Office, particularly Permanent Under-Secretary James Stephen. Stephen sought to investigate the form and extent of Māori land-holding and to restrict the company's acquisition of Crown land through appropriate purchase fees.[46] As it turned out, events swung in favor of the company's position, not through the ideological force of stadial theory and Vattelian *jus gentium*, however, but as a result of a political transformation in the British administration: specifically, the appointments of Viscount Howick (Earl Grey) to head the Colonial Office (1846) and George Grey as governor of New Zealand (1845), both notable supporters of the New Zealand Company. It was this political change that provided the ideology with the political force that allowed it to shape George Grey's land distribution policy: the policy of extensive government land purchases as a means of extinguishing broad native title and reconstructing this title in terms of the reserved proprietorship of limited horticultural holdings[47] As Hickford comments: "What was at stake was not merely control of the rationale for policy but the manner in which it would be executed in practice irrespective of legal niceties.... the question of defining public policy (and the history of its practice) had much to do with power and authority over those processes that beget desired outcomes in the first place."[48]

Finally, we can observe that even if—perhaps especially if—the colonial effectivity of *jus gentium* concepts of sovereignty and property hinged upon their deployment within contested programs for the shaping of a political and juridical order, it is anachronistic to imagine that this order was based on the ideological character of these ideas: that is, on their function of occluding a global form of justice based in true conceptions of sovereignty and property common to both British and Māori cultures. In contrast to the case of the Australian Aborigines, acknowledgment of Māori capacities for agriculture, commerce, and organized warfare had indeed led to a recognition of their sovereignty—hence their capacity to enter into the Treaty of Waitangi in 1840—if only for the purposes of ceding this sovereignty to the British Crown. As John Pocock has argued, however, despite the Treaty's bilingual formulation, there was no way for its *jus gentium* concepts of sovereignty and property to achieve the cultural translation of the Māori idea of "belonging to the land." The latter was not based in the European juridical culture of alienable personal rights that was in the process of defining native title. Rather it was grounded in such cultural practices as burying the placenta of new-borns in the land to which they will belong—the word *whenua* meaning both "land" and "placenta"—such that land-holding is understood in terms of belonging to the community of ancestors that is personified by the land's present occupants.[49] This kind of knowledge was inaccessible to eighteenth- and nineteenth-century European philosophical anthropology—wedded as it was to rights as subjective capacities of "rational and sociable" individuals—and would become available only via twentieth-century ethnology and ethno-linguistics: disciplines that were themselves the contingent outcome of reflection taking place within the cultural bridgeheads formed through colonization.[50]

If we place the radically ethnocentric Māori conception of land-belonging alongside the radically Eurocentric conceptions of sovereignty and property found in *jus gentium*—recalling, for example, Vattel's entirely metaphysical conception of sovereignty as the political authority exercised by and for a self-perfecting nation-person—then there is no reason to think that the clash between the British and the Māori could have been rendered morally intelligible within a common normative juridical order.[51] We have already seen that the candidates for such an order to which critical historiography appeals today—the "universal justice" of free national self-determination, Kantian cosmopolitan right, or the deconstructive dissolution of the colonizing "self" and its "other"—are themselves neither more nor less than the instruments of rival European metaphysical cultures; they are hence historical symptoms of European cultural and political hegemony. This is not to argue, however, that European and Māori conceptions of authority and land-holding represent mutually sealed universes of discourse, only that we must pay attention to the "windows" of communication between them. I have argued that one such window was formed when the fragmentation of European metaphysics helped give rise to a contextual historiography capable of showing the "regionality" of this metaphysics. A second was opened when the establishment of inter-cultural bridgeheads—such as the Treaty of Waitangi itself—allowed diverse peoples to encounter each other's metaphysics and cosmogonies on the disenchanted plains of an unfinished history.

Notes

1. Research for this chapter was made possible by the award of an Australian Professorial Fellowship. A longer version was presented at the "Transpositions of Empire" symposium, held in Prato April 20–22, 2009. I am grateful to the other participants, especially to my co-organizer, Shaunnagh Dorsett, and to Mark Hickford, Barry Hindess, David Saunders, Shaun McVeigh, and Gary Wickham for their comments.
2. Antony Anghie, *Imperialism, Sovereignty and the Making of International Law* (Cambridge: Cambridge University Press, 2005), pp. 8–12.
3. For a recent example, see Georg Cavallar, "Vitoria, Grotius, Pufendorf, Wolff and Vattel: Accomplices of European Colonialism and Exploitation or True Cosmopolitans?," *Journal of the History of International Law*, 10 (2008), 181–209.
4. A founding statement is provided in Charles Henry Alexandrowicz, *An Introduction to the History of the Law of Nations in the East Indies* (Oxford: Clarendon Press, 1967). More recently this paradigm can be found in

Anghie, *Imperialism, Sovereignty*; S. James Anaya, *Indigenous Peoples in International Law* (Oxford: Oxford University Press, 2004); and Brett Bowden, "The Colonial Origins of International Law: European Expansion and the Classical Standard of Civilization," *Journal of the History of International Law*, 7 (2005), 1–23.

5. See Anaya, *Indigenous Peoples in International Law*, ch. 1; Anghie, *Imperialism, Sovereignty*, pp. 1–31; Bowden, "The Colonial Origins of International Law"; Henry Reynolds, *Aboriginal Sovereignty: Reflections on Race, State, and Nation* (St Leonards, NSW: Allen & Unwin, 1996); and Bruce Buchan, "The Empire of Political Thought: Civilization, Savagery and Perceptions of Indigenous Government," *History of the Human Sciences*, 18 (2005), 1–22.
6. Anghie, *Imperialism, Sovereignty*, p. 16; Reynolds, *Aboriginal Sovereignty*, pp. 39–59; and Bruce Buchan, "Civilisation, State Sovereignty and War: the Scottish Enlightenment and International Relations," *International Relations*, 20 (2006), 175–92.
7. Robert A. Williams Jr., *The American Indian in Western Legal Thought: The Discourses of Conquest* (New York: Oxford University Press, 1990), pp. 6–8; Reynolds, *Aboriginal Sovereignty*, pp. 60–85.
8. Anghie, *Imperialism, Sovereignty*, pp. 269–70; Bruce Buchan, "Traffick of Empire: Trade, Treaty and Terra Nullius in Australia and North America, 1750–1800," *History Compass*, 5 (2007), 386–405.
9. The modern iteration of this doctrine can be found in James Brown Scott, *The Catholic Conception of International Law* (Washington DC: Georgetown University Press, 1934); and James Brown Scott, *The Spanish Origin of International Law: Francisco de Vitoria and his Law of Nations* (Washington, DC: Georgetown University Press, 1932). It was revived for postcolonial use in Alexandrowicz's *History of the Law of Nations* in 1967 and forms the basis of Anaya's *Indigenous Peoples in International Law* (2004) and Reynolds' *Aboriginal Sovereignty* (1996), while also informing Anghie's *Imperialism, Sovereignty and the Making of International Law* (2004). It can also be found in the implacable defense of Vitoria's *jus gentium* in Brian Tierney, *The Idea of Natural Rights: Studies on Natural Rights, Natural Law and Church Law, 1150–1625* (Atlanta: Scholars Press, 1997), pp. 255–87.
10. Kant's own articulation of the principle of cosmopolitan right—in terms of rational beings inhabiting a physical globe—has been reworked by Rawls and Habermas. Unlike the Catholic natural law doctrine, here the focus is not on universal national self-determination but on global democratic will-formation, seen most clearly in John Rawls, *The Law of Peoples* (Cambridge, MA: Harvard University Press, 1999); and Jürgen Habermas, "Does the Constitutionalisation of International Law Still have a Chance?," in *The Divided West*, ed. Ciaran Cronin (Cambridge: Polity Press, 2006), pp. 155–93.
11. Gayatri Chakravorty Spivak, *A Critique of Postcolonial Reason: Toward a History of the Vanishing Present* (Cambridge, MA: Harvard University Press, 1999), p. 203.

12. See, for example, Peter Fitzpatrick, "Terminal Legality: Imperialism and the (De)composition of Law," in *Law, History, Colonialism: The Reach of Empire*, ed. Diane Kirkby and Catharine Coleborne (Manchester: Manchester University Press, 2001), pp. 9–25; Anghie, *Imperialism, Sovereignty*, pp. 8–9, 31–32; and, more generally, Spivak, *A Critique of Postcolonial Reason*; and Edward Said, *Culture and Imperialism* (New York: Knopf, 1993).
13. See Knud Haakonssen, "German Natural Law," in *The Cambridge History of Eighteenth-Century Political Thought*, ed. Mark Goldie and Robert Wokler (Cambridge: Cambridge University Press, 2006), pp. 251–90; and Ian Hunter and David Saunders (eds.), *Natural Law and Civil Sovereignty: Moral Right and State Authority in Early Modern Political Thought* (Basingstoke: Palgrave, 2002).
14. See, J.G.A. Pocock, "Gibbon and the History of Heresy," in *Histories of Heresy in Early Modern Europe: For, Against, and Beyond Toleration*, ed. John Christian Laursen (Basingstoke: Palgrave, 2002), pp. 205–20.
15. See, Anthony Pagden, *The Fall of Natural Man: The American Indian and the Origins of Comparative Ethnology* (Cambridge: Cambridge University Press, 1982); and John L. Comaroff and Jean Comaroff, *Ethnography and the Historical Imagination* (Boulder: Westview Press, 1992).
16. Onuma Yasuaki, "When Was the Law of International Society Born?—an Inquiry of the History of International Law from an Intercivilisational Perspective," *Journal of the History of International Law*, 2 (2000), 1–66, p. 7.
17. See, for example, Pagden, *The Fall of Natural Man*; James Tully, "Placing the *Two Treatises*," in *Political Discourse in Early Modern Britain*, ed. Nicholas Phillipson and Quentin Skinner (Cambridge: Cambridge University Press, 1993), pp. 253–82; Jörg Fisch, *Die europäische Expansion und das Völkerrecht: Die Auseinandersetzungen um den Status der überseeischen Gebiete vom 15. Jahundert bis zur Gegenwart* (Stuttgart: Steiner, 1984); and Wilhelm G. Grewe, *The Epochs of International Law* (Berlin: De Gruyter, 2000), pp. 141–62.
18. As has been argued by Koskenniemi in Martti Koskenniemi, "The Advantage of Treaties: International Law in the Enlightenment," *Edinburgh Law Review*, 13 (2009), 27–67.
19. Dieter Schwab, "Der Staat im Naturrecht der Scholastik," in *Naturrecht und Staat: Politische Funktionen des Europäischen Naturrechts (17.–19. Jahrhundert)*, ed. Diethelm Klippel and Elisabeth Müller-Luckner (Munich: Oldenbourg, 2006), pp. 1–18; Tierney, *The Idea of Natural Rights*, pp. 43–77.
20. For Protestant scholastic natural law, see Hans-Peter Schneider, "Christliches Naturrecht," in *Die Philosophie des 17. Jahrhunderts, Band 4*, ed. Holzhey and Schmidt-Biggemann, pp. 813–35. For Catholic see Tierney, *The Idea of Natural Rights*, pp. 288–315. See also Annabel S. Brett, *Liberty, Right and Nature: Individual Rights in Later Scholastic Thought* (Cambridge: Cambridge University Press, 1997).
21. Knud Haakonssen, "Protestant Natural-Law Theory: A General Interpretation," in *New Essays on the History of Autonomy: A Collection Honoring J.B. Schneewind*, ed. Natalie Brender and Larry Krasnoff (Cambridge: Cambridge University

Press, 2004), pp. 92–109; Haakonssen, "German Natural Law"; and Hunter, *Rival Enlightenments*, ch. 4.

22. Grewe, *The Epochs of International Law*, pp. 317–63.
23. Cf., Anaya, *Indigenous Peoples*, ch. 1; Anghie, *Imperialism, Sovereignty*, pp. 1–31; and Bowden, "The Colonial Origins of International Law."
24. See, Franciso de Vitoria, "On Civil Power," in *Franciso de Vitoria: Political Writings*, ed. Anthony Pagden and Jeremy Lawrance (Cambridge: Cambridge University Press, 1991), pp. 1–44.
25. Vitoria, "On the American Indians," pp. 231–92, at 233–38, 284–86.
26. Williams, *The American Indian*, pp. 96–118.
27. Tierney, *The Idea of Natural Rights*, pp. 290–301.
28. Michael J. Seidler, "Pufendorf and the Politics of Recognition," in *Natural Law and Civil Sovereignty*, ed. Hunter and Saunders, pp. 235–51.
29. For more, see Hunter, *Rival Enlightenments*, pp. 148–96; and Horst Dreitzel, "The Reception of Hobbes in the Political Philosophy of the Early German Enlightenment," *History of European Ideas*, 29 (2003), 255–89.
30. Samuel Pufendorf, *The Law of Nature and of Nations in Eight Books*, trans. C.H. Oldfather and W.A. Oldfather, 2 vols. (Oxford: Clarendon Press, 1934), II.iii.23, pp. 226–29. Cf., Koskenniemi, "The Advantage of Treaties," pp. 47–53.
31. Pufendorf, *The Law of Nature*, III.iii.9, pp. 363–66.
32. Emer de Vattel, *The Law of Nations, or, Principles of the Law of Nature, Applied to the Conduct and Affairs of Nations and Sovereigns*, ed. B. Kapossy and R. Whatmore (Indianapolis: Liberty Fund, 2008), pp. 74–79.
33. Ibid., pp. 507–8, 644–47.
34. Ibid., pp. 129, 487, 507–8.
35. Ibid., pp. 130, 214–16.
36. For the contrary view, see Reynolds, *Aboriginal Sovereignty*, pp. 51–54.
37. Vattel, *Law of Nations*, pp. 128–31, 131–39, 198–203.
38. Ibid., pp. 174–80, 474–75.
39. Martti Koskenniemi, *The Gentle Civilizer of Nations: The Rise and Fall of International Law 1870–1960* (Cambridge: Cambridge University Press, 2002), pp. 413–36.
40. See in particular P.G. McHugh, *Aboriginal Societies and the Common Law: A History of Sovereignty, Status, and Self-determination* (Oxford: Oxford University Press, 2004); and the remarkable essays collected in *Histories, Power and Loss: Uses of the Past—a New Zealand Commentary*, ed. Andrew Sharp and P.G. McHugh (Wellington: Bridget Williams Books, 2001); and J.G.A. Pocock, *The Discovery of Islands: Essays in British History* (Cambridge: Cambridge University Press, 2005). See also Mark Hickford, "'Decidedly the Most Interesting Savages on the Globe': An Approach to the Intellectual History of Māori Property Rights, 1837–53," *History of Political Thought*, 27 (2006), 122–67; Mark Hickford, "John Salmond and Native Title in New Zealand: Developing a Crown Theory on the Treaty of Waitangi, 1910–1920," *Victoria University of Wellington Law Review* 38 (2007), 853–924; Damen Ward, "A Means and Measure of Civilisation: Colonial Authorities and

Indigenous Law in Australasia," *History Compass*, 1 (2003), 1–23; and Damen Ward, "Constructing British Authority in Australasia: Charles Cooper and the Legal Status of Aborigines in the South Australian Supreme Court, c. 1840–60," *The Journal of Imperial and Commonwealth History*, 34 (2006), 483–504. See too the papers by Dorsett, Hickford, Sharp and Ward in this volume.

41. For the contrary view—that Australian Aboriginal forms of authority and land-relation were immediately conceivable via European juridical conceptions of sovereignty and property, and were then willfully obscured in order to achieve dispossession—see the discussions of indigenous sovereignty and land ownership in Henry Reynolds, *The Law of the Land* (Sydney: Penguin Books, 1988); and Reynolds *Aboriginal Sovereignty.*
42. For a helpful statement and exemplification of this position, see P.G. McHugh, "The Common-Law Status of Colonies and Aboriginal 'Rights': How Lawyers and Historians Treat the Past," *Saskatchewan Law Review* 61 (1998), 393–42.
43. For illuminating discussions of this issue, see Andrew Sharp, "History and Sovereignty: A Case of Juridical History in New Zealand/Aotearoa," in *Cultural Politics in the University in Aotearoa/New Zealand*, ed. M. Peters (Palmerston: Dunmore Press, 1997), pp. 158–81; and Richard P. Boast, "Lawyers, Historians, Ethics and the Judicial Process," *Victoria University of Wellington Law Review*, 28 (1998), 87–112.
44. Chitty in Emer de Vattel, *The Law of Nations, or Principles of the Law of Nature, Applied to the Conduct and Affairs of Nations and Sovereigns*, ed. J. Chitty (London, 1834), pp. 1–2, fns. 10–11, pp. 166ff, fn. 107.
45. Hickford, "Decidedly the Most Interesting Savages," pp. 123–33.
46. Ibid., pp. 151–55.
47. Ibid., pp. 160–65.
48. Ibid., p. 152.
49. J.G.A. Pocock, "Law, Sovereignty and History in a Divided Culture: The Case of New Zealand and the Treaty of Waitangi," in *The Discovery of Islands*, pp. 226–55. For a parallel argument from the Māori perspective, see Te Maire Tau, "Matauranga Māori as an Epistemology," in *Histories, Power and Loss*, ed. Sharp and McHugh, pp. 61–74.
50. See J.G.A. Pocock, "*Tangata Whenua* and Enlightenment Anthropology," in *The Discovery of Islands*, pp. 199–225.
51. For a different view of this issue—in the Canadian context—see Mark Walters' chapter in this volume.

Chapter 2

Justice and Imperialism

On the Very Idea of a Universal Standard

Duncan Ivison

I

In the modern era, imperialism refers to relations between states and peoples in which one state is able to effectively impose, constrain, dominate, and exploit others in ways that affect their most important interests.[1] This can occur either directly or indirectly, formally or informally. Of course, it is never complete and there is always room to maneuver on the part of those subject to these relations of power. However, that room to move can be severely limited. The imposition of "metropolitan law" within an imperial political order can be defined in terms of its inherently hierarchical structure: one state is hegemonic and its will trumps other legal and normative systems. The independence of any other legal orders is, therefore, by definition contingent and shifting, depending on the interests of the imperial power.

In the fields of political theory and public law, the structure of imperialism is associated above all with the period of formal Western imperialism stretching from the sixteenth century (at least) until the mid- to late twentieth century and the various movements and processes of decolonization. However, it has also been associated with developments *since* decolonization, especially the rise of the United States and the new global political, legal, and economic order formed in its wake. This "new imperialism" is associated with the United States and its allies working with (and at times against) an informal league of cooperating and competing sovereign states and transnational corporations, as well as a complex of global institutions such as the International Monetary Fund (IMF) and the World Bank (WB), and transnational legal regimes such as the General Agreement on Tariffs and Trade (GATT). There remains considerable debate about the extent to which various responses to this form of imperialism—among them, the discourse of moral cosmopolitanism—manage to escape or remain entangled within imperial relations. Here is one formulation of this kind of concern:

> [cosmopolitan discourse] is abstract and utopian in the worst sense...the sovereignty-based model of international law appears to be ceding not to cosmopolitan justice but to an imperial project of dominance and indirect control of key "peripheries." The world's sole superpower makes good use of cosmopolitan discourse in its efforts to marginalize international institutions and undermine international law, especially law restraining the use of force and the legal principles of non-intervention and self-determination. What we face is not a simple effort to evade international law by a powerful actor, but rather a serious bid to reorient it in an imperial direction—under the heading of "global right."[2]

How does empire become transposed onto justice? There are two kinds of question here, one historical the other conceptual, though they are often entwined. First, we may ask whether there are particular arguments about justice that were subsequently used in the justification of empire or colonialism. Or, we may seek to trace the conceptual structure of arguments justifying imperialism to their roots in particular philosophical views, debunking their supposed universalism.[3] Second, we may ask about the very nature of the concept of global justice and the values it expresses in relation to other important values. Is the very *notion* of global justice imperialistic, just because it claims there are universal values applicable to everyone everywhere, whatever their particular ways of life or worldviews?

The form of justice I am concerned with here is *distributive* or *social* justice. The challenge of global or international justice is the extension of this framework from the domestic to the global sphere. How do you reconcile a deep commitment on the part of liberal egalitarianism to *moral* egalitarianism with an assumption that distributive justice applies only to those who share membership (usually citizenship) in a territorial state.

The central question of this chapter lies at the intersection of the historical and conceptual questions. I am interested in the historical question about the relationship between particular conceptions of justice and the justification of imperialism and actual imperial practices. But I am also interested in the conceptual questions: the tension between the demand for universal principles (or at least standards) of justice and moral particularism; the idea that there may well be principles of justice, but that they apply only within states or "peoples" or hold only among individuals who stand in certain practice-mediated relations. The broader, normative issue at stake is something like this: Liberals are committed to tolerating cultural diversity and value pluralism, along with something like what Rawls calls the "fact of reasonable pluralism."[4] Reasonable pluralism is a "fact" for Rawls, at least within liberal democratic states, given the free exercise of our reason. If people exercise their reason freely, we have no reason to expect that they will all agree on the same comprehensive view of the good, or on fundamental questions of morality. Within liberal democratic states this picture presents an acute problem for the egalitarian liberal: according to at least some conceptions of liberalism, a state will be legitimate only to the extent that the exercise of coercive power is based on reasons that no one could reasonably reject. But what kinds of reasons are these, and how could they not fail to be comprehensive in some way?

If the task is daunting *within* liberal democratic states, it is positively Herculean when turning to the global sphere. Here we have to contend with diversity not only between individuals but also between "peoples," to use Rawls's phrase. Do peoples have a collective right to determine their own political arrangements free from interference, including the distribution and allocation of various rights and resources within that collective? How should liberals respond to this kind of diversity? How much difference should be tolerated? How universal can (or should) principles of justice be? What would the *grounds* of such principles be?

If you believe that there are universal standards that apply to all individuals (and groups) then you must be committed to seeing those principles or standards realized in some way. And thus an imperial dimension to considerations of justice might enter here. It comes with the very idea of a universal standard, whether that standard is understood in terms of basic human rights or as an egalitarian redistribution of resources. Is it possible to hold all societies to a common standard that is thick enough to protect important human interests and yet not grounded in a particular set of cultural values that would mean essentially imposing one way of life on another?

In what way could the very idea of a universal standard be potentially imperialistic? It may involve the justification of the imposition of European ways of life, or liberal political orders, on non-European and non-liberal societies. What is wrong with that? One argument is that it denies the capacity of those peoples to exercise their collective freedom, which in turn is a necessary condition of the legitimacy of domestic and international political and legal orders to which we assume they are subject. Of course, the appeal to the value of collective freedom—or to what James Tully calls their *democratic* freedom—is itself an appeal to a universal value.[5] So what makes the latter more acceptable or less imperialistic than the former? The details of that argument will have to be evaluated elsewhere, but the gist of it lies in the idea that the laws and norms people are subject to must always be open to criticism, negotiation, and modification. The suggestion by scholars of both formal and informal imperialism is that this participatory and reflexive freedom of negotiation has been subverted by imperialistic practices and ideologies that have their origins in early modern and modern political thought.

A crucial question here is whether the debunking of supposedly universal political forms (such as we find in Kant) invalidates the very idea of global justice itself. It's one thing to say a *particular* constitutional form is universal or not; it's another to deny there are any universals whatsoever. Every argument has its origins in some particular cultural form, but does that mean there are no claims or values that can be vindicated across cultures? What would the structure of a conception of global justice be that took plurality and history seriously?

II

So what are the crucial features of the legitimating ideology of an imperialistic mode of global justice? There are many potential sources, but Kant looms large, especially along two dimensions: (1) the normative and juridical language of an international system of constitutional states; and (2) a philosophy of history of humanity's progress through various stages of development from savagery to civilization and modernization. The metanarrative that Kant presents is not only of the right normative order of states in the international system but also a philosophico-historical account of their movement toward that destination. The normative theory is provided most prominently in *Perpetual Peace* (1795), but undergirded by the moral philosophy of the *Groundwork to the Metaphysics of Morals* (1785) and the first part of the *Metaphysics of Morals* (the *Rechtslehre*) (1797). The philosophico-historical account is provided, among other places, in "Idea for a Universal History from a Cosmopolitan Viewpoint" (1784).

Kant also plays an important role in the history of distributive justice in at least two ways, although he is not a theorist of *social* justice per se. First, he offers a powerful philosophical defense of the equal worth of all human beings. This is a crucial premise required for linking equality with distribution. Respect for the rights of others means all of us will have duties to ensure each can exercise their freedom (compatible with the freedom of others). Thus everyone has, as Kant put it, "a right to enjoy the good things of this world" (27: 414). If morality is understood under the aegis of law as command, then what is owed to others—including the poor—is owed as a matter of right, not beneficence or charity, and not based on an assessment of people's needs. Although no defender of the modern welfare state, Kant did, in fact, see it as part of the role of the state to "constrain the wealthy to provide the means of sustenance to those who are unable to provide for the most necessary natural needs." He also supplies one strand of the notion that each of us has a set of potentials for fully free action that can be realized only in certain natural and social circumstances. These two premises—that each of us is owed certain things by right in order to realize our "potential"—aren't explicitly linked in Kant's moral and political theory, but they would be developed much more extensively by later political philosophers.

The second broad influence Kant has is in relation to the *scope* of justice. His delineation of the domain of "cosmopolitan right" provides a way of conceiving of the interdependence between domestic and international justice. Kant's conception of "cosmopolitan right" thus continues to shape contemporary debates over the nature of global justice and human rights.[6] Critics, however, have been quick to point out that far from embodying genuinely a priori principles that could reasonably be adopted by people everywhere, Kantian and neo-Kantian cosmopolitan justice represents a parochial, historically particular (and peculiar) set of highly contestable claims: in other words, it offers only a false universalism.[7] Kant's cosmopolitanism is thus vulnerable to the very charge of imperialism his defenders and interpreters claim he provides a bulwark against. Before exploring these claims directly, I want to try to lay out the structure of Kant's argument as charitably as possible in order to try to identify what many liberal interpreters, in particular, have found so compelling about it.

One of Kant's most powerful ideas is that human beings possess an innate worth that can never be traded off against other ends—even ends we might find extremely desirable or valuable for all kinds of reasons. Human beings possess *dignity* or, in another formulation, human beings should never be treated as a "means" but always as "ends" in themselves. But what does this mean? How can it provide guidance for action in the complex and conflicted world of politics? One thing Kant's approach does is anchor claims about rights in what he calls "pure practical reason." People have rights, and others have duties to respect them, in virtue of a theory of justice that is derived from a particular account of the relation between reason and freedom. Duties are morally basic, not needs or interests. And those duties are tied to a view about the nature of human freedom.

In the *Groundwork of the Metaphysics of Morals*, Kant says that "what has a price can be replaced by something else as its equivalent; what on the other hand is raised above all price and therefore admits of no equivalent has a dignity."[8] This he associates with our fundamental rational being, our *humanity* (4: 434). It's one thing to act out of fear, or to be constrained by others to act as a means to an end, but it's another thing to set an end for oneself—to act genuinely freely. The appeal to dignity here isn't so much an appeal to a principle of action as it is to an *attitude* that we should take up toward others. Elsewhere in the *Groundwork* Kant expresses it another way: "I say that the human being and in general every rational being exists as an end in itself, not merely as a means to be used by this or that will at its discretion" (4: 428). Appealing to the fundamental dignity of human beings is now a familiar way in which we talk about the rights. In fact, it's written into Article 1 of the *Universal Declaration of Human Rights*. But what follows from it?

For Kant, morality involves rational agents imposing a law on themselves that at the same time provides a motive for them to obey. What does this mean? The basic idea is that morality presupposes freedom. To think of myself as free is to think of myself as able to act according to self-legislated principles. To be self-governing in this way is to be autonomous.[9] But what is the moral law and how can it show us what we ought to do (and not do)? In order to be consistent with our autonomy, the moral law must be formal, or a priori, that is, we must be capable of acting on it merely by thinking its idea, independently of all interests or purposes we might have—hence the idea of moral duties as flowing from the "categorical imperative." To say that an imperative—a principle for action—is "categorical" is simply to say that its bindingness does not depend on the pursuit of some end set independently of it.

But this is only the beginning. Kant provides two further formulas, one that draws our attention to those affected by our actions, and another from the perspective of our being a member of a community that so wills. The second formula states, "So act that you use humanity whether in your own person or that of another, always at the same time as an end, never merely as a means" (4: 429). This says that the ends of others, as long as they are morally permissible, set limits to our own and that we must respect them. In doing so we are respecting others as "ends in themselves," that is, not using them as "things" or coercing them for our own purposes. This is a good way of making sense of Kant's appeal to the inherent dignity of "humanity" with which we began above. The duties that the moral law will prescribe will be—just given their form—coordinate with the rights of others (or at least, so he claims).

The third is the "formula of autonomy": "the idea of the will of every rational being as a will giving universal law (4: 431), and that "all maxims from one's own lawgiving are to harmonize with a possible kingdom of ends" (4: 436). This third formula instructs us to think of ourselves as members of a society of beings whose permissible ends are respected in the right way, as ends in themselves rather than as ends for some particular purpose. We should act to help bring about such a community of harmonized ends.

None of these formulas are intended as moral algorithms that tell us how to act in each and every situation, whatever the context. But put together, they add up to a powerful set of rules or norms against which to test our actual or intended behavior. In particular, they act as a set of constraints on our tendency to excuse ourselves from the demands of reason we place on others. And they structure how we should think about our rights as well as the rights of others.

How does morality relate to the establishment of civil society and to politics more generally? On the one hand, Kant is faced with a familiar question: If human beings are fundamentally free and equal, how can they be legitimately subject to coercion? It should be clear now that Kant cannot help himself to the kind of argument Hobbes makes about the genesis and legitimacy of the state—namely, that people in pursuit of the minimal morality of social peace are driven through mutual fear to appoint a sovereign power whose laws will compel them to be mutually peaceful. And this raises the very difficult question about the ultimate relation between morality and politics in Kant, or more precisely, between morality and right (or justice).

Right is distinguished from ethics in three basic ways: it is the subject of external legislation; it relates only to duties of justice ("perfect" as opposed to "imperfect" duties); and it is concerned only with the external actions of others rather than their moral will. The crucial question, however, is the extent of the dependence of Kant's political theory on the metaphysics underpinning his moral philosophy, as much of the force of the criticism of Kant's cosmopolitanism stems from pushing hard against this connection. There are generally two ways of making sense of this relation. First, one could argue that we should see Kant's theory of right (and thus ultimately his political theory) as derived from his ethical writings. Second, one could argue that we should distinguish sharply between his ethical theory and his theory of right. Let us consider the second more closely.

III

The political upshot of Kant's argument in the *Rechtslehre* is something like this: If I am autonomous in the way Kant suggests, then no other external authority—whether the state, the church, or "society"—has the right to (or even could) impose *moral* obligations on me. In principle at least, I am both free and able to impose moral obligations on myself and in doing so provide myself with the motive to act in accordance with them. Freedom is conceived of as *independence*: I am free in the sense that I can set my own purposes, as opposed to having them set for me. Moreover, I am truly independent only when I am not dependent on others for granting or allowing me to possess what is truly mine. If I have to depend on the benevolence of others, at least with regard to what is mine by right, then my autonomy as a moral agent is undermined. Kant thinks that it follows from this view of human agents as self-governing, autonomous moral beings that social and political arrangements have to be organized in a certain way. Each of us should have the freedom in which to determine our own actions. Others should not be allowed to interfere with our moral autonomy by telling us what morality requires. Nor should they be allowed to undermine our independence by using us as a means for their own purposes (for example, by defrauding us) or by depriving us of our means (by controlling our person or harming us). To do this is to treat someone as a means to purposes other than their own—to treat them as a "thing" instead of a person.

Ethics concerns how a human being regulates her own conduct according to self-given laws, as we've seen. The theory of right, however, concerns the rational standards for externally coercive laws and the framework within which laws are applied in society. A crucial difference between ethical duties and political duties (imposed by right), of course, is that the latter can be coercively enforced, but the former cannot. Why? Justice has to do only with *external* relations, not internal motives. The ethical and the political share similar ends, but different motives; they are continuous, but at the same time distinct.[10] In other words, right concerns the concrete, observable actions taken by us that affect other agents. As Kant says, "in this reciprocal relation of choice no account at all is taken of the matter of choice, that is, of the end each has in mind with the object he wants. . . . All that is in question is the form. . . . and whether the action of one can be united with the freedom of the other in accordance with universal law" (6: 230). Thus, every action is "right" Kant declares, "if it can coexist with everyone's freedom in accordance with a universal law, or if on its maxim the freedom of choice of each can coexist with everyone's freedom in accordance with a universal law" (6: 230). Kantian politics doesn't require so much the right kind of *willing* (as Kantian morality does) as the right kind of *acting*, which can be achieved through what Kant calls the "principle of universal reciprocal coercion." Still, respect for persons is supposed to provide a crucial limiting condition for politics. Part of the whole point of establishing public right is to create the conditions in which people will be treated as ends and not means in their unavoidable interactions with others.

For Kant, each of us has what he calls an "innate right" of humanity: a "right of humanity in our own person." It is this aspect of Kant's moral and political theory—grounding law and politics in the innate rights of man—that is considered to be the core of Kantian politics for many readers today. But what does Kant mean when he says we have innate rights, and how is our having them supposed to shape politics? Each of us has the right of *independence* from others (and equal to others) innately, that is, "by nature," independently of any affirmative act to establish it (6: 236–7; see also 8: 290). Not only do we have an innate right to our person, which is crucial to our setting and pursuing any kind of end in the first place, but we also have rights to usable things and to establish various kinds of rational relations.

But if we are all equally free, then how can we interact in ways that don't compromise our independence? Since we are all fundamentally free and equal, nobody should have the power to interfere with or control how I set my purposes, except insofar as it's required to preserve the freedom of others. This is *private right*: the right to make something external one's own. Kant relates it to three categories: property, contract (i.e., our capacity to transfer our rights), and status, or asymmetrical but rightful relations with others, such as masters/servants, parents/children, teachers/students (6: 254–5).

IV

Consider Kant's theory of property, which is central to his general account of political legitimation. Free beings must be able to choose objects to use for their own purposes, as means toward their ends. Kant thinks of the "surface of the earth" as a common possession of all and that each of us has by nature the will to use it (6: 261–2). This is a "practical rational concept," not a historical fact as it tends to be conceived in the natural law tradition. And he will move from the possibility of unilateral acquisition to this idea of original possession in common, as opposed to the other way round, as it was for the natural lawyers. However, the limited nature of the earth's surface is also crucial to his argument and supplies an important premise for the cosmopolitan scope of his theory of right:

> Since the earth's surface is not unlimited but closed, the concepts of the Right of a State and of a Right of nations lead inevitably to the Idea of a Right for all nations or cosmopolitan Right. So if the principles of outer freedom limited by law is lacking in any one of these three possible forms of rightful condition, the framework of all others is unavoidably undermined and finally collapse. (6: 311)

To deny the possibility of exclusive possession would be to unjustifiably restrict the freedom of persons. (6: 251). Here Kant distinguishes between "phenomenal" and "intelligible" possession. The first applies to objects we are in immediate physical contact with and control, like the computer on which these words are being written. When something I physically possess is taken away from me or damaged against my will, I am being coerced unjustifiably. But this is also true of objects that aren't in my immediate physical possession, but which form part of my "intelligible" or rational possession (of "concepts of the understanding": 6: 253): objects secured through a *relation* between rational wills. Relations of right specify relations between *subjects*, not just between subjects and objects. I can claim something as rightfully mine only if others recognize the legitimacy of my claim, and it is this idea that Kant is referring to with regard to intelligible possession; that is, when I say I own something I mean this to hold even if I don't actually have physical control of it (6: 246). Thus for Kant, ownership has to do with my intention to occupy land, for example, and to bring it under my will, not with my current actual possession, or the way I've used it, or the fact that I've invested my labor in it, as was the case for Locke.

Pure practical reason tells us how we should interact as rational wills: exercise your freedom in a way compatible with the freedom of all. But reason also tell us, given the fact that the world is finite, that some of our actions will unavoidably limit what others would otherwise be able to do. The principle of right provides a (supposedly) formal principle for resolving those conflicts, but one informed by certain empirical facts as well. Thus, even if it is the case that I can institute rational relations with others to secure nonphysical ownership, I cannot do so on the basis of my judgment *alone* as to what should be the case. My possessing something will have consequences for your freedom. As Kant puts it, "a unilateral will cannot serve as a coercive law for everyone with regard to possession that is external and therefore contingent, since that would infringe upon freedom in accordance with universal laws" (6: 256).

This means we are necessarily subject to the principle of right, to justice. Therefore, what is wrong with remaining in the state of nature is that it is a state of indeterminacy about the boundary between mine and thine.[11] We know we have to respect each other's freedom and property, but we need a mechanism for determining what that actually entails. We cannot fulfill our duty to "harm no one" (see section II above) without the determinacy provided by a civil order. Neither can we, *in principle*, establish unilaterally the intelligible possession that is a necessary aspect of the exercise of our freedom in a finite world we share with other agents. Unilateral judgment is incompatible with the innate rights of humanity. This is what Kant means by the "*a priori* idea of a general and united will" (6: 258). It is not just that we are likely to disagree over property (contra Locke), but that we must already be in the right relationship for my act to have significance for you.[12] I need to acquire means for my purposes, but your freedom must be respected in the process (6: 250–1; 6: 312). These two requirements can be satisfied only in a "rightful" condition, and the same holds true for contractual and "status" relations.

Interestingly, Kant does allow for an intermediate stage of possession, what he calls "provisional right." In a state of nature, something may be able to be seen as mine (or thine) but only "provisionally"; that is, "in anticipation of and preparation for the civil condition." Possession in the civil condition, however, is "conclusive" (6: 256–7).[13]

To remain in a state of nature, then, is to subject oneself to the potential interference of others, which is to live in a way incompatible with one's autonomy (6: 255–6). It follows from our being free that to be subject to the right kind of coercive authority is not only permissible but required. Doing so is the only way to make our freedoms mutually compatible. Thus we have a duty to enter into the civil condition (6: 256). This gives rise to the social contract, as distinct from private contract. The social contract grounds the "right of men to live under public coercive law, through which each can receive his due and can be made secure from the interference of others." (8: 289) But the notion of a contract is not doing any real work here. It is as if the initial violation of others' equally valid claims to freedom is provisionally legitimate (*lex permissiva*), as a means to engendering (internal, reflective) recognition on the part of the first acquirers that a unilateral will cannot serve as the basis for coercive law (6: 256). The legitimacy of the state flows from what it does (or should do), as opposed to our having literally consented to it, or from the conditionality of mutually incurred obligation on the part of each party to the agreement. To use an abstract Kantian formulation, the state as an *idea*, not as embodied in any particular empirical or historical manifestation, is justified in terms of its role in enabling and coordinating our freedom and, over time, the promotion of moral ends (like peace). Political right, in general, is grounded in the natural principles of respect for autonomy.

The enforcement of rights, in other words, has a distinctly public character in Kant's political theory. It is not just that the private enforcement of rights is inconvenient or likely to lead to conflict (as both Hobbes and Locke suggest) and, therefore, prudentially warranted, but that it is fundamentally incompatible with our status as free and equal. Even if it never did lead to conflict, private enforcement is wrong. The only imposition of force compatible with our freedom is one that issues from an "omnilateral" as opposed to unilateral will. The only rights I can have are those compatible with a system of rights in which your rights are guaranteed as well, including their mutual enforcement.

But Kant also says we have a duty to establish not just any common authority but rather a *republican* political order, one compatible with our innate rights. Formally he defines it as "the political principle of separation of the executive power (the government) from the legislative power" (8: 352, 354). But it is also a regime in which the sovereign will of the people is represented to the ruling power, which is then charged with implementing it.

Our innate rights, thinks Kant, help explain the kind of powers the state has, as well as the nature of our obedience to it. For one thing, the justification has to be formal in order to be universal. Free persons (ideally conceived), concerned to protect their freedom, can only ever agree (ideally, not actually) to enter a civil condition in which their freedom is secure. So a state is never justified in seeking to promote the happiness of its citizens, only their freedom (8: 290–1). Nor is a state justified in appropriating the property of its citizens to help meet the needs of landless or poorer citizens. As we've seen, as a matter of private right, no one can be made to serve as the means for another, just as no one has a right to means that are not already their own. As a matter of public right, the state is not justified in using me as a means for promoting social justice or substantive equality, even if I can afford it and others are in genuine need. However, the state still needs enough authority to make the division between "mine and thine" determinate and rightful, that is, to "hinder the hindrances" to our freedom, and this ends up justifying considerable state power.

V

A problem with Kant's account, however, is the extent to which it is dependent on a comprehensive and hence potentially particularistic metaphysical anthropology. The conception of ideal rational beings at the heart of his account—independent of being determined by any kind of sensible impulse—has attracted criticism ever since he first made the argument. Kant's work is replete with indications, however, that he is not so naïve about politics and, moreover, sees a crucial role for freely willed human action in relation to it, although it is not immediately clear how much weight these remarks bear on his wider argument about the relation between morality and politics. One of the most notorious examples can be found in *Perpetual Peace*:

> The problem of setting up a state... is solvable even for a people of devils (if only they have understanding). It is this: A set of rational beings who on the whole need for their preservation universal laws from which each is however secretly inclined to exempt himself is to be organized and their constitution arranged so that their private attitudes, though opposed, nevertheless check one another in such a way that these beings behave in public as if they had no such evil attitudes. (8: 366)

"Mere" legal order is thus possible through natural incentives, as Hobbes showed. But Kant also clearly indicates (here and elsewhere) that it's not enough (can only ever be provisional), and that progress through enlightenment includes the transition from mere legal order to a civil society in which one's autonomy is genuinely respected. The transition from the state of nature to civil society includes a stage in which a legal order may be in place, but not yet just. Still, it ought to be respected if it promotes the *possibility* of eventual rightful possession under a truly just civil authority.

A more "political" reading of Kant is that there is some independent value to the notion of external freedom such that each of us has an enlightened interest in establishing a political and legal order in which our lives are determined by our own choices, rather than those coercively imposed by others.[14] To borrow from Rawls, it would be that the appeal to external freedom in the *Rechtslehre* could be grounded on a "freestanding" as opposed to comprehensive conception. For Rawls, a comprehensive conception relies on "conceptions of what is of value in human life, as well as ideals of personal virtue and character that are to inform our non-political conduct."[15] The claim would be, then, that we can read the *Rechtslehre* as somehow detachable from Kant's moral philosophy and transcendental idealism. More precisely, the claim would be that even if it's true that Kant sees his doctrine of *Recht* as the only one that fits his moral philosophy, it doesn't follow that his right or justice cannot stand without that moral philosophy.[16]

There are deep challenges for such a reading, however. Ian Hunter, for example, has argued that we need to see Kant's entire philosophical approach as a historically specific intellectual or spiritual exercise aimed at forming the kind of self that the philosopher must become if he is to accede to the principle of right as a metaphysical truth. Kant is engaged, in other words, not in the philosophical project of justifying metaphysical truth, but in "the grooming of the intellectual deportment required to accede to such truth."[17] In short, Kant's metaphysics needs to be treated as a contingent historical form, the product of a specific regional set of intellectual practices and institutions, as opposed to a valid claim about the structure of human understanding.

We must be careful to avoid something like the genetic fallacy here. Unveiling the historical specificity of an argument says nothing in itself about its ultimate validity. It denaturalizes the concept and renders it more contingent, but it does not in itself refute it or even suggest we should abandon it. Contingency does not entail arbitrariness. It may well refute certain *beliefs* we have about the concept or theory, but equally it may not.[18] A genealogy of a concept or theory can be debunking, but also vindicatory.[19] It will depend on how that genealogy sits within the self-understanding of the tradition or community of interpreters involved, or for whom the argument or concept has significance. What historical reflection can do is debunk the seeming obviousness of our assumptions about the problem at hand. In doing so it can generate not necessarily a new set of answers as much as a new set of questions. And it can pluralize conceptual possibilities in ways no amount of conceptual analysis can provide. Arguments and theories can spill over the bounds of their historical specificity in a range of different ways. They can be put to work in new circumstances, sometimes with surprising results.

Recall the distinction between "freestanding" and "comprehensive" doctrines. The problem with comprehensive doctrines—for Rawls, this includes Kant's doctrines—is that they are socially divisive and unable to gain the reasoned assent of individuals understood as free and equal. If a conception of social justice depends on the state extracting resources from individuals in order for them to be redistributed, and if that conception is grounded in a "comprehensive" view, then the danger is that state power will be required to maintain that shared understanding (through public education etc.) and it will be seen as alien or illegitimate in the eyes of those with different comprehensive views. Since the presence of a diversity of comprehensive views is unavoidable in free societies, such a doctrine could be sustained only through state "oppression."[20]

The liberal reading of Kant depends on the plausibility of an interpretation of the *Rechtslehre* as "free-standing" in some way, given the independent value of something like external freedom understood as independence or "non-domination."[21] Liberal cosmopolitan readings of Kant then depend on the scope of justice that Kant's argument implies and which I have attempted to highlight above. The "fact of proximity," as I suggested above, or the spherical limits of the earth's surface, seems to point to the unavoidability of developing transnational standards for evaluating the behavior of states and other actors in relation to individuals' basic rights (or claims) to freedom. The interdependency between property rights and political legitimation also points to the issue of a politically adequate motivational basis for justice: *Cognitivist* Kantians appeal to the more robust metaphysical account of the nature of our political agency, given what they take to be the need for a fundamental change in our thinking regarding our obligations of justice. The *political* Kantian appeals to a form of enlightened self-interest.

This returns us to the challenge of imperialism, since the same argument applies, *mutatis mutandis*, to a purportedly global theory of justice. The most peculiar (and difficult) aspect of Kant's argument here is the extent to which his notion of the "cosmopolitan intent" of history plays a central role in the argument of the *Rechtslehre*. For critics such as Hunter or Tully, it presents a picture in which mankind's perfection will be realized on earth through a philosophical history in which nature itself will perfect man using empirical means in accordance with history's hidden cosmopolitan purpose.[22] Man's asocial sociability, including his tendency to engage in expansionary wars and colonization, along with an ethos of competitive individualism, leads to the development of institutions and processes that moves the world closer to the normative ideal outlined in the definitive articles of *Perpetual Peace*. This makes colonization seem to be a necessary stage in the development of the human species toward the realization of Kant's vision of a world order of republican states. The violence inherent in colonialism is unjust, but the consequences seem to provide a necessary stage in the development of perpetual peace. It also seems to present a cosmopolitan future in which there is only one legitimate constitutional form, embedded within a body of international law that extends equal recognition to other similarly constituted states but permits intervention into the affairs of non-republican states, which are treated as essentially outside of the law.

This philosophical history seems hard to reconcile with any kind of liberal interpretation of the cosmopolitan structure of Kant's argument in the *Rechtslehre*. Therefore, it must be either read completely *out* of that argument—which seems difficult to do—or read down in such a way that the appeal to the teleology of man's asocial sociability bears considerably less philosophical weight than Hunter's or Tully's reading suggests.[23]

VI

If we have good reason to worry about the Kantian structure of cosmopolitan argument in its either "metaphysical" or "political" mode, then are there other ways of conceiving of the nature of global justice? There are, and to conclude I set out some broad distinctions as a way of beginning to think differently about global justice.

Charles Beitz has pointed to the difference between "social liberalism" and "cosmopolitan liberalism."[24] Social liberalism takes a two-level conception of international society that embodies a division of labor between the domestic and international. States take responsibility for "their" people, while the international community is concerned with the conditions in which those societies can flourish. Cosmopolitan liberals, however, seek principles that are acceptable from a standpoint in which everybody's prospects are equally represented, without representing the standpoints of "societies" per se. Three crucial principles are usually appealed to here: the fundamental moral worth of individuals (as opposed to nations, tribes, or ethnic or cultural groups); their fundamental equality; and the existence of obligations binding on all. In addition to the difference between social liberals and cosmopolitan liberals, Beitz and other scholars distinguish between "moral" and "institutional" cosmopolitanism.[25] The three principles alluded to in the previous sentence amount to a form of moral cosmopolitanism. Institutional cosmopolitanism entails a commitment to certain global political institutions. So one could be a moral cosmopolitan without being an institutional cosmopolitan. The claim would be that moral cosmopolitanism is not committed, as Caney claims, to "any specific empirical or explanatory claims about what forces shape the global realm."[26]

In yet another attempt to map the domain, Thomas Nagel has distinguished between a "political" and "cosmopolitan" approach to global justice. The cosmopolitan approach is close to what Beitz describes. The "political" approach suggests that states "give the value of justice its application, by putting the fellow citizens of a sovereign state into a relation they do not have with the rest of humanity, *an institutional relation* which must then be evaluated by the special standards of fairness and equality that fill out the content of justice."[27] What I want to draw attention to here is the suggestion of justice being an *institution-dependent* concept. Perhaps a better way of making sense of this idea is to say that principles of justice hold only among individuals who stand in certain "practice-mediated" relations with each other.[28]

A practice-independent approach to thinking about the nature of justice would be one in which the contingent, practice-mediated relations in which we find ourselves should not affect or change the justifying reasons and premises underpinning the content and scope of justice. The intuition that justice should be grounded on the premise that we should seek to mitigate the effects of brute bad luck—or people's "circumstances" (as opposed to their choices)—on our life prospects is practice-independent in this sense. The appeal is to moral values alone. The institutions and practices to which they are meant to apply play no role in the content, scope, and justification of the principles.

Practice-dependent theorists, however, think that our living under certain institutions (whatever their origins) or our sharing specific kinds of practice-mediated relations should have a bearing on our thinking about justice. A practice-dependent theorist is committed, therefore, to saying that a conception of justice rests at least as much on an interpretation of actually existing institutional systems as it does on common values: the content, scope, and justification of the conception will be determined, in part, by the role it is meant to play given those institutions and practices.[29] Although this might allow for principles of justice with less than global scope, it would not be limited to *only* such principles: there could well be principles that are global—or at least transnational—given the nature of the practices or institutions at issue. In fact, I think this is very likely to be the case. We might call this a form of non-cosmopolitan global justice.

The difference between cosmopolitan and non-cosmopolitan global justice hinges, ultimately, on differing interpretations of the role, legitimacy, and normative distinctiveness of the state (or other non-state but effective political entities) and its relation to the interests—including the rights, liberties, and responsibilities—of individuals. The cosmopolitan liberal infers from moral cosmopolitanism that if the ultimate unit of moral concern is the individual, then only individuals have intrinsic moral worth and our principles of justice should reflect this. However, states can be said to retain normative relevance for a theory of justice without thinking either that they *ought* to always do so, are the *only* collective political entities that could do so, or that this requires giving up on some plausible interpretation of respecting the equal worth (or agency) of individuals, including non-citizens. A non-imperialistic doctrine of universal right needs to reconcile these different intuitions without appeal to either the hidden hand of teleology, or a radical disjuncture between a cosmopolitan heaven and a devilish earth.

Notes

1. Research for this chapter was supported by a grant from the Australian Research Council. I am grateful to Andrew Fitzmaurice, Henry Reynolds and especially Ian Hunter for their suggestions and help.
2. Jean L. Cohen, "Sovereign Equality vs. Imperial Right: The Battle over the 'New World Order,'" in *The Modernist Imagination*, ed. Peter E. Gordon, A. Dirk Moses, Samuel Moyn and Elliot Neaman (New York: Berghan Books, 2009), pp. 346–67 (p. 353).
3. See, for examples, the various postcolonial critiques of European philosophical universalism discussed in Ian Hunter's chapter in this volume. Hunter's own argument offers a different version of this critique.
4. John Rawls, *Political Liberalism* (New York: Columbia University Press, 1993).
5. James Tully, *Public Philosophy in a New Key, Vol. II: Imperialism and Civic Freedom*, 2 vols. (Cambridge: Cambridge University Press, 2009).
6. See James Bohman and Matthias Lutz-Bachman, *Perpetual Peace: Essays on Kant's Cosmopolitan Ideal* (Cambridge: MIT, 1997); Katrin Flikschuh, *Kant and Modern Philosophy* (Cambridge: Cambridge University Press, 2000).
7. Tully, *Public Philosophy*; also Hunter's chapter in this volume.
8. *Immanuel Kant: Practical Philosophy*, ed. and trans. Mary J. Gregor (Cambridge: Cambridge University Press, 1996), 4: 434. English translations of Kant are taken from the Gregor Cambridge edition. All subsequent citations of Kant are given in text, using the volume and page numbers from the Berlin Academy edition—Immanuel Kant, *Kants Werke: Akademie Textausgabe* (Berlin: De Gruyter, 1902).

9. J.B. Schneewind, *The Invention of Autonomy: A History of Modern Moral Philosophy* (Cambridge: Cambridge University Press, 1997).
10. Patrick Riley, *Kant's Political Philosophy* (Totowa, NJ: Rowan & Littlefield, 1982), pp. 100, 173; see also Robert Pippin, "Mine and Thine? The Kantian State," in *The Cambridge Companion to Kant and Modern Philosophy*, ed. Paul Guyer (Cambridge: Cambridge University Press, 2006), pp. 416–46 (p. 434).
11. This phrase is from Pippin's "Mine and Thine?" pp. 432–33.
12. I am indebted here to Arthur Ripstein, "Private Order and Public Justice: Kant and Rawls," *Virginia Law Review*, 92 (2006), 1391–1438.
13. See Elisabeth Ellis, *Kant's Politics: Provisional Theory for an Uncertain World* (New Haven: Yale University Press, 2005).
14. Thomas Pogge, "Is Kant's *Rechtslehre* a Comprehensive Liberalism?," in *Kant's Metaphysics of Morals: Interpretive Essays*, ed. Mark Timmons (Oxford: Oxford University Press, 2002), pp. 133–58.
15. Rawls, *Political Liberalism*, p. 175.
16. Pogge, "Is Kant's *Rechtslehre* a Comprehensive Liberalism?"
17. See Ian Hunter, "The Morals of Metaphysics: Kant's *Groundwork* as Intellectual *Paideia*," *Critical Inquiry*, 28 (2002), 908–29.
18. Hunter for example, may not be making a claim about the ultimate truth value of Kant's moral philosophy, so much as offering an alternative description that attempts to deconstruct its claims to transcend historical particularity.
19. See Bernard Williams, *Truth and Truthfulness* (Princeton, NJ: Princeton University Press, 2002).
20. Rawls, *Political Liberalism*, p. 37.
21. On freedom as non-domination see Philip Pettit, *Republicanism: A Theory of Freedom and Government* (Oxford: Oxford University Press, 1996).
22. See Tully, *Public Philosophy*, II, pp. 145–49; 15–42.
23. For example, Ellis, *Kant's Politics.*
24. Charles Beitz, "International Liberalism and Distributive Justice," *World Politics*, 51 (1999), 269–96.
25. See Simon Caney, *Justice Beyond Borders* (Oxford: Oxford University Press, 2005).
26. Ibid., p. 6.
27. Thomas Nagel, "The Problem of Global Justice," *Philosophy and Public Affairs*, 33 (2005), 113–47 (p. 120).
28. Amartya Sen, *The Idea of Justice* (Cambridge, MA: Harvard University Press, 2009); Bernard Williams, *In the Beginning Was the Deed* (Princeton, NJ: Princeton University Press, 2005).
29. See Ibid..

Part II

Transpositions of Empire

Chapter 3

The Legalities of English Colonizing

Discourses of European Intrusion upon the Americas, c. 1490–1830

Christopher Tomlins

European colonizers began refining their plans for the New World almost from the moment of Columbian landfall. Conventionally the English are absent from this story, latecomers by ninety years.[1] But the New World early attracted English attention. Henry VII had offered Columbus English patronage for his first voyage westward in 1492. Before the end of the decade the Crown twice issued letters patent to John Cabot and his sons to search out provinces of "heathen and infidels" unknown to Christians.[2] Cabot made landfall on the far northern mainland and laid claim to Newfoundland and Labrador, all as the renewed voyaging of Columbus and Vespucci was directing Iberian attention southward. Throughout the sixteenth century English fishing fleets were seasonal visitors to the fisheries and shores of Newfoundland. When Martin Frobisher resumed voyaging under Crown patronage in 1576 it was again to the far north: Labrador, Baffin Island, and Greenland.

Renewed Crown interest in the North Atlantic was prompted in good part by the work of scholars and propagandists of empire such as the Tudor mathematician and geographer John Dee and the two remarkable cousins both named Richard Hakluyt. None wrote from first-hand experience. Each mobilized discourses of Christianity and commerce, and of geography and law, to plot transoceanic expansion.[3]

Dee was instrumental in encouraging Crown investment in Frobisher's first voyage. His subsequent treatise, "The Limits of the British Empire," presented to Elizabeth I in 1577–78, sustained Crown interest in Frobisher's voyaging and resulted in the grant of letters patent to Sir Humphrey Gilbert licensing voyages of discovery and conquest to Newfoundland.[4] Dee combined a geographer's analysis of Spanish claims in the Central and South Atlantic with conjectural histories of a millennium of British oceanic voyaging to advance claims of British *imperium* and *dominium*—sovereignty and its exercise—to virtually the entire Northern Atlantic littoral.[5] Many of his arguments were recapitulated six years later by the younger Hakluyt, whose "Discourse of Western Planting" was presented to Elizabeth I in support of Sir Walter Ralegh's petition for letters patent licensing further expeditions of discovery and conquest, for which the elder Hakluyt prepared instructions and advice.[6]

Dee's writings on Atlantic empire offered the Tudor monarchy the New World as a site onto which to project English sovereign desire. Sixty years earlier, in 1516, Sir Thomas More's *Utopia* had also inserted the New World into the English imaginary, somewhat distinctly, as a site upon which to project an ideal civic order: an insular commonwealth founded on an invading monarch's deliberate acts of conquest and material transformation.[7] These distinct strands of metropolitan discourse upon the New World—of sovereign possession and of idealized creation or improvement—intertwine in the works of propagandists for colonization such as the Hakluyts and Sir George Peckham, whose commentaries on early English voyaging drew upon the repertoire of contemporary legalities to establish the legitimacy and justice of the outcomes that projectors of colonies contemplated. They merge more completely in the letters patent and charters by which the English Crown licensed agents in schemes of Western planting that would actually realize the Crown's transatlantic sovereign claims: chartering, that is, expressed *both* Crown prerogative *and* formal approval for the actual detailed designs that projectors created.[8]

The European Law of Colonizing

The legalities of English Atlantic expansion have their origins in sixteenth-century intra-European debates, conceptually indebted to the Roman law of nature and nations, which examined the claims of European sovereigns to *imperium* and *dominium* over transatlantic territories and their indigenous populations. Fifteenth-century Iberian expansion into the cis-Atlantic had identified the evangelization of all humanity as its purpose and the divine mandate of the Roman Church, rendering all ultimately subject to papal jurisdiction, to its authority. To this was joined an additional papal role of mediation between rival Iberian powers. Both impulses found expression in fifteenth-century papal bulls, notably *Romanus Pontifex* (1455) mediating Portuguese and Castilian competition for ascendancy in the Eastern Atlantic, and *Inter Caetera* (1493) granting the unified Spanish monarchy of Ferdinand and Isabella the territorial fruits of Columbus' first transoceanic voyage.[9]

Inter Caetera created a form of delegated spiritual guardianship that granted title to the discovering Christian prince, who was commanded in turn to instruct the inhabitants in the Catholic faith. Growing controversies over the treatment of indigenous populations under this authority provoked serial reexaminations of the basis of Spanish New World rule, culminating in two lectures delivered in 1539 by Francisco de Vitoria, the University of Salamanca theologian and canon lawyer: *De Indis Recenter Inventis* (On the Indians Lately Discovered) and *De Iure Belli Hispanorum in Barbaros* (On the Law of War Made by the Spaniards on the Barbarians). Vitoria's lectures were critical reexaminations of the basis upon which the Spanish claimed "sway" over the peoples and territories of the New World. They have been interpreted as a successful attempt to free Spanish expansion from any specific reliance on *Inter Caetera* for justification and to represent it instead as legitimate conquest grounded on natural law and law of nations reasoning.[10] Whether that interpretation is justified we shall see. Intended or not, one effect of discarding the specific authority of *Inter Caetera* as the legal basis of Spanish rule was to render the natural law language of "legitimate conquest" generally available to any Christian nation desirous of advancing and realizing New World claims.

Vitoria was an exponent of Thomistic theology, the infusion of later-medieval Christianity with Aristotelian philosophy derived from the work of St. Thomas Aquinas. In *De Indis* he drew four conclusions. First, the papacy had no determinative capacity in matters temporal; hence the papal grant to Spain had no foundation. Second, all temporal rule throughout the world was informed by the law of nature and nations. Third, the Indians of the New World were true owners and could not be dispossessed whether by papal fiat or Christian discovery, or by any human law without consent or cause. As social and reasoning creatures they knew the law of nature and nations, enjoyed its rights and protections, and could be held to its obligations: notably, the duty to grant those who traveled peaceably among them "natural society and fellowship," unhindered commerce, access to all that was held common to both natives and strangers, and opportunity to evangelize. Fourth, persistent Indian breaches of the law of nations in the face of Spanish forbearance created grounds for the Spaniards to wage just war, up to and including seizure of "the provinces and sovereignty of the natives." Acts without justification under the authority of *Inter Caetera* became, notionally, justifiable under the authority of *ius gentium* and the doctrine of just war.[11]

Proponents of English Atlantic empire—Dee and the Hakluyts—would take advantage of Vitoria's case against the authority of *Inter Caetera* to limit or undermine the legitimacy of the papal gift and establish openings for English sovereign claims. Dee labored to establish *Inter Caetera*'s irrelevance to the North Atlantic while simultaneously assembling positive evidence of ancient English *imperium* there, hence commensurate jurisdictional capacity in the English Crown to make grants by letters patent in realization of that historical *imperium*.[12] The younger Hakluyt followed Dee but added that the bull could not in any case establish a basis for any Spanish claim to territories beyond those the Spanish had actually discovered and occupied, for "God never gave unto the Popes any such … aucthoritie to give away kingdoms of heathen princes."[13]

For both Hakluyts, as for Dee, Christian evangelizing was the point of departure for transoceanic colonizing.[14] When it came to detailed planning, however, evangelism was of minor significance. As the younger Hakluyt wrote, "the meanes to sende suche as shall labour effectually in this busines ys by plantinge … Colonies." In *that* business, the promise that "Westerne discoveries" would strengthen "this Realme of Englande" held center stage.[15] His cousin was no different, listing as the purposes of Ralegh's first voyage to Virginia, "To plante Christian religion. To trafficke. To conquer. Or … all three." Though his reasoning favored "trafficke" (trade), the elder Hakluyt doubted the indigenous population's desire or capacity to engage in trade. And so "trafficke" takes on something of the appearance of evangelism in his cousin's "Discourse," a worthy goal but dependent for its realization upon a prerequisite—planting. Hakluyt's "Inducements" altered the meaning of "trafficke" from bilateral exchange to the colonizer's appropriation of local resources and production for export. Attention fixes on "the soile and climate," and how to "man it, to plant it, and to keepe it."[16]

Evangelizing and commerce thus end up serving the objective of planting. Vitoria had allowed that persistent indigenous refusals in either arena might provide justifications for conquest as breaches of the law of nature and nations. The elder Hakluyt offered what was in effect a formal briefing on how *ius gentium* rendered indigenous resistance to "juste and lawfull Traffique" a "wronge" that could be lawfully revenged by conquest:

> Yf we fynde any kinges readye to defende their Tirratoryes by warre and the Countrye populous desieringe to expel us that seeke but juste and lawfull

> Traffique, then ... [we may] be revenged of any wronge offered by them and consequentlie maye yf we will conquere, fortefye and plante.[17]

Terra Nullius?

Neither the propagation of Christianity nor the spread of commerce was cited in the Crown's letters patent to Gilbert (1578) and Raleigh (1584). Instead, they licensed voyages of discovery and conquest of "remote, heathen and barbarous lands ... not actually possessed of any Christian Prince, nor inhabited by Christian People." Both stated the Crown's purpose as the realization of dominion within its claimed *imperium*. Both enjoined the licensee to take actual possession: "to inhabit or remaine there, to build and fortifie."[18]

By crafting claims using the language and concepts of Roman law, the English improved the chances of acquiescence in their activities among European competitors.[19] It has also been contended that English colonizers chose a Roman law idiom because it allowed them to mobilize the potent concept of "*terra nullius*."[20] But *terra nullius* is a doctrinal invention after the fact; it has distracted attention from the more potent resources represented in the law of war.

Roman law offered no grounds on which acquisition of sovereignty could be defended without the law of war as a crucial ally.[21] Vitoria had found no basis for Spanish "sway" over the Indians in claims of either temporal *imperium* or papal donation. What Vitoria *had* allowed was that the Spanish might claim just cause to wage wars of conquest, could those wars be founded upon the Indians' failure to abide by their duties and obligations under the law of nature and nations. Vitoria was certainly aware of Roman law's so-called occupant's title, granting "things that belong to nobody... [to] the first occupant according to the law of nations," but accorded it little significance. In classical commentary it was confined to the case of *ferae bestiae* (wild beasts) to which had been annexed certain inanimate objects found in public places. This was how the matter was discussed in *De Indis*. Nowhere did Vitoria grant first occupancy any credibility as a basis for *territorial* acquisition.[22]

In the early English letters patent the significance of occupant's title appears somewhat enhanced. The Crown directs its agents specifically to territories within its notional North Atlantic *imperium* "not actually possessed of any Christian Prince, nor inhabited by Christian People," indicating it would limit its claims to territories over which it might realize *dominium* without disturbing other European claimants in actual possession. By remaining studiously silent about non-Christian occupants, notwithstanding clear knowledge of their existence, the Crown appeared to hold that land without specifically *Christian* possessors was indeed either vacant or should be thought as good as vacant.[23] So the question that arises is whether there was any contemporary conception of first occupant's title that the English could apply to New World territories in such fashion or, for that matter, whether contemporary expositors of the meaning of sovereign possession failed to acknowledge non-Christians.

In his treatise on the law of war, first published in parts during the late 1580s and thus contemporary with the renewal of English voyaging, Alberico Gentili, the Italian humanist who taught civil law at Oxford, held that seizure and occupation of vacant places was "a law of nature." So exiles might take possession of the places they came to dwell in "which were then without inhabitants."[24] Gentili cited Justinian's *Digest* to support the claim that "unoccupied land... is the property of no one," although the passage cited says nothing so precise.[25] This certainly looks like a concept of *terra nullius*. But it was not, as Gentili's next sentence acknowledged: though unoccupied, "such lands belong to the sovereign of that territory" who retained jurisdiction over them.[26]

Roman law allowed that things "presently belong[ing] to no one" might become "by natural reason the property of the first taker." Though such things were almost invariably animate,[27] the *Digest* recognized certain other things. First, "gems, stones, and pearls found on the seashore," because seashores were themselves no one's property.[28] Second, "things captured in war."[29] The *Digest* makes but one reference to *land* in the category of things open to a "first taker," namely "an island arising in the sea," meaning the physical aftermath of rare volcanic or tectonic events—the appearance of literally new land.[30] Because the island arises in the sea, which "by the law of nature" is "common to all,"[31] it is analogous to a pearl on the seashore. Neither island nor pearl can be annexed to any prior structure of ownership. The *Digest* deals extensively and minutely with islands arising in rivers by sedimentation or natural changes in water courses. No such land is ever open to appropriation by a first taker; ownership is determined by the structure of ownership of proximate land.[32]

Ownership and possession, whether of land or things, are quite distinct concepts in the *Digest*. Possession might be claimed mentally, as by an owner, but it could not be asserted against others except by actual control. Control did not create title, except where it was long and undisputed, but it did signify exclusivity of possession as long as the possessor retained actual standing, no matter who the "lawful" owner might be. Possession, then, was an active condition of control; ownership, an assertion of legal title. Title could not be vacated by another's intervening possession; but ownership de jure could not secure possession, in fact, if the interloper was determined.[33]

Indigenous Sovereigns?

Gentili touches on the distinction between possession and ownership in identifying unoccupied land as simultaneously vacant for possession and "belong[ing] to the sovereign of that territory." A large question arises, however, from his further observation that with *belonging* went *jurisdiction* over those who intrude upon vacant lands.[34] Did English colonizers occupying vacant New World lands subject themselves to the jurisdiction of the sovereign of *that* territory? And who was sovereign in the North American case?

So far as the English Crown was concerned the answer was, of course, itself. The obvious competitors with the English Crown for sovereignty were indigenous princes. And indeed, by licensing its agents for voyages of *conquest* as well as discovery the Crown appeared to concede that indeed it was *not* clearly sovereign, that it contemplated seizing territory from indigenous princes by force. Still, did European colonizers pay any heed to the "sovereignty" of transoceanic indigenous princes? On the basis of a lengthy analysis of Vitoria's 1539 lectures, Anthony Anghie has argued that they did not. Vitoria identified certain characteristics of indigenous societies as manifestations of sovereignty but denied Indians "the most characteristic and unique powers of the sovereign," namely the power to "engage in a just war"—the only war lawful under *ius gentium*.[35]

Anghie's analysis is debatable. Vitoria defines a state as "a perfect community," complete in itself, not part of another, with its own laws, councils, and magistrates.[36] In *De Indis* Vitoria found that Indian communities manifested statehood; before the intrusions of the Spanish they had exercised "true dominion" throughout their territories. Indeed, both the logic of *De Indis* and particular observations of fact suggest that, from Vitoria's point of view, even after the intrusions of the Spanish the Indians retain sovereignty unless and until they give the Spanish a just cause for wars to take it from them.[37]

In *De Indis* Vitoria allowed that Indians' violation of their duties and obligations under the laws of nature and nations might constitute a basis upon which "Indians and their lands could have come … into the possession and lordship of Spain."[38] His "empirical" discussion of alleged Indian violations, however, leaves few actual grounds to support Spanish claims. In *De Iure Belli*, Vitoria shifts to the question of whether Spanish "seizure and occupation" of Indian lands might be better defended under the law of war "so as to give more completeness" to his previous lecture.[39] He touches little on the particulars of Spanish action; the objective is to discuss the law of war as such, particularly the concept of just cause. Vitoria probes four main questions: Do Christians may make war at all? Where lies authority to initiate war? What furnishes just cause for war? What constitutes just prosecution?

Christians may indeed make war, whether purely defensive wars to resist aggressors or wars initiated to avenge wrongs. Defensive war might be waged by *anyone*. However, only states and their princes might initiate wars. The personal right to self-defense ceases the moment the immediate threat has passed, but a state enjoys continuing authority to defend itself and to prosecute wars to avenge wrongs and "protect the public weal."[40]

Wars could be just only as vengeance for a substantial wrong done. Mere *belief* that a cause was just was insufficient. Yet, though in error, if a belligerent were convinced by "invincible ignorance" that its cause was just then its war indeed *was* just "in the sense of being excused from sin by reason of good faith, because invincible ignorance is a complete excuse."[41]

Finally, the prosecution of war was just only up to the point necessary to "the defense and preservation of the State," and the restoration of "peace and security."[42] Innocents might not be deliberately slaughtered or punished, for just wars avenged wrongs done and the innocent (by definition) do no wrong. Nor should the innocent be despoiled in their property or persons, unless required by the conduct of the war. Here Vitoria distinguished, prudentially, wars against non-Christians from wars among Christians: it was a received rule of Christendom that Christians do not become slaves in right of war. So "enslaving is not lawful in a war between Christians," only capture for the purpose of ransom.[43]

Might one slaughter the guilty? "In the actual heat of battle ... all who resist may be killed." After victory the guilty might still be killed, for the justice of the war lies in avenging their wrong. If peace and security could not be had except by destroying all enemies then all who could bear arms might be destroyed—but again, for prudential reasons, not in wars between Christians, for like enslavement such would be to the ruin of Christianity. So also cities might be sacked, property seized, territory occupied, but all only in proportion to the necessities of prosecuting the war, for otherwise to overthrow the enemy's sovereignty and depose "lawful and natural princes" would be "utterly savage and inhumane."[44]

Vitoria's discussion establishes the following: First, anyone, including Indians, might justly wage defensive war. Second, a wrong having been done them, Indian princes might wage just wars against other Indians, and also, Vitoria appeared to concede, against the Spanish. Even without just cause, invincible ignorance would excuse the Indians from fault in waging an unjust war against the Spanish. Third, the Spanish might wage just war against the Indians, but only provided a prior and serious wrong had been done them. Fourth, to remain just, war in a just cause had to be prosecuted in a manner proportionate to the wrong suffered, and only to the extent required to restore peace and security.

Vitoria was quite ready to hold Indians inferior to Christians in their capacity to exercise sovereignty.[45] But he did not deny Indian sovereignty. He held that Indian sovereignty could justly be infringed only when the Indians had provided prior cause by violating the law of nature and nations—the same condition that governed the justice of wars among Christians.

Alberico Gentili's treatise on the law of war, written half a century after Vitoria, seems at first sight a better fit for Anghie's analysis. Gentili addressed Spanish warfare in the New World only incidentally. But in one aspect Gentili indeed represented the status of New World people as exceptional, justifying exceptional methods against them in precisely the fashion Anghie suggests.

Gentili's theory of war was quite distinct from Vitoria's. First, "war" as such meant *by definition* "a *just* and *public* contest of arms" between two equal parties (*hostes*). Second, war could only be "waged by sovereigns."[46] The proposition invoked a foundational assumption. Mankind as a whole belonged to a *societas gentium*—"a community of States"—among which relations were analogous to relations among individuals within a single nation-state.[47] Human *societas* encompassed all—Christian, infidel, and barbarian—so long as they were identifiable as politically organized nations (sovereigns or sovereign peoples).[48] All identifiable as such might wage just war. Those not thus identifiable were excluded from *societas gentium* and hence from the law of nations and of war. Who were they? Pirates, brigands, rebellious slaves, brutes. Pirates were the epitome of the excluded—"the common enemies of all mankind." But all such were "no more deserving of consideration in establishing a code of laws than wild beasts."[49] And here Gentili endorsed "those who say that the cause of the Spaniards is just when they make war upon the Indians," for "against such men ... war is made as against brutes."[50] In virtually every other respect Gentili expressed as much or more doubt about the sufficiency of Spanish justifications as Vitoria. To the extent he approved the Spanish cause, the sole basis he adduced was the Indians' apparent inhumanity—their alleged brutishness.

English Designs

Whether or not Crown licensing of English voyages of "conquest" as well as "discovery" in its earliest letters patent was an implicit admission that indigenous non-Christian sovereigns were in place in the lands in question, colonizers' advisors certainly acknowledged both the presence and authority of local sovereigns, for they advised reaching strategic accommodations with them en route to gaining dominion over them.[51] Yet the first decades of actual English attempts also saw their discourse of intrusion undergo a transformation. The articulation of English claims qua European rivals remained consonant with intra-European dispositions of transoceanic acquisitions inflected by Roman law. But as a set of techniques for achieving goals on the ground colonizing acquired a distinct English idiom, in which, increasingly, attention focused on the possession of territory to the exclusion of its inhabitants.

The gestation of this English idiom can be traced to early sixteenth-century humanism; its roots lay in the same fecund soil of the law of nature and nations, to which it annexed vernacular English inflections. Its shift in emphasis was necessarily relative rather than absolute, for—inconveniently—indigenous inhabitants remained obstinately present. Yet for all those remainders, what is surely a distinguishing characteristic of the English colonizing project's impact on the North American mainland is the extraordinary thoroughness of its reinvention—legal, political, and material—of the terrain upon which projectors seated their colonies.

Two hints of this English narrative are detectable in Gentili's *De Iure Belli*. We have seen that Gentili showed some disposition to exclude the New World's indigenous inhabitants from human society, to label them brutes and as such place them among the common enemies of mankind. Elsewhere, Gentili muses on the New World itself as "unoccupied" and uncultivated, likened to "the wilderness of primeval times."[52]

Both ideas—an immense expanse of land, and a scattering of inhabitants who were actually or virtually brutes—resonate much more strongly in Sir George Peckham's near-contemporary *True Reporte of the Late Discoueries* (1583). Peckham was clearly familiar with Vitoria's 1539 lectures and attended carefully to the lawfulness of English intrusions whether for commerce or evangelization. But he was mostly preoccupied by the extraordinary opportunity to possess land. Throughout the *True Reporte* the "Sauages" appear in marked counterpoint to their abundant land. They balance precariously on the edge of humanity: sometimes "miserable and wretched," sometimes "silly souls," sometimes "Pagans" who are "grosse" and "barbarous" and "horrible Idolat[ors]." But whether miserable or incapable or horrible, in Peckham's imagination indigenous inhabitants were mostly incidental. Strikingly, it is the land itself that summons the English. It "dooth" he wrote "(as it were with arme aduaunced) ... stretche out it selfe towardes England onelie ... praying our ayde and helpe," seeking liberation from the ignorance of its current inhabitants so that it might realize its destiny to "yeeld things necessary for mans lyfe."

The inhabitants, meanwhile, would be rendered fit for their new circumstances, "reduced frō vnseemly customes ... to a wel gouerned common wealth ... taught mecanicall occupations, artes, and lyberal Sciences."[53]

Here Peckham presses More's *Utopia* into direct alignment with Vitoria's and Gentili's later examinations of the legalities of colonizing. First, recall that Utopia itself was a perfected society begun in the conquest of lands inhabited by "rude and wilde people."[54] Whenever pressure of population demanded expansion beyond its original bounds, Utopia reproduced itself by sending exiles to "build up a town under their owne lawes in the next land where the inhabitauntes have much waste and unoccupied ground." They would invite the inhabitants to join with them, but if refused the Utopians would "dryve them out ... And if they resiste and rebel, then they make warre agaynst them. For they counte this the most juste cause of warre, when anye people holdethe a piece of grounde voyde and vacaunt to no good nor profitable use."[55]

Utopia's disquisition upon the legalities of conquest and expulsion was, however, exceedingly brief. More's main subject was Peckham's other concern, the civic design—the "wel gouerned common wealth"—that would obliterate all trace of the rude and the wild. More's model commonwealth typified what Engin Isin has termed "eutopolis," the ideal of the city, or *civitas*, a perfected social and jurisdictional order.[56] Seventeenth-century English projectors treated civic humanism's eutopolitan ideal virtually as a blueprint for settlement.[57] Their charters are explicit designs for the spatial embodiment of politico-legal order created to receive and organize a migrating population. Over the course of a century they shift the focus of English colonizing from the discovery and conquest of unknown lands and transformation of barbarous peoples that framed European expansion in the sixteenth century, to *settlement* and *improvement*: the creation of new *English* commonwealths to be inhabited by one's own migrants, the transformation that is of *oneself*.

Given that the legal fate of "grounde voyde and vacant" was not governed by any Roman law "doctrine" granting unoccupied land to a first taker, what were the bases of English arguments? There were two: first, unlike those encountered by the Spanish, the Indians of the northern mainland exhibited none of the appurtenances or capacities of sovereignty[58]; second, what determined whether land was available was less title or actual inhabitation and more *use*.

The second argument was a crucial humanist innovation in natural law thinking.[59] It was articulated—briefly, we have seen—by More. It was reiterated more vigorously by Peckham and Gentili. It underwent rapid generalization in the early seventeenth century as Virginia Company propagandists took up the idea.[60] The slippage from habitation to use was expedient. What was the difference, John Donne asked in his famous 1622 sermon before the Virginia Company, between "land never inhabited, by any, or utterly derelicted and immemorially abandoned"—land that the law of nature and nations declared available for occupation—and land that *was* inhabited but whose inhabitants "doe not in some measure fill the Land, so as the Land may bring foorth her increase for the use of men." Donne's answer—no difference at all. Land could be simultaneously inhabited and vacant. In effect Donne takes Gentili's observation that "the rule which governs a private citizen in his own state ought to govern a public citizen, that is to say a sovereign or a sovereign people, in this public and universal state formed by the world" and transforms it into a rule of mutual responsibility to *manure* the world. Gentili's rule cast out of *societas gentium* those whose behavior proved them brutes; Donne's cast out those who did not improve their land.[61] The capstone comes in the most famous of all the early modern treatises on the law of war, Hugo Grotius's *De Iure Belli ac Pacis*, which quietly adds *uncultivated land* to the class of things that might be made *property* by first takers, the *Digest*'s tightly restricted list notwithstanding.[62]

English writers disclaimed intent to dispossess. "There is no intendment to take … by force that rightful inheritance which they haue," wrote Robert Gray.[63] This begged, of course, the immense question of what land counted as "rightful inheritance" and what as merely vacant and available for English possession. The answer of the first governor of Massachusetts Bay, John Winthrop, was predictable and typical. Use gave title. Land appropriated peaceably and improved was land rightfully possessed.[64] Only such land of which the Indians themselves had likewise gained actual possession by use, Winthrop allowed, was land closed to English occupation; if the English wanted that land they must purchase it. But even then, Indian right was inferior: Indians had only a natural right of ownership, never the civil right that the creation of commonwealths had earned the English.[65]

Once the era of mass migration was under way, by the 1620s in the Chesapeake and the 1630s in New England, the pressure of migrants upon indigenous inhabitation became persistent and relentless. Nevertheless, Stuart Banner has argued, Indian property rights were not denied; Indian lands, cultivated or not, were purchased, not seized.[66] Purchase was expedient, for war was costly, particularly in the earliest years when colonists clung rather desperately to their beachheads. But purchase was not a concession of sovereignty. The English were always at some pains to deny the possibility that "their" Indians had real sovereigns or even elementary civility.[67] And, even if Indians did have sovereigns and "government," what meaning did it carry? If, as Grotius claimed, in the seventeenth century's property regime "every right comes *to* the state *from* private individuals," the absence of "meum and tuum" amongst these particular individuals suggested they had precious few rights to convey. Absent a prior individual property right, what were indigenous sovereigns actually empowered to govern?[68]

Local sovereigns might be tolerated in their exercise of jurisdiction over those on the territory they claimed as "theirs," but if they obstructed the entry of others, or free passage, or the occupation of uncultivated land, they "will have violated a principle of the law of nature and may be punished by war."[69] The law of nature expressed the new property regime. The objective of war to vindicate the law of nature might be limited to the insistence that local sovereigns allow access and occupation as well as the conversion of waste to property by individuated cultivation. Or, more aggressively, it might be to overthrow that local sovereignty altogether and establish a new "jurisdiction over territory" that would complement rather than obstruct the new property regime by punishing those who stood in its way. For as Grotius wrote, "kings and those who possess rights equal to those kings"

> have the right of demanding punishments not only on account of injuries committed against themselves or their subjects, but also on account of injuries which ... violate the law of nature or of nations in regard to any persons whatsoever. For liberty to serve the interests of human society through punishments ... now after the organization of states and courts of law is in the hands of the highest authorities ... has taken this right away from others ... .
>
> And for this cause Hercules was famed by the ancients because he freed from... tyrants the lands which ... he traversed, not from a desire to acquire but to protect, becoming ... the bestower of the greatest benefits upon men ... [in] the common interest of the human race.[70]

Labors of Hercules

An epic humanist heroism—restoration of existential justice, freeing lands for cultivation in the common interest of the human race—elevated expeditions of conquest *and* improvement. English colonizers counted themselves engaged in just such a process and had the documents to prove it. "Many cases may be put, when not only *Commerce*, and *Trade*, but *Plantations* in lands, not formerly our owne, may be lawfull," John Donne would advise departing Virginia adventurers in 1622, "And for that ... [you have] your *Patents*, your *Charters* ... ."[71]

The earliest letters patent delegated the implantation of new jurisdictional authority upon the territories they granted to crown assignees invested with law-making authority. They were sufficient to establish a model for English colonization as a process that throughout the following century would use law to project onto the mainland elaborately detailed English designs that appropriated American territory to an English epistemology: English politics and economics, English representations, English purposes. Colonial charters mapped both territory and the institutional and cultural forms in which authority would be applied to (and within) that territory. Carefully expressing the claim that territory was legitimately appropriated by use, all were catalogs of intense creative activity.

From the early 1620s, English charters also embraced and anticipated massive transfers of population as colonization's purpose. Clearly the first to do so was Sir William Alexanders's "New Scotland" grant. Its emphasis lay on colonization as an act of *self*-renewal undertaken by a population "led forth into new territory, which they may fill with colonies."[72] The sentiment became commonplace.[73]

With growing emphasis on command of territorial expanse and the importation of population to fill and improve it, what had English charters to say of indigenous populations? Local populations, always slighted, were increasingly subject to conceptual and physical expulsion. This is particularly noticeable as a theme of the patents drawn up after the so-called Jamestown massacre of March 1622. Indigenous populations quite suddenly cease to appear as inhabitants of the territories in question with whom accommodations might be reached and become implacable enemies threatening them from outside. The original Virginia patent had only glanced at the "people living in those parts" and had not displaced them, suggesting rather they would be beneficiaries of English colonizing. In abrupt contrast, the Avalon patent, the first granted after the massacre, licensed the expulsion of indigenous populations from the territory they inhabited and authorized perpetual war against them. Describing the lands granted as "not yet husbanded," the patent acknowledged they were "in some parts ... inhabited." It then separated inhabitants from land by renaming them barbarian invaders against whose "Incursions ... as of other Enimies, Pirats and Robbers" the proprietor was empowered "to make warre ... even [beyond] the Limmits of the said Province and ... vanquish and take them and ... putt them to death by the Lawe of war, or ... save them" (enslave them) as he might think fit.[74] The clause clearly recalls Gentili's classical identification of mankind's "common enemies" beyond *societas gentium*.[75] Nothing like it appears in any previous charter. It would appear subsequently in all major seventeenth-century charters in "standardized" form, with minor modifications to fit the circumstances of the particular grant.[76] One can observe the completeness of the conceptual displacement achieved over the course of the century in the Georgia Charter of 1732, which declares the objectives of colonizing "to settle ... our provinces in America," to cultivate lands "at present waste and desolate," and to defend them from "Indian enemies ... neighboring savages" on the other side of the "unsettled" frontier awaiting opportunities to "la[y] waste with fire and sword and great numbers of English inhabitants, miserably massacre[d]."[77]

Conclusion

Legally, the indigenous would remain on the other side of a westward-advancing frontier. A half century after the Georgia charter they were dislocated once more in the U.S. Constitution, in which they became generic "Indian Tribes," neither "foreign" nor "domestic," neither within "the states" nor in any civic sense within the United States.[78] "To leave them in possession of their country, was to leave the country a wilderness," said Chief Justice Marshall in *Johnson v M'Intosh* (1823), reiterating the 200-year-old trope of heroic improvement. To govern them as a distinct people "was impossible ... they were ready to repel by arms every attempt on their independence." Instead, as white population advanced, "that of the Indians necessarily receded."[79] Discovery had given the Crown "an exclusive right to extinguish the Indian title of occupancy," whether by purchase or conquest. Though it might appear pretentious to claim title by conquest, "if the property of the great mass of the community originates in it, it becomes the law of the land and cannot be questioned."[80]

The claim would not reach its apogee until the middle of the nineteenth century. It was Roger Taney, not Marshall, who would complete the argument by holding that from the outset the continent had been "divided and parcelled out, and granted by the governments of Europe as if it had been vacant and unoccupied land," that indigenous inhabitants, therefore, occupied land on sufferance, subject to the dominion of European governments and their successors.[81] But what was the practical difference? "The power now possessed by the government of the United States to grant lands, resided, while we were colonies, in the crown, or its grantees. The validity of the titles given by either has never been questioned in our Courts. It has been exercised uniformly over territory in possession of the Indians. The existence of this power must negative the existence of any right which may conflict with, and control it." The Crown had claimed sovereignty in the colonies and that sovereignty had been transmitted to its successors. When the sovereign makes claims, the sovereign's courts will do the sovereign's bidding. "Conquest gives a title which the Courts of the conqueror cannot deny."[82]

The words were enough of a conclusion to a matter already settled.

Notes

1. This essay summarizes themes discussed at much greater length in chapters 3 and 4 of Christopher Tomlins, *Freedom Bound: Law, Labor and Civic Identity in Colonizing English America* (Cambridge and New York: Cambridge University Press, 2010).
2. Letters Patent to John Cabot, in *The Federal and State Constitutions, Colonial Charters, and other Organic Laws of the States, Territories and Colonies Now or Heretofore Forming The United States of America*, ed. Francis Newton Thorpe, 7 vols. (Washington, DC: Government Printing Office, 1909), I, pp. 45–47 (p. 46).
3. On Dee, see Ken MacMillan, *Sovereignty and Possession in the English New World* (Cambridge: Cambridge University Press, 2006), pp. 50–78. On the Hakluyts, see Peter C. Mancall, *Hakluyt's Promise: An Elizabethan's Obsession for an English America* (New Haven: Yale University Press, 2007).
4. MacMillan, *Sovereignty and Possession*, pp. 51–53; "Letters Patent to Sir Humfrey Gylberte" (June 11, 1578) in Thorpe, *Federal and State Constitutions*, I, p. 49. Gilbert's voyage was delayed until 1583.
5. MacMillan, *Sovereignty and Possession*, pp. 54–66.
6. Richard Hakluyt (the younger), "Discourse of Western Planting," and Richard Hakluyt (the elder), "Inducements to the Liking of the Voyage Intended towards Virginia" (1585), both in *The Original Writings and Correspondence of the Two Richard Hakluyts*, ed. E.G.R. Taylor, 2 vols. (London: for the Hakluyt Society, 1935), II, pp. 211–326, 327–38; "Charter to Sir Walter Raleigh" (1584) in Thorpe, *Federal and State Constitutions*, I, p. 53.
7. Andrew Fitzmaurice, *Humanism and America: An Intellectual History of English Colonization, 1500–1625* (Cambridge: Cambridge University Press, 2003), p. 1.
8. Christopher Tomlins, "The Legal Cartography of Colonization, the Legal Polyphony of Settlement: English Intrusions on the American Mainland in the Seventeenth Century," *Law & Social Inquiry*, 26 (2001), 315–47.
9. *Romanus Pontifex* (January 8, 1455) and *Inter Caetera* (May 4, 1493), both in *European Treaties Bearing on the History of the United States and Its Dependencies to 1648*, ed. Frances Gardiner Davenport (Washington, DC: Carnegie Institution, 1917), pp. 13–26, 72–78.
10. Sharon Korman, *The Right of Conquest: The Acquisition of Territory by Force in International Law and Practice* (Oxford: Oxford University Press, 1996),

p. 54. The critique of Vitoria as apologist for Spanish conquest may be traced to Samuel Pufendorf, *De Jure Naturae et Gentium Libri Octo* (1688), trans. C.H. Oldfather and W.A. Oldfather (Oxford: Clarendon Press, 1934), p. 364–66.

11. Francisco de Vitoria, "On the Indians Lately Discovered," in Francisci de Victoria, *De Indis et De Iure Belli Relectiones*, ed. Ernest Nys (Washington DC: Carnegie Institution, 1917), 115–62 (pp. 135–38, 151–54, 155, 156).
12. MacMillan, *Sovereignty and Possession*, pp. 49–78.
13. Hakluyt (the younger), "Discourse," pp. 250, 307.
14. MacMillan, *Sovereignty and Possession*, pp. 62–63; Hakluyt (the younger), p. 211; Hakluyt (the elder), "Inducements," p. 327.
15. Hakluyt (the younger), "Discourse," p. 215.
16. Hakluyt (the elder), "Inducements," pp. 332–34.
17. "Pamphlet for the Virginia Enterprise" ascribed to Richard Hakluyt (the elder), in Taylor, *Writings and Correspondence*, II, pp. 339–43 (p. 342). For the same argument at greater length, see Sir George Peckham, *A True Reporte of the Late Discoueries* (London, 1583), sigs. C_2v-D_4v.
18. "Charter to Sir Walter Raleigh" (1584), p. 53. Note the slight but significant change in expression from Henry VII's letters patent to Cabot, from provinces of the heathen previously unknown to Christians to heathen provinces unpossessed by Christians.
19. MacMillan, *Sovereignty and Possession*, pp. 13–15.
20. Ibid., pp. 33, 106.
21. As we shall see, with one rare exception Roman law no more hypothesized the possibility of land existing outside a state of sovereignty than English common law.
22. Vitoria twice alludes to *ferae bestiae* in *De Indis*, on the first occasion (pp. 138–39) to deny its applicability, on the second (p. 153) to observe that under the law of nations the Indians are obliged to extend to the Spaniards access to objects that the Indians themselves recognize as open to all comers.
23. In the Gilbert and Raleigh patents there was no explicit intimation that the territories in question were unpossessed and uninhabited—simply that they were not possessed by *Christian* princes or inhabited by *Christian* peoples. Evidence of Crown knowledge that the lands in question were inhabited is manifest in the documents and memorials prepared in support of the issuance of the patents, which refer to heathen inhabitants, barbarians, savages and so forth—and in the patents themselves, which refer to "heathen and barbarous lands."
24. Alberico Gentili, *De Iure Belli Libri Tres* (1612), trans. John C. Rolfe (Oxford: Clarendon Press, 1933), p. 80.
25. See *The Digest of Justinian*, ed. Theodore Mommsen, Paul Krueger and Alan Watson (Philadelphia: University of Pennsylvania Press, 1985), book 41.1.3.
26. Gentili, *De Iure Belli Libri Tres*, p. 81.
27. *Digest*, book 41.1.3, 41.1.5.
28. Ibid., book 41.2.1.1.
29. Strictly speaking, only free men could be appropriated (enslaved) by a "first taker" in war; like wild animals, those who escaped would regain their

freedom. Property taken from the enemy indeed became the property of the taker, but this was rather a forced conversion of what was already property than a first taking. See *Digest*, book 41.2.1.1, 41.1.7, 41.1.5.7.
30. *Digest*, book 41.1.7.3.
31. *The Institutes of Justinian*, trans. J.T. Abdy and Bryan Walker (Cambridge: Cambridge University Press, 1876), p. 78.
32. See, for example, *Digest*, book 41.1.7.1–6, 41.1.29, 41.1.30.1–4.
33. Ibid., 41.2.1; 41.2.3.1–9.
34. Gentili, *De Iure Belli Libri Tres*, p. 81.
35. Anthony Anghie, *Imperialism, Sovereignty and the Making of International Law* (Cambridge: Cambridge University Press, 2004), pp. 26, 28, and generally 13–31.
36. Vitoria, "On the Indians or on the Law of War," in Francisci de Victoria, *De Indis et De Iure Belli Relectiones*, ed. Ernest Nys (Washington DC: Carnegie Institution, 1917), 163–87 (p. 169).
37. Vitoria, "On the Indians Lately Discovered," pp. 127–28. Vitoria's consideration of the lawful titles whereby the Indians might fall under Spanish sway assumes, for example, the existence of a sovereign indigenous lawgiving entity that betrays its obligations (pp. 153, 157–59). Note also Vitoria's acknowledgment of indigenous sovereignty in the case of the Tlaxcaltec-Spanish alliance (p. 160).
38. Vitoria, "On the Indians Lately Discovered," p. 160.
39. Vitoria, "On the Indians or on the Law of War," p. 165.
40. Ibid., pp. 167–68.
41. Ibid., p. 173.
42. Ibid., pp. 171–72.
43. Ibid., p. 181.
44. Ibid., pp. 182–83, 186.
45. Vitoria, "On the Indians Lately Discovered," pp. 160–61.
46. Gentili, *De Iure Belli Libri Tres*, pp. 12 (emphasis supplied), 15.
47. Ibid., p. 67.
48. Ibid., pp. 53–57, 397–403.
49. Ibid., pp. 7, 22, 22–26.
50. Ibid., p. 67.
51. See, for example, Hakluyt (the elder), "Inducements," pp. 329–30.
52. Gentili, *De Iure Belli Libri Tres*, p. 81.
53. Peckham, sigs. B_4r-v, C_3r-C_4r, F_3r.
54. Thomas More, *The Utopia of Sir Thomas More, Ralph Robinson's Translation*, ed. George Sampson (London: G. Bell and Sons, 1910), p. 83.
55. Ibid., pp. 102–3.
56. Engin Isin, *Being Political: Genealogies of Citizenship* (Minneapolis: University of Minnesota Press, 2002), p. 160. On the discourse of *civitas* in European expansion, see, for example, Anthony Pagden, *Lords of All the World: Ideologies of Empire in Spain, Britain and France, c.1500–1800* (New Haven: Yale University Press, 1995), pp. 18–28.
57. See generally Robert K. Home, *Of Planting and Planning: The Making of British Colonial Cities* (London: Chapman & Hall, 1997), pp. 8–35.

58. See, for example, William Symonds, *Virginia. A Sermon Preached at White-Chappel, in the Presence of Many, Honourable and Worshipfull, the Adventurers and Planters for Virginia, 25 April 1609* (London: printed by J. Winder for Eleazar Edgar, 1609), p. 15. William Strachey *The Historie of Travaile into Virginia Britannia: Expressing the Cosmographie and Comodities of the Country, Togither with the Manners and Customes of the People*, ed. R.H. Major (London: printed for the Hakluyt Society, 1849), p. 47.
59. Richard Tuck, *The Rights of War and Peace: Political Thought and the International Order from Grotius to Kant* (Oxford: Oxford University Press, 1999), pp. 49–50.
60. See, for example, Strachey, *Historie of Travaile*, p. 19.
61. John Donne, *A Sermon Preached to the Honourable Company of the Virginian Plantation. 13° November 1622*, p. 11 <http://www.lib.byu.edu/dlib/donne/ [accessed August 22, 2009]; Gentili, *De Iure Belli Libri Tres*, p. 68.
62. Hugo Grotius, *De Jure Belli ac Pacis Libri Tres* (1625), trans. Francis W. Kelsey (Oxford: Clarendon Press, 1925), p. 192.
63. Robert Gray, *A Good Speed to Virginia* (London, 1609), sig. c_4r.
64. See David Grayson Allen, "Vacuum Domicilium: The Social and Cultural Landscape of Seventeenth-Century New England," in *New England Begins: The Seventeenth Century*, ed. Jonathan L. Fairbanks and Robert F. Trent (Boston: Museum of Fine Arts, 1982), pp. 1–10 (p. 1).
65. For Winthrop's distinction between natural and civil rights of property see his "General Observations for the Plantation of New England" (1629, multiple drafts), and the "Reasons to be considered for iustifieinge the vndertakeres of the intended Plantation in New England," in *Winthrop Papers*, ed. Stewart Mitchell, 6 vols. (New York: Russell & Russell, 1968), II (1623–30), pp. 111–24, 138–45.
66. Stuart Banner, *How the Indians Lost Their Land: Law and Power on the Frontier* (Cambridge, MA: Harvard University Press, 2005), pp. 10–84.
67. Gray, *A Good Speed to Virginia*, sig. c_4r.
68. Ibid; Tuck, *Rights of War*, p. 92.
69. Tuck, *Rights of War*, p. 106; Grotius, *De Jure Belli*, pp. 196–205.
70. Grotius, *De Jure Belli*, pp. 504–5.
71. Donne, *Sermon*, p. 11.
72. "Charter in Favor of Sir William Alexander" (1621), in *Sir William Alexander and American Colonization*, ed. Edmund F. Slafter (Boston: Prince Society, 1873), pp. 127–28, 136–37.
73. Sir Robert Heath's 1629 Carolina patent talks of "the multitude of people thronging thither." Cecilius Calvert wanted to plant "a numerous Colony of the English Nation" in Maryland, his father "a very great and ample" one in Newfoundland. See, Thorpe, I, p. 72; III, p. 1677; *Collection and Commentary on the Constitutional Laws of Seventeenth-Century Newfoundland*, ed. Keith Matthews (Canada: Memorial University of Newfoundland, 1975), p. 39.
74. "A Grant of the Province of Avalon," in Matthews, *Collection and Commentary*, pp. 53–54.
75. Gentili, *De Iure Belli Libri Tres*, pp. 15, 22.

76. See, for example, Thorpe, *Federal and State Constitutions*, I, p. 73 (Carolina); III, p. 1630 (Maine); III, p. 1682 (Maryland); V, p. 2751 (Carolina); V, p. 3042 (Pennsylvania).
77. Ibid., II, p. 765.
78. *United States Constitution*, art. I, §2, cl. 3, and §8 cl. 3; art. IV, §3 (1789). This point was reinforced in *Cherokee Nation v. Georgia*, 30 U.S. 1 (1831).
79. *Johnson v M'Intosh*, 21 U.S. 543 (1823), p. 590.
80. Ibid., pp. 587, 591.
81. *United States v. Rogers*, 45 U.S. 567 (1846), p. 572.
82. *Johnson v M'Intosh*, 21 U.S. 543 (1823), pp. 588–89.

Chapter 4

The Uses of the Rule of Law in British Colonial Societies in the Nineteenth Century

John McLaren

I

Despite the narrower version associated with Alfred Venn Dicey in the late nineteenth century,[1] the rule of law in the late eighteenth and early nineteenth century was a highly tensile notion. Its meaning varied depending on who was employing it and for what purpose.[2] In one guise or another the rule of law embraced: (1) the right to justice by the judgment of one's peers conceded by King John in *Magna Carta*, and trial by jury (both elements of claims of an Ancient Constitution)[3]; (2) *habeas corpus*, a protection solidified during the latter half of seventeenth century[4]; (3) freedom from suspension of or dispensation from laws of Parliament secured in the settlement associated with the Glorious Revolution of 1688[5]; (4) the independence of the judiciary established by the *Act of Settlement,* 1701[6] and, its corollary, the right to a trial according to law and established legal procedures involving the application of rational principles; and (5) freedom from intrusion and arrest by the invocation of general warrants developed by the courts during the mid-eighteenth century.[7] Closely allied and overlapping with the rule of law were a series of "constitutional rights," some of which seemed settled, at least in Britain, such as no taxation without representation and the right to petition the Crown, and others that were contested—freedom of the press, freedom of association, freedom of assembly, freedom of conscience, and freedom of religion. The rule of law was a permeable net of processes, principles, and ideals that embodied the values of government according to law, justice under the law, and claims to individual liberty.

My starting point is that, in the absence of a written constitution, the discourse of the rule of law mobilized a set of standards by which to judge the performance of those possessing governmental and judicial authority. I suggest, too, that where courts stood on these rights both reflected and influenced the political and legal culture of imperial governance, as well as the politics and law in various colonial jurisdictions, and how narrowly, broadly, or manipulatively the rule of law was construed within them.

Liberty was a shared constitutional and legal concept in the eighteenth-century Anglo-American world.[8] It lay at the crux of a balance between licentiousness and arbitrary power. Debates over the nature of liberty and of the rule of law had divided political and legal opinion in mid-eighteenth-century Britain.[9] On the one side there were those government or court Whigs committed to the deployment of liberty as the guarantor of order, status, and deference (an "ordered liberty"), and as the basis for resistance to "faction." For these forces a narrow conception of the rule of law that tied legitimacy to the observance of the formal requirements of justice generally sufficed. On the other side were the country Whigs and populist Wilkites, who saw liberty as a necessary bulwark against arbitrary and corrupt government, whether that of a monarch or of Parliament. The rule of law for these people was a more expansive notion encompassing constitutional protection of rights, the criteria for resisting corruption and arbitrariness, and effective mechanisms for the redress of grievances.

These ideological tensions were in time to be replicated in the debates between Loyalists and Patriots in the American colonies, both before and during the War of Independence, and in Ireland in the 1780s when Irish Whigs believed (erroneously as it turned out) that they had secured constitutional independence.[10] In the West Indian colonies the rule of law was trumpeted, with all the rhetorical fervor of seventeenth-century supporters of the *Ancient Constitution*.[11] However, designed to undergird the exclusive rights of the white population, it was, in fact, an inversion of the concept in any liberal sense.

What of the relationship between the "subject" peoples of the colonies and the rule of law during the eighteenth century? There is clear evidence of a poly-jural reality in the eighteenth-century British Empire whereby other systems and conceptions of law were recognized, and which encouraged and produced negotiation across jurisdictional boundaries and between legal systems. In the case of territories acquired by conquest of or cession by other European powers, such as Quebec and Grenada, strategic and pragmatic considerations argued in favor of the preservation of at least part of the preexisting legal system.[12] A similar policy prevailed in the case of territories, India being the prime example, in which ancient legal systems already coexisted with English law, originally introduced under extraterritoriality agreements, particularly in matters of personal law relating to marriage and inheritance.[13] In the case of Aboriginal communities, British imperial policy during the eighteenth century tended toward recognition of their sovereignty, their customary title to land, and their autonomy in conducting their own governance and law.[14] The relations between these nations and the European newcomers were, in theory, if not always in practice, a matter for negotiation through treaties and diplomacy.

One population constituted a clear exception to this policy of positive poly-jurality. Slave populations lay outside the rule of law as understood by the European colonists who employed and exploited them. Slaves had little or no protection from the traditional law of their dominators. They were considered by their owners to lie outside the common law and its protections and, as property, were subject to the latter's largely uninhibited discretion as well as brutal locally devised slave codes.[15]

A notable and common element in the constitutional ordering of the British Empire at the close of the eighteenth century, one that flew in the face of domestic British understandings of the rule of law, was the absence of judicial independence. Throughout that century, British colonial judges were appointed at pleasure, not, like their English counterparts, during good behavior.[16] The reason was simple. Judges, particularly chief justices, were seen as important players in colonial government in which the separation of powers was only hazily discernible.[17] In addition to fulfilling judicial functions, they were often key members of executive and legislative councils and acted as close advisers to governors. In the absence of legal talent elsewhere in the community they were also in some instances required to draft legislation and regulations.[18] Given these important administrative and legislative roles, it was considered imperative that they be loyal to the colonial regime in terms of political alignment. London sought to ensure that the terms of judicial employment provided the local colonial government with the power to remove a jurist who had become an embarrassment by inappropriate political activity, or who brought the administration of justice into disrepute. Appointment at pleasure allowed for prompt decisions ridding colonies of disruptive jurists. The main instrument for achieving this end was *Burke's Act* of 1782.[19] This differential treatment of the colonial judiciary was to be an irritant in the nineteenth-century empire.[20]

II

What of the fate of rule of law thinking and its embodiment of constitutional values in Britain's Second Empire? Not surprisingly, given the deep psychological commitment of those of British heritage to the rhetoric and discourse of liberty and to the rule of law, the conception was as alive and well in the Second as it had been in the First Empire. Moreover, despite the realities of a war-torn nation and an imperial government preoccupied with state security and committed to controlling and emphasizing the dependency of the colonies in the century's early decades, the liberal constitutionalist interpretation of the rule of law was as much in evidence as the narrower, conservative legalistic construction. Inverted constitutionalist interpretations of the rule of law employed by white settlers continued in or spread to the Caribbean and other territories with multiracial populations controlled by a minority of Europeans.

As Canadian politico-legal historian Greg Marquis has indicated, the cultural reasons for acceptance of English legal culture in the colonies are not hard to find.[21] For populations uprooted to a new land with whose past they had no connection, it was natural to transpose their own history and how they idealized it to their new surroundings. Ironically, the process was assisted by the writings of one of the leading conservative advocates of the ordered British constitution, William Blackstone. In his famous *Commentaries on the Laws of England* he had lauded both the constitution and English law as embodying an ordered liberty and elevating the rule of law over that of men, something that was the envy of other nations.[22] Although no friend of factionalism or dissent, Blackstone, through his appeal to history that explained the blessings of the "rights of freeborn Englishmen," and his emphasis on the central values of liberty of person, property, and security, provided a rich and flexible source of rhetorical and discursive inspiration to individuals and communities trying to make sense of their cultural identity in distant lands. In Blackstone there was something for almost everyone regardless of where they were located on the political spectrum.

Marquis provides a series of examples of how settlers in the nineteenth-century Canadian Maritime colonies constructed their history and sense of constitutional entitlement out of their memories of English history. He notes,

> Rather than seeing themselves as residents of an imperial backwater, Maritime British North Americans took solace in a thousand-year history that was elevated to a form of civil religion.... The presumed antiquity of English and legal and political institutions, which produced in the 17th

> century a school of thought known as the Ancient Constitution, lent prestige to local political questions. Both proponents and opponents of change found refuge in the past....The cornerstone of English liberty, the common law, as an ancestral gift was not to be taken lightly, it was a birth right to be guarded.[23]

The impact of Blackstone's *Commentaries* as a guide to the substance of English law and procedure and as a stimulus to constitutional contention was to be assisted by a phenomenon of empire—the networking and peripatetic careers of colonial officials.[24] As Bridget Brereton and John Bennett have demonstrated in their biographical work, the movement between colonies of judges with developed views on law and constitutionalism influenced legal and political discourse in those possessions.[25] Moreover, judges who needed to test their understanding of the law were not shy about making contact with their counterparts in other colonies who might have faced similar issues.[26]

III

The examples of the variable use of rule of law discourse and rhetoric by both imperial and colonial interests that follow are drawn from the writer's research on judicial tenure and accountability in British North America and the Caribbean. They demonstrate how ubiquitous, tenacious, open-textured, and tensile the concept was.

In Canada, major issues of constitutional debate and even political dissension were framed by rule of law discourse, and it was invoked by groups and movements as diverse as Tories, Liberals, radicals, imperialists, nationalists, loyalists, Orangemen, Roman Catholics, and striking trade unions. In the West Indian colonies, both those with representative assemblies, such as Barbados and Jamaica, and those that were newly acquired Crown colonies, such as Trinidad, the rule of law, although given a liberal spin, was primarily invoked by the ruling elite, whether to maintain or secure political and economic dominance.[27] However, there is also evidence that the peculiarly English discourse of liberty was being invoked by nonwhite leaders, especially those of the Creole or "free coloured" populations, to argue for some recognition of their rights.[28]

In reviewing the status of the remaining British North American colonies in the wake of the American War of Independence, the lesson that William Pitt the Younger and his secretary of state responsible for the colonies, William Grenville, drew was that the thirteen colonies had enjoyed too much liberty in their political and legal arrangements.[29] The new constitutional order in the flagship possessions of Lower and Upper Canada, established in 1791, although giving the superficial impression of replicating the combination of executive rule and local legislative authority that had marked the structure of government in the old empire, was, in fact, designed to impose close British control. London sought to ensure this through the grant of clear executive powers over the legislative bodies in the colony, the dominance of appointed legislative councils over elected assemblies, and a degree of fiscal independence bestowed on governors.[30] Pitt and Grenville also imagined that the dominance of Loyalists in Upper Canada would make for a peaceful and orderly polity resting comfortably under the providential benefits of British rule and English law. In its sister province it was supposed that the mutual interest of both the colonial government and its English commercial supporters, on the one hand, and the traditional *Canadien* political and religious elite, on the other, was in order and stability, and that the latter groups would impress this message on their constituents.[31]

In the two Canadas British assumptions about the populations of these territories, that they were basking loyally and gratefully in the roseate glow of peace, order, and good government of the eighteenth-century British constitution, proved naive. In Upper Canada, the presence of differing shades of opinion among Loyalists over what it meant to be a North American in political and legal terms—as well as later migration of Americans, Britons, and Irish to the territory—created a diverse ideological mix.[32] In Lower Canada differences in ethnic and religious culture inevitably worked against the new order. In both colonies tensions over the administration of justice and constitutional values were quick to surface, manifesting themselves in battles between conservative executives and their local supporters on the one hand, and reformers and radicals on the other.[33]

The colonial judiciary was not immune to these ideological conflicts, as the case of Robert Thorpe demonstrates. An Irishman of Whig sensibilities, he was appointed puisne justice of the Court of King's Bench of Upper Canada in 1805. He quickly allied himself with a disaffected group of Irish immigrants who were critical of the conduct of what they considered to be a haughty and uncaring colonial government in managing land settlement, sidetracking the Assembly on fiscal matters, and introducing the draconian *Sedition Act* of 1804.[34] In his charges to grand and petty juries, the judge appealed to the "rights of freeborn Englishmen," the constitutional struggles of seventeenth-century England, and the writings of Blackstone.[35] When he was elected to the Assembly and assumed the mantle of the leader of the opposition, Lieutenant Governor Francis Gore lost patience and removed him from office, a decision confirmed by Thorpe's patron and secretary of state for the colonies, Lord Castlereagh.[36]

However, this was not before Thorpe had penned a manifesto for responsible government for the colony, drawing on Irish Whig ideas about compact constitutionalism.[37] Although Thorpe himself was to suffer silencing as a North American judge, his ideological inspiration was to be revived by more moderate and judicious reformers in the province in the 1820s and beyond.[38]

In Lower Canada the judiciary was allied to the conservative ruling elite during the first twenty years of the life of the colony. In this possession serious tension existed between the executive and judiciary on the one hand, and the increasingly French-speaking and reformist Assembly on the other.[39] The reformers who blended liberal British constitutional discourse and French revolutionary inflection became outraged at the special measures taken against their leaders by Governor Sir James Craig in 1810.[40] In particular, they decried the arrest, seizure, and detention of lawyer Pierre-Amable Bedard and other members of the Assembly associated with the reformist newspaper *Le Patriot*. Most galling to these interests was the involvement of the chief justice of Quebec, Jonathan Sewell, a conservative Loyalist, as the close adviser and even unofficial "prime minister" to Craig, and his manipulation of the justice system in corrupt ways to silence the opposition.[41] Sewell, along with the chief justice of Montreal, James Monk, was also suspected, with some justification, of designs to substitute English private law for the civil law of Quebec. The judges' actions and words became grist for the mill in the Assembly's attempt to impeach the two of them in 1814–1815.[42] In a series of indictments that read like a bill of impeachment from seventeenth-century England, Sewell was accused inter alia of "traitorously and wickedly [endeavoring] to subvert the Constitution and established Government of the... Province," and of introducing "an arbitrary, tyrannical Government against Law, which he had declared by traitorous and wicked opinions, counsel, conduct, judgments, practices and actions."[43] Both justices were charged with interfering with French law and its application.[44] In response, Monk astutely shifted the focus of imperial attention from the Assembly's charges to the judiciary as protectors of order and stability in the colony. In the result, the judges were vindicated.[45] The conservative British government of Lord Liverpool refused to consider the charges of political manipulation against Sewell. Moreover, the Privy Council found no substance in the allegations against either judge of seeking to subvert the civil law of Quebec. Faced with tension between the forces of law and order and representatives of dissent and faction, there was in the imperial halls of power no contest. The only concession to reformist criticisms of the administration of justice through all of this was that London persuaded itself in 1810 that allowing judges to sit in the Lower Canadian Assembly was no longer good policy.[46]

Elite *hauteur*, manipulation of the levers of colonial governance and law, and an obsessive fear of disloyalty among the population were evident in Upper Canada in the years after the War of 1812. The law officers of the Crown and most of the judges were associated with a group described as the Family Compact—including colonial officials, businessmen, and churchmen—committed to preserving and replicating their own high Tory, anti-democratic values in the governance of the colony.[47] For the Crown lawyers the justice system was a legitimate instrument for neutralizing or even ridding themselves of those with a different vision of society. The exclusivist views of these men did not go unchallenged, however. The presence of reformist lawyers, such as William Warren Baldwin, in the Assembly in the early 1820s was to introduce the discourse of a more liberal constitutional tradition, drawing strength from eighteenth-century English country Whigs, Irish Whig ideology, and expansive readings of Blackstone. Baldwin went on the attack against the *Sedition Act*. He argued that as long as the Act, with its provisions for summary arrest and banishment, remained in force Upper Canadians were "without a constitution, at least a free one." "The statute," he continued, "remained in force not only in the face of Magna Carta, but directly in the face of all the statutes made for the liberty and protection of the subject."[48] Baldwin began asserting that the *Constitution Act* of 1791 represented a compact between the Crown and people of Upper Canada (reflecting his own Irish Whig heritage and the influence of Thorpe's thinking), a compact that could not be altered without the consent of the governed. This latter point represented a position close to that of the English reformist and radical Whigs of the mid-eighteenth century.[49] Here were the seeds of what became in a short time the reformers' manifesto for the grant of responsible government.

The issue of partiality in the administration of justice in the province came to a public head in 1828, through the intervention of puisne judge John Walpole Willis, recently appointed from England.[50] The latter challenged Attorney General John Beverley Robinson in court for the law officers' failure to launch prosecutions in serious cases of assault and vandalism by Tory supporters. Willis dressed down Robinson for failure to do his duty and threatened to refer the matter to His Majesty's government. The clear implication of the judge's comments was that discretion to prosecute did not extend to serious breaches of the peace, and that the law officers were bound to act regardless of the circumstances and the identity of the culprits. Robinson, relying on English practice, in his later justification of the law officers' decisions, made it clear that Crown lawyers were perfectly justified in exercising discretion in whether or not to prosecute.[51] Moreover, the alleged offenses were ones in which it was expected that the *victims* would take the initiative in prosecuting, not the Crown. The attorney general was arguing that both he and the solicitor general had complied with the formal requirements of the law, and that was all that was demanded of them.

Willis's relations with the governing elite deteriorated even further. This happened when the judge challenged the legality of the Court of King's Bench sitting with less than three judges under the *Court of King's Bench Act* of 1794 and refused to sit on a bench with any fewer.[52] The patience of the colonial executive having been tried to the limit, Lieutenant Governor Peregrine Maitland removed Willis from office in July 1828, a decision approved by secretary of state for the colonies, William Huskisson.[53]

The Willis "scandal" was used by the reformers in the Assembly to petition the British government for responsible government. This was warranted, they claimed, because of subversion of the wishes of the Assembly, "the constituted guardian of our rights and liberties," by the existing clique of government placemen.[54] The document also complained of the all too cozy relationship between the judges and the executive as well as their partiality, and it advocated appointment "during good behaviour" and the judges' exclusion from both the Executive and Legislative Councils. Although the British government of the day was nowhere close to contemplating responsible government for its North American colonies, it did show a willingness to rethink the relationship between the judges and the executive. The new chief justice, John Beverley Robinson, was excluded from the Executive Council on orders from Westminster.[55] From 1834 onward judges to the colony were appointed during good behavior, and ten years later judges had been excluded from all executive and legislative bodies in the province.[56] This was a pattern to be later adopted in all the settler colonies of the empire that were granted responsible government between 1848 and 1856.

IV

In the multiracial colonies Great Britain had acquired during the wars against the French, and their Spanish and the Dutch allies, between 1796 and 1815, imperial policy on governance was even less yielding than in British North America. These territories comprised European, Creole, African, and remnant indigenous populations. In most of them chattel slavery was practiced. Because of the challenges and complications surrounding the grant of representative government in these territories, the British government decided that they would be given Crown colony status, typically ruled by a governor with full plenary powers.[57] Initiating legislation for the colonies lay with Westminster, and, although a governor might have the benefit of working with an appointed council, the latter had only an advisory role. Not without some dithering, the European legal systems of civil justice introduced by imperial predecessors were left in place. At the same time English criminal justice, which was chauvinistically trumpeted as more humane than that of France, Spain and Holland, replaced the previous system. The multiracial slave colonies inherited from the First Empire were allowed to keep their representative assemblies. In the case of the slave colonies in general, a new and disturbing factor for the white elite in those territories was the meteoric rise of the antislavery movement in Britain and the pressure being put on government and Parliament to abolish the slave trade.[58] Ironically, then, in an era of political conservatism and deep anxieties about security of state and empire, a new rhetoric and discourse of freedom and the equality of humankind was superimposed on British imperial law and politics.

The contentious issue of whose law should prevail in bi-jural colonies existed in several possessions wrested from other European empires other than Quebec—for example, Trinidad, Demerara, and St. Lucia.[59] In Trinidad, which the British had wrested from the Spanish in 1796, the question of whether Spanish law should subsist or be replaced by English law became a bone of contention between the island's British planters and merchants on the one hand, and the first professional chief justice on the other.[60] George Smith—like Thorpe, a protégé of Lord Castlereagh—had persuaded his patron to allow him to write his job description as senior judge in the colony in 1808.[61] Smith sought to combine in his office several discrete Spanish offices. He favored the retention of the existing legal system, which he saw as in some ways superior to English law in property matters and in its treatment of slaves. The judge had ties to James Stephen Senior, a committed antislavery advocate described by his enemies as "the evil genius of the Colonial Office."[62] Smith, like Stephen, was strongly opposed to the grant of a representative assembly for the colony, which both feared would give planters and merchants the power to entrench a more oppressive slave economy than it already possessed.[63] Smith's view brought him into direct conflict with those commercial interests, the governor (Thomas Hislop), and the island's law officers.[64] The vigorous and increasingly intemperate debate was suffused with rule of law rhetoric and discourse, with Smith asserting the need for respect for judicial independence and the virtues of Crown colony government in protecting the non-European population, and his opponents, the "rights of freeborn Englishmen," which could be guaranteed only by an Assembly representing their interests and the inherent virtues and liberality of English law. Smith, who became increasingly difficult to live with, was suspended by

Hislop from a number of his posts in 1811, a decision confirmed by the Privy Council two years later.[65]

Ironically, Smith's view on governance and law were largely adopted by Lord Liverpool's government when it constituted Trinidad as a Crown colony and approved the continuation of Spanish law as the dominant system on the island in 1811.[66] One of its prime motives in choosing close control of the colony was a concern to protect the "free coloured" population who had petitioned the king for the recognition of their rights as loyal subjects of the Crown.

The abolition of slavery within the British Empire in 1834 was in theory meant to introduce former slave populations to equality under the law and the benefits of British justice. The colonial office recognized that this process would not be self-executing and took some steps to try and reduce the influence of a highly partial administration of justice in these territories by the planter magistracy through the appointment of stipendiaries from England.[67] This short-lived experiment did little to cure the basic problem of discriminatory administration of justice in these possessions. Although Britain took the moral high-road in abolishing slavery, the government subverted that position by both compensating the planters and supporting the continuation of plantation economies in these territories. The result was that the power and authority of the social and economic elite was broadly sustained, and their control over the sources of labor continued.[68] The black population remained outside the political mainstream, as did most of the "colored" or Creole population. Although some steps were taken in particular colonies to revise the local courts' system to make it more sensitive to the needs of these people, they continued by and large to be on the receiving end of the administration of justice, be it the criminal law or master and servant legislation.[69]

For those former slaves who continued to work on the plantations, although protected from the excessive harshness of the slavery codes, they were still regimented and closely regulated.[70] Many, in fact, refused to provide wage labor, preferring to eke out an independent existence on their small plots of land. The same draconian treatment was meted out to newcomers to the plantations, the indentured laborers imported from India and China, with the encouragement of the imperial government, to fill the labor deficit caused by the refusal of former slaves to work in this environment.[71] Often subject to overwork, exploitation, and neglect, they could expect little or no sympathy from the planter magistracy.[72] The fact that the empire-wide system of master-servant law was administered by magistrates meant that to a great extent it operated outside the surveillance of superior courts.[73]

The planters continued to be haunted by fears of revolts. One of the most notorious episodes of Caribbean history during the nineteenth century was the Morant Bay Rebellion in Jamaica in 1865 and the brutal treatment of actual and suspected rebels in its wake. The actions of the governor, Edward Eyre, invoking martial law and supporting its vigorous and indiscriminate enforcement, proved that the rule of law was meaningless when minority white populations felt themselves in mortal danger from their subjects of color.[74] This episode, which was labeled by ultra-imperialists as yet another example of the untrustworthy character of non-European subjects, produced a shift in imperial policy toward the multiracial empire. London sought to secure greater imperial control in multiracial colonies by vesting plenary powers in governors, abolishing or reducing the powers of legislative bodies, and reacting unfavorably to internal bickering between governors and chief justices.[75] Although by this time in white settler possessions judges had secured at least formal independence from executive power, they were still viewed as key players in executive government in colonies with majority nonwhite populations and expected, above all else, to be loyal and compliant. Those who did not play the game were viewed with alarm.

Chief Justice Joseph Beaumont, who had grown up in an antislavery family, was dispatched to British Guiana in 1863.[76] He quickly became embroiled in conflicts with the governor, Francis Hincks, and the latter's friends among the planter elite. Among the judge's concerns was the harsh treatment of indentured workers in the colony, which along with Trinidad had received the lion's share of this new labor pool. When he overturned the decisions of magistrates in cases of worker discipline, on what his enemies considered technicalities, and sought to exercise supervisory control over the administration of justice in the lower courts, the temperature began to rise.[77] It reached boiling point after Beaumont sought to establish his authority over gaol delivery and the process of commutation of sentences; he then committed for trial William Campbell, the clerk of the Supreme Court, for tampering with the relevant judicial records. Beaumont alleged that the colonial executive was behind this.[78] Hincks suspended the jurist from office, action that was abruptly countermanded by the secretary of state for the colonies, Edward Cardwell. The governor in justifying his actions sought to paint himself as the protector of peace and order in the colony and as the fearless foe of the sort of agitation and violence that had recently plagued Jamaica. Beaumont then proceeded with the Campbell case and imprisoned a hostile newspaper editor for contempt in his vituperative references to the judges sitting on that hearing. Hincks and his friends in the Assembly (the Court of Policy) lost patience and forwarded a petition for the jurist's removal from office.[79] The matter was then referred to the Privy Council. In 1868 that body recommended the chief justice's removal, having found him guilty of "proofs of indiscretion and a want of judicial temper." His conduct was characterized as calculated "to embarrass the Executive Government rather than promote the ends of justice."[80]

Beaumont returned to England and to practice, embittered at his treatment. He set out his frustrations in *The New Slavery* in which he described the abuses of justice committed against indentured workers in the colony and the difficulties he had faced in securing fair and decent treatment for them.[81] His protestations may not have been entirely in vain. London, responding to the complaints of his friend, George Des Voeux, a former stipendiary magistrate in Guiana who supported Beaumont's attempts to bring justice to the estates, established a royal commission to consider the indenture system in the colony. This body recommended changes to the system of which the former judge would have approved and some of which were implemented.[82]

Although there may have been some sympathy for the stand taken by Beaumont and his likes in official imperial circles, the tensions he was seen as having created with executive power in British Guiana were ultimately considered unacceptable. Judicial independence of the type exhibited by this judge was no longer palatable. Although the consolidation of political power in these territories was prompted in part by the desire to clip the wings of the planter elite, the result was for decades the freezing of further constitutional development of the relationship between these colonies and the metropolis.[83] Moreover, with a main objective of the colonial mission as preserving law and order, the traditional centers of social and economic power in these possessions continued to exercise influence.

V

By the last third of the nineteenth century there were two distinctive trajectories in British imperial policy toward its colonies. In the case of the settler (now predominantly white) colonies a significant degree of self-government had been granted by the concession of responsible government (and in the case of Canada, dominion status from 1867).[84] With that move on the part of London, government and law (including the administration of justice) became largely a local responsibility. Accordingly, interpretation of the rule of law and its scope was left largely to political and legal players in the possessions in question.

In these "white" jurisdictions, whatever the relationship between new constitutional forms and the rule of law in its different hues, the concept continued to be contested terrain. In many ways, as in Britain in the eighteenth century, the focus of contention shifted from the risk of autocracy associated with powerful, seemingly untrammeled executive authority to the dominance of local legislative assemblies. Although increasingly democratic in their composition as representatives of white male settler populations, these bodies could and did prove narrow-minded and exclusionary when it came to dealing with the "other" within their societies, especially in matters of race and ethnicity.[85] Independence of the judiciary, formally granted to all of these possessions, could produce detached and balanced judgments in some instances. However, it was compromised in others by an identity of judicial sentiment on race and class with mainstream opinion in white society, and by the political nature of appointments to the bench.[86]

The second trajectory was that of closer imperial government and supervision of the multiracial empire, primarily through the exercise of the royal prerogative, administered by governors with plenary powers. In the last three decades of the century advocates in Britain of a liberal and inclusive notion of the rule of law and the protections of the common law were clearly on the defensive as the imperial agenda came under the influence of the pessimistic, even apocalyptic, proponents of racial superiority and the need to keep the "untrustworthy," "mutinous," and inherently "dangerous" colored populations under close control.[87] Although to some extent balanced by more benign notions of trusteeship and the guidance of subject populations, this mindset often undercut judicial independence in these territories, as the pressures for loyalty and compliance became stronger and put off to some distant point in time greater political freedom for majority populations.

The acceptance of the rule of law in a liberal sense was imperfectly realized in the nineteenth-century British Empire, despite spirited individual judicial attempts to champion it. This reality was reflected in the white settler colonies in the effects of majoritarian democracy, in which issues of race tended to confine the application of the rule of law to the European populations of these territories. Throughout the multiracial colonies, although the blessings of the rule of law might be proclaimed by imperial officialdom, the reality on the ground was often that the influence of minority European populations that controlled the economic and, either directly or indirectly, political destinies of these possessions subverted its unconditional application to the "subject" peoples.

That having been said, it can also be argued that the efforts of colonial jurists to champion judicial independence were not entirely in vain, whether in a substantive or symbolic sense. The short-lived judicial careers of men such as Thorpe and Willis were important in pointing the way to necessary changes in the imperial constitution and the role of the judiciary in the colonial state. Judges such as Smith and Beaumont provided impetus to the idea that differences in race, ethnicity, and culture should not stand in the way of the evenhanded administration of justice in multiracial colonies. As Martin Wiener has demonstrated in his study of criminal justice in several British colonies between 1870 and 1935, advocacy of the ideal of equality before the law and resistance to discrimination in its application continued to be pressed by individual judges, lawyers, imperial and colonial politicians, and not least the subject peoples, with increasing intensity and some success during that period.[88] Bearing out Lauren Benton's assertion that "subject" peoples were adept at turning the cherished ideals of their colonial masters against them, representatives of these communities deployed British rule of law rhetoric and discourse in demanding that the principles, rights, and protections associated with it be extended to them.[89] In time, during the twentieth century, the values and ideals associated with the rule of law were to become elements in political and legal arguments for independence from colonial rule.

Notes

1. A.V. Dicey, *Introduction to the Study of the Law of the Constitution* (London: St. Martin's Press, 1961), pp. 183–203.
2. Roy Porter, *English Society in the Eighteenth Century* (Harmondsworth: Penguin, 1982), p. 149.
3. *Magna Carta* (1215), articles 29 and 30. In *Bushell's Case* (1670) 6 State Trials 1006 (K.B.) Vaughan CJ denied a power in the judiciary to imprison jurors for verdicts which they considered perverse and against the evidence.
4. *Habeas Corpus Amendment Act* (1679) 31 Car. II, c. 2.
5. *Bill of Rights* (1689) 1 Will. & Mary, Sess. 2, c. 2.
6. *Act of Settlement* (1701) 12 & 13 Will. III, c. 2, s.3.
7. See *Leach v. Money* (1765) 19 State Trials 981 (K.B.); *Entick v. Carrington* (1765) 19 State Trials 1045 (C.P.).
8. John Phillip Reid, *The Concept of Liberty in the Age of the American Revolution* (Chicago: University of Chicago Press, 1988); Janice Potter, *The Liberty We Seek: Loyalist Ideology in Colonial New York and Massachusetts* (Cambridge, MA: Harvard University Press, 1983).
9. H.T. Dickinson, *Liberty and Property: Political Ideology in Eighteenth-Century Britain* (London: Methuen, 1977), pp. 121–92.
10. Alan J. Ward, *The Irish Constitutional Tradition: Responsible Government and Modern Ireland, 1782–1992* (Washington DC: Catholic University of America Press, 1994), pp. 15–29.
11. Andrew Jackson O'Shaughnessy, *An Empire Divided: The American Revolution and the British Caribbean* (Philadelphia: University of Pennsylvania Press, 2000), pp. 116–21.

12. Helen Taft Manning, *British Colonial Government after the American Revolution 1782–1820* (London: Oxford University Press, 1933; repr. Hamden CT: Archon Books, 1966), pp. 293–96.
13. Lauren Benton, *Law and Colonial Cultures: Legal Regimes in World History, 1400–1900* (Cambridge: Cambridge University Press, 2002), pp. 127–49.
14. See P.G. McHugh, *Aboriginal Societies and the Common Law: A History of Sovereignty, Status, and Self-determination* (Oxford: Oxford University Press, 2004), pp. 61–116.
15. Hilary McD. Beckles, "The 'Hub of Empire': The Caribbean and Britain in the Seventeenth Century," in *The Origins of Empire*, ed. Nicholas Canny (Oxford: Oxford University Press, 1998), pp. 218–40 (pp. 231–33).
16. John McLaren, ""Men of Principle or Judicial Ratbags? The Trials and Tribulations of Maverick Colonial Judges in the 19th Century"; or "A Funny Way to Run an Empire," *Windsor Review of Law and Social Issues*, 27 (2009), 145–67.
17. See Shaunnagh Dorsett's chapter in this volume.
18. F. Murray Greenwood, *Legacies of Fear: Law and Politics in Quebec in the Era of the French Revolution* (Toronto: Osgoode Society, 1993), pp. 24–34; Peter Oliver, "Power, Politics and the Law: The Place of the Judiciary in the Historiography of Upper Canada," in *Essays in the History of Canadian Law Vol. VIII: In Honour of R.C.B. Risk*, ed. G. Blaine Baker and Jim Phillips, 10 vols. (Toronto: Osgoode Society, 1999), VII, pp. 441–68 (pp. 450–51).
19. (1782) 22 Geo. III, c. 75. Under s. 3 of the Act the judge had a right of appeal to the Privy Council. In colonies with representative assemblies an alternative procedure was for the Assembly to petition the Privy Council to remove a colonial jurist. It was also open to London, using the prerogative, to recall a troublesome judge.
20. Leonard Woods Labaree, *Royal Government in America; A Study of the British Colonial System before 1783* (New Haven: Yale University Press, 1930), pp. 389–400.
21. Greg Marquis, "In Defence of Liberty: 17th-Century England and 19th-Century Maritimes Political Culture," *University of New Brunswick Law Journal*, 42 (1993), 69–94.
22. William Blackstone, *Commentaries on the Laws of England*, 4 vols. (Oxford: Clarendon Press, 1765–1769; facsimile version Legal Classic Library: Birmingham ALA, 1983), I (1765), pp. 49–52, 63–73, 123–26, 130–31, 134–36.
23. Marquis, "Defence of Liberty," pp. 77–78.
24. See Zoe Laidlaw, *Colonial Connections 1815–45: Patronage, the Information Revolution and Colonial Government* (Manchester: Manchester University Press, 2005); David Lambert and Alan Lester eds., *Colonial Lives across the British Empire: Imperial Careering in the Long Nineteenth Century* (Cambridge: Cambridge University Press, 2006).
25. Bridget Brereton, *Law, Justice and Empire: The Colonial Career of John Gorrie 1829–1892* (Kingston, Jamaica: Press University of the West Indies, 1997); J.M. Bennett, *Sir Francis Forbes: First Chief Justice of New South Wales 1824–1837* (Annandale, NSW: Federation Press, 2001).

26. J.M. Bennett, *Sir John Pedder: First Chief Justice of Tasmania* (Annandale, NSW: Federation Press, 2003), pp. 94–95. The author notes the correspondence between Pedder and Justice John Walpole Willis in Melbourne on issues of criminal libel and contempt of court.
27. Gad Heuman, "The British West Indies, 1815–1914," in *The Oxford History of the British Empire, Volume III: The Nineteenth Century*, ed. William Roger Louis (Oxford History of the British Empire Series, ed. A. Porter, 5 vols.) (Oxford: Oxford University Press, 1999), III, pp. 470–94 (pp. 474–76); Bridget Brereton, *A History of Modern Trinidad 1783–1962* (London: Heinemann, 1981), pp. 42–44; James Millette, *Society and Politics in Colonial Trinidad* (London: Zed Books, 1985).
28. Brereton, *A History of Modern Trinidad*, pp. 43–44; Millette, *Society and Politics*, pp. 264–66.
29. John Manning Ward, *Colonial Self-Government: The British Experience 1759–1856* (Toronto: University of Toronto, 1979), pp. 1–3; Robert Fraser, "'All the Privileges Which Englishmen Possess': Orders, Rights and Constitutionalism in Upper Canada," in *Provincial Justice: Upper Canadian Legal Portraits*, ed. Robert Fraser (Toronto: Osgoode Society, 1992), pp. xxi–xcii (pp. xxi–xxii, xxv–xl, xlvii–xlviii).
30. See *Constitution Act* (1791) 30 1 Geo. III, c. 31, ss. XIII, XXV1, III.
31. See Greenwood, *Legacies of Fear*, pp. 43–55.
32. Fraser, "'All the Privileges,'" pp. xxiv–xxxii.
33. Ibid.
34. John McLaren, "The King, the People, the Law…and the Constitution: Justice Robert Thorpe and the Roots of Irish Whig Ideology in Early Upper Canada," in *People and Place: Historical Influences on Legal Culture*, ed. Jonathan Swainger and Constance Backhouse (Vancouver: UBC Press, 2006), pp. 11–24 (pp. 15–16); and "The Rule of Law and Irish Whig Constitutionalism in Upper Canada: William Warren Baldwin, the 'Irish Opposition', and the Volunteer Connection" in *Essays in the History of Canadian Law: A Tribute to Peter Oliver*, ed. Jim Phillips, R. Roy McMurtry and John T. Saywell (Toronto: Osgoode Society, 2008), pp. 320–52.
35. McLaren, "The King, the People," p. 19. The correspondence relating to Thorpe is in Douglas Brymner, "Political State of Upper Canada in 1806–7," in *Report on Canadian Archives, 1892*, ed. Douglas Brymner (Ottawa: Public Archives of Canada, 1893), pp. 32–136.
36. McLaren, "The King, the People," p. 18.
37. K.D. McRae, "An Upper Canadian Letter of 1829 on Responsible Government," *Canadian Historical Review*, 31 (1950), 291–96.
38. See McLaren, "Rule of Law," pp. 334–40.
39. Fernand Ouellet, *Lower Canada 1791–1840* (Toronto: McClelland & Stewart, 1980), pp. 52–94.
40. Jean-Marie Fecteau, F. Murray Greenwood, and Jean-Pierre Wallot, "Sir James Craig's 'Reign of Terror' and Its Impact on Emergency Powers in Lower Canada," in *Canadian State Trials: Law, Politics and Security Measures, 1608–1837*, ed. F. Murray Greenwood and Barry Wright, 3 vols. (Toronto: Osgoode Society, 1996), I, pp. 323–78; Greenwood, *Legacies of Fear*, pp. 213–46.

41. Greenwood, *Legacies of Fear*, p. 237.
42. Evelyn Kolish and James Lambert, "The Attempted Impeachment of the Lower Canadian Chief Justices, 1814–1815," in Greenwood and Wright, *Canadian State Trials*, I, pp. 450–86.
43. Ibid., pp. 450–51.
44. *Proceedings in the Assembly of Lower Canada on the Rules and Practice of the Courts of Justice and the Impeachments of Jonathan Sewell and James Monk Esquires* (1814) are included in Greenwood and Wright, *Canadian State Trials*, I, pp. 688–94. For the charges against Monk, see pp. 694–96.
45. Kolish and Lambert, "The Attempted Impeachment," pp. 469–75.
46. Ibid., p. 460.
47. Jane Errington, *The Lion, Eagle and Upper Canada: A Developing Colonial Ideology* (Montreal and Kingston: McGill-Queen's Press, 1987), pp. 92–96.
48. McLaren, "Rule of Law," pp. 334–35.
49. Ibid., pp. 335–36.
50. Robert Hett, "Judge Willis and the Court of King's Bench in Upper Canada," in *Ontario Historical Society*, 65 (1973), 19–31; Leo Johnson, "John Walpole Willis's Judicial Career in Upper Canada, 1827–28; The Research Impact of Computerized Documentation on an Non-controversial Theme," *Ontario History* 85 (1993), 141–66.
51. See Paul Romney, *Mr. Attorney: The Attorney General for Ontario in Court, Cabinet, and Legislature 1791–1899* (Toronto: Osgoode Society, 1986), pp. 137–39.
52. Hett, "Judge Willis," p. 26.
53. Ibid., p. 28. Willis unsuccessfully appealed his removal. The evidence for both Maitland and the former judge can be accessed in *Printed Papers in Indian and Colonial Appeals*, folio series (P.C.I.C.A.), Vol. 15 (1829) in the Archives of the Judicial Committee of the Privy Council, 12 Downing Street.
54. Petition by Dr. Baldwin and others to King George IV on the case of Justice Willis. July 1828, Canadian Institute for Historical Microreproductions, No. 41338.
55. Romney, *Mr. Attorney*, p. 151.
56. Peter Oliver, "Power, Politics," pp. 456–57.
57. John Manning Ward addresses the issue in *Colonial Self-government*, pp. 82–123. See especially pp. 82–91.
58. J.R. Oldfield, *Popular Politics and British Anti-Slavery: The Mobilization of Public Opinion against the Slave Trade* (Manchester: Manchester University Press, 1995).
59. Manning, *British Colonial Government*, pp. 365–67 (St. Lucia); pp. 367–75 (Demerera/Berbice–British Guiana); pp. 346–63 (Trinidad); pp. 401–8 (Cape Colony); pp. 453–55 (Ceylon); pp. 469–73 (Mauritius).
60. Millette, *Society and Politics*, pp. 230–66; Brereton, *Modern Trinidad*, pp. 32–51.
61. Millette, *Society and Politics*, pp. 230–33.
62. Ibid., p. 253.
63. Ibid., pp. 234–35, 246–49.

64. Ibid., pp. 236–60.
65. Manning, *British Colonial Government*, p. 388.
66. Millette, *Society and Politics*, pp. 264–66; Brereton, *Modern Trinidad*, pp. 43–44.
67. W.L. Burn, *Emancipation and Apprenticeship in the West Indies* (London: Jonathan Cape, 1937).
68. William A. Green, *British Slave Emancipation: The Sugar Colonies and the Great Experiment* (Oxford: Clarendon Press, 1976); Mary Turner, "The British Caribbean. 1823–1838: The Transition from Slave to Free Legal Status," in *Masters, Servants and Magistrates in Britain & the Empire, 1562–1955*, ed. Douglas Hay and Paul Craven (Durham, NC: University of North Carolina Press, 2004), pp. 303–22.
69. Anthony De V. Phillips, "Emancipation Betrayed? Social Control Legislation in the British Caribbean (with special reference to Barbados), 1834–1876" *Chicago-Kent Law Review*, 70 (1994/5), 1349–72.
70. Heuman, "British West Indies," pp. 478–83.
71. Ibid., pp. 484–85.
72. Walton Look Lai, *Indentured Labour, Caribbean Sugar: Chinese and Immigrants to the British West Indies, 1838–1918* (Baltimore: Johns Hopkins University Press, 1993), pp. 87–141; Basdeo Mangru, *Indenture and Abolition: Sacrifice and Survival on the Guyanese Sugar Plantations* (Toronto: TSAR Publications, 1993), pp. 17–42.
73. Hay and Craven, *Masters, Servants*, pp. 54–58.
74. See Rande Kostal, *A Jurisprudence of Power: Victorian Empire and the Rule of Law* (Oxford: Oxford University Press, 2005); Julie Evans, *Edward Eyre: Race and Colonial Government* (Dunedin, NZ: University of Otago Press, 2005), pp. 99–150.
75. Heuman, "The British West Indies," pp. 487–88.
76. Basedo Mangru, "The Hincks-Beaumont Imbroglio: Partisan Politics in British Guiana in the 1860s," *Boletin de Estudios Latinoamericanos y del Caribe*, 43 (1987), 99–114. Documentation relating to the Beaumont Case may be found at P.C.I.C.A, Archives of the Judicial Committee of the Privy Council, Vol. 68 (1868).
77. Mangru, "Hincks Beaumont," pp. 99 100.
78. Ibid., pp. 101–2, 104–7.
79. Ibid., pp. 109–10.
80. Ibid., pp. 111.
81. Joseph Beaumont, *The New Slavery: An Account of the Indian and Chinese Immigration to British Guiana* (London: W. Ridgeway, 1871).
82. British Guiana, *The Inquiry as to the Treatment of Immigrants* and *The Dispatch of the Secretary of State and Mr. Des Voeux's Letter* (Demerara: The Colonist Office, Georgetown, 1870). See also George William Des Voeux, *Experiences of a Demerara Magistrate, 1863–1869* (Georgetown, BG: Daily Chronicle, 1948).
83. Heuman, "British West Indies," pp. 487–88.
84. The debates in imperial circles and the negotiations in the various colonies are addressed in Manning Ward, *Colonial Self-government*, pp. 247–329.

85. Robert A. Huttenback, *Racism and Empire: White Settlers and Colored Immigrants in the British Self-Governing Colonies, 1830–1910* (Ithaca, NY: Cornell University Press, 1976); John McLaren, "The Burdens of Empire and the Legalization of White Supremacy in Canada 1860–1910," in *Legal History in the Making: Proceedings of the Ninth British Legal History Conference Glasgow 1989*, ed. W.M. Gordon and T.D. Fergus (London: Hambledon Press, 1991), pp. 187–200; McHugh, *Aboriginal Societies*, pp. 117–214.
86. On controversies relating to the Canadian judiciary, see Jonathan Swainger, *The Canadian Department of Justice and the Completion of Confederation 1867–78* (Vancouver: UBC Press, 2000), pp. 98–122.
87. Catherine Hall, *Civilizing Subjects: Colony and Metropole in the English Imagination, 1839–1867* (Chicago: University of Chicago Press, 2002), p. 25.
88. Martin J. Wiener, *An Empire on Trial: Race, Murder, and Justice under British Rule, 1870–1935* (Cambridge: Cambridge University Press, 2009).
89. Benton, *Law and Colonial Cultures*, pp. 253–65.

Chapter 5

"*Your Sovereign* and *Our Father*"
The Imperial Crown and the Idea of Legal-Ethnohistory

Mark D. Walters

I

This chapter is about historical narrative, the shifting uses of language over time, and the relevance of diverse cultural perspectives for our understanding of the legal history of imperial sovereignty—and for these reasons I shall begin with a story.[1]

In the spring of 1764, messengers arrived at an Anishinaabe village with an invitation to its inhabitants from Sir William Johnson, the Crown's representative for Indian affairs in the northern parts of British North America, to attend a feast at Niagara to establish peace. The villagers reacted with both hope and fear. The journey from their home at the *Sault*, or falls, between Lakes Huron and Superior to Niagara would be long, and they doubted Johnson's sincerity. Village elders decided to consult the spirits or *manitous*.[2]

The villagers, or Saulteurs as they were known, constructed a moose-skin tent. As the sun set, an elder entered the tent and the villagers gathered around. The tent began to shake and anguished voices from inside were heard. During the shaking-tent ceremony, or *jiisakiiwin* as the Anishinaabeg called it, Mikinaak the Great Turtle would reveal what the manitous knew. The village chiefs offered tobacco and asked whether it was safe to go to Niagara. There was a long silence, and then a feeble voice gave the answer. The Turtle assured them that they would be safe and Johnson would fill their canoes with presents.

Sixteen Saulteurs set out for Niagara. As they navigated through the islands of Lake Huron they felt a sense of spiritual unease. They saw a rattlesnake on one of the islands—a manitou—and they addressed it as grandfather and asked it to fill Johnson's heart with sentiments of charity. But the manitou seemed displeased, and angry waves later threatened their bark canoes. They sacrificed two dogs to appease the spirits.

The Saulteurs crossed Lake Huron safely and navigated the rivers leading inland before leaving their canoes and striking out on foot. They struggled for two days through forests thick with mosquitoes before emerging at the Toronto trading house on the shore of Lake Ontario. Here they made new canoes from elm bark for the trip across the lake to Niagara. On the morning of their departure, the Saulteurs, painted in bright colors to signify their peaceful intentions, held a council and sang songs that would protect them from danger.

They arrived at Niagara later that day. The sight must have astounded them. On one side of the river was the stone fortress, built by the French but now possessed by the British. On the other bank were the encampments of over a thousand delegates from nations all around the Great Lakes and beyond, the largest such gathering ever held.[3]

The treaty council would extend over many days. Finally, on the last day of July, Johnson and his officers left the fort and crossed the river to formalize the treaty at the native encampment. With promises of peace, friendship, justice, security, and prosperity, he gave the assembled chiefs "the great Covenant Chain," a belt of wampum shells "23 Rows broad, & the Year 1764 worked upon it," and then he distributed valuable gifts for them to take home to their people.[4] In subsequent treaty councils, chiefs would hold the same belt in their hands, recite the story of the meeting at Niagara, and implore "our Great Father"—the king—to honor the promises then made.[5]

What should we make of this story? How is it relevant to our understanding of the legal history of Imperial sovereignty in North America? What, in particular, did the characterization of the king as "Father" mean? It is tempting to understand this expression in the sense that it has in modern Western societies. As historians such as Quentin Skinner and J.G.A. Pocock have argued, however, that temptation must be resisted. Statements such as this one are, Skinner insists, speech-acts that can acquire meaning only through an examination of what speakers were *doing* in speaking as they did. To know the historical meaning of a statement, Skinner argues, we must "surround the particular statement ... with an intellectual context that serves to lend adequate support to it," a context reconstructed from "the complete range of the inherited symbols and representations that constitute the subjectivity of an age."[6] For Pocock, the relevant contexts for understanding the languages of the past extend beyond a consideration of what speakers were *doing* to an examination of the "paradigms" of discourse that both enabled and restricted what they *could* do. "[O]nly after we have understood what means he had of saying anything," Pocock writes, can we begin to understand what a speaker "meant to say, what he succeeded in saying, what he was taken to have said, or what effects his utterance had in modifying or transforming the existing paradigm structure."[7]

From these contextualist perspectives, the account of the Saulteur journey—the shaking tent, the snake-manitou, the songs—is much more than an interesting story. It is part of the cultural texture against which the words expressed and recorded at treaty councils must be interpreted. Historical contextualism, at least in this context, involves ethnography. The interpretation of the history of relationships between peoples in colonial settings, including their legal relationships, must involve the distinctive methods associated with *ethno*history.

Synthesizing legal history and ethnohistory is hardly straightforward, especially within the contextualist framework articulated by scholars such as Skinner. Legal interpretation tends toward unity, continuity, and coherence within normative orders. Contextualism resists these interpretive tendencies. Attributing a common or shared meaning to a statement such as the "King is father" is, for the contextualist, problematic. In Skinner's view, history is nothing but "a variety of statements made by a variety of different agents with a variety of different intentions . . . ."[8] To complicate matters further, the anthropological component of ethnohistory is linked to traditions of synchronism and structuralism—the static and persistent "ethnographic present"—that compete with the diachronic, dynamic view of the human condition generally adopted by historians.[9] In short, if there is a legal-ethnohistorical style of interpretation at all, it is one that strains to contain interpretive tendencies that pull in different directions.

This chapter is an attempt at legal-ethnohistory. I first examine the ways in which the imperial Crown in British North America was generally conceived as a father by both common law and indigenous legal traditions. I then consider intercultural discourse in the colonies of Upper and Lower Canada in the 1820s and 1830s, with reference as well to the larger imperial discourse concerning "aborigines" in British settlements at this time, with a view to reconstructing the legal meaning, or meanings, of the imperial Crown. I conclude with some brief observations about the possibilities for legal-ethnohistory as a distinctive style of historical interpretation.

II

The description of the Crown by a Cree speaker from west of Lake Superior in 1816 as "*your Sovereign* and *our Father*" captures the ambiguous legal character that the imperial Crown had in British North America.[10] The imperial Crown seemed to have a double life.

One of the imperial Crown's identities was determined by the common law of England. At the dawn of the seventeenth century, the common law already embraced conceptions of Crown, sovereignty, and empire that would provide legal sustenance for the subsequent flourishing of English and later British imperial power. Weaving history and myth together, judges found the imperial quality of the Crown of England in its very origins: the English Crown was forged, wrote Sir Edward Coke, when the several regional kings within England "melted" their respective crowns "to make one imperial diadem."[11] The English Crown, as a composite or imperial Crown, appeared destined to extend its sovereign reach to distant places and peoples.

For common law judges, Crown sovereignty implied reciprocal obligations between subject and sovereign: subjects were bound to "obey and serve" the king and the king was bound to "govern and protect" his subjects.[12] The subjects' allegiance was a sacred "faith" internalized as a quality of "the mind and soul of man"; it was submissive and reverential, the subject always "inferior" to a sovereign "superior."[13] Within Coke's vision of the constitution, the "Crown" emerged as a "hieroglyphic"—a symbol or metaphor.[14] In his political capacity, the king was "mysticall," "immortal," and "invisible," omnipresent throughout the empire and divisible amongst its many dominions.[15] But in his natural capacity, the king was a single person whose endowments of "soul" and "body" enabled him to dispense justice and judgment according to right and equity, a unifying focus of allegiance for diverse peoples with diverse laws across an expanding empire.[16]

The peoples indigenous to North America did not view sovereignty or kings this way. These were non-state societies governed through councils of chiefs and elders representing networks of clans or extended families within and between villages. Political order was intimately connected to spiritual order, and both were oriented toward relations of kinship. Kinship transcended temporal and physical boundaries: trees, water, and animals were infused with spiritual life—with *manitous*—and survival necessitated spiritual balance with them through constant gift-giving. Peaceful relations with the elements of the natural world and peoples within that world meant establishing and maintaining relationships of spiritual-kinship by creating reciprocal obligations of care. To give or receive presents was to renounce the status of alien and to become kin. The snake-manitou met by the Saulteurs on their way to Niagara was a grandfather and gifts were needed to ensure its good thoughts. This episode is not unrelated to the message of the Great Turtle given in the shaking tent, that the Crown's representative would fill their canoes with presents. To establish political relations was to create obligations of care between members of an extended family. To have a wealthy king as father meant having a caring relation who would provide gifts, offer counsel, and ward off danger.[17]

Understanding the historical treaty references to the king as father in North America is not simply a matter of acknowledging that indigenous customary law was able to clothe the king with a certain status as father and the common law was not, for the common law had metaphors of its own and the "Crown as father" was one of them. The king was, by virtue of the common law, "*parens patriæ, et paterfamilias totius regni*"—the king was *father of the people*.[18] The *parens patriæ* metaphor had symbolic power, but like the father motif within indigenous customary law, it had practical implications too. Indeed, these implications were similar: both legal traditions associated parental status with the value of *care*. "Of necessity," common lawyers said, "the State must place somewhere a superintending power over those, who cannot take care of themselves...."[19] The parental metaphor was most apt in relation to the Crown's special powers over children. At common law, "the Crown, as *parens patriæ*, was the supreme guardian and superintendent over all infants," and so the lord chancellor could make vulnerable children wards and assert royal discretion over their property and other interests.[20]

In short, two legal conceptions of political order, both expressed through distinctive metaphors, myths, and symbols, came into contact at treaty councils in North America. Linguistic usage gave distinct legal meanings to words such as *father* in both systems. But despite differences a shared normative world took shape.

At a very practical level, linguistic differences had to be bridged through the translation of words from one language to another. A complete ethnohistorical analysis of the expression "Crown as father" (or "mother") would, therefore, involve an analysis of aboriginal languages and their translation by treaty interpreters—a task beyond the scope of this chapter. We may gain some sense of that process, however, by comparing two mid-nineteenth-century accounts of Anishinaabe or "Chippeway" language written by John Summerfield and Thomas McKenney.

The Anishinaabe language falls within the Algonquian language group. It has words for chief, father, and mother but, it seems, no words for king or queen. The Summerfield and McKenney accounts identify the Anishinaabe root word for father and its various possessive forms in the same way, though with different spellings. Summerfield says the root word for father is *oose* and variations include *noose* (my father), *koose* (your father), and *koosenon* (our father).[21] The account published by McKenney says that the root word for father is *oaoas'emau* and variations include *nósa* (my father), *kose* (your father), and *ko'sanaun* (our father).[22] Summerfield says the root word for mother is *ogah*, and variations include *negah* (my mother) and *kegah* (your mother).[23] Both accounts give the same word for chief, namely, *o'geeman* or *ogemah*.[24] What is interesting, however, is that both accounts also attempt to provide an Anishinaabe word for king, but one account links that word with chief and the other with father. Summerfield translates *kecheogemah* as "King, or great Chief."[25] The word *kecheogemah* is formed by the addition of the prefix *keche*, which means "great," to the word for chief, or *ogemah*. The McKenney account, however, links the word king with father. It translates *ko'sanaun* as "King ... Our father."[26] To summarize, both accounts translate "our father" in the same way, as *koosenon* or *ko'sanaun*, but one account also links this word to king whereas the other looks to *kecheogemah*, literally "great chief," as the nearest Anishinaabe word.

As Skinner reminds us, we must look to the conventional usage of words in historical context, not dictionaries, to know the full meanings of historical speech-acts. But a simple form of linguistic analysis can provide a starting point. The Summerfield analysis suggests that even though the Anishinaabeg did not have a word for king, such a word could be created by adding together the Anishinaabe words for great and chief. But this assumes that the speaker wishes to capture a meaning for king that is close to the Anishinaabe idea of political leader associated with their word for chief. What is striking about the treaty council records from the seventeenth to the nineteenth centuries, however, is that the Crown is consistently referred to as father or mother rather than chief or great chief. Anishinaabe chief Kakkewaquonaby, or Peter Jones, who served as a translator at treaty councils, wrote in 1861 that his people referred to the king as "*Ningeche Noosenon*," which, he said, means "Our Great Father," and to the queen as "*Ningahnon*," which he translated as "Our Great Mother."[27] Jones' reference to *Noosenon* appears to be the equivalent of the word for "our father"—*koosenon* or *ko'sanaun*—in the accounts we examined above.

By addressing the Crown as *koosenon* (or *noosenon*) in treaty councils, rather than using the words for chief or great chief, Anishinaabe speakers presumably wished to convey a meaning of king that was associated in some way with their conception of father. But what was that sense of father? When they used that word at Niagara in 1764, what (Skinner would have us ask) were they *doing* in using that word?

One thing that they were *not* doing was submitting to Crown sovereignty—or at least the Crown's representative, Sir William Johnson, did not think that they were.[28] Johnson conceded that it was common for people to describe Indians as subjects of the Crown, but, he insisted, the Indians themselves would never have consented to that status. "It is necessary to observe," he wrote, that "no Nation of Indians have any word which can express, or convey the Idea of Subjection"; "they often say, we acknowledge the great King to be our Father ... [but] our People too readily adopt & insert a Word [i.e., sovereign] very different in signification, and never intended by the Indians ... ."[29]

By this time the use of kinship terms in structuring political relations between settler and indigenous societies already had a long history. Indeed, the Crown was not the only European member of extended aboriginal families. European officials dealing with Indian nations generally became brothers or fathers by means of adoption and renaming. The governors of New France were fathers called *Onontio*; the governors of New York were brothers called *Corlaer*; William Johnson was brother *Warraghiyagey*, and so forth.[30] By renaming an official whose authority and powers were alien to aboriginal legal traditions, native peoples were, in essence, remaking the image of that official to fit within their understandings of what political leaders were. Once integrated within the aboriginal network of kinship, an official became obligated, like any family member, to contribute to the spiritual and material well-being of his relations in proportion to his abilities and their needs.

Johnson tells us what indigenous leaders did *not* mean when they addressed the king as father. It is through additional ethnohistorical analysis that we may begin reconstructing what they *did* mean. Our brief overview of common law and indigenous legal traditions permits some tentative conclusions. We may say that the legal traditions of the societies that met in treaty councils in North America embraced rather different conceptions of the king as father. There was the king as *parens patriæ*, a sovereign king who enjoyed a common law *power of discretion* over vulnerable wards. There was also the king as *koosenon* (to use the Anishinaabe word), an indigenous father with *duties of care* arising in customary law from a relationship of spiritual kinship with independent children. As we shall see, however, it would be easy for officials to slip from one sense of father to the other.

III

The end of the American revolutionary war brought settlers into what was left of British North America. As Indian territories were surrendered and settled in colonial Canada, aboriginal ways of life became precarious. Communities were vulnerable to levels of poverty, malnutrition, and disease that they had not previously experienced, just when traditional systems of spirituality and governance were increasingly undermined by missionaries and colonial officials. If context determines the historical meaning of words, then a new context for the word father, or *koosenon*, as applied to the Crown, was perhaps emerging.

Still, law and legal forms have a conservative quality and legal meanings rarely crumble at the first sign of a new social or political context. In its legal or normative sense, the concept of Crown as father or *koosenon* enjoyed at least some autonomy from the dramatic cultural changes occurring around it. Regulations issued to the Imperial Indian Department in 1783, and in force until the 1820s, directed officers to follow the general principles for intercultural engagement developed by Sir William Johnson, which included respecting aboriginal customary methods of council discourse when conferences were held and making regular distributions of presents. Officers were to assure Indians "of the King's Paternal Care and Regard" so long as they acted "as good and obedient Children," but officers were also reminded that, "as these People consider Themselves and in fact are free and independent," their affairs were to be "governed by Persuasion and Address" rather than coercion or command.[31] It may be said, then, that the imperial Crown itself accepted the aboriginal status of father or *koosenon*.

But how long could this understanding of the Crown survive in the face of social and political change within the colony? In fact, the parental metaphor was still used, and indeed it permeated all levels of official contact between peoples, throughout the first half of the nineteenth century. The Crown's representatives—governors, lieutenant governors, and governors general—were fathers, as were the superintendents general and deputy superintendents of the Indian department. "Children," said an Indian department official addressing Anishinaabe chiefs in 1818,

> I presented your Paroles to your Father Pish-ki-ask [Col. Claus] he forwarded them to your Father at Montreal [Sir John Johnson], and Sir John himself laid them before your Father at Quebec [Commander of the Forces] and ... your Father at Quebec, as you wished, desired me to carry them across the great Salt Lake to your Great Father [the King] ....[32]

There were, in other words, layers of fatherly care in this relationship. The practice of adopting and renaming officials seems to have continued. In 1815, for example, the Mohawks met with Sir Francis Gore, the lieutenant governor of Upper Canada, and "agreed to give him an Indian name agreeable to our Custom"; Gore thus found himself adopted into the Turtle clan and named "our Father the Great Turtle."[33]

But did fathers still have the role that they used to have? There is indeed evidence that the customary understanding that fathers gave their relations resources and advice, but not commands, survived well into the nineteenth century. A suggestion by the Munsey Delawares of the Thames River in Upper Canada in 1820 that they might refer to Indian department officials as brothers rather than fathers drew a sharp rebuke: "if they had no Father here," they were told, "they could not expect to receive Presents as Children ... ." But childhood did not mean subjection in this case, at least not in relation to internal matters. The Delawares were also told that they were to "consider themselves subject to our Laws if they committed any outrages or offences on our Lands," but "any outrage among themselves committed on their own Lands they might punish or compromise as they thought fit."[34] Similarly we find the chiefs of the Grand River Six Nations in Upper Canada in 1827 expressing "thanks for Our Great Fathers bounty in the Annual distribution of Presents" and gratification for "the Paternal regard which Our Great Father at Quebec has shewn," while at the same time denying the application of "the Civil Law, which we do not consider in force in our territory, except in cases of Murder."[35] These statements should be considered in light of the fact that colonial judges in Canada at this time were still uncertain about whether colonial courts had jurisdiction over matters arising between Indians on Indian lands.[36]

The essence of the covenant chain relationship—reciprocal obligations of care and respect coupled with a measured distance and autonomy—was thus still evident in the early decades of the nineteenth century. Still, fathers in this relationship were not above using their position as provider to pressure acceptance of their advice. After a violent disagreement over hunting territories erupted between members of different nations in Lower Canada, Indian department deputy superintendent general Henry Charles Darling met with chiefs in 1827 and asked them to "listen to what advice your Father sends through me" concerning "your interfering with Each other in your Hunting Grounds." "If the Custom of your Nations makes this an Offence," said Darling, "Your Father can only advise you, One and all, to discontinue it," and "young men" should be "admonished by the Chiefs not to trespass anymore"; however, he continued, if they did not follow this advice the "Bounty of your great Father in England" would be "entirely discontinued … ."[37]

Treaty council discourse, however, was not immune to the significant social changes occurring within colonial Canada. There was an increasing air of desperation in the addresses of many chiefs as the nineteenth century progressed. After seeking to establish his dignity, saying that although "small" he was "head of many Nations to the North," an Anishinaabe chief stated in an 1827 council,

> Father … when your Children saw the melancholy predicament to which they were reduced, they with one voice called out, where is our Father, where is our Father, who has brought us up & cherished us. Oh! Father Oh! Father you cast us off, you cast all your own Children [off] … .
>
> Father. Stretch out your arm, as mine is long enough to be able to take you by the hand—we are in a deplorable condition. This is the state in which your children are, they hold out the hand to you … .[38]

Voices of desperation such as this one reflected the hard new reality for indigenous people that accompanied settlement of their country. For their part, imperial and colonial officials were concerned that the presents distributed to

Indians annually—items useful primarily for hunting—represented a wasteful expense that only encouraged traditional but now unsustainable ways of life, and that Indians were thus exposed to poverty and disease. At the same time, it was increasingly difficult to prevent settlers from possessing Indian lands through trespass and unlawful bargains. For British officials concerned about the morality of colonization—and there were some—these problems cried out for government intervention. It was this moral concern that informed the shifting use of the words "Crown as father."

In general, English law as applied in Canada was assumed to include traditional common law principles concerning the royal prerogative. In an 1830 case unrelated to Indian affairs, the chief justice of Upper Canada stated that the principle that "the king is *parens patriæ* is one of the first principles of our constitution … ."[39] Like its counterpart in England, the colonial Court of Chancery thus "represent[ed] the sovereign in her capacity of *parens patriæ*" and asserted authority to act "for the benefit of infants … ."[40] The common law doctrine of *parens partriæ* was, therefore, one element of the general legal context within which officials considered aboriginal legal status in Canada. Indeed, it proved to be a powerful one. As the solicitor general for Lower Canada reported in 1836, the Indians were regarded "in the same situation as Minors" and thus unable to convey land titles.[41] "The Indian Tribes," wrote the superintendent general of Indian affairs in 1844, are "under the especial tutelage and protection of the Government by reason of their unfitness for business and their imprudence and ignorance of the ways of the world … ."[42]

These statements show indigenous peoples to be children and the Crown to be father in a sense very different from the sense of father and children found in aboriginal customary law and manifested through treaty encounters. It might be said that these officials did not know or care about aboriginal customary conceptions of the Crown, and they simply imposed the idea of *parens patriæ* onto the Crown-Indian relationship on the assumption that it was analogous to the guardian-ward relationship that the Crown had with respect to vulnerable children. Perhaps this was true of some officials at the time. Certainly, it was true of judges later on. There is no hint, for example, that in 1916 when Justice Lyman Duff held that in relation to Indian lands the governor general "does not represent the Crown as proprietor but as *parens patriæ*," he was in any way influenced by aboriginal conceptions of the Crown as father.[43] But in the 1820s and 1830s, when the treaty rhetoric of father was still a feature of colonial public discourse, we can see that a complex relationship between the different senses of Crown as *koosenon* and as *parens patriæ* did exist.

The views of Henry Charles Darling are worth examining in this respect. As we saw above, Darling appeared to invoke the treaty conception of Crown as *koosenon* in an 1827 council. But Darling also held the view that

Indians were "considered Minors, under the Guardianship of the Crown," and so, for example, contracts made with them were not valid unless approved by the governor—an assertion of the common law conception of Crown as *parens patriæ*.[44] That Darling mixed the two ideas together is suggested by an 1828 report that he wrote in response to the imperial government's proposal to abolish Indian presents and the Indian department. In the report, Darling observed that in Canada an Indian was "little better than a child" with respect to land reserved for his use, and the Indian department was thus needed to protect Indians from being "daily plundered by their designing and more enlightened white brethren"—a statement consistent with the common law conception of Crown as *parens patriæ*. But Darling went on to say that "the Indians pride themselves on their fidelity and adherence to the cause of their great father," and that in their view "a total suppression of their great father's bounty would be considered a cruel infraction of custom, which, from its duration, has attained in their estimation to the sacred character of a treaty"—language consistent with the idea of Crown as *koosenon*. If the "protection of their great father be withdrawn," Darling concluded, "the consequences ... would be ruinous & destructive to the Indian ... ."[45] Taking these statements together, we may say that Darling was, in effect, running the two languages of the Crown together, the indigenous *koosenon* evolving subtly into the common law *parens patriæ*. This shift in linguistic usage does not appear to have been malicious or even consciously appreciated. The two legal languages pertaining to the Crown both had something to do with care and protection, and it would have been natural for anyone familiar with both usages to blend them together.

Darling's report had a considerable impact. Upon reading it, Sir George Murray, the secretary of state for the colonies, concluded that presents should continue, but in the form of agricultural implements that would encourage civilization among Indians.[46] Policy discussions followed, leading to Murray's decision in 1830 to move Indian affairs from military to civil control. As he informed the governor general of Canada, Indian policy had until that point been premised upon "the advantages which might be derived from their friendship in times of war," but it was now appropriate in light of "moral duty and sound policy" to focus instead upon "gradually reclaiming them from a state of barbarism ... ."[47]

The development of a proactive civilization policy represented paternalism of a whole new order. But, as Darling's report suggests, old and new legal languages about the Crown as father tended to run together. As aboriginal communities struggled to cope with social change, their own statements were sometimes ambiguous in this respect. Particularly influential were the views of chief Peter Jones, or Kakkewaquonaby, whose Credit River Mississaugas had been devastated by disease, malnutrition, and alcoholism but were now prospering in a small, self-governing village near Toronto.[48] Writing to the colonial secretary, Lord Goderich, in 1831, Jones explained how his and other communities had accepted the "blessings of civilized life." He praised missionaries for teaching them to "pray for our great father the King" and thanked their "great father" for "taking a new way with us, and giving us useful things as presents … ." What they now needed, he said, were title deeds to their lands so they could cultivate their farms secure in the knowledge that they would not be taken away from them, though he added that these titles should be inalienable to "any white man" without a "license from our father the governor." Jones closed his letter by expressing on behalf of his people their "love and attachment" to "our great father the King," and their desire "that the chain of friendship"—a reference to the covenant chain treaty—"may always be kept bright and strong … ."[49] The language of treaty discourse, the language of the Crown as *koosenon* or *ningahnon,* was used, but in ways that were also suggestive of the Crown as *parens partriæ*.

There was little doubt as to which version of the Crown imperial officials in London saw in these statements. Calls for a civilization policy were favorably received at the Imperial center. The humanitarian-evangelical movement that produced the Clapham Sect had turned its attention from ending slavery in the empire to addressing the plight of aboriginal peoples in British settlements.[50] Pressure for a unified humanitarian policy for aboriginal peoples across the empire culminated with the 1837 report of the parliamentary select committee on "Aborigines" in British settlements. The report famously concluded that the British Empire had been "blessed by Providence" with commercial, military, intellectual, moral, and religious advantages that were destined for the "higher purpose" of bringing "civilization and humanity, peace and good government, and, above all, the knowledge of the true God, to the uttermost ends of the earth," and, in particular, to the "untutored and defenceless savage … ."[51] Among the specific recommendations made in the report was that the "protection of the Aborigine" be regarded as a trust "peculiarly belonging and appropriate to the Executive Government," as administered by the Crown's representatives within each colony rather than local colonial legislatures.[52]

The committee considered evidence from British colonies around the world, and evidence from Canada featured prominently. Passages from Darling's 1828 report were cited, and a description by Jones of the successes at his Credit River village was held up as a "remarkable instance of the power of the gospel in reclaiming savages … ."[53] Jones' 1831 letter to Lord Goderich was also cited.[54] Finally, an Anishinaabe chief from Upper Canada, Shah Wundais, or John Sunday, appeared in person to give evidence before the committee, stating that "we are very anxious to have a writing from our Great Father, as we call our King here, so that we may hold the land by it."[55]

The parliamentary committee, therefore, had ample evidence before it of the distinctive aboriginal language from Canada of Crown as father. But the report itself reveals no outward signs that the committee appreciated the traditional meaning of that phrase for indigenous peoples, and its recommendations were wholly consistent with Crown paternalism of the common law *parens patriæ* variety. That indigenous peoples in Canada themselves referred to the Crown as father seems to have reinforced the committee's vision of the Crown as protector of aboriginal peoples throughout the empire, if only indirectly or implicitly. In its reports in later years, the successor to the select parliamentary committee on aborigines, the (extra-parliamentary) Aborigines Protection Society, would continue to advocate paternal Crown control of indigenous peoples in British colonies and would use to this end statements from Indian chiefs in Canada expressing thanks for the protection of their "great mother the Queen."[56] The paternalistic and moralistic ideas advanced by these groups were received sympathetically in a colonial office run by the likes of Lord Glenelg and James Stephen, humanitarians closely linked by family ties to Wilberforce and the Clapham Sect.[57] Over time, this brand of moralistic paternalism would be woven with other strands into the theory and practice of empire.[58] On an abstract level, it would inform theories of liberal imperialism developed by utilitarians such as J.S. Mill.[59] In practical terms, it would justify particularly aggressive—indeed oppressive and abusive—government policies, such as the Indian residential school system aimed at the forced assimilation of aboriginal peoples into Euro-Canadian society.[60]

It is beyond the scope of this chapter to further follow the narratives relating to the Crown and indigenous peoples in Canada. It is perhaps sufficient to observe that the common law mind, at least in Canada, would have difficulty in reconciling the idea of aboriginal peoples as both dependent children and autonomous nations. As of 1950, judges still insisted that the Crown's care of Indians was essentially beyond judicial scrutiny: that "aborigines are, in effect, wards of the State whose care and welfare are a political trust of the highest obligation."[61] In 1984, the Supreme Court of Canada changed tack somewhat and held that the Crown's duties of protection and care in relation to aboriginal peoples are not, at least not always, a mere political trust; in some instances these duties amount to legally enforceable "fiduciary" duties.[62] But the Crown's fiduciary duty to aboriginal peoples in Canada has been held to be only "some restraint on the exercise of sovereign power."[63] There is, in other words, no indication that judicial ideas about the Crown and its duties have been informed in anyway by the indigenous conception of Crown as father/mother or *koosenon/ningahnon*. The logic of *parens patriæ* prevailed and still informs modern Canadian law pertaining to aboriginal peoples and their rights.

IV

My examination of the expression "Crown as father" in this chapter has been an attempt to pursue the legal history of imperial sovereignty using an ethnohistorical method. I have attempted to engage in an interpretive process that might be called "legal-ethnohistory." At the same time, I have attempted to follow, at least in a loose way, a contextualist approach to the interpretation of past statements and languages of the sort advocated by historians such as Quentin Skinner and J.G.A. Pocock. As I observed at the outset, the application of this brand of contextualism to the past statements of indigenous peoples in colonial settings actually *requires* the adoption of an ethnohistorical method—that is, a method that combines historical, anthropological, linguistic, and ethnographic analyses.[64] But legal, ethnohistorical, and contextualist readings of the past may not always fit neatly together; indeed, they may at times pull in rather different interpretive directions. While the contextualist may resist the notion that cultural ideas are durable over time, the ethnohistorian, especially one adopting techniques of "cultural upstreaming," may not;[65] and while the legal historian may emphasize the continuity of normative concepts, at least within unified jurisdictional and cultural narratives, both contextualists and ethnohistorians may resist the assumptions about interpretive coherence and unity underlying that approach. A legal-ethnohistorical perspective must embrace, but at the same time modify, each of these schools of historical method.

At the center of legal-ethnohistory is an openness to the possibility that not all human attempts at developing shared normative meanings in the face of deep cultural divisions were failures. Representatives of different nations did sometimes speak to each other as if there existed certain normative standards capable of disciplining the exercise of political power.[66] In these instances, it is incumbent upon the legal historian to make the best sense of those statements, and this will include taking seriously the possibility that common rules, principles, guidelines, and customs—or, in the broad sense, *law*—existed for two sets of people independently of the particular utterances or statements or speech-acts that they made, and that this law might, therefore, represent a standard with at least some temporal durability against which past statements or speech-acts may be judged. This is the unique perspective law can add to ethnohistory and contextualist history. The ethnohistorian and the contextualist may conclude, as Francis Jennings did, that the covenant chain treaty relationship was "legally ambiguous" and, given its "bicultural membership," it has to be "defined twice."[67] A *legal*-ethnohistorical examination may reach the same conclusion, but not without first attempting to reconstruct an explanation of the covenant chain that honors the explicit commitment of its participants to a shared or common normative structure.

Looking back to the legal history of the imperial Crown in colonial Canada from a legal-ethnohistorical perspective, a number of tentative conclusions can be drawn. First, the unique aboriginal legal perspective on the status of the Crown as father was different from and should not be confused with common law conceptions of the Crown as father. Second, historical actors, both aboriginal and non-aboriginal, began to speak in a way that tended to blur the lines between these two different senses of the Crown as father. Third, legal meanings, at one level, were thus fragmented, ambiguous, and even confused, and misunderstandings about the uses of legal language may have influenced the larger discourse concerning the Crown and "aborigines" across the British Empire in the 1830s, as well as legal assumptions concerning the Crown's fiduciary duty to aboriginal peoples in Canada developed much later. Fourth, and most importantly, despite the contested and divided way that historical actors spoke, they assumed that a shared legal conception of the imperial Crown existed and provided a foundation for intercultural normative order, and that this legal conception of the imperial Crown was defined, in large part, by indigenous legal traditions. What is the precise legal character of this inter-societal conception of the Crown? Does it still exist? If so, what is its normative significance for the state of law today? These are all questions that legal-ethnohistory makes possible for further legal and historical analyses.

Notes

1. I wish to acknowledge the funding support for the research in this essay provided by the Social Sciences and Humanities Research Council of Canada, including the support provided through a Jules and Gabrielle Léger Fellowship. My thanks also to Professor Darlene Johnston for her helpful suggestions as I was writing this essay, and to the participants of the "Transpositions of Empire" symposium, held in Prato, Italy, April 20–22, 2009, for their comments.
2. The story told in this and following paragraphs is taken from Alexander Henry, *Travels and Adventures in Canada and the Indian Territories between the Years 1760 and 1776* (New York: I. Riley, 1809), pp. 165–81. On Anishinaabe ceremonies, see Michael Angel, *Preserving the Sacred: Historical Perspectives on the Ojibwa Midewiwin* (Winnipeg: University of Manitoba Press, 2002), pp. 31–32, 232.
3. Sir William Johnson to the Lords of Trade, August 30, 1764, in *Documents Relative to the Colonial History of the State of New York*, ed. E.B. O'Callaghan, 15 vols. (Albany: Weed, Parsons, & Co., 1856–1861), VII, pp. 648–50.
4. "Conference with Indians," Niagara, July–August 1764, in *The Papers of Sir William Johnson*, ed. J. Sullivan, 14 vols. (Albany: State University of New York, 1921), XI, pp. 309–10.

5. For example, Minutes of a Council held at Drummond Island, July 7, 1818, National Archives of Canada (NAC), RG 10, vol. 35, pp. 20381–88.
6. Quentin Skinner, *Visions of Politics: Regarding Method*, 3 vols. (New York: Cambridge University Press, 2002), I, pp. 42, 102.
7. J.G.A. Pocock, *Politics, Language and Time: Essays on Political Thought and History* (New York: Atheneum, 1971), p. 25.
8. Skinner, *Regarding Method*, p. 85.
9. Mary W. Helms, "Time, History and the Future of Anthropology: Observations on Some Unresolved Issues," *Ethnohistory*, 25 (1978), 1–13 (pp. 4–5); James Axtell, "Ethnohistory: An Historian's Perspective," *Ethnohistory*, 26 (1979), 1–13 (pp. 2–3).
10. Edward Ellice, *The Communications of Mercator Upon the Contest Between The Earl of Selkirk and the Hudson's Bay Company on the one side, and the North West Company on the Other* (Montreal: W. Gray, 1817), p. 55.
11. *Calvin's Case* (1608), 7 Co. Rep. 1a, p. 23b.
12. Ibid., pp. 4b–5a.
13. Ibid., pp. 25a.
14. Ibid., pp. 12a.
15. Ibid., pp. 11b, 12b, 10a.
16. Ibid., pp. 11b, 12b.
17. This is a simple outline of some common features shared by complex and diverse societies. See in general Diamond Jenness, *The Indians of Canada*, 6th edn. (Ottawa: National Museum of Canada, 1963); Alan D. McMillan, *Native Peoples and Cultures of Canada: An Anthropological Overview*, 2nd edn. (Vancouver/Toronto: Douglas & McIntyre, 1995).
18. *Case of Monopolies* (1602), 11 Co. Rep. 84b, p. 85b.
19. *De Manneville v. De Manneville* (1804), 10 Ves. Jun. 52, p. 64.
20. *Eyre v. Countess of Shaftsbury* (1722), 2 P. Wms. 103, p. 104.
21. John Summerfield, *Sketch of Grammar of the Chippeway Language, to Which Is Added a Vocabulary of Some of the Most Common Words* (Cazenovia, NY: J.F. Fairchild, 1834), pp. 21, 27.
22. Thomas L. McKenney, *Sketches of a Tour to the Lakes, of the Character and Customs of the Chippeway Indians, And of Incidents Connected with the Treaty of Fond du Lac; Also a Vocabulary of the Algic, or Chippeway Language* (Baltimore: Fielding Lucas Jun'r, 1827), pp. 488, 490.
23. Summerfield, *Sketch of Grammar of the Chippeway Language*, pp. 32, 30, 27.
24. McKenney, *Sketches of a Tour to the Lakes*, p. 490; Summerfield, *Sketch of Grammar*, p. 31.
25. Summerfield, *Sketch of Grammar*, p. 26.
26. McKenney, *Sketches of a Tour to the Lakes*, p. 490.
27. Peter Jones (Kah-ke-Wa-Quo-Na-By), *History of the Ojebway Indians; with Especial Reference to Their Conversion* (London: A.W. Bennett, 1861), p. 208.
28. Sir William Johnson to the Lords of Trade, October 30, 1764, in *Documentary History of the State of New York*, ed. E.B. O'Callaghan, 15 vols. (Albany: Weed, Parsons, & Co., 1849), II, pp. 670–74.

29. Sir William Johnson to Thomas Gage, October 31, 1764, in *Papers of Sir William Johnson*, ed. Sullivan, XI, pp. 394–96.
30. Gilles Havard, *Empire et Métissages: Indiens et Français dans le Pays d'en Haut* (Sillery: Septentrion, 2003), pp. 205–39, 359–414; Allen W. Trelease, *Indian Affairs in Colonial New York: The Seventeenth Century* (Lincoln: University of Nebraska Press, 1997), p. 116; Fintan O'Toole, *White Savage: William Johnson and the Invention of America* (New York: Farrar, Straus & Giroux, 2005), p. 69.
31. Instructions for Sir J. Johnson, Supt. Gen. Ind. Affrs, February 6, 1783, The National Archives, London (TNA), CO 42/44, fol. 95–97.
32. Minutes of a Council held at Drummond Island with the Ottawas, Chipawas and Winabagos, July 7, 1818, NAC, RG 10, vol. 35, pp. 2038–388, 20476–77.
33. Proceedings of a Meeting with the Indians residing at the Grand River, Burlington Heights, November 12, 1815, NAC, RG 10, vol. 31, pp. 18642–43.
34. George Ironside to Col. W. Claus, November 25, 1820, NAC, RG 10, vol. 38, pp. 21489–21491.
35. Proceedings of a Council of the Six Nation Indians, October 19, 1827, NAC, RG 10, vol. 44, pp. 23430–23434.
36. Mark D. Walters, "The Extension of Colonial Criminal Jurisdiction over the Aboriginal Peoples of Upper Canada: Reconsidering the *Shawanakiskie* Case (1822–26)," *University of Toronto Law Journal*, 46 (1996), 273–310.
37. Proceedings of a Grand Council held at Caunaghwaga, October 5, 1827, NAC, RG 10, vol. 663 (no page numbers).
38. Minutes of a Council held at the Garrison of York, September 17, 1827, NAC, RG 10, vol. 44, pp. 23403–23406.
39. *Rex v. Allan, McGill and Jarvis* (1830–31), 2 U.C.Q.B. (O.S.) 90 (Upper Canada Queen's Bench), para. 9.
40. *Anonymous* (1858), 6 Gr. 632 (Upper Canada Court of Chancery), p. 632.
41. Report of Mr. O'Sullivan, Solicitor General of Lower Canada to Earl of Gosford, Gov. Gen, January 5, 1836, NAC, RG 10, vol. 7, pp. 3346–47.
42. S.P. Jarvis, Ch. Supt. Ind. Dept., to Major Winniett, Supt. Six Nations, March 29, 1844, NAC, RG 10, vol. 508, pp. 154–55.
43. *Canada (Attorney-General) v. Giroux* (1916), 30 D.L.R. 123 (Supreme Court of Canada), p. 139.
44. H.C. Darling, military secretary to Sir P. Maitland, Lt. Gov. Upp. Can., January 13, 1824, NAC, RG 10, vol. 16, p. 12457.
45. Maj. Gen. H.C. Darling to Earl of Dalhousie, Gov. Gen., "Report Upon the Exact State of the Indian Department," July 24, 1828, enclosed in Earl of Dalhousie to Sir George Murray, Sec. of State for the Colonies, October 27, 1828, in British Parliamentary Papers, *Papers Relative to the Aboriginal Tribes in British Possessions* (London: House of Commons, 1834), V, no. 617, p. 30.
46. Sir George Murray, Sec. of State for the Colonies, to Sir James Kempt, Gov. Gen. and Commander of the Forces, December 3, 1828, in *Papers Relative to the Aboriginal Tribes in British Possessions*, p. 36.

47. Sir George Murray, Sec. of State for the Colonies, to Sir James Kempt, Gov. Gen., January 25, 1830, in *Papers Relative to the Aboriginal Tribes in British Possessions*, pp. 87–89.
48. Mark D. Walters, "'According to the Old Customs of Our Nation': Aboriginal Self-government on the Credit River Mississauga Reserve, 1826–1847," *Ottawa Law Review*, 30 (1999), 1–45.
49. Kakkewaquonaby, alias P. Jones, Indian Chief and Missionary, to Lord Goderich, Sec. of State for the Colonies, July 26, 1831, in *Papers Relative to the Aboriginal Tribes in British Possessions*, pp. 135–136.
50. Ernest Marshall Howse, *Saints in Politics: The 'Clapham Sect' and the Growth of Freedom* (London: Allen & Unwin, 1953), p. 7.
51. Great Britain, Parliamentary Select Committee, *Report from the Select Committee on Aborigines (British Settlements)* (London: House of Commons, 1837), VII, no. 425, p. 76.
52. Ibid., p. 76.
53. Ibid., pp. 6–8, 47.
54. Ibid., p. 6.
55. Ibid., pp. 28–29, "Minutes of Evidence."
56. *The Third Annual Report of the Aborigines Protection Society* (London: P. White & Son, 1840), pp. 18–19. Also *The Second Annual Report of the Aborigines Protection Society* (London: P. White & Son, 1839), pp. 10–11.
57. Ronald Hyam, *Britain's Imperial Century, 1815–1914*, 2nd edn. (London: Macmillan, 1993), p. 83; Richard Brent, *Liberal Anglican Politics: Whiggery, Religion, and Reform, 1830–1841* (Oxford: Clarendon Press, 1987), p. 269.
58. Peter Adams, *Fatal Necessity: British Intervention in New Zealand, 1830–1847* (Auckland: Auckland University Press, 1977), pp. 13, 57, 92, 93.
59. See W.P. Morrell, *British Colonial Policy in the Mid-Victorian Age* (Oxford: Clarendon Press, 1969), p. 15; Eileen P. Sullivan, "Liberalism and Imperialism: J.S. Mill's Defense of the British Empire," *Journal of the History of Ideas*, 44 (1983), 599–617.
60. John S. Milloy, *A National Crime: The Canadian Government and the Residential School System, 1879 to 1986* (Winnipeg: University of Manitoba Press, 1999).
61. *St. Ann's Island Shooting and Fishing Club Ltd. v. The King*, [1950] S.C.R. 211 (Supreme Court of Canada), p. 219.
62. *Guerin v. Canada*, [1984] 2 S.C.R. 335 (SCC).
63. *R. v. Sparrow*, [1990] 1 S.C.R. 1075 (SCC), p. 1103.
64. Bruce G. Trigger, "Ethnohistory: Problems and Prospects," *Ethnohistory*, 29 (1982), 1–19.
65. William N. Fenton, "Ethnohistory and Its Problems," *Ethnohistory*, 9 (1962), 1–23.
66. For a different view, see Ian Hunter's contribution to the present volume.
67. Francis Jennings, *The Ambiguous Iroquois Empire: The Covenant Chain Confederation of Indian Tribes with English Colonies* (London: W.W. Norton & Co., 1984), p. 373.

Chapter 6

The Justification of King Leopold II's Congo Enterprise by Sir Travers Twiss

Andrew Fitzmaurice

It was Sir Travers Twiss, more than any other international lawyer of his generation, who furnished the legal justification for the creation of King Leopold II's Congo Free State.[1] Leopold's colonial venture was notoriously one of the most brutal episodes in the history of colonization. The justification for his occupation of the Congo required all of Twiss' legal ingenuity and obliged him to manipulate a number of doctrines in international law. One of those innovations is the focus of this chapter: namely, his argument that private associations can assume sovereignty, in this case through establishing colonies.[2]

Like many international jurists of his generation, Twiss was during most of his career attached to Emer de Vattel's view of the law of nations as a closed club of sovereign states. According to Vattel, and according to Twiss and most of his contemporaries, private individuals and associations that did not rise to the status of sovereign states had no rights and no voice within that system. According to this view, almost all peoples on the globe apart from European states, or former European colonies, had little or no place in international life, although there were gray areas such as the Ottomans and Japan. The indigenous peoples of Africa, America, and the Pacific had few rights other than property rights. But a further consequence of this view was that private associations led by Europeans must also have no voice in international life or in the law of nations.

At a crucial point in his career, Twiss reversed his long-held Vattelian attachment to the monopoly of sovereign states in international society and launched a legal and diplomatic campaign to have Leopold's International African Association recognized as a state, even though the association possessed nothing like territorial competence in the Congo and performed few or none of the duties required of states. The reasons for this reversal can be linked to the dramatic unraveling of Twiss' personal and professional life in the 1870s.

In 1862 Twiss was at the height of his career and was one of the most eminent civil and international lawyers of his generation. In this year, at the age of 53, Twiss married Marie van Lynseele, who, at 22, was 31 years his junior. She was the "smart and handsome" daughter of a Polish nobleman. They married in Dresden. On returning to London, Marie Twiss was presented to Queen Victoria at the Court of St. James. But Sir Travers and Lady Twiss were dreadfully unlucky. Their paths crossed with a bankrupt lawyer, Alexander Chaffers, who proved to be perhaps the most vexatious litigant of Victorian England. Chaffers was so vexatious that he later inspired the *Vexatious Actions Act* in 1896.[3] But Twiss was one of his first victims. Unfortunately for the Twisses, Chaffers had known Lady Twiss prior to her marriage. He had known her, he claimed, as a notorious London prostitute, in which capacity she had met Sir Travers. She was in reality not Marie van Lynseele but a French woman called Marie Gelas, a "heroine of the demi-monde," as Chaffers described her, and the daughter, not of a Polish nobleman, but of a French artisan.[4] Gelas was the "inmate of a score of London dens" including Holborn Casino.[5] It appears that for some time in the 1860s Chaffers successfully blackmailed Twiss with this knowledge. By the late-1860s Twiss refused to pay more. Chaffers then sent letters revealing the truth to the lord chamberlain, the chief functionary at the Royal court, and to Twiss' employers, including the archbishop of Canterbury and the bishop of London. Finally, he made a statutory declaration in Chelsea police station recounting his claims. Twiss had hesitated for a long time about whether to sue on a charge of libel with a view to extort money. His longtime friend and employer A.C. Tait, the archbishop of Canterbury, now told him he could delay no longer.[6]

The libel case, as the *Annual Register* reported, was the talk of the town for a fortnight in March 1872—indeed it was reported in detail in newspapers across the globe.[7] Chaffers mounted what was in Victorian England a kamikaze defense. He argued that he knew Lady Twiss was "a woman of the town," of course, because he had first picked her up on April 15, 1859, in Regent Street "between 9 and 10 o'clock in the evening" and "accompanied her to her lodgings" where he paid her a sovereign for two hours of her time.[8] Thereafter he continued to enjoy her company for a number of years, even after her marriage. Twiss himself, Chaffers revealed, had been one of his wife's clients and prior to their marriage kept her as his mistress at the rate of five pounds a week. When key witnesses for the Twisses refused to appear, their case collapsed. It appeared that, regarding identity as a mantle, the Twisses had reinvented Maria Gelas as Marie van Lynseele.

Twiss' career was destroyed. He offered to resign his post as vicar general to the archbishop.[9] The resignation was accepted without hesitation.[10] He was also obliged to resign as chancellor of the diocese of London, as queen's advocate general, the equivalent of attorney general in civil law; and he resigned as Regius professor of civil law. All of these posts were salaried. For her part, Lady Twiss' presentation at court was revoked—an unprecedented reprimand from the Court of St. James.[11]

Twiss was ruined as well as devastated.[12] But it was revealing of his temperament, when he wrote to Archbishop Tait after fleeing into exile in Lausanne, that he complained not of humiliation but of the fact that he had lost his sinecures. He no longer possessed, he pointed out, the means to support himself or his wife. He spoke not of the morality of the case but of the services he had performed for the state and the services he could still perform. Importantly, given his later services for Leopold, at this lowest ebb of his career he spoke about his "future chances of usefulness in some humbler department of life" and he expressed a desperation to reestablish the means to support his "family."[13] He wrote in similar vein to John Jackson, the bishop of London.[14] Jackson scrawled across the top one of Twiss' letters concerning the scandal, "*Twiss*: The man I believe to be a *little mad* but thoroughly indignant."[15] Twiss was thus not only guilty of gross moral turpitude but also ridiculous. It was Leopold who would eventually grant Twiss the opportunity for redemption. This story is not only about the development of particular doctrines in international law but also about Twiss' use of those doctrines to justify the occupation of the Congo and at the same time gain personal redemption. As he himself stated in his letters to Tait, he was desperate to return to employment and public service. His doctrine concerning the ability of private associations to assume sovereign powers was tailored not only to Leopold's needs in the Congo but also to his own needs. Twiss' support of private associations in international law was against the grain of contemporary thought, but it was only through making this argument that he could be of service to Leopold and so return to public life.

In his career prior to 1873, Twiss' Vattel-like attachment to the supremacy of sovereignty was nowhere more apparent than in his discussion of occupation, for example, in the chapter "The Acquisition of Territory by Occupation" in his 1846 treatise *The Oregon Territory*.[16] In this work, he had argued that the right of occupation rests upon what he described as an "axiom of natural law," namely "*quod enim ante nullius est, id ratione naturali occupanti condeditur.*" But this right of the first taker, he warned, was reserved to sovereign bodies only, not to private individuals, and in this sense he followed Pufendorf and Vattel in making the law of occupation subject to sovereignty. A nation, he argued, may delegate its sovereign authority to establish a colony by occupation to an individual or agent.[17] But, he stressed, "the colonists must be sent forth *by the public authority of the nation*, otherwise they will possess no national character, but will be considered to be a body of *emigrants*, who have abandoned their country."[18] He agreed that, of course, an individual may occupy a vacant country and thereby exercise rights of *dominium*, or property, but he or she cannot claim "empire" or sovereignty. To do so, he argued (paraphrasing Vattel), would be "rash and ridiculous" "as against other nations."[19]

In the late-1870s European colonial powers showed intensifying interest in central west Africa. Due to its impenetrable terrain, the area known as the Congo had previously been free from the colonization that had embraced much of the north and south of Africa. The sole route into the region from the west was up the rivers, particularly the Congo, but the massive volume of water running out of those rivers impeded European sail boats as well as canoes from navigating their waters. This situation was changed by the explorations of Henry Stanley and David Livingstone and, more importantly, by the invention of steam-powered boats that could prevail against the current. For the first time Europeans could penetrate deep into the continent from the west and there was panic about who would first be able to exercise the rights of occupation.

King Leopold II of Belgium failed to interest the Belgian government in his ambition to establish a colony in the Congo. Undeterred, in 1876 he held a geographical conference on the need to civilize Africa to which he invited representatives of all the major occidental nations. At this conference, Leopold declared that for Belgium to rest politically neutral would be a condemnation to sterility and decadence.[20] At the same time he created the International African Association for furthering the civilization of central Africa. And he also enlisted the services of Henry Stanley to further the interests of the association in the Congo.

Leopold faced significant political and legal obstacles to his ambitions, particularly insofar as the acceptance of the international community was concerned. To overcome these obstacles he needed a legal complement to Stanley. He accordingly enlisted Sir Travers Twiss. Twiss was not chosen by chance—he shared the same antipathy to neutrality as Leopold, as well as the same sense of *Realpolitik*. His knowledge of international law was equal to any of his contemporaries, but owing to his ostracism from public life he needed Leopold as much as Leopold needed him.

From 1878 the question of the legal status of the Congo was put by the European president of the International Red Cross, Gustave Moynier, to the members of the *Institut de droit international* as requiring urgent attention.[21] In the absence of a legal framework, he feared that the increasing competition between the various European interests acting in the Congo could quickly lead to conflict. He was also concerned about the legal status of the indigenous peoples. Writing in the *Revue de droit international* in 1883, the Belgian Emile De Laveleye agreed with Moynier.[22] Laveleye's opinion carried great weight. He was one of the founders of the *Institut de droit international*, its vice president, and a highly respected international lawyer.[23] He proposed that the Congo River and the adjoining territory should be declared neutral as had been the case for the Danube following the Vienna Congress. Laveleye's proposition was supported. Moynier responded that he found it very "persuasive."[24] Moynier also warned against the exploitative nature of the behavior of the "blancs" on the Congo as well as making cynical comments about the "zeal" of the "nations civilisées" for the inhabitants of the region.[25] As it attracted growing support, Laveleye's proposal for neutrality in the Congo threatened to undermine completely his own king's ambitions.

Without revealing that he was employed by Leopold, Travers Twiss immediately responded to Laveleye's proposal (and to Moynier) with four essays published in 1883: two in the *Revue de droit international*, and one in the *Law Magazine and Review*, which was republished as a pamphlet in England.[26] These essays outlined the points that Twiss argued were necessary to avoid full-blown conflict between the European powers in the Congo and that, if followed, would justify the elevation of Leopold's International African Association into a colonial state. Central to his argument was, first, a rejection of neutrality and, second, the claim that a non-state association could assume sovereign power.

On the first point, Twiss condemned Laveleye and Moynier's argument for the neutrality of the Congo as dangerous. Neutrality, he argued, was merely a euphemism for anarchy. In neutral territory, nobody can use arms to impose authority. What the Congo needed, he said, was the "continual presence of an armed ship of one or other of the nations."[27] Twiss acknowledged that there were many conflicting national interests in the Congo, but he argued that, if peace was to be maintained, those interests must be constrained by a legal framework that was sanctioned by force. Here Twiss' arguments were consistent with the character of the international law he had promoted all his career: namely, a law that was sanctioned by force and driven by self-preservation.

Twiss had furnished only part of the argument that could justify the elevation of Leopold's International African Association from an exploitative commercial enterprise into a legal authority with a status in the law of nations. On the second point, he was to resolve the question of whether a private association could exercise sovereignty. Clearly, because

Leopold was obliged to act without the support of the Belgian government, he needed to be able to create a colonial state with a private organization. In an era in which state powers jealously defended their rights to determine all matters, it was difficult to justify private organizations as proper authorities for establishing colonies. It is true that in the colonial record there were plenty of examples of private organizations that had conquered first and received the approval of the state only later. But in eighteenth- and nineteenth-century international law such practices were frowned upon. For a statement of the classic position of nineteenth-century international law one need not go further than the chapter Twiss wrote forty years earlier in his 1846 treatise *The Oregon Territory.*[28] As we have seen, he agreed that, of course, an individual may occupy a vacant country and thereby exercise rights of *dominium*, or property, but he or she cannot claim "empire" or sovereignty. To do so would be "rash and ridiculous."

It was precisely this rash and ridiculous position that Twiss found himself justifying on behalf of Leopold forty years later. Indeed, it would seem that Lady Twiss was not the only dissimulator in the Twiss family. Leopold had failed to persuade the Belgian state to establish a colony and he had no license from the state to undertake the venture himself. In the second of his 1883 essays in the *Revue de droit international,* Twiss argued that at least four of the contemporary United States of America had begun as privately established colonies without license from a sovereign.[29] He then turned, more contentiously, to medieval precedents. There was, Twiss argued, a medieval chivalric order that had "rendered service to civilisation in defending Christian countries against the invasion of Arabs and Ottomans."[30] This was the medieval sovereign order of St. John of Jerusalem that had been founded by the private association of the Hospital of St. John of Jerusalem. This order, moreover, had adopted territorial sovereignty in transforming themselves into the Knights of Malta, taking possession of the island of Malta.[31]

Twiss' efforts met with immediate success. Moynier responded to Twiss on September 4, 1883 in an *Institut* meeting at Munich and his response was published in *Annuaire de l'institut de droit international.*[32] Moynier had been persuaded by Twiss that neutrality for the Congo would be undesirable and withdrew his support for Laveleye's proposal.[33] Laveleye sent a letter to the same meeting, in which he too capitulated to Twiss' opposition to neutrality.[34] In December 1883, the Belgian jurist Égide Arntz, also writing to justify Leopold's claims, cited Twiss' claim that private associations could make treaties that establish sovereign states.[35]

Not everybody was persuaded. It is routinely argued that prior to the Berlin Conference nobody suspected Leopold's intention to turn the International African Association into a colonial state.[36] If this were so, and if we did not know that Twiss was in Leopold's pay, Twiss' arguments would appear in a rather innocent and perhaps slightly naïve light. There was, however, in the British Foreign Office strong opposition to Leopold that included skepticism of his intentions and a realistic and damning appraisal of his cynicism, particularly in the memos of Thomas Lister, who was the assistant under-secretary of state for foreign affairs, and Leopold's fiercest critic in the Foreign Office. The Portuguese government, which had most to lose from the success of the International African Association, also brought attention to numerous abuses by Leopold's agents in the Congo, even in the years leading up to the Berlin Conference. In the year prior to the Berlin Conference a forty-four-page tract was published anonymously in Brussels that made it clear that Leopold's intentions were no secret and that Twiss' efforts were not at all disinterested.[37] The author accused Leopold of seeking a colonial empire for Belgium. Although Belgium was a constitutional monarchy, Leopold still wielded great influence and there was consequently good reason to seek anonymity. According to the author of this tract, if Belgium acquired a colonial empire it would lose its neutrality. "Who would believe," the author stormed, that anybody would wish to spend millions civilizing central Africa out of a "simple love of humanity." In any case, the author argued, a neutral but colonial Belgium was a contradiction and was politically imprudent, not to say dangerous.[38]

If any doubt remained about the implications of Twiss' role in this drama, the title of this tract was *Sir Travers Twiss et le Congo* and it devoted its forty-four pages to a point-by-point refutation of Twiss' legal pronouncements on the question. The author declared that "it is to give sovereign rights to this commercial Association that Sir Travers, stirring the ashes of the past, has had to reach as far as the middle ages in order to find the model of a sovereign civilising institution . . . One must have the grand personality of Sir Travers Twiss to not see in that proposition a challenge against good sense."[39] The author became even more heated:

> We will not trust inept friends, the example invoked further of the sovereign order of Saint John of Jerusalem, better known under the name of the order of the Knights of Malta, is even more unhappy. Moreover, what are we doing almost at the dawn of the twentieth century, invoking the old European customary law and why search examples from the night of the past which modern law has for a long time repudiated.[40]

In conclusion the author argued that to recognize

> as a rule of international law the right of a private association to exercise sovereignty would be a monstrous juridical heresy. Facts have sometimes

> conferred certain privileges upon associations, but to demand today the recognition of absolute rights, without them even being exercised in fact, as is the case in the Congo, this would seem to us to leave the path of serious juridical debate.[41]

It is striking that the author felt not only that the legal justification of Leopold's enterprise would be key to the success of his ambitions but, moreover, also that Twiss' particular contribution would be decisive.

In May 1884, Twiss responded to his attacker with a third article on the Congo in the *Revue de droit international*.[42] In this article, Twiss addressed himself almost exclusively to the question of whether a private association can create a sovereign entity. Remarking that he had been accused of a "monstrous heresy" by the anonymous attacker, Twiss responded by turning to more modern examples of private associations that had acquired the right to exercise sovereignty in an uncivilized country.[43] Clearly stung by the accusation that he was pursuing a rather medieval understanding of relations between Europeans and non-Europeans, he recounted the story of the American Colonisation Society that had established the colony and subsequently founded the state of Liberia. The previous month, in April 1884, Twiss had published a second edition of his major work of legal theory, *The Law of Nations Considered As Independent Political Communities*. This text, like all of Twiss' prior work, held a strong commitment to Vattel's understanding of the supremacy of sovereignty in the law of nations. In the new edition, however, Twiss added a preface in which he made an appeal for recognition of the sovereignty of the International African Association in the Congo. Here again he cited Liberia as a precedent that "tend[s] to show that the juridical difficulty, which has been suggested to be in the way of private associations forming settlements in Africa, and acquiring for their settlements full rights of dominion—the right of Empire over the territory ceded to them—is without foundation."[44] Thus, in order to justify Leopold's enterprise, Twiss was prepared to fracture the polemical force of his major work of legal theory. Indeed, he appeared to have timed the new edition of the text largely in order to add weight to his case for the International African Association.

But Twiss' legal justification of the ambitions of Leopold's International African Association remained contested and still left a mountain to climb in order for Leopold to gain the recognition he desired. By 1884 the United States of America had effectively recognized that sovereignty in the Congo lay with the International African Association. In order to make his case to the Americans, Leopold employed both Twiss and the Belgian jurist Égide Arntz.[45] In his legal briefing to the U.S. Senate Committee on Foreign Relations concerning "Occupation of the Congo country in Africa" in

March 1884, Arntz based his legal arguments largely on Twiss' authority. By November 1884 Bismarck had secretly followed the lead of the Americans in recognizing Leopold's sovereignty in the Congo, but Leopold had still not gained the support of the majority of European states.

As the tensions mounted in equatorial Africa, however, Leopold's ambitions were not even the main focus of attention. The French and German governments contrived together to call a conference in Berlin in order to check not Leopold but what they mistakenly believed to be Britain's territorial ambitions in the Congo, which they thought had been revealed in the treaty between Portugal and Britain. Bismarck called the members of the community of nations to a conference in Berlin at which the principles of colonization were to be agreed upon and the fate of the Congo decided.

Britain sent five official delegates to the Berlin conference.[46] They were led by Sir Edward Malet, the British ambassador at Berlin, and otherwise included senior representatives of the Foreign Office and Colonial Office. But the British government also sent an unofficial advisor: namely, Sir Travers Twiss. Twiss, who had not been permitted to hold public office in Britain since the scandal of 1873, had managed to get himself invited.[47] Malet was clearly surprised by this invitation that appears to have been issued by Lord Granville, the foreign secretary, but over the next two months he leaned heavily on Twiss for advice.[48] The extraordinary aspect of the British government's decision to use Twiss in this capacity is that they were apparently aware of his services for Leopold, although possibly not of their full extent. Although the British came to recognize the claims of the association, the interests of Leopold and Britain were to a large degree in conflict. Twiss, therefore, managed to be working for two opposing sides in the negotiations. The British government may simply have decided that it was better to have Twiss in both camps, where they could (and did) get information from him about Leopold's actions and intentions, rather than having him working only against them. It would perhaps have been worse if he had been outside the tent than inside. But having placed Twiss in this position, they also increased his usefulness to Leopold for the same reasons.

The German and British delegations at the Berlin conference discovered that their aims were closer than they had previously thought. Both sought free trade in the Congo basin. For this reason, Bismarck concluded by the time the conference opened that the best means to secure free trade was to grant sovereign rights to Leopold's International African Association. Moreover, the International African Association, whether or not a state, was one of the powers at the Berlin conference and it was clear to Bismarck that all the agreements made at the conference would lack authority if the association did not have sovereign power. He then set about persuading Britain on these points, while concealing the fact that he had already recognized the sovereign rights of the association. The British, although generally positive in their attitude to the International African Association, took the position that it was too early to grant it sovereignty and withheld their approval.

It was at this juncture that Twiss intervened by informing his colleagues in the British delegation, who clearly did not have the same access to information, about Leopold's and Bismarck's agreement.[49] Somewhat disconcerted at having been secretly trumped, Malet nevertheless persuaded Lord Granville, the secretary of state, to follow suit and he obtained permission to "negotiate a treaty with the Association to recognise its flag as that of a friendly government."[50] It should perhaps come as no surprise that the person who was then charged with the duty of drafting this treaty was Travers Twiss.[51] The treaty was signed on December 16, 1884. By the end of the conference in February 1885, all the other powers present except one (namely, Turkey) had followed Britain and Germany and recognized the sovereignty of the International African Association over the Congo. The Congo Free State was now born in all but name although it was, to adapt Voltaire, neither free nor, properly speaking, a state. At the same time that Leopold achieved this personal triumph, the conference adopted that the principles of effective occupation applied to all colonial claims, thus dashing Portugal's ambitions.

Anticipating recognition of his new state, Leopold had already commissioned its constitution before the conference at Berlin commenced. The person he chose to draft the constitution of the Congo Free State was Sir Travers Twiss. In the draft, the new state was to be called "L'Afrique Equatoriale." Playing the role that the British government clearly had hoped he would take, Twiss in November 1884 provided Sir Julian Pauncefote, the permanent under-secretary of state for foreign affairs, with an advance view of the draft constitution.[52] The constitution contained the legislative, judicial, and bureaucratic offices that were to be expected in an era of metropolitan and colonial political reform. Writing two weeks after Pauncefote had received the constitution, Thomas Lister, the assistant under-secretary of state for foreign affairs, commented, "The constitution is I believe the work of Sir T. Twiss." He added, "It is a highly coloured sketch of a Bureaucratic Utopia."[53] But the extraordinary aspect of this constitution was that it granted absolute power to the king of the Congo state. In this regard it confirmed all the fears that had been expressed by Leopold and Twiss' anonymous attacker. According to the constitution, Leopold could suspend laws and officers of the state "a sa discretion."[54]

The Berlin conference had been called to resolve three issues, these were formalized as "Three Bases" to be negotiated between the powers: the first was the question of free commerce in the Congo basin; the second was the matter of free navigation on the Congo and Niger rivers; and the third was to determine the rules regarding effective occupation. In January 1885, negotiations over the Third Basis broke down. Broadly, the Third Basis stated that an occupying power would recognize its obligation to maintain the territory it occupies, including establishing sufficient authority to maintain peace, to administer justice and respect for rights, and to create the conditions for freedom of commerce and movement.[55] It was decided to establish a commission to settle the wording (the British, for example, wanted protectorates excluded from this rule). It seems that at this point Twiss' role at the conference passed from being unofficial to official, because he was appointed as the chair of the commission that was given the task to determine the wording of the Third Basis.[56]

The distillation of exactly what principles regarding occupation had been established at the Berlin conference was left, in its aftermath, to the members of the *Institut de droit international*. Indeed, this problem consumed discussions at the meetings of the *Institut* as well as their publications for many years to come.[57] One of the most controversial issues concerned the right of private associations to assume sovereign powers. Twiss' anonymous attacker was not the only jurist to express his displeasure at the precedent established by the transformation of the International African Association into the Congo Free State. Other jurists were persuaded that private associations could assume sovereign status.

As late as 1915, T.J. Lawrence, a member of the *Institut de droit international*, wrote that there were three circumstances through which new "international persons" were admitted to the family of nations. The first occurs when a civilization that had previously been regarded as barbarous becomes recognized as sufficiently civilized to participate in public law. Lawrence cited Turkey as an example. The second, and the most frequent case of admission into international society, was when a community splintered off from a larger body. All the examples he cited were colonies, such as the United States, achieving their independence. For the third case for admission to the society of nations, Lawrence accepted Twiss' argument that it is possible "a new body politic" could be "formed by civilized men in districts hitherto left to nature or to savage tribes." Here he gave the example of Dutch farmers in South Africa and cited the second edition of Twiss' *Law of Nations* on the creation of Liberia. But the majority of Lawrence's discussion of this point concerned the creation of the Congo Free State. Lawrence condemned the fact that the peoples of the Congo Free State had lived in a "state of virtual slavery," but he accepted entirely the proposition championed by Twiss—that a private association can be "turned into an international person."[58]

In 1889 Frantz Despganet, the French jurist who wrote extensively on protectorates and colonial occupation, took an ambivalent position on the legitimacy of the Congo Free State. He insisted categorically upon Vattel's (or, for that matter, Grotius's) rule that "sovereignty is an attribute that belongs exclusively to states," so "when we are concerned about the acquisition of the right of government or sovereignty, international law cannot recognise in private people a right to achieve an occupation." This constraint would seem clear enough, but Despagnet then conceded that private individuals ("particuliers") could organize a state on a territory they occupy and then enter into international agreements. This, he noted, was the process followed in the creation of Liberia and Congo Free State. Despagnet accordingly bent Vattel to contemporary practice.[59]

A contemporary of Lawrence, the great German jurist Lassa Oppenheim was far less sanguine about the transformation of private associations into states. The "so-called Congo Free State," he said, was "a State of quite a unique character" and he included it in a discussion of doubtful claims to membership in the society of nations. It had, in any case, "lost its membership" of that society, as he pointed out, when it was absorbed by Belgium in 1908.[60] Similarly, writing the year after the Berlin conference, the prominent Swiss political scientist Johann Caspar Bluntschli declared that private individuals can take possession of new territories only under the authority of a state. If they act without that authority, the state must ratify their acts in order for them to be recognized in international law.[61]

Other jurists, such as Charles Salomon, wrote vehement attacks on the precedent established by the creation of the Congo Free State. According to Salomon, contemporary colonizing practices were characterized by an abuse of the rule of law that threatened to revive absolutism. This concern was particularly strong in relation to the Congo because Leopold's state, based upon a private company, was ruled more by prerogative than by law—and Twiss, as we have seen, had legitimized prerogative power in his constitution for the new state. A revival of absolutism through the creation of states out of private companies was precisely the problem to which Twiss' anonymous Belgian attacker had drawn attention. According to jurists such as Salomon and Gaston Jèze, European peoples had fought centuries of bloody wars against their sovereigns precisely for the purpose of overturning absolute rule, only to see it being recreated in the colonies with the possibility that such prerogative powers could be repatriated.[62] Salomon agreed that private individuals could form a community, but they must do so through an organic process of politics and law. First they must create private property and then slowly they may form the customs and institutions that would give them the basis for a state.[63] According to Salomon, the practices employed in the Congo did not conform to these principles. The Congo Free State did not go through a process of gradual development. It was partly based upon treaties that were made between a private association and tribes with limited or no sovereignty to cede.[64] A private association, such as the International African Association, could acquire only territory in private international law—that is, they could acquire property, not sovereignty.[65]

In light of these debates, it is important to return to the common representation of the jurists of the *Institut de droit international* as naïve or indifferent when compared with the Machiavellian figure of Leopold and the larger political reality that Leopold represented.[66] This question of whether Twiss and his generation were naïve or disengaged is vital to the matter of whether they were deliberately shaping the conventions of international law to the practice of international relations in general and to colonial practice in particular. If the jurists were naïve then the degree to which they were responsive to changes in practice is questionable. There are at least three grounds of evidence pointing to the fact that Twiss, in the case of the Congo, was not only not naïve but also opportunistically adapting international law to practice. First, anyone who had read the anonymous Belgian's attack on Twiss could not have believed that Leopold's ambitions were open to a solely philanthropic interpretation and, therefore, he could not have acted naïvely in relation to them. We know that Twiss had read this attack because he paraphrased it in his third article on the Congo for the *Revue de droit international*.[67] Second, if we compare Twiss' thoughts on whether private associations or individuals can establish colonies as recorded in his *Oregon territory* and also as expressed in the Vattel-like character of his *Law of Nations*, we can see that he changed his position on this matter in order to make the case for Leopold. Third, to argue that Twiss or any of the other international lawyers of his generation were naïve is to ignore the often heated debates and divisions between them on precisely such questions as whether private associations can assume sovereignty. Many lawyers believed that Leopold and other colonial powers were seeking what they described as absolutism, while their opponents, such as Twiss, were happy to provide an apology for prerogative forms of rule.

The international lawyers of the *Institut de droit international* could never, of course, agree on any set of rules with which to govern the society of nations, although not for want of trying. Twiss' proposal that private associations could exercise sovereign powers was not, in the long term, accepted by the majority of his colleagues. But the debate opened sufficient legal space to enable Leopold and the International African Association to go ahead and occupy the Congo with force. Under Leopold's rule, millions of the Congolese peoples died, most of the rest were enslaved. At the same time, Twiss was redeemed. Directly after the Berlin conference, Leopold opened the Brussels meeting of the *Institut de droit international* on September 7, 1885, and in turn he received an encomium in his honor as a champion of the humanitarian cause in Africa.[68] At the same meeting, Laveleye, whose theory of neutrality for the Congo Twiss had demolished, stepped down from his position as vice president of the *Institut*. In his place Travers Twiss was elected. Twiss, thereafter, sat on numerous commissions and published prolifically. Most pleasing of all, perhaps, King Leopold honored him with an "Order of Leopold" for his services in creating the Congo Free State. Twiss was too old by this time to resume public office in Britain but his honor had been restored, and it had been restored, ironically, not by rejecting his wife's imposture but by following her example.

Notes

1. Earlier versions of this chapter were presented at the "Transpositions of Empire" symposium, held in Prato April 20–22, 2009, and at the Sawyer Mellon Seminar, "Atlantic Justice in the Pacific World: Property, Rights, and Indigeneity," July 17, 2009 at the University of Sydney. I am grateful to the participants on both occasions for valuable feedback.
2. Twiss' role in nineteenth-century international law has attracted attention in recent years. See Martti Koskenniemi, *The Gentle Civilizer of Nations. The Rise and Fall of International Law 1870–1960* (Cambridge: Cambridge University Press, 2004), pp. 132–33 for Twiss on the rights of Oriental nations in international law and p. 143 on Twiss and the Congo; Jennifer Pitts, "Boundaries of Victorian International Law," in *Victorian Visions of Global Order*, ed. Duncan Bell (Cambridge: Cambridge University Press, 2007), pp. 67–88, pp. 71–72; and Caspar Sylvest, "'Our Passion for Legality': International Law and Imperialism in Late-Nineteenth-Century Britain," *Review of International Studies*, 34 (2008), 403–23. Sylvest provides the most sustained analysis of Twiss' role in justifying Leopold's Congo venture: Sylvest, "Our Passion for Legality," pp. 408–15.
3. Michael Taggart, "Alexander Chaffers and the Genesis of the Vexatious Actions Act 1896," *Cambridge Law Journal*, 63 (2004), 656–84.
4. Alexander Chaffers, *The Twiss Libel Case* (London: Alexander Chaffers, 1873), p. 2.
5. "A Pitiless Persecutor," *Chicago Daily Tribune*, May 27, 1882, p. 3. Holborn Casino, or "Casino de Venise," was a popular location for prostitutes, see William Acton, *Prostitution, Considered in Its Moral, Social and Sanitary Aspects in London and Other Large Cities* (London: John Churchill, 1857), p. 102.

6. A.C. Tait to Twiss, November 10, 1871, Lambeth Palace Library (LPL), Tait MSS 176. See also: Tait to Twiss, March 17, 1872, LPL, Tait MSS 184, fol. 86.
7. *The Annual Register: A Review of Public Events at Home and Abroad for the Year 1872* (London: Rivingtons, 1873), pp. 14–16.
8. Testimony in the Twiss case was reported verbatim in *The Times* over the course of the first half of March 1872. See *The Times*, March 2, 1872, p. 11; March 4, 1872, p. 11; March 8, 1872, p. 11; March 14, 1872, p. 11. For Chaffers' affidavit see: "FOREIGN," *Chicago Tribune*, March 16, 1872. Believing the newspaper editors to be against him, and seeking vindication, Chaffers printed his own account of the case: Chaffers, *The Twiss Libel Case.*
9. Twiss to Tait, March 19, 1872, LPL, Tait MSS 184, fols. 90–91.
10. Reports of the Twiss case comment that he resigned all his posts. This was not quite the case. It would appear that to some degree he was pushed: A.C. Tait, March 18, 1872, LPL, Tait MSS 184, fol. 89.
11. Taggart, "Alexander Chaffers and the Genesis of the Vexatious Actions Act 1896," p. 659. See also Lord Chancellor to Tait, April 15, 1873, LPL, Tait MSS 184, fol. 94, announcing that Lady Twiss' presentation at court had been "cancelled."
12. Twiss to Tait, Lambeth LPL, Tait MSS 184, fols. 92–93, addressed Basle, La Swisse: "My Dear Lord Archbishop, I felt myself compelled to leave London by the consciousness that my mind would have given way under the weight of the calamities, which have so suddenly overtaken me if I had remained there. In fact, I was hardly responsible for my actions when I left, so completely were the nerves of my brain disordered."
13. Twiss to Tait, n.d., LPL, Tait MSS 184, fols. 92–93, addressed Basle, La Swisse: "in giving up my offices I have given up the income which has been the support of my family and of many who depended upon me, and I am anxious that no additional mark of the Queen's displeasure should be inflicted upon me... and destroy my future chances of usefulness in some humbler department of life."
14. There were a series of letters concerning the scandal, see: LPL, Jackson MSS 33, fols. 141–61.
15. April 11, 1871, LPL, Jackson MSS 33, fols. 140–41.
16. Travers Twiss, *The Oregon Territory* (New York: D. Appleton & Co., 1846), pp. 111–14.
17. Ibid., p. 112.
18. Ibid.
19. Ibid.
20. G. Rolin-Jaequemyns, "Œuvre de l'Exploration et de la Civilisation de l'Afrique Centrale," *Revue de Droit International*, 9 (1877), 318–19.
21. *Annuaire de l'Institut de Droit International*, septième année (1885), pp. 237–38.
22. Emile de Laveleye, "La Neutralité du Congo," *Revue de Droit International*, 15 (1883), 254–62.
23. Laveleye was vice-president of the *Institut*, see *Annuaire de l'Institut de Droit International*, septième année (1885), p. 238; and Koskenniemi, *Gentle Civilizer*, p. 60.

24. See, for example, Moynier in the *Annuaire de l'Institut de Droit International*, septième année (1885), p. 239 on the "persuasive" argument put by Laveleye on "neutralisation."
25. Moynier in the *Annuaire de l'Institut de Droit International*, septième année (1885), p. 239.
26. Travers Twiss, "La Libre Navigation du Congo," *Revue de Droit International*, 15 (1883), 437–42 ; "La Libre Navigation du Congo. Deuxième Article," *Revue de Droit International*,15 (1883), 547–63; "An International Protectorate of the Congo River," *Law Magazine and Review*, 250 (1883), 1–20; *An International Protectorate of the Congo River* (London: Pewtress & Co., 1883). The July 24, 1883 essay was also presented to the *Institut de Droit International* the following year and then reprinted in its *Annuaire* in 1885, see Travers Twiss, "La Libre Navigation du Congo," *Annuaire de l'Institut de Droit International*, septième année (1885), pp. 242–49.
27. Twiss, *International Protectorate of the Congo River*, p. 12.
28. Twiss, *The Oregon Territory*, pp. 111–14.
29. Twiss, "La Libre Navigation du Congo. Deuxième Article."
30. Ibid., p. 552.
31. Ibid. On p. 551 he also gives the example of the Teutonic order to the same purpose.
32. "Mémoire lu à l'Institut de Droit International, à Munich, le 4 Septembre 1883, par M. Moynier," in *Annuaire de l'Institut de Droit International* septième année (1885), pp. 250–74.
33. Ibid., p. 253.
34. *Annuaire de l'Institut de Droit International* septième année (1885), pp. 274–75.
35. Arntz's article ("Argument of Professor Égide Arntz") is reprinted in Henry Wellington Wack, *The Story of the Congo Free State* (New York: Knickerbocker Press, 1905), pp. 516–27.
36. Most recently Caspar Sylvest and Martti Koskenniemi. See Sylvest, "Our Passion for Legality," p. 411: "In some ways, the most arresting part of the story…lies in Leopold's success in convincing nearly everyone of his peaceful, philanthropic intentions"; p. 415: "Twiss was, of course, only one (and not the most important) among the moralists fooled by Leopold. But is it not only his naïvety which is representative"; and Koskenniemi, *Gentle Civilizer*, pp. 157–65. This also seems to be the position of earlier scholarship. See, for example, Jesse Siddall Reeves, *The International Beginnings of the Congo Free State* (Baltimore: Johns Hopkins University Press, 1894), p. 71; and also to some degree S.E. Crowe's *The Berlin West-African Conference, 1884–1885* (London: Longmans, Green & Co., 1942).
37. Anon., *Sir Travers Twiss et le Congo. Réponse à la Revue de Droit International et de Législation Comparée et au Law Magazine and Review, par un Membre de la Societé Royale de Géographie d'Anvers* (Bruxelles: Office de Publicité, 1884).
38. Ibid., pp. 5–6. My translation.
39. Ibid., p. 39.

40. Ibid., p. 40.
41. Ibid., p. 40.
42. Travers Twiss, "La Libre Navigation du Congo. Troisième Article," *Revue de Droit International*, 16 (1884), 237–46. He named his attacker the "anonymous publicist" and the "Portuguese lawyer" even though he knew that the author was Belgian writing in defense of Belgian interests rather than the Portuguese.
43. Twiss, "La Libre Navigation du Congo," pp. 238–43
44. Travers Twiss, *The Law of Nations Considered as Independent Political Communities*, 2nd edn. (Oxford: Clarendon Press, 1884), pp. xii–xiii. He wrote also of having met President Joseph Jenkins Roberts, the first President of Liberia, at a dinner party at the home of Édouard Drouyn de Louys, the French statesman and Minister of Foreign Affairs, in Paris.
45. Koskenniemi, *Gentle Civilizer*, p. 143.
46. Crowe, *The Berlin West-African Conference, 1884–1885*, p. 99.
47. It was Lord Granville, the foreign secretary, who wrote Twiss' letter of introduction to Malet. See Lord Granville to Malet, The National Archives, London (TNA), November 14, 1884, FO 84/1814.
48. Malet to Lord Granville, November 12, 1884, TNA, FO 84/1814, fol. 310: "I have been requested by the German Government to send in the names of the British Plenipotentiaries and Delegates to the Conference. Having heard incidentally that Sir Travers Twiss and a geographer are to be associated with me, I beg your Lordship to inform me on the point before I send in the list." Granville responded that "Sir T. Twiss" should not "be put on the Official List of Delegates" (TNA, FO 84/1814, fol. 309v).
49. Crowe, *The Berlin West-African Conference, 1884–1885,* p. 144.
50. Ibid., p. 147.
51. Ibid.
52. Julian Pauncefote, "Memo, 6/11/84," TNA, FO 84/1814, fol. 222: "Sir Travers Twiss has handed me for Lord Granville's information this copy of the Draft Constitution of the new state to be founded by the King of the Belgians under the name of L'Afrique Equatoriale. JP. 6/11/84."
53. T.V. Lister, "Memo, 23/11/84," TNA, FO 84/ 1815, fol. 214. Sylvest, in "Our Passion for Legality," p. 414, notes that Twiss is "reported to have drafted the constitution of the Congo Free State" adding that "This is claimed by several sources" although Sylvest himself has "not succeeded in recovering the constitution." Lister's memo would appear to put the authorship of the constitution beyond doubt and a copy, provided by Twiss, is available in the same Foreign Office documents.
54. "West African Conference. Confidential. Projet.—La Constitution de l'Etat.—L'Afrique Equatoriale," TNA, FO 84/1815, fols. 80–81.
55. Rapport de la Commission Chargée d'Examiner le Projet de Déclaration Relative aux Occupations Nouvelles sur les Côtes d'Afrique, TNA, FO 84/1820, fols. 233–38.
56. Edward Malet to Granville, January 19, 1885, TNA, FO 84/1820, fol. 58: "On Saturday a restricted Committee with Sir Travers Twiss in the chair met to agree upon the ultimate wording of the 3rd Basis."

57. Twiss, as always, was at the forefront of this effort, see for example: Travers Twiss, "Le Congrès de Vienne et la Conférence de Berlin," *Revue de Droit International*, 17 (1885), 201–17.
58. T.J. Lawrence, *The Principles of International Law*, 6th edn. (Boston: D.C. Heath & Co., 1915, first published 1895), pp. 83–87.
59. Frantz Despagnet, *Cours de Droit International Public*, 2nd edn. (Paris: Librairie de la Société du Recueil Général des Lois et des Arrêts, 1899), p. 434.
60. L. Oppenheim, *International Law a Treatise. Volume 1, Peace*, 3rd edn., ed. Ronald F. Roxburgh (London: Longmans Green & Co., 1920), I, pp. 35, 78, 143.
61. Johann Caspar Bluntschli, *Le Droit International Codifié*, 4th edn. (Paris: Librairie Guillaumin, 1886), p. 176.
62. Charles Salomon, *L'Occupation des Territoires Sans Maître* (Paris: A. Giard, 1889); Gaston Jèze, *Etude Théorique et Pratique sur l'Occupation* (Paris: V. Giard & E. Brière, 1896).
63. Salomon, *L'Occupation des Territoires*, pp. 163–88.
64. Ibid., p. 174.
65. Ibid., p. 170.
66. See, for example, Koskenniemi, *Gentle Civilizer*, p. 163.
67. Sylvest, "Our Passion for Legality," accuses Twiss of naïvety but does not mention his "La Libre Navigation du Congo. Troisième Article."
68. "Vote d'une adresse à S.M. Léopold II, Roi des Belges, Souverain de l'Etat Indépendant du Congo," *Annuaire de l'Institut de Droit International*, huitième année (1886), pp. 17–19.

Part III

Frontiers of Justice

Chapter 7

Samuel Marsden's Civility

The Transposition of Anglican Civil Authority to Australasia

Andrew Sharp

I

It is appropriate that the study of the colonial transposition of British government should focus on an array of impersonal and abstract instruments—sovereignty, occupation, the rule of law, natural rights—not least because such instruments can have quite concrete effects in establishing the terms of intelligibility and argument for the exercise of colonial rule. It is no less appropriate, though, that such study should also investigate the much less abstract and impersonal issue of the "character" or "persona" of those charged with wielding such instruments in the concrete exercise of government. Eighteenth-century English society remained firmly under the sway of the Anglican settlement of religious civil war, which had installed broad-church Anglicanism and the common law as the two central pillars of social government.[1] It also remained a society of "offices"—that is, a society in which duties and rights were packaged in interlocking role-specific bundles—such that the exercise of social authority was no abstract matter. It required rather the cultivation of a specific character or persona—the office-specific personality of the king, magistrate, parson, midwife, philosopher, husbandman, and so on—that formed the condition for successful occupancy of an office and the exercise of its social powers.[2] The colonial transposition of English social authority thus took place in and through the movement of particular "official" personages: governors, lawyers, missionaries, soldiers, and magistrates. It is no surprise then that the office through which the combined authority of Anglicanism and common law was concretely exercised in England—the dual office of clergyman and justice of the peace—should have had such decisive importance for the exercise of this authority in colonial Australia and New Zealand. It was as the occupant of this double office that Samuel Marsden (1765–1838) earned his celebrated or notorious place in the history of colonial Australia and New Zealand. He personified the mix of evangelical rectitude and judicial implacability that was required by the "character" of his office, even though this has been reduced to the level of personal foible by an often unsympathetic later historiography. At first, especially before the Macquarie years, Marsden's character was, naturally enough, largely judged by his fellow settlers as a function of his personality. It was after all a society in which roles were unclearly differentiated and taken ad hoc by those who would and could fill them; and so appearance, energy, and temperament counted for much. Few appreciated his office and character: what he lived for and habitually practiced. What is remarkable is that a politics (and later, a historiography) of personality continued to provide the frame for judging Marsden's actions, even after New South Wales had become an extended society in which offices and personae had become, in fact, more determinative than individual temperament. In attempting to understand the early stages of the transmission of English legal and religious culture to New South Wales, then, it is vital to study the man's office and the character cultivated for it, without reducing these to personal foible, for it is in the character of pioneers—the *auctors* of a new or transplanting society—that lodge the deep structures of control that they bring with them.

Today the colonial magistrate and Anglican minister Rev. Samuel Marsden is infamous in Australia as the "flogging parson": fat, flush-faced, rolling in landed wealth, aggressively pious, worldly, black-hating, and hypocritical. In New Zealand, which he visited seven times from 1814 to 37, his reputation is better. He has been known—though with increasing embarrassment—as a founding father of the state. He directed the missionaries who brought the rudiments of Christianity and civilization to the savage New Zealanders, and he established the friendly relations with them that made the consensual foundation of the New Zealand state possible. But he was a supplier of muskets as well as hoes and axes; he did not really understand the impact of the Christian presence and teaching on his audience; too many of his missionaries combined unpleasingly narrow piety with unscrupulous land-grabbing.[3]

Marsden's Australian infamy and the New Zealand embarrassment stem from adventitiously allied Catholic, liberal, and mercantile-colonialist traditions. These traditions were present nearly from the beginning, and they all rejected evangelical protestant Christianity as a way of life. Elements of each have been adopted by modern historians as nicely corresponding with their high valuations of national self-determination and individual skin color. They approve equality, liberty, toleration, and democracy and have no truck with subordination and the settled duties of station; so they cannot condone Marsden's anti-Catholicism and his admiration of authority. Nor do they appreciate his resistance to European colonization in the South Seas when undertaken for the accumulation of wealth and power rather than the spread of the gospel; though they applaud the self-reliance and industry of the settler, they prefer their priests (if they must have them) to be poor. They are ambivalent about the value of Europeans' remolding native races. Historians of both countries have, therefore, rather disliked Marsden, sometimes allowing that dislike to obscure the religious and political culture that formed his judgments and governed his actions.

Many of Marsden's generation, though, *did* support the export of protestant Christianity.[4] In London in May 1809, Rev. Legh Richmond preached to the annual meeting of the Church Missionary Society to Africa and the East (CMS). He took as his text the injunction of Jesus in John 11:16 to "Feed my sheep." He urged his hearers to extend their financial support to the organization's ramifying missions and to pray for their success. One of his congregation, Marsden himself was home, busy organizing an Anglican mission to New Zealand. In his sermon, with a striking eloquence that was long remembered,[5] Richmond, appropriately to the occasion, imagined a "statesman," a "merchant," a "natural philosopher," and a "curious traveler" examining a world map from their separate points of view. (It is notable that he did not imagine a "colonist," an uncommon and unattractive figure at the time).[6] The Christian "beholds the world's map" in a very different way from the others. "He has a subject of investigation far beyond them all. What they have overlooked and disregarded, is everything to him." He looks for "the visible kingdom of Christ"; then he will see "how small a part of those immense tracts of country which the map presents to his view, so much as know whether there be any Christ!"

In fact Marsden had seen the world exactly this way when he first left for New South Wales in 1793. His diary of the seven-month voyage out records his single-minded commitment to bring the gospel to the convicts and to the heathen natives of "New Holland."[7] The salvation of souls was to be his life's work. So it was not a new man who left England for the last time in 1809 to the strains of the "Old Hundredth" Psalm.[8] It was simply one who was reinvigorated by an eighteen-month stay in his homeland and who now had further flocks in mind: the New Zealanders, and the growing numbers of convict, free, and freed settlers in New South Wales.

"I believe that God has gracious designs towards New South Wales, and that his gospel will take root there, and spread amongst the heathen nations to the glory of his grace."[9]

This chapter is a sketch of Marsden's world, drawn up in terms that he and his evangelical fellows understood and adopted. Though far from conclusive, it sets the scene for an act of historical revisionism. It does so by displaying some of the mental freight that Marsden brought with him in the store-ship *William* when he first landed in Sydney Cove in March 1794—along with 260 tons of pork and beef and many necessary iron tools for the home, the farm, and the workshop.[10]

II

Product of a West Yorkshire background in the cottage woolen industry, the forge, and the small farm, Marsden intended to transplant his civilization as well as his Christianity. He immediately joined his senior chaplain, Rev. Richard Johnson,[11] in pastoral duties to the scattered settlements of the penal colony. But both men soon also took up plots of land and proceeded to farm them with great success[12]; more pertinently here, both acted as administrators of secular law, as Justices of the Peace.

The source of their religious knowledge was the bible. Their legal textbook was the Rev. Richard Burn's *Justice of the Peace, and Parish Officer* (1755 etc.), interpreted according to local custom and the orders and proclamations of succeeding governors. In line with normal English understandings, Marsden and Johnson regarded the teachings of (Anglican) Christianity and the English common law as jointly and harmoniously authoritative. Both required respect for God and for one's neighbor, so that Sabbath-breaking and idolatry were as rightly to be punished by the magistrate as killing, stealing, adultery, fraud, and perjury. Good law and policy would also enforce the rules of "social morality" that governed the unequal domestic, labor, and political relations between husband and wife, parents and children, masters and servants, and magistrates and subjects. This they learned from their English clerical sponsors: men like Revs. Miles Atkinson, Joseph Milner, and Thomas Dikes from Yorkshire; Charles Simeon and Isaac Milner of Cambridge; Thomas Robinson of Leicester; and John Newton and Thomas Scott of London.[13] Their lay sponsors such as William Wilberforce, MP for Yorkshire, and his agent, Dr. William Hey of Leeds, attempted the "reformation of manners," if necessary by legal enforcement, to similarly biblically defined ends.[14] And while more worldly powers in Westminster and Sydney might not believe in a "vital" or "serious" Christianity, they certainly believed in Christian teaching as a means to social order.[15] Even Marsden was capable of a Gibbonesque remark: "It is well known that all civilizations have found it expedient for the maintenance of good government... to inculcate upon the minds of their subjects all due respect for religion, whether their national religion were false or true."[16] To a man, the chaplains' friends in England supported Pitt's repression of radicalism at home.[17]

Marsden and Johnson lamented and excoriated the many sins and crimes of New South Wales.[18] Among the convicts, broken Sabbaths were spent drinking, gambling, rioting, and having irregular sexual liaisons. The expense of these led to fraud, theft, the desertion of illegitimate children, the bearing of false witness in courts, assault, murder, and very likely death by hanging. Horrid blasphemies filled the air. The clergymen's loud laments were doubtless designed to obtain more resources from England; however, their agony was real enough, for criminality was not the only issue: they believed that eternal damnation was the consequence of sin. In the end, an ill and dispirited Johnson could stand it no more and departed the colony in 1800, leaving Marsden by himself.

Although Marsden professed anxiety that some of his religious friends at home might doubt the wisdom of his mixing the professions of clergyman and magistrate, he accepted Governor Hunter's request that he become a JP.[19] Order was essential; Hunter had no established settler class to call on that might command the respect of the inhabitants; Johnson had been a JP before and was willing to serve again; it was common enough in England for clergy to be JPs[20]; his English sponsors committed to the "reformation of manners" by magisterial enforcement if necessary. And so Marsden thought it right to administer the law as a magistrate for three separate terms: first under Hunter and King from 1796 to 1806, then (more reluctantly) under Macquarie from 1812 to 1818, and finally for a few months under Brisbane in 1822. He was to be followed into this mixture of professions in Australasia and Tahiti by other clergy and missionaries into the 1820s.[21]

Under Hunter and King, Marsden was among the most prominent magistrates of the colony, burdened with a great number of administrative as well as pastoral and judicial tasks. His experience led him to offer his thoughts in three extended papers around 1806, intended for King, his successor William Bligh, and the authorities in England.[22] The papers discussed unmarried convict women living with men, the toleration of the Catholic religion among the Irish convicts, and the trade in spirituous liquors. As a recent writer has shown, Marsden's opinion of the morals and law-abidingness of convict women was low; he disapproved of the military élite's trading and monopoly in hard liquor as a medium of exchange; and most of all he abhorred the Irish Catholic convicts.[23] Each was excoriated as a corrupting source of sin and crime.

Hunter and King felt the same about the Irish: the two continually complained to Downing Street of those among them who were sent out for their parts in the 1798 rebellion. They were "ignorant, obstinate, and depraved," "turbulent and worthless characters," "insolent, refractory, and troublesome," "perjurers," "wicked and disaffected," "discontented," and of "troublesome spirit." Above all they were "seditious."[24] Marsden, reflecting on his and his fellow magistrates' experience of Irish unrest,[25] wrote in his Irish paper:

> The Toleration of the Catholic Religion would not only be dangerous to the present Inhabitants; and to the Government; but also to the rising Generation; and would lay the Foundation for future internal Wars and commotions. The Catholics who have Children...would bring them up in their own Persuasion; and would instil into their Minds all the Hatred against Church and State, which they themselves possess.

It is in this context of shared fear, taken in conjunction with Marsden's religious conviction that social order should be enforced through law, that his notorious reputation as the bigoted "flogging parson" is best considered. The primary evidence is scarce, but it is clear that during insurrection scares in September 1800 he (with Richard Atkins JP) ordered Pat Galvin to be severely flogged in an attempt to force him to give information as to the location of a cache of pikes. "General" Joseph Holt—an Ulster protestant—gave a vivid account of the consequence:

> The first hundred were given on his shoulders, and he was cut to the bone between the shoulder blades, which were both bare. The doctor then directed the next hundred to be inflicted lower down, which reduced his flesh to such a jelly that the doctor ordered him to have the remaining hundred on the calves of his legs. During the whole time Galvin never even whimpered or flinched, if, indeed, it had been possible for him to have done so. He was asked, "where the pikes were hid?" Galvin answered that he did not know, and that, if he did, he would not tell. "You may hang me," said he, "if you like; but you shall have no music out of my mouth to make others dance upon nothing [i.e., hang]."

Galvin was put into a cart and sent to the hospital. One other man had already received three hundred lashes; three others now each received one hundred.[26]

There is reason to doubt most of Holt's account of the day in question, yet Marsden and Atkins undoubtedly did order Galvin's flogging, and after the fashion described. Marsden reported it coolly to King, regretting only that the victim had not talked and was too ill to be sent down to Sydney for further interrogation.[27] There is no doubt either that under Macquarie

Marsden's magistracy was "stamped with severity." Commissioner Bigge reported it as such in 1822,[28] and Marsden never had any wish to deny it—only that he did not "torture" men, remitting lashes for information about criminal accomplices and the location of stolen goods.[29]

There was, in fact, nothing unusual in Galvin's flogging, and if his political opponents had not accused Marsden of cruelty in the 1820s in the course of feuds with him it is unlikely that the question of his excessive cruelty would have ever been raised.[30] Flogging was established as a common form of discipline in New South Wales, derived from naval and military custom rather than English domestic law, and a regular means of proceeding in the absence of viable options. The records of military discipline down to the mid-nineteenth century make mainland New South Wales's practices seem relatively moderate when convicts are regarded in a similar light as soldiers—as under another legal régime.[31] And although it is hard to gauge the severity of the floggings until the *Sydney Gazette* began publication in 1803, in the *Gazette*'s pages there is no hint that Marsden had done anything unusual: twenty-five lashes were very common and hardly worth reporting. Sometimes, though, the number was especially emphasized for its deterrent effect, and from 1803 to 1806 there are abundant records of punishments of 300, 500, 800, and 1,000 lashes being administered.[32] Nor was Marsden's order to flog Galvin harsh compared with the fate of the ringleaders of the 1800 plot, decreed by others. A military committee recommended "severe corporal punishment," followed by their removal to "some secluded isle belonging to the territory" and their being "employed in hard labour, and ordered to the strictest discipline to reduce them to due obedience, subordination, and order." Five men were to be flogged 1,000 times each in Sydney; four were to be flogged 500 times each at Parramatta. Governor King approved. There was no subsequent objection from Downing Street.[33] Marsden was acting in conformity with the legal norms of the time and place.

Marsden also thought he was acting in a Christian way according to biblical injunction and never resiled from his belief in corporal punishment as warranted by divine command as well as justified by its deterrent effects. As he told the secretary of the London Missionary Society (LMS), "Where Crimes are committed against Society, Punishments must be inflicted to prevent as far as possible their Repetition."[34] St. Paul taught that the magistrate did not "bear the sword in vain" and was a "terror to evil doers."[35] The Old Testament was full of the punishments prescribed to the Israelites by their ordained leaders: crucifixion; hanging, stoning, fire, the rack, the sword, the precipice, the saw, the tearing to pieces by thorns, the plucking out of eyes, the cutting off of hands and feet.[36] The injunctions in Proverbs not to "spare the rod" lest the child be spoiled would have seemed to Marsden to be merciful in comparison.[37] And if flogging a man was more than the mere "rod" to children, what he had to deal with in the Galvin case was armed rebellion, the greatest of crimes against society and the subject of severe condemnation in the church's *Homily on Disobedience*.[38] It is unsurprising, therefore, to find that the milder Richard Johnson also ordered floggings.[39]

III

If Marsden's recourse to flogging was in keeping with both judicial norms and Christian teaching, nonetheless his preferred means of reform was not the lash but Christian education. This was his prescription in his papers on the Irish, women, and liquor. In his imagined future colony, military and civil officers would not depart New South Wales when their time was done. They would remain. There would also be an increase in numbers of the (very few) free settlers currently in the colony. They would supply the essential "men of property," evidently graziers; however, they would be few in number compared with the "lower orders" or "lower classes." A few of these would constitute the body of the military while the rest would be engaged in agriculture. Among them would be "industrious" proprietor farmers who would have their own houses, servants, and field laborers, all modestly paid. Urged on by moral and religious duty, they would engage in the "useful and honest occupations" of raising "sheep, hogs, grain and poultry," so as to support their wives and families. They would also, by way of a money economy, support a body of mechanics such as "naylors, smiths and carpenters." Most of the lower orders would have been recruited from convicts whose time had expired or who had been pardoned—others would be recruited from seamen and soldiers—but Marsden was far from imagining the convict population away from New South Wales. Among them, "punishment should beget Repentance and Reformation and reclaim the unfortunate Criminal from the Paths of Vice."

All would sedulously attend church on the Sabbath. "Protestant clergymen," "supported by the executive power" and aided by a modest handful of schoolteachers, would shape and develop this ideal society. "The only effectual means to prevent the increase of bad Characters is to countenance and support the Protestant Religion as by law established; that Religion tending so much to inform the Judgement, improve the morals and ameliorate the Heart."

Marsden argued that when the convicts arrived, their religious opinions were scarcely discernable, let alone distinguishable:

> By living together in Prisons, and during a long voyage to N.S. Wales, the different religious Sentiments which they imbibed from their Education or

> Parents, are generally obliterated; and they acquire similar habits of acting and thinking, independent of their former various opinions and Education. The Catholic and the Quaker, the protestant Dissenter, and Churchman; the Baptist and the Jew can scarcely be distinguished one from another in a religious and moral Sense."

On the Sabbath, therefore,

> the Clergy...should studiously avoid introducing any political Subject whatever into their public discourses; and all controverted religious opinions. The Gospel should be preached in simple plain and scripture Language, and the duties of practical Religion pressed strongly upon the Consciences of their Hearers. The minister should consider his Congregation as one nation; and one People that he may be guarded against national Prejudices in all his public Addresses. For however much he may condemn in his own Judgment that Spirit of Rebellion which stimulated many of the Irish Convicts to commit those acts of Violence for which they now suffer, yet New S. Wales is not the place to discuss publickly from the Pulpit these political Evils.

School teachers would join the clergy in that task: "Men of tolerable Education and good Morals, who would willing devote their time and Study to instruct the rising Generation."

Marsden was, then, an integrationist, pursuing a protestant and rural ideal. He considered it possible to transform the population by the application of a non-doctrinal ethical Christianity, hardly considering, until much later, possible Catholic, dissenter, and even Methodist objections to the Anglican church's dominating the colony. And these sentiments were consistent with his record. He had recruited schoolteachers and (mainly dissenting) pastors for New South Wales among the LMS refugees from Tahiti and Tonga and organized their payment by both governors and the Society for the Propagation of the Gospel. He had agitated for the building and maintenance of churches and schools. He had played a major part in the founding of a female orphan school, and a female factory for secluding and educating young women in useful productive skills. In London he was to promote the continuation and extension of his program of Christian education and the reform of sexual relations.[40]

Until about 1815, Marsden may be seen as bringing religion to the aid of law and order and commending both as instruments for the production of a civil society in New South Wales. But when he returned in 1810, he found himself increasingly at odds on various fronts with Governor Macquarie. Soon one of the few men in authority he could consistently admire was Ellis Bent: judge advocate, a Christian, and his friend. But Bent died young, at 32. In November 1815, Marsden delivered a panegyric to him: his text, 2 Chronicles xxix 10–11.[41] The chapter spoke of King Hezekiah's restoring to Israel the worship of the true God and religious governance. For Marsden, Hezekiah was the model of the godly magistrate, as was Bent: "A truly pious man will not be satisfied in merely serving God in his closet. He will exert his influence to bring others to a sense of their duty." Priests were dedicated to the Christian ministry, but "all who are possest of authority—parents, magistrates, governors & kings should use that authority for the promoting of virtue and religion." "In these relations few equalled, and none... excelled him [Bent], as many of you can testify."

But if Bent was a rare epitome of human excellence, Macquarie was not. Responding to the sermon, the governor gave Marsden "a severe lecture... stating that it was blasphemous to speak so highly of any man."[42] More likely what lay behind the dressing down was Marsden's claim that the blame for the evils besetting the colony—namely drought and the death of Judge Bent—was to be laid at the governor's doorstep because of his neglect of religion and legal justice. The two never met again socially.

In 1817 Marsden came to see even more clearly a now-evident tension between the law of God and the will of an anti-Christian, if not Satanic, autocrat. The trouble began when J.T. Campbell, Macquarie's colonial secretary, allowed the publication of a letter signed "Philo Free" in the *Sydney Gazette*. The letter jested at and attempted to degrade Marsden and the missionaries in the South Seas. They were hypocrites and traders—even of muskets and powder—for their own profit.[43] From then on there was no turning back in the feud between the governor and the clergyman, Marsden strongly hinting at the devilish characteristics of his superior (the "enemy," the "liar," the "roaring lion," the "calumniator"). He wrote to his friends in the LMS and the CMS, "Our Enemy is powerful; and must be powerfully opposed."[44]

This is not the place to relate the details of Marsden's further clashes with Macquarie, or the ramifications of his hounding of Dr. Henry Grattan Douglass from 1822 to 1828, stemming from an alleged sexual liaison of Douglass with a female convict. It is enough to note that Marsden showed that he was very willing to fight to preserve his professional reputation as a clergymen and for his and the missionaries' vocation as the bringers of religion and Christianity to the poor suffering heathen. He always, though, felt mortified at the very thought that he had ever acted without legal warrant—he still saw no conflict between civil government and religion and remained committed to a prosperous, civilized colony, one that would increasingly come to imitate England's law and constitution.

IV

We can further re-balance our historical understanding of Marsden by shifting our attention to his attempts to Christianize and civilize the natives of New Zealand. Here his sense of the difficulties facing him was every bit as great as in New South Wales, but his aggressive assertion of his status and authority was restricted only to certain of his missionaries. He told the CMS in 1820 that

> All the difficulties in New Zealand that I have met with have been in governing the Europeans. They will not do what is right. They will not live in unity and brotherly love. The love of money, the thirst for pre-eminence, the want of industry, and zeal for the good of the heathens, have greatly mitigated against the success of the mission.[45]

In 1820, he urged Rev. John Butler to use strong measures, when, as head of the mission in the Bay of Islands, he could not control his men.[46] By the same token, soon after, he would not tolerate Butler's own weakness and insubordination, and he was implacable against Thomas Kendall and William Yate for their greater sins of adultery and homosexuality.[47] But with the New Zealanders Marsden was a benign figure, always interested in them and their affairs, anxious to do them good, and a peacemaker.

It was partly because he simply admired them as a highly intelligent race in general and was attached to (or wisely respected) several of them in particular—such as Maui,[48] Ruatara,[49] Te Morenga,[50] and Hongi Hika.[51] His published journals and (often-private) letters were full of praise for them—their kindness to their children and women, their respect for marriage, and their distaste for bad language: "We do not see the New Zealanders drinking or swearing and fighting and murdering each other, as is the case in civil society... Nor did I ever hear of a private murder unless theft, adultery, or some crime had been committed meriting that punishment according to their laws."[52] They lived in relatively settled communities, were interested in agriculture and trade, and displayed curiosity and great capacity for learning. They displayed sporadic hopes for peace and a government among themselves, and their oratory on public matters was comparable with the ancient Greeks'. Their courage in the wars (of which he disapproved) was exemplary.[53] They were altogether a superior people to the convicts in New South Wales, not to mention the aboriginals, who were "a nomad or a wandering people, always moving from place to place in search of food, or from mere love of change... They offer no prayer, and have no worship or sacrifices. Civil government is unknown; authority in the tribe depends on personal strength or cunning."[54] After serious attempts to civilize them until 1807, he decided there was little benefit in spending scarce resources in attending too much to them.[55] By contrast the New Zealanders were a "noble race,"[56] "far advanced and apparently prepared for receiving the Knowledge of Christianity more than any other savage nations I have seen."[57]

He thought it obvious and lamentable that the New Zealanders had many evil customs: not only cannibalism and the keeping of slaves, which were the worst,[58] but also their persistent holding of grudges that acted as causes of war of revenge, their superstitious avoidance of proximity with the dying, their fear of curses and other *tapu* (forbidden things), their ascription of guilt to communities rather than individuals, their blood sacrifices, thieving habits, tattooing, and polygamy. And although they were of a loving and quiet disposition, they could give way to furious and murderous rage when their passions were roused, or to a fit of suicidal depression induced by jealousy or despair.[59] Marsden usually tried unsuccessfully to dissuade them gently from these things while insisting it was not his intention to interfere with their customs or their government.[60] (After all, the New Zealand chiefs displayed "the character of our ancestors,"[61] and all men and women were "one blood.")[62] Customs varied: he told Te Morenga that, if he went to England, the English would not kill him for his many wars and his cannibalism "merely because the habits of his country were bad"; at the same time he criticized Kendall before a group of chiefs as acting "contrary to" the European's own "customs and laws."[63]

Marsden made no attempt to suppress the dark side of the natives' lives. He either recorded them with composure or, when comparing them with European customs, did so ironically where he saw it was the Europeans' fault, and jestingly if the fault was the New Zealanders'.[64] In fact, his dominant emotional reaction to the New Zealanders' savagery was the Christian pity his detractors in New South Wales thought he should have displayed to infidel officers, ignorant common apostates, and wandering heathen aboriginals. Anger and disgust were out of the question for him because he was convinced that the New Zealanders lay under the dominion of Satan.[65] They were helpless victims of their situation. He witnessed Ruatara about to die: "What horrors do these poor people suffer when they come to die!"[66] He saw their fear of *makutu* (curses): "In such strong chains of superstition does the Prince of this World bind the dark minds of these poor Heathen captives!"[67] He saw the dead in battle being mourned: "What hardships do these poor heathen suffer under the dominion of the Prince of Darkness!...These poor creatures sorrow as those without hope."[68] "Nothing," he concluded, "but the Gospel of our blessed God can effectually provide a remedy for their spiritual and temporal bondage."[69]

It was at a recurring point in his thinking that Marsden turned to consider the "means and instruments" by which the Lord's preordained will would be done; it was at this point that he considered the introduction of civilization and law into New Zealand. Christianity was the end, civilization and law the means. When proposing the mission to the CMS in London he had, in the light of his experience of the LMS missions, insisted that the civilization of the heathen in the South Seas must precede their evangelization—not as a moral priority, but as a causal one. In a famous public letter, he wrote of the New Zealanders:

> Though they appear to be a very superior people in point of mental capacity...yet they must not be considered by any means as favourably circumstanced for the reception of the gospel, as civilized nations are, even though strangers to the doctrines of divine revelation. Commerce and the arts, having a natural tendency to inculcate industrious and moral habits, open a way for the introduction of the gospel, and lay the foundation of its continuance when once received.[70]

The first missionaries to New Zealand thus were not clergymen at all, but laymen: two artisans and a schoolteacher. This idea was to be criticized by subsequent generations of the missionary community, even by Marsden's most sympathetic biographer.[71] He had his reasons though, uncolored by later fears of white settler takeover.[72] When in 1801 he had set out to advise the LMS after the flight of their first missionaries, he argued that their efforts would continue to be in vain until they brought the Tahitians to a standard of civilization so that they might understand the scriptures. But before that could happen, they must also be persuaded—no easy or obvious task—of the superiority of the civilization of the missionaries: "If Missionaries suppose they are coming out to a people already prepared for the reception of the Gospel and that they have only like the primitive Apostles to proclaim the glad tidings of Salvation to effect the Conversion of the Heathen, they are greatly deceived."[73]

It was on the imperative to civilize that in New South Wales Marsden opened his house and farms to the natives of the South Seas,[74] founded seminaries for them,[75] and (unsuccessfully) advocated a settlement of New Zealanders near Port Stephens.[76] For the same reason he encouraged trade with the islands and New Zealand—the trade for which he was criticized by Philo Free—and attempted to introduce agriculture, as well as in New Zealand flax weaving and the "simple arts" of the ropemaker, flax spinner, sawyer, blacksmith, and carpenter. Trade in their products and better (iron) tools would improve their habits of industry. The natives would have to work for what they wanted.[77] As he wrote to the LMS, "A nation without Arts and Commerce will never be a religious nation.... If the natives of Otaheite and the neighbouring Islands were employed in growing Cotton, making Sugar, Cordage, &c &c they would be more likely to form religious Habits, and be more moral and regular in the whole of their Conduct."[78] The New Zealanders, though less in need of this discipline than the Otaheitians, should learn to labor for their living and thus escape the wiles of Satan. "To give a man a spade is not like giving him 100lb of potatoes to supply his immediate wants, but is furnishing him with the means of raising many hundreds."[79] And so Marsden sought to provide the material bases of a civilization there, harboring a final vision of a society that was something like that of his idealized New South Wales: a small class of *rangatira* (chiefs)—perhaps under a single king[80]—would own the bulk of the land; the rest would labor for them, or on their own small holdings. An artisan class would emerge. An agricultural and Christian civilization would be established, advised by the missionaries.

He spoke often with the New Zealanders about the virtues of agriculture, commerce, and civilization, contrasting them with their state of continual wars.[81] British Law should be introduced, though only for the purpose of protecting the natives against the depredations of Europeans. Marsden was always clear and urgent on the need for this and championed the New South Wales Government Orders of 1813 and 1814 threatening legal penalties against British and colonial ships and crews who insulted and injured natives of the South Pacific Ocean and New Zealand.[82] He continued to agitate for their protection when it became evident that the governors of New South Wales were powerless; he advocated the presence of a gunboat to deter the depredations of seamen and convicts.[83] But he approved of a European colony only if it were to be made up of "real Christians,"[84] or of British soldiers to protect the New Zealanders. He only lukewarmly welcomed settlement of any kind, was in no hurry,[85] and did not imagine Professor Belich's "explosive colonisation" for a moment.[86] By 1831 he had come to advocate the establishment of a British resident Bay of Islands,[87] but this did not mean that he ever ceased wishing the New Zealanders to govern themselves.[88] In 1837, he met "many chiefs whom I had formerly known. Many were enquiring after the Saviour and a large number attended religious worship. I had much important conversation with them on the subject of religion and civil government. They have no established laws amongst them, and they feel the want of a government." He would propose British protection of the natives when he returned home.[89] The policy of the CMS in 1838 (quoting Marsden just after his death) was that missionary "influence" should not give way to colonization and the "coercive Authority" of imposed British sovereignty.[90]

Here then is a beginning of revising the anachronistic and invidious portrait of Marsden as the "flogging parson." If he ordered floggings in New South Wales it was not from any personal failing but from the manner in which he combined the offices of minister and magistrate in accordance with the forms of Anglican civil authority that he personified in the new colony. In New Zealand where he had freer reign he envisaged the protection and further civilization of already noble people, albeit in keeping with Christian-European conceptions of nobility and civility. Marsden was no less a child of his times than his modern critics.

Notes

1. J.C.D. Clark, *English Society 1660–1832: Religion, Ideology and Politics During the Ancien Regime*, 2nd edn. (Cambridge: Cambridge University Press, 2000).
2. Conal Condren, *Argument and Authority in Early Modern England: The Presupposition of Oaths and Offices* (Cambridge: Cambridge University Press, 2006).
3. On Marsden historiography—and other unfinished themes raised here—see my forthcoming, *Civilisation and the Prince of Darkness: Samuel Marsden in Australasia* (New Zealand: Penguin, forthcoming). The best biography of Marsden is A.T. Yarwood, *Samuel Marsden. The Great Survivor*, rev. edn. (Melbourne; New York: Oxford University Press, 1996).
4. See initially, *Christian Missions and the Enlightenment*, ed. Brian Stanley (Grand Rapids and Cambridge, UK: Curzon Press, 2001); Elizabeth Elbourne, "The Foundation of the Church Missionary Society. The Anglican Missionary Impulse," in *The Church of England c. 1689–c.1833: From Toleration to Tractarianism*, ed. John Walsh, Colin Haydon and Stephen Taylor (Cambridge: Cambridge University Press, 1993), 247–64.
5. T.S. Grimshawe, *A Memoir of the Rev. Legh Richmond*, 4th edn. (London: R.B. Seeley and W. Burnside, 1828), p. 217. *Proceedings of the Church Missionary Society*, irregular vols. (London: Church Missionary Society 1801–1921), II (1805–9), pp. 405–58.
6. Emphasized by James Belich, *Replenishing the Earth: The Settler Revolution and the Rise of the Anglo-World, 1783–1939* (Oxford: Oxford University Press, 2009), pp. 145–48.
7. Samuel Marsden, Diary July 27, 1793–July 15, 1794. Mitchell Library [ML] C245.
8. Marsden to Avison Terry, August 31, 1810, National Library of New Zealand [NLNZ], MS Papers 453, fold. 1.
9. Marsden to Mrs Good, August 1, 1809, qtd. in J.B. Marsden, *Memoirs of the Life and Labours of the Rev. Samuel Marsden of Paramatta* (London: Religious Tract Society, 1858), p. 63.

10. Dundas to Grose, June 31, 1793 and enclosure, in *Historical Records of Australia: Series I, Governors' Despatches to and from England* [*HRA*], ed. Frederick Watson, 26 vols. (Sydney: Committee of the Commonwealth Parliament, 1914–1925), Series 1, I, pp. 441, 443–44. Also in *Historical Records of New South Wales* [*HRNSW*], ed. A. Britton and F.M. Bladen, 7 vols. in 8 (Sydney: various publishers 1892–1901), II, pp. 50, 53.
11. On Johnson see James Bonwick, *Australia's First Preacher: The Rev. Richard Johnson* (London: Sampson Low Marston & Co., 1898); Neil K. Macintosh, *Richard Johnson, Chaplain to the Colony of New South Wales* (Sydney: Library of Australian History, 1978).
12. Samuel Marsden, *An Answer to Certain Calumnies in the Late Governor Macquarie's Pamphlet* (London: Hatchard, 1826), pp. 8–12. Also available at <http://nla.gov.au/nla.aus-vn1803578> [last accessed February 22, 2010].
13. For example, Miles Atkinson, *The Necessity of National Reformation: A sermon occasioned by the present critical state of the nation, preached at the parish-church of Leeds, July 11th 1779* (London: Leeds: John Binns; J. Wallis, 1779); John Newton, *Political Debate on Christian Principles* (Edinburgh; London: John Ogle; J. Johnson, 1793); Thomas Robinson, *A Christian System Unfolded in a Course of Practical Essays* (London: F.C. and J. Rivington; J. Hatchard, 1805), esp. III, pp. 111–79, 199–203; Thomas Scott, *Essays on the Most Important Subjects of Religion* (London, 1794), pp. 51, 255–78.
14. A useful contemporary account of their ideas is John Scott, *An Account of the Societies for the Reformation of Manners and the Suppression of Vice* (Hull: W. Rawson, 1807), esp. p. 48. Recent studies: J. Innes, "The Reformation of Manners Movement in Later Eighteenth-Century England," in *Transformation of Political Culture. England and Germany in the Late Eighteenth Century*, ed. Eckhart Hellmuth (London: Oxford University Press, 1990), pp. 57–118, and M.J.D. Roberts, *Making English Morals: Voluntary Association and Moral Reform in England, 1778–1886* (Cambridge: Cambridge University Press, 2004), pp. 107–34.
15. Instructions to Governor Phillip of April 25, 1787 in *HRNSW*, II, p. 90; also in *HRA*, Series 1, I, p. 14; III, p. 635; and Wilberforce to Dundas, August 7, 1792, in *HRNSW*, I, part 2, pp. 633–35.
16. Marsden, to Hunter, August 11, 1798, in *HRNSW*, III, pp. 440; and in *HRA*, Series 1, II, pp. 186.
17. See their biographies in *ODNB*.
18. See especially Richard Johnson, *An Address to the Inhabitants… in the Colonies Established in New South Wales and Norfolk Island* (London, 1792); Marsden to Atkinson, September 17, 1796, qtd. in *The Letters and Journals of Samuel Marsden 1765–1838* [*LJ*], ed. J.R. Elder (Dunedin, NZ: Otago University Council, 1932), pp. 31–33; Johnson to Hunter, July 5, 1798; Marsden to Hunter, August 11, 1798, in *HRNSW*, III, pp. 432–37, 439–42.
19. Marsden to Atkinson, September 17 and 18, 1796, qtd. in Elder, *LJ*, pp. 29–34.
20. Thomas Skyrme, *History of the Justices of the Peace*, 3 vols. (Chichester: Barry Rose, 1994), vol. 3, chap 11; John Walsh and S. Taylor, "Introduction: The

Church and Anglicanism in the 'Long' Eighteenth Century," in *The Church of England c. 1689–c.1833*, ed. Walsh et al., pp. 7, 28, 60.

21. Revs. Robert Knopwood (Van Diemen's Land) in 1803, John Jefferson (Tahiti) in 1804, Henry Fulton (New South Wales) in 1810, William Cartwright (New South Wales) in 1810, Mr. Thomas Kendall (New Zealand) in 1814, and Rev. John Butler (New Zealand) in 1819.
22. ML MSS 18 on microfilm CY369. Electronic version: < http://acms.sl.nsw.gov.au/item/itemDetailPaged.aspx?itemID=423135 >.
23. See Michael Saclier, "Sam Marsden's Colony: Notes on a Manuscript in the Mitchell Library, Sydney," *Journal of the Royal Australian Historical Society*, 62 (1966), 94–113.
24. Hunter and King to Portland, various letters,1796–1798: in *HRNSW*, II, pp. 184–86; III, pp. 175, 348, 359, 506, and *HRA*, Series 1, I, p. 674; II, pp. 129, 237, 613–15.
25. G.W. Rusden, *Curiosities of Colonization* (London: [s.n.], 1874), pp. 62–71; *HRA*, Series 1, II, pp. 575–83, 637–51, and *HRNSW*, IV, pp. 119–30, 234–38. Cf. pp. 209–10, 228–29.
26. *Memoirs of Joseph Holt, General of the Irish Rebels in 1798*, ed. T. Crofton, 2 vols. (London: Henry Colbourn, 1838), II, pp. 119–22.
27. Marsden to King, September 30, 1800, in *HRNSW*, IV, pp. 235–36, and *HRA*, Series 1, II, pp. 638–39.
28. House of Commons, *Report of the Commissioner of Inquiry into the State of the Colony of New South Wales* (1822), p. 91; John Ritchie, *Punishment and Profit: The Reports of Commissioner John Bigge 1822–1823* (Melbourne: Heinemann, 1970), p. 174.
29. Samuel Marsden, *Statement Including Correspondence between the Commissioners of the Court of Enquiry, the Rev. Samuel Marsden* (Sydney: Robert Howe, 1828). See also *Sydney Gazette*, May 19, 1828, and May 21, 1828, p. 2; May 23, 1828, pp. 2–3; August 5, 1828, p. 2; October 24, 1828, p. 2; and November 10, 1828, p. 2. The *Gazette* is at <http://newspapers.nla.gov.au/ndp/del/home>.
30. Though there may have been an independent convict tradition to that effect: Samuel Sidney, *Three Colonies of Australia* (London: Ingram, 1852), pp. 40–41.
31. J.R. Dinwiddy, "The Early Nineteenth Century Campaign against Flogging in the Army," *English Historical Review*, 97 (April 1982), 308–31.
32. *Sydney Gazette*, for example, August 7, 1803, p. 4; December 18, 1803, p. 4; May 20, 1804, p. 4; October 2, 1803, p. 2; April 6, 1806, pp. 2 and 4; May 11, 1806, pp. 3 and 4; August 3, 1806, p. 3; and October 10, 1806, p. 1.
33. *HRNSW*, IV, pp. 225, 236–38, and *HRA*, Series 1, II, pp. 614–15, 626, 650–51.
34. Marsden to Hardcastle, November 5, 1801, in School of Oriental and African Studies, London: CWM/LMS Collection. Australia. Incoming Correspondence. [CWM, Australia Incoming], 1,1, C.
35. *Romans* xiii 1–4.
36. I quote Alexander Cruden's *Concordance* (of which Marsden inherited a copy from Johnson), sub "punishment."

37. *Proverbs* xiii 24; xix 18, xxii 15, xxiii 13–14. Also *Hebrews* xii 5–11. Quoted by Scott, *Essays*, p. 268.
38. See Church of England, *Sermons or Homilies Appointed to Be Read in Churches* (Oxford: Clarendon Press, 1802).
39. John F. Nagle, *Collins, The Courts & the Colony* (Sydney: University of New South Wales, 1996), pp. 186–92.
40. See "Dr Good's Summary of the Character and Labours of the Revd. Samuel Marsden," in Olinthus Gregory, *Memoirs of the Life, Writing, and Character of John Mason Good* (London: H. Fisher and Son, 1832), Appendix to Sect III. Taken from the *Eclectic Review*, 5 (1809), 988–95. Also published in *Evangelical Magazine*, 17 (1809), 498–503, and Supplement, pp. 537–39.
41. Marsden Papers, ML C244, pp. 17–40.
42. Marsden Papers, ML C244, p. 17.
43. *Sydney Gazette*, January 4, 1817, p. 3. Another adverse letter: January 11, p. 2. The affair is summarized in *Report of the Commissioner of Inquiry*, pp. 20–33.
44. Marsden to George Burder, May 17, 1817, CWM, Australia Incoming, 1, 6, D, cf. Marsden to Pratt, July 12, 1819, Hocken Library, Dunedin [HL], MS 56, p. 168.
45. Marsden to Pratt, September 22, 1820, in Elder, *LJ*, pp. 331–32. Cf. pp. 140, 341, 343–46, 354–55.
46. Marsden to Butler, September 19, 1820, HL, MS 57, p. 18.
47. Elder, *LJ*, pp. 344–47, 351, 379–80, 391–403, 421–22, 518–19, 531–32, 534–35, 537 and Marsden to Coates, September 10, 1832, HL, MS 57, p. 22; Judith Binney, *The Legacy of Guilt: A Life of Thomas Kendall*, 2nd edn. (Wellington: Bridget Williams Books, 2005). On Yate, see Marsden to Coates, CMS, December 13, 1836, onward in Birmingham University, Church Missionary Society Archive.[CMS Arch], Section III: Central Records. Part 7: CMS Minutes, 1799–1837
48. Woolls, *Short Account*, p. 43. Cf. Elder, *LJ*, p. 159.
49. Anne Salmond, *Between Worlds: Early Exchanges between Maori and Europeans 1773–1815* (Auckland: Penguin, 1997), chap. 17.
50. Elder, *LJ*, pp. 155, 261, 388–89 and *passim* see index.
51. Ibid., pp. 146, 201, 336–37, 376, 380–81, 383. Marsden to Hongi, February 16, 1824 and July 26, 1824, NLNZ, MS Papers 453, fold. 2.
52. Elder, *LJ*, pp. 407–8. Cf. pp. 128, 388. 477–78.
53. Ibid., pp. 128, 135, 170, 219, 386–87, 389, 471.
54. J.B. Marsden, *Memoirs*, pp. 79, 81.
55. See *Sydney Gazette*, November 2, 1804, p. 2; *The Memoirs of James Hardy Vaux, including his Vocabulary of Flash Language*, ed. Noel McLaughlan (London: Heinemann, 1964). Marsden's later, pessimistic opinion is best expressed in a letter to Archdeacon John Scott, December 2, 1826 in CWM, Australia Incoming, 2, 3, C; and Marsden to Hankey and Burder, February 24, 1829, CWM, Australia Incoming, 2, 6, A. See also his practical objections in L.E. Threlkeld, *A Statement Chiefly Relating to the Formation and Abandonment of a Mission to the Aborigines* (Sydney: Robert Howe, 1828).

56. Marsden to John Terry, October 26, 1810, Private Papers Samuel Marsden 1765–, ML, II Correspondence, fol. 2; Marsden to Avison Terry, October 7, 1812, Private Papers Samuel Marsden 1765–, ML, II Correspondence, fol. 5; Marsden to George Burder, September 6, 1816, CWM, Australia, Incoming 1, 6, B; Marsden to Pratt, March 4, 1817, HL, MS 56, p. 54.
57. Marsden to Pratt, November 19, 1811, in *Marsden & the New Zealand Mission* ed. P. Harvard-Williams (Dunedin, NZ: University of Otago Press, 1961), pp. 35–37.
58. Elder, *LJ*, Cannibalism: pp. 29, 129, 173–74, 215, 267, 285, 373, 408–10. Slavery, pp. 105, 387, 477.
59. Ibid., pp. 116–17, 119, 156, 159–60, 162–64, 167, 171–74, 208–9, 211–12, 272–73, 277, 350, 352–53, 371, 372, 408, 465–66, 477–79, 483–85.
60. Ibid., pp. 199, 352.
61. Ibid., pp. 185–87, 231. He thought they might be descended from the ancient Jews (pp. 219–20, perhaps p. 325), showing the point to be historical not racial.
62. Ibid., p. 353.
63. Ibid., pp. 267, 351, 353–54.
64. Ibid. Ironically: pp. 129 ,165–67, 214. Jestingly: pp. 114, 190, 203, 271. But horrified: pp. 152–53, 177.
65. Ibid., pp. 60, 135, 151, 183, 232, 277, 287, 309, 354, 362, 365, 372, 379–80, 407–8, 422, 464, 479, 484, 489.
66. J.B. Marsden, *Memoirs*, p. 109.
67. Elder, *LJ*, p. 277.
68. Ibid., p. 365, quoting *Ephesians* ii 12. See also pp. 196, 215, 244, 378.
69. Ibid., pp. 386–87.
70. Woolls, *Short Account*, pp. 21–24; J.B. Marsden, *Memoirs*, pp. 56–57; CMS, *Proceedings*, II (1805–9), pp. 361–64; Elder, *LJ*, pp. 166–67.
71. J.B. Marsden, *Memoirs*, pp. 41–44, 56–58. Cf. Alexander Strachan, *The Life of the Rev. Samuel Leigh, Missionary to the Settlers and Savages of Australia and New Zealand.* (London: Wesleyan Missionary House, 1870), pp. 83–87; Lancelot Thelkeld to Burder and Hankey, March 27, 1826, CWM, Australia Incoming, 2, 4, B; Marsden to Hankey February 24, 1829, CWM, Australia Incoming, 2, 6, A.
72. As expressed by the leaders of the missions in 1837: D. Coates, J. Beecham and W. Ellis, *Christianity the Means of Civilization; Shewn in Evidence before a Committee of the House of Commons* (London: R.B Seeley, W. Burnside, 1837).
73. Marsden to Captain William Wilson, January 30, 1801, enclosed in Marsden to Hardcastle, August 15, 1801, CWM, Australia Incoming, 1, 1, C.
74. Especially the New Zealanders: Elder, *LJ*, p. 365. Cf. pp. 128–30, 134, 159–63, 165, 181, 197, 206, 218, 239,234, 243–48, 253, 289, 305, 329, 352, 355, 358, 354–55, 362–64, 375, 385–87, 446–49, 539.
75. Marsden to Pratt, October 9, 1810 in Harvard-Williams, *Marsden & the New Zealand Mission*; Marsden to Pratt, January 20, 1817, HL, MS 56, p. 38; Marsden to Pratt, February 20, 1819 in Elder, *LJ*, pp. 233–34; John Butler

to Pratt, July 10, 1819, in *Missionary Register* (July 1820), 8, 305; Marsden to Pratt, February 21, 1824, HL, MS 57, 114; Marsden to William Kemp, March 10, 1824, Auckland Library, NZMS 741, 4.

76. Marsden to Darling, September 14, 1827, NLNZ MS Papers 453, fold. 3; Marsden to Coates, November 12, 1827, CMS Arch, 9, p. 519.
77. Marsden to Burder, October 17, 1814, CWM, Australia Incoming, 1, 5, B; Marsden to Burder, June 9, 1815. CWM, Australia Incoming, 1, 5, C; Elder, *LJ,* pp. 130, 166–67, 170, 176, 187, 230–31, 370–71.
78. Marsden to Burder, June 9, 1815; CWM, Australia Incoming, 1, 5, C.
79. Elder, *LJ,* p. 371.
80. Ibid., pp. 383, 388.
81. Ibid., pp. 114, 187, 192–93, 196, 208, 260, 272, 280, 285–86, 290, 347, 352–53, 471.
82. *Historical Records of New Zealand*, ed. Robert McNab, 2 vols. (Wellington: Government Printer, 1908–14), I, pp. 316–17, 329–30. Elder, *LJ,* p. 207.
83. Marsden to Pratt, November 6, 1815, HL, MS 55, p. 40.
84. Marsden, Cartwright and Youl to Pratt, March 27, 1817, in Elder, *LJ,* pp. 226–28.
85. Marsden to Pratt, March 30, 1817, in Elder, *LJ,* p. 229. Cf. pp. 261, 364.
86. Belich, *Replenishing the Earth,* pp. 9, 178–79, 183, 221, etc.
87. Elder, *LJ,* pp. 497–504, 523.
88. Ibid., pp. 113–14, 141–42, 290, 295, 330, 332, 335, 383, 388, 439, 532, 543. On the episode at pp. 141–42 where in 1814 the missionaries deny an intention to take land and government from the New Zealanders, see *Report from the Select Committee of the House of Lords, Appointed to Inquire into the Present State of the Islands of New Zealand* (1837) pp. 10–12, and John Liddiard Nicholas, *Narrative of a Voyage to New Zealand*, 2 vols. (London: J. Black and Son, 1817), I, pp. 39–44.
89. Marsden to Coates, March 27, 1837, in Elder, *LJ,* pp. 518–24.
90. *Report from the Select Committee of the House of Lords*... [on the] *Present State of the Islands of New Zealand*, pp. 271–72 Cf. pp. 243–55, esp. 247, 251, 263–72, 273–75, 340.

Chapter 8

The Limits of Jurisdiction

Law, Governance, and Indigenous Peoples in Colonized Australia

Mark Finnane

In events well known and controversial in Australia, the last year of the Howard government (1996–2007) saw a federal "intervention" in one of its own territories with the aim of restoring order in Aboriginal communities.[1] Under the mandate of an "Emergency Response" the government designed a comprehensive program of policing (including military aid to the civil power), welfare reform, and criminal law amendment. The response comprised both material and symbolic elements. Among the latter was a widely publicized announcement that "customary law" would no longer be an excuse for criminal behavior. Some months later the Commonwealth Parliament amended the Crimes Act to delete a requirement passed only in 1994 (with bipartisan support) that a court take account of "cultural background" in sentencing decisions. Today the Crimes Act directs that

> a court must not take into account any form of customary law or cultural practice as a reason for: (a) excusing, justifying, authorising, requiring or lessening the seriousness of the criminal behaviour to which the offence relates; or (b) aggravating the seriousness of the criminal behaviour to which the offence relates.[2]

Such a determined government attack on "customary law and cultural practice" more than two centuries after the British settlement of Australia prompts us to consider how such traces of indigenous authority and even assertions of jurisdiction have survived. For it will be argued here that far from being resolved in 1836, the question of indigenous amenability to imported British criminal law in Australia remained surprisingly open. Historians as well as jurists have generally agreed that when the New South Wales Supreme Court affirmed in the case of *R v Jack Congo Murrell* in 1836 that "the aboriginal natives of this Colony are amenable to the laws of the Colony for offences committed within it against the persons of each other and against the peace of our Lord the King," a line was drawn against the survival of indigenous law. The most subtle recent inquiries into the extension of British jurisdiction over Australian indigenous peoples in the first half of the nineteenth century stress the evidence of early colonial legal pluralism, while concluding that *Murrell* marked the turning point. The courts in New South Wales as in Georgia, argues Ford, completed in the 1830s "what they had started a decade before: they perfected settler sovereignty by subordinating indigenous jurisdiction."[3] Similarly for McHugh, the assertion of Crown sovereignty in *Murrell*, with its subsequent affirmation by the imperial and colonial authorities, brought to an end a period during which there had been a fitful recognition of "Aborigines being outside colonial jurisdiction."[4] For Dorsett and McVeigh, "*Murrell* commenced the process of erasing the legal memory of a time in which the common law's jurisdiction was anything other than complete and unified."[5] These accounts enrich our understandings of the plurality of early nineteenth-century legal worlds but unite with long-established views acknowledging the authority of *Murrell*.[6]

In what follows I do not seek to displace the significance of *Murrell* as legal authority for the principle of British jurisdiction over Aboriginal crimes committed among themselves (or *inter se*). Rather I want to explore the limitations of that assertion of a comprehensive and untrammeled jurisdiction when confronted by the practical circumstances of governing in colonial and postcolonial conditions in Australia. In the brief space available here I consider some of the ways in which successive generations of Australians—governors and governments, settlers and their institutions, and indigenous peoples—confronted the reality of persisting Aboriginal difference in customs, norms, and perspectives: difference that is from those holding among the ascendant settler populations. The persistence of that difference helps to explain why, more than two centuries after British settlement, Australian governments might still be seeking to terminate recognition of "customary law or cultural practice" in determination of criminal guilt.

It will be suggested that the persistence of Aboriginal difference in criminal law was in part an effect of contradictions and shortcomings in criminal justice procedure. It was also a product of the competing demands and interests of the various domains of governance—religious governance through the missions, and administrative governance through reserves, policing powers, status distinctions, and population controls—in which indigenous peoples were rendered as objects of potential transformation into self-governing citizens. These were domains of governance before or beyond which criminal jurisdiction was another threshold. Although indigenous peoples shared this subjection with some other status groups in the increasingly saturated government of populations (juveniles, for example, or mentally ill people), they brought to this arrangement something else altogether: a different linguistic, cultural, and ethical universe, with its attendant structures of law and mentality, constituting worlds of difference from the settler populations. If the integrity and autonomy of those indigenous cultures was challenged, and in very many cases shattered, the historical displacement nonetheless was uneven. That unevenness is expressed in the evidence reviewed here of the way in which indigenous practices, beliefs, and norms challenged the certitudes of criminal jurisdiction.

After considering briefly the significance of the assertion of sovereign command and the extension of jurisdiction over Aborigines in early New South Wales, I examine some of the ways in which criminal jurisdiction was constrained in its encounter with indigenous peoples, both by the illegibility of their practices and perspectives and by its tension with the regimes of social governance that developed in Australia. This theme is explored first in the colonial and early postcolonial conditions of Queensland—one of Australia's three northern jurisdictions—and second in the unique conditions of the Northern Territory, a federal territory administered by the Commonwealth government from 1911 and to this day. The case materials gathered here from both judicial and administrative domains suggest that in northern Australia in the late colonial era and especially after the federation of the Australian colonies, there was continuing disquiet in government about the means, ends, and impacts of criminal justice routines applied to Aboriginal people. A twentieth-century discourse of customary law developed as a loose set of propositions about the rules, norms, and practices of indigenous societies that constituted a legacy of pre-settlement life. In changing political and policy contexts there even emerged attempts to recognize the continuity of such law through modifications of procedure and sentencing outcomes.[7] Far from *Murrell* resolving the jurisdictional question in 1836, it appears that it was only the beginning of a protracted and still incomplete argument about the place of indigenous peoples in settler Australia's law.

I

For nearly 50 years following the first settlement at Sydney in 1788 it was unclear whether colonial courts could exercise jurisdiction over Aborigines committing offences against settlers or their own. The erosion of early attempts at conciliation between the invading settlers and indigenous people of the Sydney region was a prelude to later conflict in which retaliation was the preferred mode of response to violence on either side. When law started to intervene, through rare cases of prosecution of Aborigines for killing settlers, the results were mixed, and disturbing to settlers as much as to Aborigines. Doubts about the practicality, the wisdom, or the justice of trying Aborigines in criminal courts were early expressed. These doubts developed as a discourse that was of remarkable longevity, even if of uneven impact. During a period in which settlers and Aborigines lived in constant contact, frequenting the streets of Sydney and the colony's few other towns, or occupying in uneasy contiguity the same lands, there were continuing aggravations to government policy that sought a measure of accommodation. Aboriginal ownership of land might not be tolerated, but there was a heavy sense of prior occupation and continuing attachment to land and customs.[8]

Long before courts came to consider whether they had a jurisdiction to try Aborigines for offences committed *inter se*, the governor of New South Wales, Lachlan Macquarie (1810–1821), embarked on a program intended to transform the Aboriginal peoples of the Sydney region into the kinds that might inhabit a British settler colony in the antipodes. His measures included institutions for the transformation of Aborigines into civil subjects (encapsulated in his Natives Institution for the education of children) and measures to enforce peace, which entailed an end to Aboriginal customs that offended contemporary notions of civility, even in the rough conditions of a convict colony.

In May 1816, following military operations against hostile Aborigines in the farming lands west of Sydney, on the periphery of settlement, Macquarie issued a proclamation aimed at curtailing Aboriginal violence. The governor's proclamation combined the promise of violent response to Aboriginal "Outrages and Barbarities' with an enticement to those who were peaceable to become settlers (through land grants) or servants, as they were inclined. But in a move designed to address the behaviour of Aborigines within the bounds of the colony's towns, he drew another line between barbarism and civilization. Here Macquarie simultaneously recognized the persisting practice of Aboriginal punishments "on Transgressors of their Customs and Manners" and proscribed them "as a barbarous Custom repugnant to the British Laws, and strongly militating against the Civilization of the Natives." The practice he objected to was the periodic assembly of Aborigines in Sydney for meting out ritualistic punishments through spearing and fighting.[9] Unlike the military operation and threats of retaliatory violence in the first part of his proclamation, Macquarie's proscription of these rituals was quasi-legislative. It rested on the assumption that Aborigines were already subject to the jurisdiction of the courts for behaviors that were formally *inter se* in character, even before the matter had been judicially decided. Under the Proclamation, "Any Armed Body of Natives" assembling for these purposes would be "considered as Disturbers of the Public Peace and shall be apprehended and punished in a summary Manner accordingly."

At the same time, we cannot read this edict as oriented only to Aborigines already within the bounds of settlement. Attached to it was a much broader objective: "The Black natives are therefore hereby enjoined and commanded to discontinue this barbarous custom not at or near the British Settlements, but also in their own wild and remote places of resort."[10] On close reading, one notices that Macquarie's proclamation sets out an ambitious set of policy objectives: determined opposition to indigenous violence against settlers; enticement to come into the fold, but on condition of abandoning their way of life, especially those repugnant customs that were now penalized in summary jurisdiction; and reformation of their way of life even in places remote from settlement.

Macquarie's sovereign command thus enjoined the indigenous people of New South Wales to behave in ways that accorded with civilized standards. But what did this mean for criminal jurisdiction? Before 1836 there was a reluctance to prosecute Aborigines. In Ford's conclusion, "local magistrates, governors and soldiers thought it impossible, inappropriate or unnecessary to bring then into court."[11] It was a missionary, Lancelot Threlkeld, who in 1836 advised the attorney-general that other Aborigines wanted Murrell and his accomplice Bummaree tried "by the English," on a charge of murdering another Aborigine.[12] Although *Murrell* settled the question of jurisdiction in New South Wales, its impact on jurisdictional practice was less evident. The possibility that assertion of jurisdiction might not be enough to bring Aboriginal offending within the purview of the criminal law in the conditions of colonial society was already contemplated by the Supreme Court in that case. But the author of the court's judgment, Justice William Burton, dismissed the problems that might flow from the assertion of jurisdiction. He thought much overrated the "difficulties and inconveniences and hardship which have been referred to as likely to arise from this decision."[13]

The difficulties to which Burton referred included the possible increase in court business that would flow from making Aboriginal offending justiciable, and the problems of testimony and evidence that already constituted an impediment to their standing in courts as witnesses. The challenges, however, were not limited to these matters. To make jurisdiction more than formal, to give it practical effect, required in the conditions of a colonial society other measures of government and policy. Over the longer term these would include the institutions of policing as well as the establishment of a court system that was capable of administering justice according to those high standards established in the judgments of the superior courts and the communications of the Colonial Office. Measures of policy followed from the discovery of how far short of competent jurisdiction the law really fell when it came to dealing with indigenous offenders. In fact, policy would need to address the conditions of an oath, the provision of interpreters, the compellability of "wives" as witnesses, the meaning of a jury of one's peers, the availability of a jury, the status of a plea of guilty, the "tariff" of punishment. Running through policy discussion—in judicial opinion, in the public media, and in government offices—would be another theme: the risk of double jeopardy for offenders who might be subject to indigenous punishments (the product of some other kind of jurisdiction) as well as those meted out in settler courts.

As in other settler polities, so in the developing Australian polity, from the mid-nineteenth-century, criminal jurisdiction constituted only one point in an increasingly complex field of social governance. From the founding of Governor Macquarie's Native Institution through the missionary endeavors of the mid- and later nineteenth century to the formal establishment of protection regimes in a number of jurisdictions in the early twentieth century, the lives of indigenous peoples were increasingly organized by systems of religious transformation, tutelage, and welfarism. As we will see below, the determination that certain behaviors constituted a criminal offence that should be managed within the systems of policing, prosecution, and punishment of the settler majority was a contingent matter. The debates around jurisdiction over Aboriginal "crime" form part of a much deeper discourse around the conditions under which indigenous peoples would be accommodated in settler societies. When Aborigines committed crime, government responded sometimes with a decision that a person was an offender, at other times with a decision that the behavior indicated a moral, educational, or psychological deficit that might be better met through a non-criminal justice response. From the beginning of settlement and persistently as settlement ranged out over Australian territory in the two centuries after 1788, the discourses framing such decisions spoke of the tribal or native or "customary" character of indigenous practices, even if they did so unevenly and uneasily. In the next section we examine how such recognition was evident in the seemingly uncongenial conditions of late colonial Queensland.

II

Detailed attention to prosecutions of Aboriginal offenders for *inter se* as well as interracial offences in the middle years of the colonial period has shown how insecure were the claims of settler jurisdiction.[14] In late colonial Queensland (separated from New South Wales in 1859), a place widely reputed to be among the worst examples of Aboriginal repression,[15] the reality of law in everyday life exhibited the continuing undercurrent of indigenous jurisdiction. Amenability to settler jurisdiction brought many indigenous *inter se* homicides to the Queensland courts from the 1860s.[16] Struggling to deal with the realities of Aboriginal difference, police, prosecutors, courts, and the executive council (responsible for clemency decisions in capital cases) were repeatedly faced with evidence that referred to experience and belief systems beyond their understanding.

Before the Supreme Court sitting in the northern city of Charters Towers in 1886, Aborigines Paddy and Wills were charged with murder of another man, Billy. The defendants and victim were described as "Aboriginal natives of Queensland." Billy was out of his country, having been recruited for employment on a pastoral station some 500 miles from his home. In indigenous space, Billy was probably in places where he was not welcome; Paddy at least was from a local people. There was counsel for defense but no interpreter; the judge later expressed some doubt about the defendants' ability to understand the trial adequately. The defense argued that the prisoners were ignorant of the laws of the country, an argument that built on evidence from the white station owner that indicated there was a "tribal" element in the killing: "generally if two blacks belonging to different tribes meet and one gets an opportunity to kill the other he will do it." There was little evidence of motive except some confessional evidence making the case more one of manslaughter. The judge told the jury "that the Prisoners' ignorance of the law, a preference for their own tribal observances was no excuse for or justification of the crime if they were satisfied of its commission, though it might be a subject of consideration by the Executive in the event of a conviction." In delivering their verdict after long deliberation, the jury found both men guilty and "strongly recommended them to mercy on the grounds of ignorance of the laws of the country."[17] This muted recognition of "tribal observances" thus affected a result that found its justification not in a discovery of motive but in a postulation of the defendants' ignorance of settler law.

For most settler Australians objectionable tribal practices were accompanied by incomprehensible tribal beliefs. The intrusion of Aboriginal belief systems into the courtroom persisted well into the years of protection regimes. In the mixed economy of the pastoral districts of northern and western Queensland, cattle stations relied on Aboriginal labor, usually employed after 1897 under the administration of the local protector (typically a police officer). At the Supreme Court sitting in Townsville in March 1913, one such Aboriginal worker, Paddy Flynn, was convicted on a charge of fatally shooting another Aboriginal man, Roderick. The two had been among a large group of fifty to sixty Aboriginals employed on western pastoral stations who congregated at Hughenden after Christmas 1911, camping around a local hotel or on the river bank. Both men were well-regarded workers. Interviewed by the police, Paddy Flynn said "that he shot Deceased because the Deceased had given him a bone or poisoned shell," a hostile act reputed to be an act of sorcery. In court the same justification led to some debate over the nature of Aboriginal belief. In spite of the strong direction of the judge regarding evidence of willful murder, the jury found Flynn guilty of murder, but with "a strong recommendation to mercy owing to delusion through prisoner's tribal beliefs." Although the rider had no legal force it was the kind of thing calculated to weigh in an executive consideration of clemency.[18] As the police inspector first reported the case, drawing on the amateur ethnography that commonly characterized police practice, "I have known for years past that Aboriginals have a strange superstition in respect to the giving of a bone, and a great many of them believe that there are certain aboriginals who have the power to kill them with a bone which has been taken from the dead body of an aboriginal."[19] The standing of such accounts of sorcery, like allusions to any kind of indigenous beliefs and practices, was unstable in the policing and court systems. Such accounts were capable of attracting notice, although they rarely provoked detailed inquiry for the purpose of establishing criminal responsibility or mitigating guilt and amenability to the penal tariff at this time of capital punishment. Yet they had the potential to persuade juries, judges, and executive council that they were dealing with other, impenetrable, worlds that needed to be judged somehow differently to the usual run of defendants.

Such cases from the judicial and executive record suggest the impediments to achieving a knowledge of beliefs and practice—a translation of one set of cultural understandings into another—that would render these indigenous people subjects of a uniform jurisdiction.[20] At the end of the nineteenth century this difference was institutionalized through the development of a comprehensive protection system. In Queensland the *Aboriginals Protection and Restriction of the Sale of Opium Act, 1897* established a model of population management that proved influential in other jurisdictions, especially Western Australia—where protection was established in 1905—and later the Northern Territory under Commonwealth administration (1911). Just at the point when the Australian colonies were federating, for what proved initially to be a limited set of national objectives—especially the protection and advancement of a "White Australia," the object of the Commonwealth's first legislative instrument—the distinctive administrative regimes of the established colonies in respect of indigenous peoples hardened. A critical result in the context we are addressing here was the preservation of a patchwork of jurisdictional arrangements in which the comprehensive jurisdiction implied in *Murrell* continued to be sacrificed to the varying demands of legal, policing, reformatory, and administrative regimes. Thus, after 1897, and beyond Federation in 1901, the amenability of most Aborigines in Queensland to the standard procedures (and procedural protections) of the criminal law was significantly affected by protection.

The extreme paternalism of this system is well known, its subjection of Aboriginal people to an absolutist welfare control with executive powers of removal from one place to another especially notorious. What is less well known is the infra-legal structure of authority in the reserves and missions administered under the regime of a chief protector. These were places in which the quotidian routines of policing and law court were set aside for the sake of transforming Aboriginal subjects into the governable and rights-bearing subjects of Australian law, at some point in the indefinite future. The scope of these regimes in objective and method may be learned from the diaries of the missionary Rev William Mackenzie of Aurukun, a mission on the western side of the Cape York Peninsula "ruled" by Mackenzie for some four decades from 1925. Mackenzie ruled his subjects with an iron fist, sometimes literally, but always with the object of effecting the transformation of individuals and community into the God-fearing citizenry that might one day emerge from his transformative regime, were they to survive its excesses. Thus evidence of abortion was not prosecuted but made the subject of homily; adulterers were lectured and punished; homicides in some cases not prosecuted but made the occasion of removal to the Palm Island settlement. Mackenzie's punishments were harsh, unorthodox, and arbitrary. They included the use of banishment, corporal punishment, flogging and beating, use of his fists, the "electro magnet," and binding the mouth with tape to stop verbal abuse and swearing. Not surprisingly, his subjects were not beyond protesting his regime. An inquiry by the chief protector, prompted by an anonymous complaint, found the punishments justified. Anthropologists visiting Aurukun were appalled by the brutality. In 1932 one of them, Donald Thomson, photographed three men and two women in chains at Aurukun, at the start of their long trek under police escort to Palm Island. Thomson aired his complaints and photograph in a Melbourne newspaper but failed to get the Presbyterian Church or government at any level to intervene.[21]

In such a domain the spaces administered under a chief protector based in Brisbane were environments in which Aboriginal difference was sustained, mostly for worse than better. The most serious interpersonal offences were indeed brought before the Queensland criminal courts between 1897 and 1940; but when the realities of Aboriginal life circumstances rendered prosecution uncertain, inconvenient, or too expensive, an alternative to the criminal court was banishment by executive order. After the Palm Island settlement was established in 1918, it not only served as a place for removal of the troublesome in other districts but also became a place of exile for those who had committed murder or manslaughter, either subsequent to formal trial and sentence or in place of these.

Prosecutors as well as police and protectors worked in and around the law to secure their objective of removing the troublesome from the fringes of white settlement and into the centers of segregated black reserves. Even into the 1930s the negotiations around difficult cases involving killings express discomfort in dealing with cultures and practices that remained opaque. In 1934 a trial of a number of Aboriginal men from the Herberton region in north Queensland went badly wrong for defense counsel and police after defense applied successfully for a separate trial of the person regarded as the principal in a killing. Sixty-five-year-old Alick Brown had died after being subjected to treatment widely reported as involving a ritual "cleaning" ceremony, during which pieces of flesh had been cut from his back. Reported in the Brisbane papers, the case was sensational and occasioned a flurry of correspondence from pastoral stations that employed some of the men. Police reports spoke of some of the defendants as Aboriginal "doctors" skilled in the use of "Aboriginal weapons of war." As one pastoralist reported in an allegation passed up the line through the police hierarchy, "both Wild Jimmy & Jacob are looked upon as Doctors amongst the other blacks... The blacks all state that what ever the Doctor's [*sic*] tell them to do they have got to do it, or else the Doctor's will kill them." While the defense tactic of applying for separate trials for the five defendants succeeded in the acquittal of the alleged principal (Jacob), the others, seemingly less culpable, were found guilty and punished with terms of imprisonment. In a remarkable commentary on the way in which such people were now caught in the tidal flows between courts, policing, and administrative regimes, the consequences of acquittal or conviction seemed to make little difference. Agreeing with the sentiments of another station owner that it would be best for "Wild Jimmy" to be "kept in confinement for the rest of his life," police before the trial had already initiated steps to have the chief protector make arrangements for their "freedom to be restricted as they are a cause of dread to the blacks and whites, who reside in the District." In the event, "Wild Jimmy" was convicted and received the heaviest sentence of five years, while the acquitted Jacob was dealt with in the alternative register of the chief protector's office. As described by the sub-inspector of police at Cairns, "The Aboriginal Department was advised of the character of Jacob, and the fact that he had been found not guilty, with the result that instructions were received that an order for his removal to Woorabinda Aboriginal Mission Station [in the south] was issued and he was escorted there."[22]

Evidence of Aboriginal ritual associated with this killing was once more a sign of the incomplete transformation of indigenous people into fully responsible subjects of the common law, justifying their continuing subordination through the Protection regime. The more intensive settlement of Queensland, reflected in its more comprehensive policing and Aboriginal protectorate, made such cases rarer than might be encountered across its western border, in a territory that since 1911 was also a responsibility of the Commonwealth government. In what follows, we see another kind of history: the distinctive combination of a majority indigenous population (their languages and cultures intact) in a jurisdiction overseen by the national government, its policies informed by new knowledges (especially anthropology). Contributing to an expanding patchwork of jurisdictions in mid-twentieth-century Australia, such regional histories render the jurisdictional uniformity announced in *Murrell* into little more than an aspiration, its comprehensive reach qualified by other forces of government and the persistence of indigenous cultures.

III

A century after *Murrell* the realities of governing in domains that were marginal to effective jurisdiction were brought home repeatedly to the Australian government by a sequence of well-publicized trials of Aboriginal men in the Northern Territory. Inside the territorial spaces of Australian jurisdiction lay domains of social life that were still little comprehended by non-indigenous observers and beyond the ken of the judiciary and policymakers. The problems presented to government policy in the administration of justice were many, and they all flowed from the persisting sense of a separate indigenous world—one in which actions and belief lay outside the realm understood within Australian courts.

Prior to 1884 there were no murder trials held in the Northern Territory, which was a territory of South Australia and was thus administered from Adelaide. The problems of administering justice in small communities on the fringes of country that was still frontier were brought home time and again from the date of the first trial in 1884 up to the eve of World War I. In 1913 the single judge of the Supreme Court sitting in the Northern Territory (since 1911 a jurisdiction under the Commonwealth) and the administrator of the territory together viewed jury trials as unreliable in their outcomes, especially in cases involving Aborigines.[23] "In my mind," wrote the administrator to the minister,

> there is no doubt that it would be impossible to secure a jury in the Territory which would convict a white man of the murder of a native solely on aboriginal evidence, no matter however strong; while there would be comparatively little difficulty in securing the conviction of a native for killing a white man on much more slender evidence. In this the Judge concurs.[24]

By 1921, the management of justice in small communities in which juries might be suborned or biased resulted in trial by jury being abolished in the Northern Territory for crimes other than capital offences.

Justice on Australia's northern frontiers proved a headache to the national government through the interwar years, especially in the 1930s. When prosecutors, police, and courts attempted to deploy the criminal law to respond to Aboriginal offending they faced intractable problems that forced constant policy change to accommodate Aboriginal difference. Were Aboriginal wives compellable witnesses? Progressive opinion in Canberra and Sydney said no, informed by an increasingly influential anthropology based on fieldwork in northern Australia. A protracted and often ill-tempered policy debate canvassed legal opinions that considered not only the prior colonial case law (of Victoria and NSW) but also cases and statute law from New Zealand and South Africa. The government finalized the matter in the *Aboriginals Ordinance 1937* by declaring that "any Aboriginal living as consort, husband or wife of any Aboriginal" charged with a summary or indictable offence was not compelled to give evidence against the person charged.[25]

Should evidence of Aboriginal custom play a role in adjudging guilt and determining punishment? A radical nostrum of the interwar years drew on Australian colonial experience in Papua and New Guinea, where Governor Hubert Murray had created a "native court."[26] In the early 1930s a "native court" for the Northern Territory was favored by some government members (especially the chief protector of Aborigines) and anthropologists. But the scheme's proposals for a completely separate jurisdiction in which the relevance of native custom to offending would be recognized and capital punishment abolished went beyond the Murray scheme and faced strong judicial objection. The result was a more modest if distinctive amendment to the Northern Territory criminal law. A 1934 amendment to the Crimes Ordinance directed the court to receive evidence as "to any relevant native law or custom" in mitigation of penalty.[27] That amending legislation also entailed a partial abolition of the death penalty, with the penalty becoming discretionary only for Aboriginal defendants convicted of murder. When the Northern Territory's sole judge (T.A. Wells) later failed to exercise his discretion and sentenced eight Aboriginal defendants to death for the murder of two white prospectors, there was a public outcry in the metropolitan southeast. Anthropologist A.P. Elkin was influential publicly and behind the scenes, urging the relevance of Aboriginal justice ("a revenge expedition") as a motive in the killings, and the government responded with clemency.[28]

Behind these policy and judicial struggles with the conditions in Australia's north, there remained other procedural challenges, a consequence of both geographical and cultural conditions. These issues were compellingly brought to attention in the 1940 prosecution of Jakala, a youth charged with the murder by spearing of an Aboriginal elder during a tribal "affray" in Arnhem Land. After the judge dismissed the jury in a protest against inadequate accommodation, it was suggested within the administration that the Crown might enter a *nolle prosequi*. This was consistent with the reluctance of other observers to see this case prosecuted: a local missionary's cabled report of the killing expressed fears that it would be "difficult prevent further loss life in revenge... [p]ersonally do not desire legal action but think removal murderer Darwin for formal questioning would satisfy everyone."[29] The response of law officers was to recommend a change in procedure for Aboriginal defendants. The discourse informing the change exhibits a remarkable degree of continuity with that which puzzled over jurisdiction in *inter se* killings a century ago. J.A. Carrodus, the long-serving secretary of the department of the interior, preferred a principle of noninterference in purely Aboriginal disputes. His advice to the minister reflected a view that killings in Aboriginal communities should be viewed contextually. Public policy should have regard primarily to securing peace and not so much the protection of individual subjects:

> I think it is a great pity that these natives were brought in for trial. The killing occurred in country which was not under control and where the natives are living according to native custom. Unless there are a large number of killings and it is essential that peace be brought about by the Government

> interference, I am of opinion that the Administration should not interfere in these tribal disputes.[30]

As in Queensland, such policy advice did not contemplate an absolute indifference to conditions on Aboriginal lands, since lurking in the background was always the possibility of the exercise of a protector's powers of removal of troublesome elements, without the difficult business of a trial to establish guilt or innocence. Such powers continued into the postwar years, amplified by the development in the Northern Territory of a new style of administration centered on the role of patrol officers in a welfare system that was intended to circumscribe the responsibilities of police. The Patrol Officer administration—its officers were trained to the task in a way unknown to the police—was interventionist but more finely attuned to procedural justice. When in 1956 a patrol officer advised Darwin that, "whether guilty or not," a suspect in the killing of two Aboriginal men might be "removed to a southern district for at least ten years," his superior annotated heavily in blue pencil, "Guilty or not ten years banishment? Democracy!"[31] In the 1959 case of Timmy, a man who feared payback in spite of his acquittal on a charge of murder, the chief welfare officer commented,

> I would respectfully point out that we would be acting in contempt of court if we were to commit Timmy to Beswick Creek [a northern Aboriginal settlement], because he was found Not Guilty in the Supreme Court and was discharged by the Judge. If we were to take further action by a committal, then it could be argued that we did not agree with the processes of law and had, in fact, pre-judged the defendant'[32]

The kind of thinking that had contemplated a native court as a solution for jurisdiction in cases of Aborigines living outside the effective boundaries of white settlement infused midcentury thinking at a number of levels in the Northern Territory administration, providing compelling evidence of negotiation between the domains of law and welfare. Evidence of the use of infanticide in desert communities during times of food scarcity resulted in a departmental consensus that "with regard to infanticide the constructive approach should be stressed rather than the punitive one."[33] An alleged killing at Ti Tree in 1954 was considered by the patrol officer investigating to be entirely explicable in terms of the cultural status of the suspected defendants:

> The defendants in this action can best be described as bush people of a semi-nomadic nature who have lived within the influence of their tribal law during the whole of their lifetime.... tribal law is still the dominating

> factor governing the lives and habits of the greater majority of natives in this District.[34]

At the heart of many murder trials in the Northern Territory in the 1950s was the dilemma of adjudication in a context of such contested cultural commitments, prompting the first sustained Australian judicial reflections on the problem. The single justice of the Territory Supreme Court in this decade was Judge Martin Kriewaldt, a judicial officer of Lutheran background.[35] Kriewaldt was determined that Australian justice should prevail over Aboriginal violence, but that its impact in penal consequences be mediated by a regard for the context of offending, mentality, and life circumstances. In 1959, not long before his premature death, and at a time when he was still composing an extended treatise on the application of the criminal law to Aborigines in the Territory, he presided over a case typical of his experience. In the western desert community of Papunya two men had died after what appeared to be a punishment spearing directed at one of them. Tried before a jury on charges of murder, one man, Timmy, was acquitted (and subsequently removed from the community for his safety) and another, Jack Wheeler, found guilty of manslaughter. In sentencing remarks, Kriewaldt J. was brief but incisive.

> I cannot allow myself to be influenced in this case by the failure of the authorities to bring well merited prosecutions in respect of the other non-fatal spearings. I have also come to the conclusion that since the criminal law is one of the means which must be used as an aid in the process of the assimilation of the Australian aboriginal into an integrated community, the sentence must give the aborigines at Papunyah notice that spearing will not be tolerated.

In coming to his conclusion that a sentence of 16 months for manslaughter was appropriate in this case, Kriewaldt balanced two considerations: one that the death was indeed accidental, since "in the majority of cases where aboriginals spear each other, death does not follow"; the other that although the defendant had little contact with "white civilization" he was then living in a government settlement and "obviously the custom of 'pay back' cannot be permitted to continue on settlements staffed by Government officials."[36]

Kriewaldt's reasoning highlighted the unease still prevailing in the exercise of criminal jurisdiction in this Australian territory. In a direction to the jury in the related prosecution of Timmy, Kriewaldt had already alluded to that unease, centered on the question of whether an "Aboriginal native" should be tried in the same court and by same rules as "a white person." As he commented, "[p]eople have argued for 150 years or more whether this is a good thing. Perhaps it is, perhaps it is not."[37] When Kriewaldt justified sentencing not on the basis of the characteristics of the offence (motive, aggravation, consequences) but on the necessity of drawing a line in the sand against the custom of "payback" surviving in a government settlement, he also illuminated the intersection of law and governance regimes. In this respect he stood in the long line of those—judges, administrators, protectors, and anthropologists—who looked to law as an instrument for the shaping of a particular type of person, and a particular kind of community: one void of Aboriginal jurisdiction. In other ways Kriewaldt's self-conscious conclusion was consistent with the development of his original contribution to an approach to sentencing that would take account of the conditions of Aboriginal life while asserting the authority of the court and government policy. In that respect he initiated a contemporary discourse that grapples still with the consequences of criminal jurisdiction over indigenous peoples in Australia.

Conclusion

In the contemporary era, pre- and post-*Mabo* (1992), the High Court of Australia has been consistent in its affirmation of the jurisdictional reach of the criminal law. *Mabo* made no difference to this fundamental postulate. When Aboriginal activist Dennis Walker optimistically challenged the jurisdiction of the court in 1994 he was slapped down without hesitation by Chief Justice Sir Anthony Mason:

> In Mabo (No.2), the Court held that there was no inconsistency between native title being held by people of Aboriginal descent and the underlying radical title being vested in the Crown. There is no analogy with the criminal law. English criminal law did not, and Australian criminal law does not, accommodate an alternative body of law operating alongside it. There is nothing in Mabo (No.2) to provide any support at all for the proposition that criminal laws of general application do not apply to Aboriginal people.[38]

Such judicial affirmations of the general reach of the criminal law do not comprehend the history on which they rest. From *Murrell* to *Mabo* the courts in Australia asserted jurisdiction but the stories briefly traced here show the distance between territorial jurisdiction's aspiration and its shortcomings in adjudicating over indigenous peoples. In the century after *Murrell* those shortcomings were recognized and addressed through the multiplication of regimes, institutional and statutory. These regimes, taking different forms across time and space, constituted a governance of indigenous peoples in which amenability to Australian criminal law was a threshold crossed in exceptional circumstances and with exceptional consequences.

The persistent intrusion of indigenous difference exhibits a remarkable continuity through more than two centuries of Australian settler history, constantly raising the possibility of an alternative body of law and practice that government policy and criminal justice institutions have struggled to understand and contain. From Macquarie's uneasy assertion of jurisdiction in 1816 to the Howard Government's ill-informed "abolition" of the so-called "customary law defence" in 2007, government in Australia has struggled to come to terms with indigenous claims and dispositions that are at odds with the immigrant cultures of the Australian settlement. The archaeological work of excavating the law as it is practiced, avoided, or subverted helps us to understand why jurisdiction remains less complete than contemplated by Burton J. in *Murrell* in 1836.

Notes

1. Research for this chapter has been assisted by the Australian Research Council (DP0771492). I am grateful to John Myrtle and Jonathan Richards for research assistance; to Ian Hunter and Lisa Ford for their comments on an earlier draft; and to the participants at the "Transpositions of Empire" symposium in Prato, April 2009 for the stimulus of their own work and conversations.
2. *Crimes Act* 1914 (Cth), s16A(2A).
3. Lisa Ford, *Settler Sovereignty: Jurisdiction and Indigenous People in America and Australia, 1788–1836* (Cambridge, MA: Harvard University Press, 2010), p. 183.
4. P.G. McHugh, *Aboriginal Societies and the Common Law: A History of Sovereignty, Status, and Self-determination* (Oxford: Oxford University Press, 2004), pp. 159–64.
5. Shaunnagh Dorsett and Shaun McVeigh, "Just So: 'The Law Which Governs Australia is Australian Law,'" *Law and Critique*, 13 (2002), 289–309 (p. 296).
6. Bruce Kercher, "The Recognition of Aboriginal Status and Laws in the Supreme Court of New South Wales Under Forbes CJ, 1824–1836," in *Land and Freedom: Law, Property Rights and The British Diaspora*, ed. A.R. Buck, John McLaren and Nancy E. Wright (Aldershot: Ashgate, 2001), pp. 93–97; Alex C. Castles, *An Australian Legal History* (Sydney: Law Book Co., 1982), pp. 526–29.
7. There is not space here to document the extensive literature, governmental and research, which developed around customary law: see especially Australian

Law Reform Commission, *The Recognition of Aboriginal Customary Laws*, Report No. 31 (Canberra: Australian Government Printing Service, 1986); Western Australia Law Reform Commission, *The Interaction of Western Australian Law with Aboriginal Law and Culture: Final Report*, Report No. 94 (Perth: Law Reform Commission of Western Australia, 2006).

8. For the most recent accounts see Grace Karskens, *The Colony: A History of Early Sydney* (Crows Nest, NSW: Allen & Unwin, 2009); Ford, *Settler Sovereignty*; Alan Atkinson, *The Europeans in Australia. A History. Volume I: The Beginning*, 2 vols. (Melbourne: Oxford University Press, 1997); Inga Clendinnen, *Dancing with Strangers* (Melbourne: Text Publishing, 2003).
9. Karskens, *Colony*, pp. 440–42.
10. Proclamation by His Excellency Lachlan Macquarie…, May 4, 1816, in *Historical Records of Australia: Series I, Governors' Despatches to and from England* [*HRA*], ed. Frederick Watson, 26 vols. (Sydney: Committee of the Commonwealth Parliament, 1914–1925), Series 1, IX, pp. 141–45.
11. Lisa Ford, "Indigenous Policy and Its Historical Occlusions: The North American and Global Contexts of Australian Settlement," *Australian Indigenous Law Review*, 12 (2008), 69–80.
12. "Miscellaneous Correspondence Relating to Aborigines, 1797–1840," State Records NSW (SRNSW), NRS 13696 [5/1161], doc 41, on-line at *Original Documents on Aborigines and Law 1797–1840*, <http://www.law.mq.edu.au/scnsw/Correspondence/documents.htm> [accessed February 9, 2010]. In this respect the case compares with that of *Rangitapiripiri* in New Zealand in 1847, indicted for murder of another Māori, who was brought in for trial by his own people: Shaunnagh Dorsett, "'Sworn on the Dirt of Graves': Sovereignty, Jurisdiction and the Judicial Abrogation of 'Barbarous' Customs in New Zealand in the 1840s," *The Journal of Legal History*, 30 (2009), 175–97 (p. 186).
13. *R v Murrell*, 1836 (Supreme Court NSW), <http://www.austlii.edu.au/au/journals/AILR/1998/27.html> [accessed February 9, 2010].
14. Ann Hunter, "The Boundaries of Colonial Criminal Law in Relation to Inter-Aboriginal Conflict ('Inter Se Offences') in Western Australian in the 1830s–1840s," *Australian Journal of Legal History*, 8 (2004), 215–36; Libby Connors, "Traditional Law and Indigenous Resistance at Moreton Bay 1842–1855," *ANZLH-Ejournal*, 107–17 (2005) < http://www.anzlhsejournal.auckland.ac.nz/pdfs_2005/Connors.pdf> [accessed February 9, 2010]; Simon Cooke, "Arguments for the Survival of Aboriginal Customary Law in Victoria: A Case Note on R v Peter (1860) and R v Jemmy (1860)," *Australian Journal of Legal History*, 5 (1999), 201–41; Damen Ward, "Constructing British Authority in Australasia: Charles Cooper and the Legal Status of Aborigines in the South Australian Supreme Court, c. 1840–60," *Journal of Imperial and Commonwealth History*, 34 (2006), 483–504.
15. For McHugh: "In Queensland Aboriginal peoples unluckily under officialdom's ken truly experienced a terrible century of suppression and confinement," qtd. in McHugh, *Aboriginal Societies*, p. 281; and see generally Rosalind Kidd, *The Way We Civilise: Aboriginal Affairs—the Untold Story*

(St Lucia, Qld: University of Queensland Press, 1997); Thom Blake, *A Dumping Ground: A History of the Cherbourg Settlement* (St Lucia, Qld: University of Queensland Press, 2001).

16. Mark Finnane and Jonathan Richards, "Aboriginal Violence and State Response: Histories, Policies, Legacies in Queensland 1860–1940," *Australia New Zealand Journal of Criminology*, 2010 (forthcoming).
17. "*R v Paddy and Wills*," 1886, Queensland State Archives [QSA], EXE/4: sentences commuted.
18. "Re death of Roderick on 30 Dec 1912," QSA, A/49730, 95N; sentence commuted to life imprisonment: see "Record of death sentences," QSA, PRI/19.
19. "Re death of Roderick on 30 Dec 1912," QSA, A/49730, 95N. For police as amateur ethnographers, see Amanda Nettelbeck and Robert Foster, *In the Name of the Law: William Willshire and the Policing of the Australian Frontier* (Kent Town, S. Aust.: Wakefield Press, 2007); and Derek John Mulvaney, Alison Petch and Howard Morphy, *From the Frontier: Outback Letters to Baldwin Spencer* (St Leonards, NSW: Allen & Unwin, 2000).
20. For more, see the contributions to the present volume by Hunter and Walters.
21. Diaries of WF Mackenzie, AIATSIS Library (Canberra), MSS 2483; for some of the context see Kidd, *The Way We Civilise*, pp. 118–22; Peter Sutton, *The Politics of Suffering: Indigenous Australia and the End of the Liberal* (Carlton, VIC: Melbourne University Press, 2009), pp. 1–5, 106–7, 178.
22. "Alick Brown Murdered," QSA, POL/512N.
23. "Trials for Murder N.T.," Judge David Bevan, December 3, 1913, National Archives of Australia [NAA], NAA: A3 (A3/1), NT1914/426.
24. "Trials for Murder N.T.," J.A. Gilruth to Minister for External Affairs (P.M. Glynn), September 27, 1913, NAA: A3 (A3/1), NT1914/426.
25. *Aboriginals Ordinance (No. 2)* 1937 (N.T.), s. 2; "Aboriginal Prisoners—Wives as Compellable Witnesses," NAA: F1 1938/536; Tony Austin, *Never Trust a Government Man: Northern Territory Aboriginal Policy 1911–1939* (Darwin: Northern Territory University Press, 1997), pp. 242–44.
26. Francis James West, *Hubert Murray: The Australian Pro-Consul* (Melbourne; New York [etc.]: Oxford University Press, 1968), pp. 38–45, 216–35.
27. *Crimes Ordinance* 1934 (N.T.), s. 2(6A).
28. Austin, *Never Trust*, pp. 226–27; and see "Alleged Murder of Kock and Arinsky by Aborigines," NAA, A659 (A659/1), 1939/1/9949.
29. "The King v Jackala," Director of Native Affairs, April 9, 1940, NAA: A432, 1940/377.
30. "The King v Jackala," minute of J.A. Carrodus, April 17, 1940, NAA: A432, 1940/377. For contrasting assessments of Carrodus see Austin, *Never Trust*, pp. 231–32; and Andrew Markus, *Governing Savages* (Sydney: Allen & Unwin, 1990), pp. 122–29.
31. "Trial of Bullfrog," NAA: F1, F1/0, 1955/172.
32. "Papunya—Tribal Killing," NAA: F1 F1/0, 1959/1502.
33. "Tribal Murders—Reports and Investigations," Walpiri 1954, NAA: F1, F1/0, 1955/172.

34. "Tribal Murders—Reports and Investigations," McCoy, November 24, 1954, NAA: F1, F1/0, 1955/172.
35. Heather Douglas, "Justice Kriewaldt, Aboriginal Identity and the Criminal Law," *Criminal Law Journal*, 26 (2002), 204–22.
36. "Papunya—Tribal Killing," sentencing remarks by Justice M. Kriewaldt, August 19, 1959, NAA: F1 F1/0, 1959/1502. For Kriewaldt's own reflections see: Martin Kriewaldt, "The Application of the Criminal Law to the Aborigines of the Northern Territory of Australia," *University of Western Australia Law Review*, 5 (1960), 1–50.
37. Kriewaldt J, "Summing up remarks, in *R v Aboriginal Timmy*, 18 Aug 1959," in John McCorquodale, *Aborigines and the Law: A Digest* (Canberra: Aboriginal Studies Press for the Australian Institute of Aboriginal Studies, 1987), p. 364.
38. *Walker v the State of New South Wales* (1994) 182 CLR 45 (High Court of Australia), para. 6.

Chapter 9

The Pig and the Peace

Transposing Order in Early Sydney

Lisa Ford

On October 29, 1795, the shooting of a pregnant pig caused a ruckus in Sydney. When Private William Faithful shot a "very fine sow," her owner, John Boston, ran into the street "in a riotous manner" demanding to know "where is the damned Villain of a Rascal who has shot my Pig."[1] Either Quartermaster Thomas Laycock or Lieutenant Neil McKellar ordered private Faithful to defend the honor of the New South Wales Corps in manly fashion. In one version, Mr. Laycock is reported to have called, "do you hear, this man calls you a Rascal, do you take that—give him a damned good threshing."[2] Faithful dutifully beat Boston on the street in front of a crowd of soldiers and convicts. Faithful was not prosecuted for breaching public order, so Boston sued Faithful, Laycock, and bystander Private William Addy for trespass in assault and battery in the court of civil jurisdiction seeking £500 compensation.

Boston v Laycock (1795) may have had inauspicious beginnings, but it ended as one of the most important decisions ever handed down in the colony of New South Wales.[3] This was because the death of Boston's pig, the street brawl, and the court's decision all revolved around a dilemma central to the constitution of the British Empire: what sort of Peace could be transposed from the metropolis to its colonial peripheries? The defendants declared that they kept a soldier's Peace in this fragile convict-ridden outpost. Boston argued for a commercial Peace where he could cuss and trade free from military tyranny. The court responded in a way that was bound to endear it to lawyers. It declared that New South Wales was not beyond the reach of the rule of law. Soldiers in Sydney, like soldiers in London, had no special right to beat civilians in defense of the Peace. Despite the fact that New South Wales was an open prison, populated with rebels and riffraff, the New South Wales Corps was bound within the King's Peace.

Behind this triumph of law lurks an important story about the legal transposition of empire. The very fact that a street brawl turned into an examination of the nature of the King's Peace in the colony is remarkable. Though the "King's Peace" is a vague term, one that has "passed into common use as a kind of ornament of speech, without any clear sense of its historical meaning," it invokes the sovereign's jurisdiction to order people in space.[4] When we think of the Peace, we think of the state's capacity to curb its everyday disturbance by brawlers, revelers, and noisy neighbors. We are thinking both of a series of porous, public performances of order and of key sticks in the "bundle of rights" constituting sovereignty.[5] These were sticks gathered by the English Crown and disputed by subjects and colonists over centuries. Indeed, as a legal idea, the King's Peace comprehends all of the mysteries of early modern state-making in the British Isles, and many of the deepest constitutional questions about empire abroad, all of which were hotly debated at the end of the eighteenth century. The litigants' efforts to define the place of soldiers in Peace-keeping in *Boston v Laycock* in 1795, then, engaged British imperial sovereignty at a time when it was in rapid flux. As a result, their dispute tells us much about the nature of British imperial order and its instantiation far from home in this period.

The King's Peace

The importance of *Boston v Laycock* as a case study in the transposition of empire rests on the fact that the King's Peace was an inherently flexible and contestable notion in the late eighteenth century. This was so first because the Peace rested on a collection of everyday performances of order that were particularly fraught on colonial peripheries. As the Peace was law *and* public spectacle it was always open to public interpretation and contest. In early New South Wales, however, the Peace was particularly open to dispute. In a convict colony graced with some soldiers, a handful of free settlers, and a skeletal justice system, every voice mattered in discussions of the nature of colonial order. Second, crown authority to keep the Peace at home and in the colonies was still deeply contested at the end of the eighteenth century and the soldiers and settlers of New South Wales had an impressive grasp of global Anglophone debates about the constitutional limits of military power.

The institutions and legal meaning of the King's Peace changed so fundamentally between Saxon times and the late eighteenth century that the term is little more than an empty shell filled with competing ideas about the mechanics of crown jurisdiction. According to Pollock and Maitland, the phrase came into use in Saxon times "when the king's protection was not universal but particular, when the king's peace was not for all men or all places, and the king's highway was in a special manner protected by it."[6] The king's jurisdiction settled only on "the king's house," the king's roads, and the "king's attendants and servants": concentrated sites or emissaries of sovereign power.[7] Margaret Kelly traces its extension over the "English Nation" to the tenth century, when Edward the Elder (900–924) and his successors made it a crime to disobey the king's orders, made local outlawry into outlawry throughout the kingdom, and began to use the language of a universal Peace.[8] The Peace was extended further when the Norman Conquest gave the king paramount title, and with it both unprecedented power over the landed gentry and the potential to intervene in local governance. Then chapters 17 to 19 of the Magna Carta sought to make the King's Courts the final arbiters of justice, at least in matters of real property law. They stipulated fixed sessions for his courts and institutionalized the principle of the local administration of royal justice.[9] The upshot, according to Fitzjames Stephen, was that "instead of being a local and exceptional state of things, [the King's Peace] became the permanent and universal guarantee for public security" in public consciousness.[10] Yet, in reality, it was still far from universal. The lore of universal Peace outstripped the reality of myriad overlapping and circumscribed jurisdictions: royal, manorial, commercial, and municipal.

Despite the language of universality, then, the medieval and early modern King's Peace relied on partial performances of order. Certain people in certain places were particularly charged with performing universal Peace. Constables and judges in courthouses were only the most obvious of these. The public in general and the urban public in particular were also crucial collaborators in performing the Peace. Trials and arrests could not occur without neighborly assertions of rights, orderly behavior, or even calling out "murder," as Boston did when Faithful struck him in 1795.[11] The importance of public collaboration to the Peace is clear in Peter Goodrich's analysis of the fourteenth-century case *William de Thorp v Mackerel and another*. In this case, Mackerel was held in contempt of court when he "pissed on" the "king's sworn clerk" who had been attacked by someone else on a street "some one and a half miles from the court" building.[12] It was not clear that he had done anything wrong. There was no law against public urination and Mackerel did not injure the clerk. Yet, a court read Mackerel's urination as a dangerous attack upon the king and his court. In so doing, it privileged law officers as bearers of the Peace and marked urban streets (like courthouses) as theaters where the Peace was to be specially performed and defended.[13] In the process, however, the court also demonstrated Mackerel's special capacity as a member of the public to challenge the King's Peace by the simplest of actions. This case suggests that every voice mattered in daily performances of the King's Peace, as did every bodily function.

Mackerel was a vindictive passerby in one of many early modern English towns. In New South Wales in 1795, the brawl between Boston and the New South Wales Corps constituted a much more obvious and important rupture of the illusion of universal Peace. *Boston v Laycock* occurred in a nascent colonial town: the only place where a plausible imitation of order could be maintained. It involved some of the most important and notorious free men in the colony: free businessmen and members of the New South Wales Corps. They represented two major and opposing interests in a settlement largely comprised of convict men and women who themselves constituted a threat to public order. When the parties to *Boston v Laycock* brawled, everyone saw. When they disagreed in court over how best to keep the Peace, everyone heard. Indeed, as the participants knew as much about the law as most of their lay judges, their arguments carried disproportionate weight in the colony. If Mackerel's urination showed the contestability of Peace in early modern England, then this public spat in early Sydney shook the little colony at its legal foundations.

The importance of *Boston v Laycock* stems not only from the fact that the colonial public had special power to perform and contest the Peace in early New South Wales. The parties asked questions of the imperial constitution that neither the public nor the government could answer. Their disagreement centered on the unresolved role of soldiers in Peace-keeping, one of the most contentious constitutional questions in the history of Britain and its empire. From the time of the Tudors and Stuarts, who strove to keep the Peace more comprehensively than any monarchs before them, the role of the military in keeping civil order figured in every major constitutional crisis in the archipelago.[14] The English Civil War and the Glorious Revolution both turned not just on the power of the king to legislate and adjudicate, but also on the practical limits of the king's power to use the military against his subjects. Likewise, the "third" English Revolution, the American War of Independence, began with a recitation of the king's failure to use soldiers appropriately to keep the Peace in North America.[15]

The role of the military in Peace-keeping was difficult to resolve because, though the distinction between military and civilian law had medieval origins, the institutions of the standing army and the centrally appointed magistracy were relatively modern. Lines between military and civilian justice had long been muddy. The medieval militia was a key component of local governance. Militiamen were organized first by sheriffs and then by constables in medieval English parishes, and local keepers of the peace oversaw not only local justice but local defense as well.[16] However, after a century of post-Reformation warfare and the advent of the Stuart monarchy, Parliament demanded that these muddy lines be redrawn. In 1628, Parliament entered into a long debate about arbitrary arrest, soldier-billeting, civilian-impressment, and the application of martial law to soldiers and civilians in peace time.[17] The administration of justice and the standing army likewise figured heavily in the debates that culminated in the 1689 Bill of Rights.[18] By 1780, the use of the military in the preservation of the Peace at home had become so fraught that Gordon rioters burned down the house of Lord Mansfield before the mayor of London felt he could call in the military to suppress the riot. Afterward the Parliament protested against the use of "soldiers against civilians in a time of peace."[19]

If the military's role in keeping the King's Peace was disputed at home; soldiers in the colonies seemed to be governed according to different rules. General Gage's liberal use of the military to keep the Peace in Quebec, New York, and Boston after 1763 precipitated the American Revolution.[20] Nor did the loss of the thirteen colonies in 1783 bring to an end the use of soldiers in Peace-keeping overseas. As Charles Townshend has noted, martial law was applied much more expansively in the colonies than in Britain, into the twentieth century.[21] No legal settlement in the metropolis in the 1780s, therefore, determined the role of the military in early New South Wales. When New South Wales was settled as a convict colony whose institutions were dominated first by marines, and then by soldiers, it seemed destined to provoke fresh conflict about the constitution of empire and the role of the military within it.

When Boston argued with the New South Wales Corps about the nature of the Peace and who could keep it in colonial Sydney, he raised one of the most important unresolved questions about crown authority at home and in the empire. Their dispute made a sensation because it was itself comprised of a series of very important breaches and performances of Peace by soldiers and free settlers in a tiny colonial town. What is most important about the case, however, are the very interesting ways that the parties defined the Peace in the colonies. Neither of them sought a simple transposition of late eighteenth-century law to New South Wales. Each acknowledged the problems attending the transposition of the King's Peace to colonial peripheries, both as a matter of law and as a matter of public performance. This is why, when they set about to define the nature and limits of military power in the colony of New South Wales, their debate echoed across the globe to London.

The Soldier's Peace

Of the four defendants in *Boston v Laycock*, Neil McKellar and William Faithful were the most vocal. In addition to questioning and cross-examining witnesses, they presented several missives to the court describing the nature of the Peace in New South Wales. These missives—which Governor Hunter feared represented views widely held in the colony—argued that a soldier's Peace predicated on honor, hierarchy, and violence was the only security against chaos in a colony filled with traitors and felons. The defense argued that William Faithful shot Boston's pig and later beat Boston because Boston threatened the soldier's Peace at a number of levels.

At the center of their defense lay a very important contention: that a soldier in New South Wales was in the position of "a Constable, or Peace Officer in England."[22] Soldiers were Peace-keepers, they argued, because New South Wales was in form and substance a military establishment and they were bound both by military law and by loyalty to the Crown to act as keepers of the Peace. They had a point. Institutionally, early New South Wales was a strange mix of martial and civilian legal institutions. According to Neal, the military's stated role in the colony was merely to protect the colony from invasion—foreign and indigenous—and to prevent armed rebellion. Everyday order was to be kept by constables, many of them convicts who answered to civilian magistrates.[23] In reality, however, the military's role in local governance was much more extensive and ambiguous.[24]

Soldiers and their military order pervaded local institutions. The colony's rudimentary court was staffed by a judge-advocate who was also a naval officer in 1795. He sat, in Boston's case, with an untrained civilian (senior assistant surgeon William Balmain) and a soldier (Captain Lieutenant George Johnston). Criminal cases were even more dominated by the military. They were heard before "six uniformed officers plus the Judge-Advocate."[25] As the courts had no courthouse and none of the other paraphernalia of civilian legal status, they likely relied on the taint of military ceremony to give them symbolic status as a keeper of orders in the colony.[26]

Government offices were distributed according to military rank. The governor of New South Wales was a military officer until the appointment of Governor Richard Bourke in 1831. As commanders in chief, governors of New South Wales wielded more power than most governors in the empire.[27] In 1795, Major Grose was second in command and lieutenant governor. When he gave "government orders," the rank and file of the New South Wales Corps understood them as military commands.[28] So, on July 17, 1793, when Grose proclaimed that "All hogs, seen in the Streets, that are not yoked, and have not rings in their noses, are ordered to be shot," his directive was read, simultaneously, as a civil and a military directive that soldiers were obliged to obey.[29] As defendant Neil McKellar put it,

> An order has been given by the Commander in Chief, that all Hogs, unyoked, and unringed, straying at large about the Town, were to be shot.—This order

> was considered as a Law... particularly addressed to the Soldiers. No Soldier therefore could pass a Hog in such Circumstances, without either destroying it, or subjecting himself to the Charge of contempt and disobedience.[30]

Quite apart from this peculiar institutional confusion, soldiers could argue that their formal duty to prevent invasion and rebellion in the colony invested them with a duty to keep the Peace in and around Sydney. The early colony was often in a state of undeclared war with Aborigines in the wilderness surrounding Sydney and soldiers were deployed repeatedly to capture or kill them.[31] More importantly, when *Boston v Laycock* was heard in 1795, the colony was filling rapidly with potential rebels. As Mark McKenna has pointed out, some 600 of 2000 "Irish convicts transported to New South Wales between 1791 and 1803 ... had been convicted of riot and sedition."[32] This was particularly worrying to free settlers, just two years after Louis XVI lost his head, and twelve years after Britain lost the thirteen colonies. Their potential for rebellion was realized in the so-called Irish Rebellion at Castle Hill in 1804.

Rebels aside, in 1795, New South Wales was essentially a colony of convicts. The convict population was concentrated in Sydney, making it a place where performances of the Peace were both important and fraught. As convicts, the vast majority of Sydney-siders had very little interest in preserving a system of government predicated on their legal subordination.[33] The convict population, moreover, mixed indiscriminately with the few free settlers and soldiers in town. From 1788 onward, Sydney-based convicts and soldiers were encouraged to shift for themselves in town for the many hours each day that they were not involved in mandatory work. Convicts earned wages for extra work, drank and gambled in their free time, built their own houses in disorder, and dressed in cheap finery.[34] They were in many respects indistinguishable from free people on the street. In such a place, as the soldier's saw it, the King's Peace could not be kept merely by neighborly behavior, litigious civilians, or civil constables who were convicts themselves.[35] Rather, the uniforms, rank, and hierarchy of soldiers were the only visible accoutrements of Peace to keep poorly regulated convicts and potential rebels in check. Where others, the governor included, saw a potential for qualified civilian order in which convicts took up the mantle of subjecthood, soldiers saw only chaotic intermingling, a breach of ordered hierarchy.[36]

Having established their special position in New South Wales, the defendants had to cast Boston's beating as an act of Peace-keeping. They did so by cataloging his breaches of the Peace. They argued, first and foremost, that Boston was himself a potential rebel whose leveling tendencies disturbed Peace in the colony. Though Boston came out with government approval to cure fish, he had associated with radicals in Birmingham and may have emigrated to avoid persecution.[37] He arrived on the ship *Surprise* with a group of Scottish radicals convicted of sedition for supporting the French Revolution.[38] Boston was singled out on that trip as a radical troublemaker. He was accused of inciting the convicts to mutiny.[39] Though no charges were laid against Boston, he arrived in New South Wales a notorious man. The defendant's noted that Boston was a threat to the colony and had "publickly [*sic*] drink [to] a Murder of his King."[40] He was a dangerous man who needed to be kept within a soldier's Peace.

Second, the defendants argued that Boston had breached the Peace by letting his pig run loose in town in defiance of an ordinance that soldiers had a special duty to enforce.[41] Major Grose had stipulated that pig's "in the streets" be shot and, as noted, soldiers took it as a military order rather than a civilian directive. However, Grose's order was not their only motivation for killing Boston's pig. The hungry sow also challenged *social* and *military* hierarchy. McKellar argued that Boston's pig had a "leveling disposition," an attribute "carefully and industriously inculcated in every part of the household of its master."[42] The pig, after all, was not on a public street when Faithful shot it.[43] Much worse, from the soldiers' point of view, it was eating Captain Foveaux's grass. Faithful killed the pig, then, "because it was amongst others destroying the property of Faithful's Master."[44] Captain Foveaux was not only his military superior, he was a man on the rise. By 1803, Foveaux was lieutenant governor at Norfolk Island and by 1809 was de facto "ruler" of the colony after the Rum Rebellion.[45] Kirsten McKenzie has recently pointed out the important role that regulating domesticated animals played in the performance of class-based hierarchy in colonial towns.[46] The killing of Boston's "very fine sow" here did more than protect Foveaux's grass and destroy Boston's asset. It preserved an order that was at once legal, social, and military.

Third, Boston breached the soldier's Peace by acting riotously. Even witnesses for Boston agreed that he had run into the street in a disorderly fashion "raging,"[47] "in a great passion,"[48] "running up," and "crying out."[49] Witnesses for the defense, most of them soldiers, cast his disorder in more ominous terms, suggesting Boston's criminality or liability in tort. Sergeant William Jamison swore that Boston came "along raving" and swearing and, in true revolutionary fashion, threatened to "cut off his [Faithful's] head."[50] Soldier-witnesses attested that Boston then struck the first blow against Faithful. Boston, in this account, was a rioter, an assaulter, or a batterer liable in civil and criminal law for his wrongs. His public spectacle of disorder, moreover, took place on a street in town before an audience of convicts. As such it was a gross threat to the soldier's Peace.

Boston's treasonous politics, his trespassing pig, and his riotous manner paled in comparison to his insult to the Corps, however. By calling a soldier a "damned rascal" he did more than hurt Faithful's feelings, he brought the legitimacy of the Corps as keepers of the Peace into question.

To keep order in New South Wales, soldiers needed to be above rebels or convicts. As Neil MacKellar pointed out,

> It has been asserted that we designed to create an invidious distinction between the Soldiers and the Civil inhabitants.—If it is meant that we intended to preserve a distinction between the loyal and determined supporters of their King, their Country and its laws—and the base and abandoned miscreants, whose secret purpose, is the destruction of the one, and the overthrow of the others.—then do I not hesitate to acknowledge it.[51]

The purpose of this distinction was to preserve the special status of soldiers as Peace-keepers. William Faithful begged that

> the Convict, all men of such turbulent and unquiet dispositions as the Prosecutor, will not be encouraged to repeat their insults by a Confirmation of a Sentence, which certainly casts the Soldier out of the Protection of the very Laws he is ordered to execute, and of which, in this Country, he is in a great measure the Guardian.[52]

Indeed, the soldiers understood honor as the basis of any sort of Peace. They reasoned that

> a Peace Officer in England would without hesitation, if called a d—Rascal for executing his Orders, have levelled the insulting Offender at his feet.—that the Peace Officer in so doing would not only, be justified in the Eye of the Law but would have it at his option still more severely to punish the Culprit both by fine and imprisonment.[53]

John Boston deserved his beating, then, because he threatened a hybrid martial order in a fragile imperial periphery. King-killers were real in 1795, and the colony of New South Wales was populated by rebels and convicts. It needed a special order that kept the leveling tendencies of men like Boston in check. Accordingly, the soldier-defendants argued, they did not breach the King's Peace when they beat Boston on a Sydney street. They kept a soldier's Peace in early New South Wales.

A Commercial Peace

Boston contended for a different sort of Peace in the colony. According to his own petitions to the court, as a businessman and a free settler, *he*, like the soldiers, had a special place in the colonial order of things. Not only was he entitled to "Public protection" as a man of commerce sponsored by the British government, he also had special claims "upon Public Patronage."[54] His special Peace was commercial in nature. It favored the freedoms and the manners of commerce over the pageantry and hierarchy of the Corps. The soldiers had breached it at a number of levels: by undermining Boston as a businessman, by maliciously killing his pig, and then by beating him in public.

Curiously, honor was just as crucial to Boston's commercial Peace as it was to the soldiers'. Boston's honor, however, had a different ethics and aesthetics. As John Smail has pointed out, commercial honor was central to eighteenth-century commerce. Commercial honor underpinned credit and its key institutions, the promissory note, and the bill of exchange. No sensible person would grant credit to a dishonorable man.[55] Yet the honor of a businessman was more robust than the soldiers' honor. Boston's commercial honor could not be threatened by a public shouting match over the death of a pig, even if violence was imminent and the words "damned Rascal" were used. Instead, commercial honor countenanced Boston's leveling pugnacity. Pugnacity merely marked him out as a "vigorous and spirited men, quick to rise to... [his] own defense."[56] Thus Boston dismissed

> with contempt...the Plea urged by the defendants, that their conduct was influenced by a jealous regard for the Honor of the Corps; what was the Honor of the Corps concerned in the pitiful dispute about the slaughter of a Pig.[57]

By insulting soldiers in the street, Boston did nothing but exercise his rights as a free man to cuss and argue. By insulting his honesty and probity, however, Boston alleged that the soldiers threatened the prosperity of the colony: the commercial Peace. Boston alleged that the soldiers' contempt for his honor "afforded a key" to both his public beating and the wrongful execution of his pig.[58] Months before he ordered Faithful to dispatch Boston's pig, Quartermaster Laycock publicly disputed Boston's honor as a businessman. One of Laycock's convict servants held a promissory note redeemable against Boston. Of course, this was a very complicated legal situation, as convict servants had dubious legal standing to enforce a contract of debt.[59] Laycock wrote to Boston demanding payment of the debt. Boston refused to pay alleging that the note was not due. Then Laycock confronted Boston in public to demand payment. In Boston's words, he had the "audacity to say on the Public Wharf in the hearing of numbers that I had robbed or swindled William Lewis of his property." He accused Laycock of endeavoring "to deprive me of what is dearer than life" (an unblemished character) and demanded that Laycock "publickly recant" his words or face a defamation suit.[60] For Boston, the Corps' attack on his pig and his person was just another phase in their conspiracy to attack his status as a free businessman in the colony: a breach of the commercial Peace.

Two subtly different notions of the Peace were in play here. Boston argued that his debt to Lewis was predicated on a contract between two equal parties, each of which was entitled to insist on fair performance of its terms. Boston's Peace assumed that convicts enjoyed a range of fundamental civil rights. In contrast, Laycock defended an aberrant hierarchy in breach of the rules of commerce. By representing Lewis, Laycock acknowledged his convict servant's legal incompetence. By demanding that Boston repay early, Laycock demanded that he meet moral rather than legal obligations. For Boston, Laycock's actions also amounted to an attempt to defend the privileged access of soldiers to most legal and illegal commerce in the colony.[61] This was so because their privileged status depended on a social hierarchy that subtly challenged the capacity of convicts to participate fully in the colonial economy and society. As Boston relied on convict customers and creditors, his business could thrive only if social and legal hierarchies remained flexible in the colony. This social and legal flexibility was incompatible with the soldier's Peace.

Boston's commercial Peace also turned on the capacity of convicts to testify. Faithful and McKellar reminded the court that convicted men were not permitted to bear witness in English courts, though convicts had been heard in Sydney from the outset.[62] The soldiers demanded, at least, that convict testimony should be dismissed when it contradicted "the evidence of a respectable Serjeant in the Army."[63] Boston argued conversely that convict testimony against respectable men and women was essential to justice in his case and to the Peace in general. His assault case turned on convict evidence that Faithful struck the first blow in their brawl. The Peace turned on convict evidence because, without it, the social matrix necessary to watch, report, and witness disorder could not be mobilized:

> If the testimony of convicts is to be rejected, the Civil and Criminal administration of the Colony must be suspended, necessity imposes their claim to admissibility, the circumstances which are to determine the credibility not of them alone, but of witnesses of every description, reside in the bosom of the Judge—necessity in the present instance acts in no respect in opposition to the common law of the land.[64]

Finally, Boston's commercial Peace rested on the rule of law. He claimed to have brought his assault suit against Faithful, McKellar, Laycock, and Addy, not only to defend his pigs, his person, and his business, but also "to vindicate the Public Justice of the Colony, to impress the Conviction that the Laws were equal to all, and that no rank in life could by impunity justify their violation."[65] Key to the rule of law in the colony, for Boston, was the subordination of the military to the civil power. Here Boston's Peace drew explicitly on the debates about military Peace-keeping that had racked both

London and the North American colonies in the late eighteenth century, causing enormous confusion about how best to prevent riot in the metropolis and goading surly Yankees into revolution in Boston.[66] In response to William Faithful's appeal to the governor, he argued that "the Appellant is a Soldier as such he is under the express control of the Civil Power, and he must be taught that an interference in the civil administration without the express and special command of the Civil Magistrate, is a breach of what are deemed the most constitutional laws of Britain, must involve him in crimes of no inferior guilt, and must subject him to superior punishment."[67]

Boston's commercial Peace used rhetoric borrowed from global Anglophone debates about the constitution of Britain and of British Empire. Yet Boston's commercial Peace, like the soldiers' Peace, was premised on a loose transposition of metropolitan order to Sydney. In his Peace, convicts were customers and witnesses. Their legal status and their punishment as prisoners of the Crown were far less important than their potential to participate in commerce with the full protection of common law courts.

The Colonial Peace

After seven days and hundreds of pages of testimony, the court gave judgment for John Boston against only two of the defendants: William Faithful for perpetrating the beating, and Thomas Laycock for ordering him to do so.[68] Yet, although the court decided for Boston, it is not clear whether it wholly endorsed his version of the events or his notion of the Peace. The court awarded only forty shillings, a fraction of the £500 compensation sought. This was not a token offering, but it was modest in the context of Boston's claim.

The court seemed to give soldiers a subtly broader role than it grants Boston in the maintenance of order in early Sydney. It reasoned that the soldiers had every right, and possibly a duty, to shoot pigs at large. Though Grose's order referred only to pigs found "in the streets," and Boston's pig was killed on private property, the court accepted that Boston's pig "could only have been shot in pursuance of that order." The court reasoned that Faithful "had done nothing more than Act in Obedience to Authorised regulation on the Settlement." Therefore, Boston "ought to have bridled his Passion."[69]

However, the court did allow convict testimony that Faithful struck the first blow against Boston, thus contradicting soldiers' testimony. On that basis it held that, though "the Military is a School of Honour, and that no term save that which brands him with the want of courage, can be more harsh in a Soldiers Ears than that of Rascal," Faithful had neither duty nor excuse to beat Boston for dishonoring him publicly. The Court had to keep "the Kings Peace" by protecting Boston from unjustified assault. Soldiers, convicts, and free settlers alike were bound by something very similar to Boston's commercial Peace.[70]

Governor Hunter confirmed the court's decision on appeal. He declared that Faithful

> ought to know, that he is as much and as safely under the protection of the laws by which we are Governed in this Country as any man or description of Men within its limits, and altho', the Soldiers as well as the Seamen in His Majesty's Service are subject in their respective Characters as Soldiers and Seaman to Martial law, they are nevertheless amenable to the Civil Power in all matters Cognizable by that power—no man within this Colony can be out of the power or lose the protection of the Laws under which we live, from the meanest of His Majesty's subjects up to the Commander in Chief or first Magistrate, we are all equally amenable to, and protected by the laws.[71]

The governor's decision did not settle the nature of the King's Peace in New South Wales.[72] When he bundled up the case materials and sent them to London, Hunter acknowledged that the question of the Peace was still open to public dispute in the colony:

> I cannot allow myself to close the letter on the subject, my Lord, without taking that opportunity of observing that I strongly suspect there are some person or persons in this colony (whose situations are probably respectable) extremely inimical to the necessary influence and authority of the civil power, and to that respect which is due from the public to the civil magistrates.[73]

He was right to worry. Soldiers went on to struggle against the civil order and the place of convicts and free settlers within it in New South Wales. The Corps deposed Governor Bligh in 1808 and continued for a long time to dominate local commerce before being overrun by free settlers and their sheep after the 1830s. The issue of what sort of Peace could be kept among convicts remained a difficult legal question in the colony, while the issue of who could control them after assignment caused an enormous rift between the first Supreme Court and Governor Darling in the 1820s.[74] Furthermore, colonists in Sydney shared their streets with indigenous people and indigenous practices of peace and order. The next major court case to discuss the nature of the King's Peace in the colony was a criminal case against an Aboriginal man named Jack Congo Murrell. *R v Murrell* (1836) began with another brawl on a small town street and ended as the first case to declare that the King's Peace was a territorial order that included indigenous violence *inter se* within its purview.

Conclusion

Boston v Laycock was a somewhat comical dispute in a tiny colonial town. Yet the case mattered because those few miserable streets on a magnificent harbor held all of the promise and peril of the British imperial project in the region. By questioning what manner of Peace subsisted in Sydney, and who was entitled to keep it, the litigants raised the question of imperial sovereignty and the role of military power within it at a moment of great uncertainty. They inserted themselves in a debate that was still being waged in London and which had recently lost Britain most of its North American colonies.

The case is important not only for the weighty questions it asked of British Empire in Sydney, but also because of what it tells us about the relationship between the public and the Peace in the colonial context. If the King's Peace is a flexible notion always mired in public performances and public disputations, then *Boston v Laycock* shows its special jeopardy on colonial peripheries where the institutions of order are scarce and the public numbers in hundreds. The case is replete with highly visible and contradictory public performances of Peace, all of which demonstrated the peculiar nature of empire in the convict colony of New South Wales. The New South Wales Corps argued that they performed Peace by strutting around Sydney in their uniforms, parading their status, and keeping rebels and convicts in their thrall. Boston argued that he performed the Peace by exercising his liberties to trade, to swear, and to assert his equality before the law. The judge-advocate and the governor claimed to perform the Peace by hearing the trial and the appeal before a poorly constituted court, held without a courtroom or a full contingent of lawyers. Each of these performances is notable because Boston and the defendants were almost as important to the Peace in Sydney as the civil court or the governor. They represented two opposed camps among a very small population of free people. They bickered, moreover, in the most important theater of order in New South Wales: Sydney.

Their argument in *Boston v Laycock* demonstrates the flexibility of the Peace on late eighteenth-century colonial peripheries. Even if the court and the governor endorsed a version of the Peace modeled closely on metropolitan understandings of the distinction between military and civilian order, no one in this case argued for a perfect transposition of the metropolitan Peace to New South Wales. Ultimately, Boston, the court, and the governor acknowledged the importance of altering the parameters of the Peace to accommodate convict commerce and convict testimony. Serving convicts might well have had few civil rights, yet the colonial establishment agreed that they too were key participants in the colonial Peace. Meanwhile, the fact that the New South Wales Corps could argue so earnestly for a soldier's Peace shows deep uncertainty about the application of metropolitan law in the colonies in general and in New South Wales in particular. Nor were the soldiers alone in their novel interpretation of the Peace. Other members of the New South Wales public too felt the special jeopardy of their colonial periphery. Indeed, the next century and a half of British imperial practice suggests that the colonial office itself continued to think of its colonies as fragile places where martial law could be declared more readily than at home. The King's Peace in these places did not follow metropolitan rules. Despite the perversity of the litigants and the insignificance of its forum, then, *Boston v Laycock* demonstrates the unsettled nature of sovereignty in the late eighteenth-century British Empire.

Notes

1. A version of this paper was presented at the "Transpositions of Empire" symposium, held in Prato April 20–22, 2009. I am grateful to Michele Ford, Shaunnagh Dorsett and Mark Finnane for their comments. James Biggs, *Boston v Laycock*, in Governor Hunter to the Duke of Portland, August 26, 1797, in *Historical Records of Australia: Series I, Governors' Despatches to and from England* [*HRA*], 26 vols. (Sydney: Library Committee of the Commonwealth Parliament, 1914–1925), Series 1, I, p. 622 (hereafter *Boston v Laycock*).
2. George Carman, *Boston v Laycock*, p. 618.
3. Bruce Kercher, *Debt Seduction and Other Disasters: The Birth of Civil Law in Convict New South Wales* (Annandale, NSW: Federation Press, 1996), pp. 26–27; T.G. Parsons, "Was John Boston's Pig a Political Martyr? The Reaction to Popular Radicalism in Early New South Wales," *Journal of Royal Australian Historical Society*, 71 (1985), 163–76.
4. Frederick Pollock and John Maitland, *The History of English Law before the Time of Edward I.*, 2 vols. (Cambridge: Cambridge University Press, 1895), I, p. 22.
5. Michael Fowler and Julie Marie Bunck call this "The Basket Approach to Sovereignty." See their *Law, Power and the Sovereign State: The Evolution and Application of the Concept of Sovereignty* (University Park, PA: Pennsylvania State University Press, 1995), pp. 70–80.
6. Pollock and Maitland, *The History of the English Law*, p. 22.
7. Ibid., pp. 22–23.
8. Margaret Kelly, "King and Crown: An Examination of the Legal Foundation of the British King" (unpublished doctoral thesis, Macquarie University, 1998), pp. 55–63.
9. J.C. Holt, *Magna Carta*, 2nd edn. (Cambridge: Cambridge University Press, 1992), pp. 127–87; and A.E. Dick Howard, *Magna Carta: Text and Commentary*, rev. edn. (Charlottesville: University of Virginia Press, 1998), pp. 12–13.

10. Fitzjames Stephen, *A General View of the Criminal Law of England* (London: Macmillan, 1863), p. 14.
11. Steve Hindle, *The State and Social Change in Early Modern England, 1550–1640* (Houndsmills, UK: Palgrave, 2002), pp. 94–97, 115.
12. Peter Goodrich, "Specula Laws: Image, Aesthetic and Common Law," *Law and Critique,* 2 (1991), 233–54 (p. 239).
13. Ibid., pp. 239–43.
14. Hindle, *State and Social Change,* pp. 94–145; Richard S. Tompson, "The Justices of the Peace and the United Kingdom in the Age of Reform," *The Journal of Legal History,* 26 (1986), 273–292 (p. 273).
15. David E. Engdahl, "Soldiers, Riots, and Revolution: The Law and History of Military Troops in Civil Disorders," *Iowa Law Review,* 57 (1971), 1–73. See also, Paul Christianson, "Arguments on Billeting and Martial Law in the Parliament of 1628," *The Historical Journal,* 37 (1994), 539–67; and the essays in *Three British Revolutions: 1641, 1688, 1776,* ed. J.G.A. Pocock (Princeton, NJ: Princeton University Press, 1980). For a detailed discussion of grievances against the King and Crown in the Declaration of Independence, see David Armitage, *The Declaration of Independence: A Global History* (Cambridge, MA: Harvard University Press, 2007), pp. 53–60.
16. Tompson, "The Justices of the Peace," p. 273; Engdahl, "Soldiers, Riots, and Revolution," pp. 3–4.
17. Christianson, "Arguments on Billeting," pp. 539–567.
18. For example, Lois G. Schwoerer, "The Bill of Rights: Epitome of the Revolution of 1688–89," in *Three British Revolutions: 1641, 1688, 1776,* ed. J.G.A. Pocock (Princeton, NJ: Princeton University Press, 1980), pp. 231–33.
19. Engdahl, "Soldiers, Riots, and Revolution," p. 32.
20. Ibid., pp. 23–28.
21. Charles Townshend, "Martial Law: Legal and Administrative Problems of Civil Emergency in Britain and the Empire, 1800–1940," *The Historical Journal,* 25 (1982), 167–95. Lauren Benton notes the importance of sites of convict transportation as havens for military law: Lauren Benton, *A Search for Sovereignty: Law and Geography in European Empire, 1400–1900* (New York: Cambridge University Press, 2010), pp. 162–221.
22. Neil McKellar, *Boston v Laycock,* p. 631.
23. David Neal, *The Rule of Law in a Penal Colony: Law and Power in Early New South Wales* (Cambridge: Cambridge University Press, 1991), p. 144.
24. Ibid., p. 145.
25. Bruce Kercher, *An Unruly Child: A History of Law in Australia* (St Leonards, NSW: Allen & Unwin, 1995), pp. 44–5, 57.
26. Ibid., p. 49.
27. Alan Atkinson, *The Europeans in Australia. A History. Volume I: The Beginning,* 2 vols. (Melbourne: Oxford University Press, 1997), I, pp. 258–59.
28. Major Grose, July 17, 1793, quoted in *Boston v Laycock,* p. 640; The Court, *Boston v Laycock,* p. 633; William Faithful, *Boston v Laycock,* p. 634.
29. Major Grose, July 17, 1793, quoted in *Boston v Laycock,* p. 640.
30. Neil McKellar, *Boston v Laycock,* p. 631.

31. Lisa Ford, *Settler Sovereignty: Jurisdiction and Indigenous People in America and Australia, 1788–1836* (Cambridge, MA: Harvard University Press, 2010), p. 45.
32. Mark McKenna, *The Captive Republic: A History of Republicanism in Australia 1788–1996* (Cambridge: Cambridge University Press, 1996), pp. 13–15.
33. Grace Karskens, *The Colony: A History of Early Sydney* (Crows Nest, NSW: Allen & Unwin, 2009), pp. 75–82. Bruce Kercher, "Perish or Prosper: The Law and Convict Transportation in the British Empire, 1700–1850," *Law and History Review,* 21 (2003), 526–84 (p. 536).
34. Karskens, *The Colony,* pp. 78–82. See also *Convicts and Colonial Society, 1788–1853, Problems in Australian History,* ed. Lloyd Evans and Paul Nicholls (Stanmore, NSW: Cassell, 1976); Grace Karskens, *The Rocks: Life in Early Sydney* (Carlton, VIC: Melbourne University Press, 1997).
35. Contrast Hindle, *The State and Social Change,* pp. 94–97, 115.
36. Contrast Karskens, *The Colony,* p. 78.
37. Parsons, "Was John Boston's Pig a Political Martyr?," pp. 167, 174. See also, J.F. Nagle, *Collins, The Courts & the Colony: Law & Society in Colonial New South Wales* (Sydney: University of New South Wales Press, 1996), pp. 257–66; Judith Iltis, "Boston, John (–1804)," in *Australian Dictionary of Biography* (Carlton: Melbourne University Press, 1966), pp. 126–27; and Dundas to Grose, February 15, 1794, in *HRA,* Series 1, I, p. 494.
38. Parsons, "Was John Boston's Pig a Political Martyr?," p. 167.
39. Ibid., pp. 167–68.
40. Neil McKellar, *Boston v Laycock,* p. 632.
41. Ibid., p. 630.
42. Ibid.
43. Boston argued on this basis that his pig had been shot unlawfully: *Boston v Laycock,* p. 640.
44. Neil McKellar, *Boston v Laycock,* p. 630.
45. Atkinson, *The Europeans in Australia,* I, pp. 310–11, 323.
46. Kirsten McKenzie, "Dogs and the Public Sphere: The Ordering of Social Space in Early Nineteenth-Century Cape Town," in *Canis Africanis: A Dog History of South Africa,* ed. Sandra Swart (Leiden, Netherlands: Brill, 2008), pp. 93–94; J.S. Palsetia, "Mad Dogs and Parsis: The Bombay Dog Riots of 1832," *Journal of the Royal Asiatic Society,* 11 (2001), 13–30.
47. Edward Collins, *Boston v Laycock,* p. 613.
48. George Carman, *Boston v Laycock,* p. 618.
49. Mark Turner, *Boston v Laycock,* p. 616; Andrew Clark, *Boston v Laycock,* p. 617.
50. Serjeant Jameson, *Boston v Laycock,* p. 620. See also Serjeant Thomas Whittle, *Boston v Laycock,* p. 623; and James Biggs, *Boston v Laycock,* p. 622.
51. Neil McKellar, *Boston v Laycock,* p. 632.
52. William Faithful, *Boston v Laycock,* p. 635. See also, Neil McKellar's address to the court: *Boston v Laycock,* p. 631.
53. William Faithful, *Boston v Laycock,* p. 634.
54. John Boston, *Boston v Laycock,* p. 604.

55. John Smail, "Credit, Risk and Honor in Eighteenth-Century Commerce," *Journal of British Studies*, 44 (2005), 439–56 (p. 449). For the particular importance of honor in nineteenth-century colonial society, see Kirsten McKenzie, "Of Convicts and Capitalists: Honour and Colonial Commerce in 1830s Cape Town and Sydney," *Australian Historical Studies*, 118 (2002), 200–22.
56. Smail, "Credit, Risk and Honor," pp. 440, 444–45.
57. John Boston, *Boston v Laycock*, p. 626.
58. Ibid., p. 625.
59. Contrast the suit of a convict to recover personal property: *Cable v Sinclair* [1788] NSWKR 1, *Decisions of the Superior Courts of New South Wales, 1788–1899*, <http://www.law.mq.edu.au/scnsw/> [accessed January 10, 2010].
60. John Boston, *Boston v Laycock*, pp. 608–9.
61. George Parsons, "The Commercialization of Honour: Early Australian Capitalism, 1788–1809," in *A Difficult Infant: Sydney before Macquarie*, ed. Graeme Aplin (Sydney: University of New South Wales Press, 1998), pp. 102–19.
62. *R v Plowman* [1789] NSWKR 1, *Decisions of the Superior Courts of New South Wales, 1788–1899*, <http://www.law.mq.edu.au/scnsw/> [accessed January 10, 2010].
63. Kercher, "Perish or Prosper," p. 536; Neil McKellar, *Boston v Laycock*, p. 631.
64. John Boston, *Boston v Laycock*, p. 638. Boston had a penchant for drama, but his observation here was astute. At key moments in the history of the colony civil order was brought to a halt by convict legal incapacity. When Jeffrey Hart Bent was appointed to administer the civil jurisdiction in the colony using emancipist clerks: C.H. Currey, "Bent, Jeffery Hart," in *Australian Dictionary of Biography* (Carlton, VIC: Melbourne University Press, 1966), pp. 87–92.
65. John Boston, *Boston v Laycock*, p. 638.
66. Engdahl, "Soldiers, Riots, and Revolution," p. 28.
67. John Boston, *Boston v Laycock*, p. 639.
68. The Court, *Boston v Laycock*, p. 633.
69. Ibid.
70. Ibid.
71. Governor Hunter, *Boston v Laycock*, p. 637.
72. Nagle, *Collins, The Courts & the Colony*, pp. 264–66.
73. Governor Hunter to the Duke of Portland, August 30, 1797, in *HRA*, Series 1, I, pp. 602–3.
74. J.M. Bennett, *Sir Francis Forbes: First Chief Justice of New South Wales 1823–1837*, *Lives of the Australian Chief Justices* (Annandale, NSW: Federation Press, 2001), pp. 57–72. Alan Atkinson, "The Free-Born Englishman Transported: Convict Rights as a Measure of Eighteenth-Century Empire," *Past & Present*, 144 (1994), 88–115.

Chapter 10

William Pember Reeves (1857–1932)

Lawyer-Politician, Historian, and "Rough Architect" of the New Zealand State

P.G. McHugh

I

In 1888 an American lawyer and socialist Edward Bellamy published *Looking Backward: 2000–1887*, a utopian novel set in the year 2000 that anticipated land nationalization, cooperative societies, piped music, and the credit card. The young hero Julian West is hypnotized into a long, deep sleep and, like Rip Van Winkle, wakes in the future. More than a century later, a Doctor Leete guides him around this transformed world, explaining all its advances, often through protracted question-and-answer dialogue. Its features include reduced working hours, easy consumerism—shopping malls included—global peace, and retirement at the age of 45 on full benefits.

The book was an immediate success "Down Under." In Australia, drovers, bushmen, navvies, and stevedores read it aloud around campfires and on the wharf-side. It quickly sold out in New Zealand. Tens of thousands of antipodeans read it, we are told.[1] Bellamy had evidently drawn on his compatriot Henry George's socialist tract *Progress and Poverty* (1879). Published just a few years before, and with identical themes, George's book had also been a huge hit. Certainly it was known to colonial politicians interested in land reform, not least for its advocacy of land nationalization and the "single tax" that sought to recover for the state what George held to be the unearned increment accruing to landowners from the increase in the value of their land owing to the presence and activity of the surrounding community.[2] However, Bellamy's literary imagination and popularism gave those ideas a new, attention-grabbing twist, transformed as they were from a lengthy economics tract to a work of fiction. In Australasia, not least, George's ideas had a shot of adrenaline that refreshed and intensified their circulation as well as provided a new accessibility.

This utopianism flourished as a literary outgrowth of what Jamie Belich has described as the era of "explosive colonization" in the Anglo world. This was a period of intense and rapid "boom-bust" economic and population growth, especially in North America and Australasia, that commenced after 1815 and peaked in the second half of the nineteenth century.[3] Anglo "settlerism" generated a very wide variety of booster literature that extolled flamboyantly and enticingly the lifestyle to be had in these lands of the proverbial milk and honey. This booster literature took many forms. It had its high-, low-, and middle-brows. It occurred in many literary forms: travelogues, essays, novels, brochures, histories, newspaper advertisements and articles, plays, revues, speeches, and the like. It drew frequently on the various ideal-society discourses, often in an indiscriminate manner, mingling the strictly utopian with Arcadian and/or land of Cockayne or Perfect Moral Commonwealth descriptions.[4] The science fiction form used by Bellamy was one especially popular manifestation of this boosterism.

This explosion was so marked that Lyman Sargent, historian of Anglophone utopian literature, insists that the nineteenth century must be divided into periods Before and After Bellamy.[5] Indeed, Sargent notes that the second half of the nineteenth century was itself an extremely and unusually rich period in the production of utopian literature, not least in Australasia and North America where Bellamy's work augmented considerably a trend that was already well in train. Even before, but especially after Bellamy, utopianism was a natural accompaniment to the phenomenon of explosive colonization. Ideal-society dreaming looked forward rather than backward in time; with its (often very detailed) constitutional blueprinting, and endorsement of a localized law-making agency—muscle that the self-governing Australasian colonies, American states, and Canadian provinces were then newly flexing—it struck a particularly resonant as well as populist chord in the Anglo political imagination of that era. Generally such literature provided an arriviste settler society with an enabling and unified future. Since the polity lacked a history, the historical self-consciousness it cultivated necessarily looked forward in time. This prospective transposition of the polity acted as an endorsement of its political agency in the present. Utopian literature—including its conservative, counteractive, dystopian forms—played with readers' sense of their community as a fresh polity fending in time and place, a key nerve-point in the psyche of explosive colonization.

Bellamy's novel spawned a legion of imitative works, most in response to its socialist message. Utopianism found especially fertile ground "Down Under." Two antipodean prime ministers of the late-Victorian era, Alfred Deakin (in a piece of juvenilia attributed only after his death) and Julius Vogel, wrote and published utopian fictions. Their message and tone was essentially conservative, validating local initiative and enterprise, whilst also harnessing it to the careful conservation and continuance of a history of reverence for extant imperial institutions, particularly the monarchy. There were also numerous published works by politicians, lawyers, journalists, and public officials, writing on and around the utopian theme, including (if not especially) its morbid dystopian counter-sphere. Figures of all political hues—capitalists, liberals, and socialists—dabbled in an idealized dreamland or dreaded a nightmarish destination. In the popularity and centrality, not to say variety, of the ideal-society trope, the thinking of these colonial figures meshed with their doing.

This chapter looks at the eastern side of the Tasman Sea, aware also that the themes invoked by kiwi protagonists were also playing out in Australia.[6] In the New Zealand setting, and even before the impact of Bellamy, the early association of the islands with a utopian paradise has been linked to the impact of the *Immigration and Public Works Act* 1870 (N.Z.), which created the post of agent-general in London.[7] The office was established to promote the colony in Britain, in particular capital investment by the city and its commercial interests at large. Before transformation (in 1905) into the now high commission, there were five agents-general, all of whom had close experience of colonial politics.[8] Of these, Julius Vogel and William Pember Reeves exerted considerable influence on the cut of New Zealand politics in the late nineteenth century. Both read and wrote after Bellamy in 1889–90, closely following the publication of *Looking Backward*. The venerable former prime minister Vogel wrote in fictional style, while the precocious Pember Reeves used Bellamy as the focus for a series of essays in his father's newspapers that were soon compiled into a forty-nine-page six-penny pamphlet.

In his book *The Ideal Society and Its Enemies* (1989) Miles Fairburn argues that in the years before 1900 the dominant variety of idealizing of New Zealand was primarily Arcadian. That is, the rhetoric promoted the islands as places of natural abundance where men without capital or of humble origins could become proprietors after only a few years in the colony. Further, Fairburn argues, the material independence of the working-man was portrayed as occurring outside a social framework. It did not depend upon working-class collective action or the mobilization of any class power. Trade unions were superfluous: "In Arcadia natural abundance had largely abolished the need for associational groups."[9] This rhetoric not only appealed to the working-class but also chimed with the middle-class, who brought capital to the colony. It promised them a land without the stresses of class antagonism and social anxiety. Fairburn unpicks this mythology, acknowledging the traction it had in the actual state of the colony where, he argues—though not uncontroversially[10]—social and political life was atomized. He writes also of the underbelly of this sunny countenance.

But Fairburn also notes the rise, particularly from the 1890s, of the centralized New Zealand state and the growing dependence of the settler society upon beneficent governmental action—ostensibly to maintain the enduring Arcadian myth of individualist rural smallholding that the long Liberal government (1891–1912) championed. He does not discuss Bellamy's book or influence, although he notes that the rhetoric and language of New Zealand boosterism shifted during the 1890s toward the perfect moral commonwealth and, most of all, utopian forms.[11] In that period, and as its population, transportation networks, and economic prosperity (and evident socioeconomic imbalances) grew, the Arcadian paradise became more utopian in flavor. It was more overtly dependent upon state intervention to perpetuate a self-depiction that was also transposed into the towns and workplace of an urbanizing settler society. Essentially, the themes of individualism, property ownership, social harmony, and egalitarianism were suburbanized to become what Austin Mitchell, many years later, described as the "Half Gallon Quarter Acre Pavlova Paradise."[12]

The reach of the state extended and consolidated in the 1890s, and so by the beginning of the twentieth century, Arcadianism, rural and urban, had segued into utopianism with its emphasis upon the central role of the state. This was also inflected, uneasily, by the local influence of Ruskin and Morris with their anti-industrial idealizing[13] and retained the motifs of small individual landholding from its earlier form, synthesizing into the land policies of the long Liberal government.[14] As Fairburn and Olssen have shown, such national self-stylization was less the deliberative activity of an intellectual elite in New Zealand than a populist imagining conducted in broad, not necessarily coherent, terms that had little regard for the intellectual provenance and subtleties of the ideal-society genres or, for that matter, of political thought at large. Indeed, it is the absence of such an intellectualized component from this activity—or rather the rarity of its occurrence—that lies at the center of this chapter and its attempt to identify key features in the thought of one influential figure of that era.

Julius Vogel and William Pember Reeves both published responses to *Looking Backward* within months of each other in 1889–90. Reacting to Bellamy, both writers explored the character of the ideal society with a strongly Pākehā (or Anglo) New Zealand orientation. The appearance of these two works so closely in time, and so focused upon the prospects of the New Zealand Pākehā polity, represented an unusual juncture in the history of intellectual deliberation upon the nature of that polity, occurring as they did at the cusp of a key state-formation period in New Zealand's short political history. Vogel's work appeared, well after his political career had ended, as a novel penned in the penury of retirement in East Mosley, England. Pember Reeves wrote a series of newspaper essays as a young journalist yet (but about) to commence his political career.

Vogel's *Anno Domini* (1889) was a capitalist utopia written primarily in the hope—unrealized—of financial gain.[15] Rejecting Bellamy's socialism, it was his loyalist paean to empire (federated, of course), capitalism and the enterprise, and to the ingenuity and moral fiber of the Anglo-Saxon race, especially of its womenfolk. The book is so thematically obvious, so lacking in self-irony and moral complexity, that it cannot but read as the manifesto of its author. As his authorial nonfictional postscript made plain, and as the novel's rather crude and pedestrian nature demonstrated, the fictional form thinly disguised its conception as Vogel's intellectual credo.

Like Vogel's work, Pember Reeves' essays idealized a destiny for the Pākehā New Zealand state, transposing it forward in time. At the outset it might be noted that Māori had no presence in either author's imagination of the settler polity's future, which was seen as shining and white, both authors inside the "pigmentopia" of the Anglo race.[16] Yet, for all the obvious self-association with his fictional voice, collocating Vogel's novel and the essays of Pember Reeves is inherently problematic. It would require more space and careful contextualization of persona, language, and authorial ambition than is possible here if one were to identify and compare their respective projections of Pākehā constitutional and political identity. Vogel's fictional utopia—his future history—was fixated with transposing a glorious imperial past into a glorious future. It will be seen that Pember Reeves' transposition is quite different: it propels forward, barely looking over its shoulder at its own past or its inherited past.

The rarity of such reflections, and the very issues surrounding a comparison of the two texts of 1888–89, indicates the difficulty of weaving a distinctly Pākehā tradition of political thought, other, perhaps, than in a disjointed and episodic manner. It may be that such a history of Pākehā political thought—one that puts the polity at the center of a history of sustained intellectual self-inquiry—is to be patched, rather than woven, and that if it occurs it can only be as a series of panels in a broader quilt of Pākehā cultural history stitched together loosely, thematically, and necessarily from a variety of sources. One cannot build or seek to find a pattern of reflection upon the political and constitutional agency of the Pākehā state that is not there, or over-egg what is.[17] What follows are what I see as the key aspects of the Pember Reeves' panels from his youth, and the impact of Bellamy's *Looking Backward* to his older self: agent-general in a form of exile in London and colonial darling of the Fabian circle surrounding Sidney and Beatrice Webb.

II

Pember Reeves, like the elder Vogel, was a believer in imperial federation, although by the time he was becoming actively involved as agent-general, very early in the twentieth century, the temperature and goals of the movement had lowered, from stronger forms of federation with a single imperial Parliament and ultimate court, to weaker, more consociational models. Active participation by Vogel and Pember Reeves in this running and rather scrambled conversation was separated by twenty years and, crucially, the white Dominions' growing experience of self-government in that time. Both had fundamentally different approaches. These were ideological as well as generational. For Vogel it was a matter of loyalism, patriotism, and veneration of institutions on grounds of their historical durability—not least in their healthy transplantation onto foreign soil—and excellence projected onward into a more glorious future. Pember Reeves, however, did not cast his belief on such a conservative and nostalgic Burkean continuum. His monarchism, if any, was virtually undetectable. For him imperial federation furthered civilization, racial superiority, and the delivery by democratic means of social justice. It looked forward not backward, propelled inexorably to its socialist destiny, and certainly not mesmerized by sentimental devotion to monarchy and a glorious past. What linked their accounts was a belief in the racial superiority of the Anglo-Saxon race.

Pember Reeves was hardly the colony's first man-of-books, though he qualifies as one of its earliest native-born. He is particularly remembered as the young minister who, only in his mid-thirties, steered through important reforming legislation early in the life of the long Liberal government, most especially in the fields of labor relations and land tenure. The preceding generation of colonial politicians that had taken the reins of self-government certainly had an intellectual component, Stout perhaps most preeminently. However, Pember Reeves was the first and remains one of the few wholehearted apostles of the centralized Pākehā state. Rather than statism being a position he came to later in his career, as did the more senior figures of Stout and Vogel in the late 1880s, he took his position from the outset, well after the divisive politics of abolition of the provinces (1876) and as the effects of Vogel's massive infrastructure investment were kicking in. The generation that preceded him and whose parliamentary twilight coincided with his comparatively brief berth in the cabinet of the 1890s—the wily and venerable Sir George Grey, the affable Ballance, the high-minded Stout, the small-farmers' hero McKenzie, the displaced Whig Rolleston, and many of the numerous Knights of Labour spread throughout the country—had plainly read their John Stuart Mill and Henry George.[18] But more than those figures, and from the start, Pember Reeves' political agenda was ideologically spurred, and he left Parliament after nine years—five as the minister of labor, 1891–96—with the reputation of an ideologue.[19]

His disposition as a reformer shone through not only his political career but also his writing. Despite his legal education he never became attached to the common law constitution of the great Whig historians, who cut such imposing figures in the intellectual milieu of the time. Neither does his writing show the constitutionalists' concern with the legal processes, forms, and constraints upon the exercise of governmental power. The past, as we will see, put Pember Reeves in no thrall. He wrote, even as an historian, with a forward gaze, as a reformer interested in ends, rather than a constitutionalist concerned with means.

III

In 1890 the young Pember Reeves MP authored a series of newspaper articles that he immediately consolidated into a six-penny pamphlet entitled *Some Historical Articles on Communism and Socialism*. These newspaper essays were sparked by the publication and ran alongside the serialization of Bellamy's novel in the *Canterbury Times* and the *Lyttleton Times*. Penned under the pseudonym of "Pharos," the articles appeared in papers owned by Reeves' father, William.

Some Historical Articles is divided into three parts and a short conclusion. The first part discusses the writers on communism and socialism, including the utopian "Socialist visionaries." The second looks at examples in practice of this form of social and political organization or "experiments," as he terms them (and titles his later book). Part III is specifically concerned with drawing lessons for New Zealand from that material, combining the theoretical and the experimental by reference—and ode—to figures such as Robert Owen, Jean Godin, and Ferdinand Lassalles,[20] who, by Pharos' account, managed successfully to integrate both. Although he opens avowing an intention not "to make converts but attract students" and to keep his sympathies, "however strong and pronounced,"[21] to himself, Pharos' support for state enterprise and interventionism is plain; his terse, pointed conclusion, as indeed his text almost from the start, sheds such pretence.

He is describing an international history of socialism—albeit a disjointed one—in which he sees his country as participating.

Opening with a quote from Henry George, Part I gives his summaries of the "more famous Ideal States" of Plato's *Republic*, More's *Utopia*, and Campanella's *Civitas Solis*, as well as passing reference to Bacon's *New Atlantis*. The introductory section ends by commending Bellamy's *Looking Backward* as "the book of the day," noting also its quick and great worldwide popularity.[22]

Part II considers past experiments in the ideal state, presenting these chronologically. His aim is to highlight the presence through time of "communistic" communities, and to show that these have not necessarily been sporadic or isolated phenomena. He demonstrates that the ideal society has been not only the subject of elevated human thought but also the object behind actual social organization. He ranges through the Spartans and Cretans on to the early Christians and the Essenes, insisting that although no system of socialism "is to be found defined or commended in the Gospels" its underlying principles are the same. He lets Christian socialists cite scripture for their purpose (presumably, like the devil?). They have Jesus, the savior and socialist, "as the greatest of their allies," unlike the Christian individualists who, "as a rule, fight shy of the Gospels."[23] Inca society is also in this group—"a despotic kingdom managed on the principles of an original, scientific, benevolent system of State socialism"[24]—as are the missionary communes in Paraguay, followed by the Russian Mir[25] and eight communistic societies of the United States, all of the latter "deeply tinctured with some sincere, if eccentric, religious belief and enthusiasm."[26]

In Part III, entitled "Socialism," Pharos moves more evidently into the modern era. His discussion focuses on England and Germany and the lessons that New Zealand can take from state enterprise in those countries, particularly Robert Owen's cooperative and Godin's profit-sharing industrial partnership. Communism requires a self-sufficing community that shuts itself off from the outside world and exerts total command and control over its members. It demands an "utter change... violent revolution" but it "cannot deal with the masses of mankind as they are." Communists "start with a fixed, settled, perfect order and arrangement" and it is into that system their disciples must fit. But there is no such thing as a perfect society, "nor anything like it is ever reached by either society or an individual at a bound." And such systems are static and inorganic. Socialism, by contrast, works toward the ideal without requiring "from each admitted member the complete surrender of all private property at the outset," although its ultimate aim is to nationalize land and capital: "Socialism will resist, not with the barricade, but with the ballot-box. It will attack, not with the rifle, but with the progressive tax. It is, in practice as in theory, the exact reverse of the red-handed individualism of the French Revolution."[27]

Condemning the State-Socialism of the Kaiser's Germany under Bismarck—"bluster, persecution and tyranny"—he notes the unconscious drift toward socialism in Britain during most of the nineteenth century. This, he insists, has also been happening in New Zealand where even those who vocally condemn it as a creed can be found actively supporting state measures and enterprise. The following passage is well known to students of New Zealand history:

> In this part of the British Empire the State is the largest landowner, the chief rent-collector, and the owner of the largest industrial "going concern"—the railways. It not only manages the Post Office, the lighthouses, the telephones, and the telegraphs, but has established a powerful Life Insurance Company. Its Public Trustee takes care of private estates. Its Land Transfer Office has taken a whole branch of business form the lawyers. The State not only provides for the sick and the aged helpless, but finds work for the unemployed and teaches, free of charge, every Child in the colony whose parents will accept State teaching... All these acts are Socialistic. All are so much State interference with private enterprise. All are so many steps onward in the march towards making industry one national thing. All show that we live in an age of unconscious Socialism.[28]

Pharos, like Bellamy, describes socialism teleologically as the inevitable collectivist end-point of human development. He raises themes, particularly that of social reform, by a piecemeal and gradual means, one that will reappear in *State Experiments* (1902).

The later work, to which we now turn, is intellectually less flamboyant and more mindful of the dark art of politics. By then the series of profound political thinkers and visionaries that so excited the young Pember Reeves as Pharos has turned into catalogues and recitations of statutory enactment in the description of which the prose is more restrained. Whereas Pharos gave his New Zealand readers an internationalist perspective and suggested that they were inextricably part of a global history of socialism, the narrative focus of *State Experiments* is markedly Anglo-Australian, with the goal of explaining experiments "Down Under" primarily to a British audience. His readership at the beginning of the twentieth century might have been larger than the colonial circulation of the late 1880s, and his angle more Anglo in focus, but his self-confidence and sense of mission and destiny remained undimmed. This blazes in the passages—highly objectionable to the modern eye—where he condemns Chinese immigrant labor and oriental culture as degraded. Despite his less exuberant prose, he writes proudly of the New Zealand achievements. At that time such recounting was his after-dinner dressage in London, where he had become the colonial show pony of the Fabian set at the beginning of the twentieth century and their dining club, the coefficients.

Though separated by only a dozen years, the two works appeared at different junctures in his life, and their readerships were vastly different. Pharos writes for a New Zealand audience, and a mainly South Island one at that, assuring them of their participation in a global history. *State Experiments* is as much a socialist manual for the British as a historical account of political agency in the southern hemisphere. In this later work his admiration for the visionaries of yore has been replaced by rhapsodies for realists. None of the former makes more than a very fleeting appearance through its two volumes, which are not without their longueurs. In his lengthy chapter on land reform, Edward Gibbon Wakefield and John McKenzie are particularly lauded as figures who hitched practical ideas (rather than lofty ideals) to gritty hard-won achievement. Now, in *State Experiments*, the narrative is a rather dry one of incremental achievement and an agenda of practicality. For the older Pember Reeves it has become less a case of what people have said than what they have done.

Pember Reeves' self-relocation from the idealism of Pharos to the dust-bowl of practical politics is seen in his characterization of the reforms of his era in government. Though "deeply tinged with socialism," these were more the product of running pragmatic adjustment than possessed of strong intellectual pedigree:

> It was not German, much less French Socialism. Here and there, no doubt, visionaries had dreams of Utopia more or less like the communities of Fourier and St Simon. Here and there might be found some student who knew of Lassalle, or through the medium of English tracts and paraphrases, had scraped acquaintance with Karl Marx. Tens of thousands read Bellamy's *Looking Backwards*. Many studied, and some borrowed from, the Fabian Essays. Such socialism as filtered through newspapers was all English and of the cautious or tentative kind.[29]

New Zealand socialism was, essentially, pragmatic, polite, and diluted. Just as the English were then being asked to distinguish between "a war" and "a sort of war," so, he said, students of state experiments in the colonies might distinguish "between socialism and a sort of socialism." Pember Reeves had always sided with and continued to support the parliamentary gradualism of the Fabians. Here, his socialism by small but sure steps was being modestly offered to the world as experimental and as driven no more than faintly by philosophy, which lies distantly and vaguely in the background. Signs this might occur were evident in Pharos, who, for example, did not see Karl Marx as "a tribune of the people" because his mission had been "to provide ammunition for other men to fire."[30] But they have become most fully articulated in *State Experiments* where the "brainworkers" who receive plaudits are the lawyer-politicians "well-read and intellectually above most of their brother members... [among whom] are found most of the few doctrinaires... [and] some of the most honourable and high-principled men in colonial politics."[31]

In this insistence upon the intellectual's participative responsibility—a Protestant emphasis upon good works and civic presence as much as on lofty thought—there appears a common theme of late-Victorian political and legal thought that cuts across the political spectrum. One finds a similar belief in active civic contribution, for example, in Pember Reeves' kiwi (and decidedly non-socialist) contemporary Sir John Salmond, who like Reeves spent a considerable amount of time (but did not exile himself) in the United Kingdom.[32] Yet, the paradox is that by this emphasis, Pember Reeves, the colonial intellectual, has become complicit in that species' marginalization:[33]

> If, then, colonial Progressives do not concern themselves with the visionary benefits or theoretical dangers of some perfectly organised socialist community, it is because they are too busy in seeing what they can make State energy do for them in experiments which have a definite purpose of immediate usefulness.

This observation is as obvious as it is, perhaps, unkind. In Pember Reeves' pantheon of heroes, there seems a clear element of self-association. His biographer, Keith Sinclair, has noted his tendency to use his writings as "disguised autobiography."[34] By the time of the publication of *State Experiments*, he was being feted in London as the intellectual helmsman of reforms that were bringing New Zealand to considerable, if momentary, international attention as the "social laboratory" of the world. Pember Reeves' national pride is plainly tinged with self-pride.

In his emphasis upon the state and practical activity, and in his evident distaste for the "individualistic," Reeves is squarely inside the mainstream of progressive political thought of his era as well as echoing the republican elements of late-Victorian imperial thought.[35] Recently Martin Loughlin has explored the reaction in the late nineteenth and early twentieth centuries against the prevailing orthodoxy of analytical legal positivism, underpinned as it was by the political values of classical liberalism and exemplified in the public sphere by the work of Dicey. He describes this new turn as a "functionalist" one that did not constitute a distinct programmatic school so much as a "style" or, to adapt Neil Duxbury's description of American legal realism,[36] mood in English legal thought. This functionalist approach was "a practical, reformist approach, offering solutions to a variety of legal challenges facing modern government and spanning the range from institutional reforms to alternative modes of interpretation and methods of legal reasoning." By his account it was a broad church and not without its contradictory elements and crosswinds, but its basic thrust was against the tenets of classical liberalism. Nonetheless, although it "no longer provided the official ideology of the twentieth-century administrative state, . . . [the] precepts [of classical liberalism] remained built into the foundations of public law thought." In challenging the atomistic assumptions implicit in the construction of individualism and by reworking the central political concepts of liberty and community, the functionalists "aimed to set in place a different, more accurate appreciation of the relationship between individual, state, and society."[37] Functionalists regarded the extending role of the state in social life as a progressive and positive trend and saw the role of the lawyer in an activist participative light. They greeted the rise of the administrative state as a step toward the positive provision of liberty. However, they also maintained, if not accentuated, a theme running through the work of Victorian liberal writers on the British constitution, Bagehot and Dicey most eminently, who saw it primarily as a place where things happened, rather than as the product of underlying design (like the American Constitution). Under that very broad umbrella one can surely put Pember Reeves.

As with the functionalists at large, Pember Reeves' works, *State Experiments* especially, offer an affirmation of legislative agency, setting out his Benthamite belief in the science of legislation deliberately shorn of its individualistic spin. In his advocacy of piecemeal legal change and reform for collectivist ends, Pember Reeves, the younger and the more mature, does not allow himself to be constrained by the traditional quality of extant institutions or by the past for its own sake. Although he is prepared to work incrementally through existing institutions and legal forms, it is not because they have an inherent legitimacy that requires their preservation, but rather because strategy is necessary since one cannot expect humans to exit or shed immediately the comfort of known institutions and practices. Although there is a distrust of the perfection of a total system, the gradual working toward collective fairness and social justice shows no sentimental attachment to extant institutions and legal forms. Thus Pember Reeves' state-centered reformism necessarily found more traction in a society that was not enraptured by a sense of its own past.

He had also shown that outlook in *The Long White Cloud* (1898), the first edition of which was completed in London a few years before *State Experiments*. Like most of his work, this book was written for a general readership and has many of the hallmarks of the later work. As an author Pember Reeves never left behind the journalist of his early career and, despite his legal education, neither did he lapse into the typical common-lawyer's love of the historical constitution. His history of the Anglo-Pākehā polity begins almost cleanly—the settlers bringing their best racial attributes but without any historical baggage. Their constitutional agency is not limited by the historical features or attributes of their form of government, on whose description he barely dwells. There is none of the constitutional historian's concern for the origins of the settlers' form of government, be it imperial and rooted in the common law, treaty, or otherwise.[38] Nor, it may be added, does Pember Reeves ever let their own short past manacle the settlers' polity. Their turbulent relations with Māori read like the report of a cricket game between two well-matched sides in which the Anglo one is destined to prevail because of its inherently superior racial attributes, a superiority that he sees Māori desiring to emulate. Doubtless this was a view buoyed from afar by his awareness of the rising political careers of new Maori leadership through James Carroll and Apirana Ngata. Guilt, another form of rumination upon the past, does not affect Pember Reeves' Pākehā polity.[39]

Pember Reeves did not give the colonial and imperial institutions of government more than a functional aspect. His commitment was to the state and empire as mechanisms for collective and civilized social justice, not as sacred relics or manifestations of a mythologized past. There was no Whiggism in his history, no cringing suggestion of institutional form so glorious, and such a tabernacle of its past, as to be incapable of present-day reform or adjustment, however small and shaped by local exigency. Indeed, his history, like his future New Zealand utopia, had what Keith Sinclair called "something domestic" about it.[40] For Pember Reeves, then, the invocation of historical legitimacy was to be shunned as a conservative tactic and impediment to reform. Nonetheless he believed in historical destiny, as well as racial ascendancy. He talked of socialism teleologically, as if it were a historical inevitability. Pharos saw Harry Atkinson, then Conservative prime minister of New Zealand, as embodying the "unconscious socialism" that was destined to prevail. *State Experiments* was a compendium of the small steps taken by practical men to that end. For Pember Reeves, socialism represented the drumbeat, the inexorable endpoint of history, and its champions were the figures who step by step gallantly marched history along its ordained path whilst the "individualists" stood impotently on the sideline.

Pember Reeves did not set out to explain the formal processes, structures, jurisdictional compasses, and constraints on public authority. That was the province (if not fixation) of the constitutional lawyer, including that of the new breed of administrative lawyer who would appear at the London School of Economics between the Wars (where Pember Reeves was director, 1908–1911).[41] For him legislative agency was taken as given and unconstrained, apart from the practical expedience of gradualism. As has been noted, description of its pathways and the nature of the administrative edifices of the state did not detain him. Rather, his conception of public law and constitutional authority was to see it as instrumental toward particular policy goals and outcomes. Ultimately his orientation was that of the politician-lawyer—the species he extolled—rather than the constitutional lawyer, either new LSE breed or old Diceyan. What interested him were the policy outcomes of the instrumental use of public authority, rather than the mechanisms for its exercise and, possibly, constraint. The common law as such barely rates mention, suggesting his agreement with the functionalists' skepticism of it as a vehicle for social progress. Pember Reeves cannot be described as a constitutional lawyer or historian.

The obvious contrast to be drawn is with Pember Reeve's contemporary Albert Venn Dicey, Britain's great mouthpiece of illimitable parliamentary supremacy, who most certainly saw himself as a constitutional lawyer. Early in the twentieth century Dicey became unnerved by the implications of this doctrine as he had previously expounded it.[42] His Britain had become a place where the likes of Pember Reeves, Webb, and their radical Fabian set threatened to put that doctrine to the mischievous ends of Home Rule, socialism, and the suffragettes. Dicey sought, therefore, to refashion it through the advocacy of referenda as a brake upon the legislative power.[43] The meddlesome Pember Reeves, however, is a template for the activist lawyer-politician of the new twentieth century, especially in the United Kingdom.[44] *State Experiments* after all was published in England for a British readership. Ultimately Pember Reeves' practical guide to the socialist state is a roadmap for his British fellow travelers. His account of an Anglo polity—unshackled by sentimental attachment to its past and steered by practical men aware of the dislocation arising from sudden change, and so taking incremental, experimental, and adaptable measures toward achievement of the ideal society—suggested the possibility of a shared Anglo-imperial history of socialism. This brings us back to his support of imperial federation, which he saw as a political and confraternal as well as rational association of states (and a race) sharing the same destiny, rather than as a constitutionally encompassed structure.

IV

It has been said that egalitarianism, authoritarianism, and pragmatism have been salient cultural attitudes toward the exercise of public power in

New Zealand.[45] Certainly those dispositions surface strongly in the works of Pember Reeves considered here. One can see those attitudes reinforcing what have been identified as the key norms of the (Pākehā) New Zealand constitution: representative democracy, parliamentary sovereignty, and the unwritten and evolving nature of the constitution.[46] Yet, as the impact of Bellamy's *Looking Backward* showed, Arcadian and, increasingly in the consolidation of the long Liberal era, utopian elements were also in the mix, downplaying, if not eliminating, the historical consciousness inside a sense of the unwritten constitution whilst boosting a sense of the polity as essentially forward-looking and chosen. It was God's Own Country, moving forward in time and destined because of the inherent qualities of its citizenry: strapping practical British stock—civic minded, industrious, and decent people of cultural and racial homogeneity, temperate people toiling respectfully and honestly in a temperate clime. These were not a people burdened by a difficult past, either inherited or of their own very recent making, but blessed with the democratic institutions of a beneficent state. Those tendencies were fixed into the Pākehā political identity as early as 1890. It was already a place of the endless golden weather, an imagined Eden always looking forward in time, of shining prospects, and from whence the serpent of history had been banished. And once he had exited New Zealand politics and joined the Fabian salons of London, Pember Reeves was able to suggest to a new readership, a British one, that this might also be achieved there. The attention his work drew was not a consequence of metropolitan interest in New Zealand for its own sake. Rather, the interest lay in the possibilities—the transpositions—it suggested for reform in England itself.

In 1902 William Pember Reeves published what is often regarded as his finest poem, "A Colonist in His Garden." The poem is a conversation between a Pākehā New Zealander and an Englishman, in which the former spurns the blandishments of "home" in England. In this poem Pember Reeves leaves the voice of the essayist and historian for a poetic dialogue that exposes overtly the tension inside *State Experiments* between the locus of political agency and reform (Anglo Australasia) and his primary readership (England). The Englishman talks to his New Zealand friend as coming from a country without history and of bland undiscriminating egalitarianism:[47]

A land without a past; a race
Set in the rut of commonplace;
Where Demos overfed
Allows no gulf, respects no height;

And grace and colour, music, light
From sturdy scorn are fled.

The colonist has the final word, but the outcome of their exchange is irresolute. The possibilities of action that come from living in a "land without a past" are not poetically transposed or seen as potentially capable of transposition. Rather, they are now "rooted" in the Anglo New Zealand soil. There is no suggestion of the possibility of shared international histories, as raised so enthusiastically by Pharos and put proudly and squarely in a more Anglo context by *State Experiments*. The colonist stresses the incommensurable particularities of the Anglo New Zealand experience. It is an early hint, put poetically and in a voice not directly his own, of Pember Reeves' retreat from the possibility of an international history of socialism, the dimming of the prospect that the publication of Bellamy's *Looking Backward* had once so excited in him:

Here am I rooted. Firm and fast
We men take root who face the blast
When to the desert come,
We stand where none before have stood…
"No Art?" Who serves an art more great
Than we, rough architects of State
With the old Earth at Strife?
"No colour?" In the silent waste
In pigments not to be effaced
We paint the hues of life.

Notes

1. William Pember Reeves, *State Experiments in Australia and New Zealand*, 2 vols. (London: Grant Richards, 1902), I, p. 68.
2. On the influence of Henry George on New Zealand politicians of the pre-Liberal era before 1891 (such as Sir George Grey, John Balance, William Rolleston, Sir Robert Stout and John McKenzie) see Frank Roger "The Influence of Political Theories in the Liberal Period, 1890–1912: Henry George and John Stuart Mill," in *Studies of a Small Democracy. Essays in Honour of Willis Airey*, ed. R. Chapman and K. Sinclair (Auckland: Auckland University Press, 1963), 153–74 (pp. 155–60).
3. James Belich *Replenishing the Earth: The Settler Revolution and the Rise of the Anglo-World, 1783–1939* (Oxford: Oxford University Press, 2009), especially chap. 5.

4. See the now classic description of ideal-society types by J.C. Davis *Utopia and the Ideal Society: A Study of English Utopian Writing, 1516–1700* (Cambridge: Cambridge University Press, 1981), pp. 20–39.
5. Lyman Tower Sargent, "Themes in Utopian Fiction in English before Wells," *Science Fiction Studies*, 3 (1976) <https://depauw.edu/sfs/backissues/10/sargent10art.htm> [accessed February 17, 2010].
6. The impact of utopian literature on Australian constitutional thought has been noted, particularly in the debate leading up to federation (1901): Helen Irving, *To Constitute a Nation: A Cultural History of Australia's Constitution* (Cambridge: Cambridge University Press, 1997), pp. 37–46.
7. Dominic Alessio, "Promoting Paradise: Utopianism and National Identity in New Zealand, 1870–1930," *New Zealand Journal of History*, 42 (2008), 22–40 (p. 22).
8. The five were Dr Isaac Featherston (1871–1876); Sir Julius Vogel (1876–1880); Sir Francis Dillon Bell (1880–1891); Sir Westby Brook Perceval (1891–1895); and William Pember Reeves (1895–1905). The office soon became regarded as the virtual peak of colonial office beyond even the premiership.
9. Miles Fairburn, *The Ideal Society and Its Enemies: The Foundations of Modern New Zealand Society 1850–1900* (Auckland: Auckland University Press, 1989), p. 51.
10. See Rollo Arnold "Community in Rural Victorian New Zealand," *New Zealand Journal of History*, 24 (1990), 3–21 (p. 3).
11. Ibid. p. 27.
12. Austin Mitchell *The Half Gallon Quarter Acre Pavlova Paradise* (Wellington: Whitcombe and Tombes, 1972).
13. Olssen, *Building the New World* at pp. 162, 191, and 219. Olssen also stresses the emphasis of non-conformist Protestant writers, such as Robert Blatchford's *Merrie England* (1893), which was also serialized in the New Zealand press of the time. Olssen notes that in the early 1890s there was a dramatic shift in attitudes toward the role of the state, especially amongst working people.
14. Tom Brooking, "Busting Up the Greatest Estate of All: Liberal Maori Land Policy, 1891–1911," *New Zealand Journal of History*, 6 (1992), 78–98 (p. 78).
15. Raewyn Dalziel, *Julius Vogel–Business Politician* (Auckland: Auckland University Press, 1991), pp. 302–3.
16. Alessio, "Promoting Paradise."
17. But see Erik Olssen "Where to from Here? Reflections on the Twentieth-Century Historiography of Nineteenth-Century New Zealand" in *The Shaping of History: Essays from the New Zealand Journal of History, 1967–1999*, ed. Judith Binney (Wellington: Bridget Williams Books, 2001), pp. 337–55 (p. 337) who sees W.H. Oliver as a New Zealand historian who, unusually, has been more interested in "ideas."
18. Frank Rogers, "The Influence of Political Theories in the Liberal Period, 1890–1912: Henry George and John Stuart Mill" in *Studies in a Small Democracy*, ed. Chapman and Sinclair, pp. 154–59. The Knights of Labour were assemblies of reform minded individuals of which there were some sixty

or so through the country in the 1880s and 1890s, modeled on the American organization in which Henry George was prominent.

19. See the classic essay by R.T. Shannon, "The Fall of Reeves, 1893–1896" in *Studies in a Small Democracy*, ed. Chapman and Sinclair, pp. 140–54.
20. Pharos, *Some Historical Articles on Communism and Socialism. Their Dream, Their Experiments, Their Aims, Their Influence* (Christchurch: Lyttleton Times Office, 1890), p. 1. London School of Economics Hutchinson Collection #1058 (copy sent by the author to 'Sydney [*sic* at p. 47] Webb).
21. Ibid., p. 1.
22. Ibid., pp. 2 and 8.
23. Ibid., p. 16–17.
24. Ibid., p. 19.
25. Ibid., p. 25: "Out of this the Russian peasant, boorish in looks and tastes though he be, has emerged one of the kindest, gentlest creatures on earth, full of capabilities for improvement and a higher civilisation." Of course, there is no suggestion of Bolshevism.
26. Pharos, *Some Historical Articles*, pp. 25–26.
27. Ibid., p. 40.
28. Ibid., p. 45. This passage is in the undergraduate compilation *Speeches and Documents on New Zealand History*, ed. W.D. McIntyre and W.J. Gardner (Oxford: Clarendon Press, 1971), pp. 191–94 (pp. 193–94).
29. Reeves, *State Experiments*, p. 68.
30. Pharos, *Some Historical Articles*, p. 42.
31. Reeves, *State Experiments*, p. 55.
32. P.G. McHugh, "Sir John Salmond and the Moral Agency of the State," *Victoria University of Wellington Law Review*, 38 (2007), 743–70 (p. 743).
33. Reeves, *State Experiments*, p. 72.
34. Keith Sinclair, *William Pember Reeves: New Zealand Fabian* (Oxford: Clarendon Press, 1965), p. 266.
35. Duncan Bell, "Republican Imperialism: J.A. Froude and the Virtue of Empire," *History of Political Thought*, 30 (2009), 166–91 (p. 166).
36. Neil Duxbury, *Patterns of American Jurisprudence* (Oxford: Oxford University Press, 1995), p. 69. His views of this movement have not been uncontroversial: Brian Leiter "Is There an American Jurisprudence?," *Oxford Journal of Legal Studies*, 17 (1997), 367–87 (pp. 375–78).
37. Martin Loughlin, "The Functionalist Style in Public Law," *University of Toronto Law Journal*, 55 (2005), 361–403 (p. 366).
38. A major contrasting and almost contemporary example is J. Hight and H. Bamford *The Constitutional History of New Zealand* (Christchurch: Whitcombe and Tombs, 1914), which locates New Zealand squarely inside the Whig imperial and constitutional paradigm of the early twentieth century, a characterization entirely absent from Pember Reeves.
39. This, of course, becomes the revision of the Pember Reeves' non-cringing historiographical paradigm of Pākehā history that occurs after World War Two, notably in the work of Keith Sinclair: see Olssen "Where to from here?"
40. Sinclair, *William Pember Reeves*, p. 212.

41. See Janet McLean, "British Idealism and the Administrative State," Paper presented at the Comparative Administrative Law Conference, Yale Law School, May 7–9, 2009.
42. There is no doubt that Dicey's constitutional thought as presented in his text *Introduction to the Study of the Law of the Constitution* (London: Macmillan, 1885) eventually became highly influential, especially after his death (1922), however the extent of its influence in his own lifetime remains a subject of academic debate.
43. M. Qvortrup "A.V. Dicey: The Referendum as the Peoples Veto," *History of Political Thought*, 20 (1999), 531–46 (p. 531).
44. For an account of the disappearance of historical consciousness and referencing from British constitutional discourse in the twentieth century and its impact (i.e., lack of a restraining influence) upon reformist lawyer-politicians of the modern era (as, notably, Tony Blair, Charles Falconer and Jack Straw) see John Allison, *The English Historical Constitution: Continuity, Change and European Effects* (Cambridge: Cambridge University Press, 2007).
45. Matthew S.R. Palmer, "New Zealand Constitutional Culture," *New Zealand Universities Law Review*, 22 (2007), 565–97 (p. 565).
46. Ibid., p. 565.
47. "A Colonist in his Garden," published in the *Monthly Review* (1902), text in *An Anthology of New Zealand Poetry in English*, ed. Jenny Bornholdt, Gregory O'Brien, and Mark Williams (Auckland: Oxford University Press, 1997), pp. 497–98.

Part IV

The Crown in Colonial New Zealand

Chapter 11

Sovereignty as Governance in the Early New Zealand Crown Colony Period

Shaunnagh Dorsett

This chapter discusses the movement of laws and the transmission of ideas across Empire.[1] In particular, it traces several ways in which sovereignty was understood in certain British intellectual contexts during the key period of the first half of the nineteenth century, and the various constructs of sovereignty that were employed in response to specific circumstances of colonial governance. The topic around which this consideration of sovereignty is organized is that of the problem of the ordering of empire and of the management of colonial relations, both between metropole and colony, and with respect to the internal legal order of one colony—New Zealand.

These matters are explored through the writings of two men—Henry Samuel Chapman (1803–1881) and George Cornewall Lewis (1806–1863). Chapman was appointed second judge of the Supreme Court of New Zealand in 1843. Both before and after this appointment he wrote on various aspects of sovereignty: Britain's acquisition of sovereignty over New Zealand/Aotearoa; the relationship of British and Māori sovereignty; and the internal legal ordering of New Zealand. These can be found in different genres of legal scholarship itself: published material, largely in the service of the New Zealand Company; extrajudicial commentary; and judgments. For his part, George Cornewall Lewis was a classicist, lawyer, and administrator and presents a different but intersecting perspective on this set of issues. In the 1830s and 1840s he published both in political theory and constitutional law, examining the notion of sovereignty and the relationship of Britain to her colonies. The lives of Chapman and

Lewis briefly intersect: both are lawyers; both are on the periphery of a particular intellectual milieu in London in the 1830s; and both attended John Austin's lectures at University College London in the early part of that decade.

Here it is possible to only briefly introduce the work of these two figures. Despite their quite different roles, there are commonalities in their writing. Like New Zealand's founding itself, both Chapman and Cornewall Lewis sit in that relatively underexplored place between the end of the "First Empire" and the rise of what might be termed "Victorian international law" from the 1860s.[2] The first part of the century is sometimes dismissed as a period of little interest for those investigating sovereignty. It is, however, a period in which a particular juridical form of sovereignty began to solidify within British theory and practice and, conversely, one in which colonial judges still looked to diverse conceptions of sovereignty in order to fashion local legal settlements.[3]

Cornewall Lewis and Chapman used particular concepts of sovereignty to perform particular tasks.[4] Both were legally trained, but both read widely in politics, philosophy, and history. For much of the history of the common law, little distinction was made between law and these other disciplines.[5] In this period, however, those distinctions become sharper. Chapman and Lewis drew on a range of disciplinary knowledges,[6] yet they wrote primarily within the genre of English jurisprudence. In fact, their method is that not only of the common lawyer, but in particular of common lawyers inspired by the new legal science of the nineteenth century. Unsurprisingly, therefore, their borrowings from other disciplinary traditions were not always precise or even particularly discerning. This was not uncommon. Judges and lawyers not infrequently referred to works of philosophy and political theory, but the ways in which they deployed them were often at odds with their original context.[7] However, they constituted sources like any other, and such usage was long part of the tradition of the common law itself and of the art of judgment.

This chapter does not trace the histories of the vocabularies in which Chapman and Cornewall Lewis talked about sovereignty, but it does draw attention to the different ways lawyers in this period still talked about and used sovereignty in structuring legal settlements, both across Empire and within a colony such as New Zealand. For both Chapman and Cornewall Lewis, sovereignty was an instrument of governance. Part I of the chapter discusses Chapman's early construction of sovereignty as a mode of organizing relations between the British Crown and the New Zealand Company, while Part II considers Cornwall Lewis's elaboration of a singular and "absolute" sovereignty (re)located in the now imperial parliament. Finally, Part III returns to Chapman, this time focusing on his legal judgments, tracing his exploration of different constructions of sovereignty and its task within the context of the governance of the new colony.

I. Discovery

After a career in Canada, largely as a newspaper man, Chapman trained at the Middle Temple in London and was called to the Bar. He was well-connected in radical circles through his writing for various publications (subediting the *London Review* and, its successor, the *London and Westminster Review*), his association with John Roebuck's *Pamphlets for the People*, and his work as an advocate for the New Zealand Company.[8] He worked as a subeditor (unacknowledged though), under Bowring, of Bentham's works[9] and he was a Benthamite utilitarian,[10] albeit with a practical, reformist bent. As a group, the "philosophical radicals" were ambivalent toward empire. As a broad generalization, they were mostly anticolonial in the period pre-1830, but after that time many became associated with the new imperial endeavors, in particular Wakefield's systematic model of colonization.[11] Chapman personally expressed broadly anticolonial sentiments, agreeing with Adam Smith that colonies were an "evil influence," not least as a burden on expenditure.[12] Nevertheless, he was strongly in favor of Wakefieldian principles of colonization, explaining Wakefield's position and commenting at some length on their advantages in the 1842 *Encyclopaedia Britannica* entry for "Zealand, new." Colonies that were not a drain on England's finances and that furnished resources were quite a different prospect.[13]

In the late 1830s, Chapman published several works on sovereignty and New Zealand.[14] Chapman built on these works after his appointment to the Bench, writing in 1845 on the "Status of the Native Races considered in relation to the sovereignty."[15] A comparison of Chapman's various works reveals that between the late 1830s and 1861 his views on sovereignty remained virtually unchanged.[16] The 1845 text, however, necessarily factors in the position of Māori. Although Māori were hardly missing from earlier discussions, their position was subordinate. This is not to say that the position of Māori could be ignored. The clear distinction of Māori on the scale of civilization from their Australian counterparts meant that any formulation of sovereignty had to take that presence into account. Through his connections with the company, Chapman had received much material on the Māori.[17] His early writings though were not primarily concerned with British sovereignty vis-à-vis the Māori, other than in so far as was necessary to establish legitimate British sovereignty, which in turn could underpin systematic settlement plans of the New Zealand Company. What was at stake was the ordering of the relations between British Crown sovereignty and the New Zealand Company's settlement plans. Chapman's audience, therefore, was the Colonial Office, government officials, and the supporters of Wakefield and the New Zealand Company.

It was the Crown's official stance in the late 1830s that the Māori had sufficient sovereignty (or sovereignties) such that consent was prerequisite to the acquisition of British *imperium*.[18] The method chosen in the end to acquire sovereignty was treaty. The capacity of "barbarous nations" to enter into legal relations had long been established, and the Colonial Office took the stance that Māori could enter into such relations.[19] However, the consent of all *iwi* (tribal groups) was not obtained, and in the end Hobson chose in addition to declare the Crown's sovereignty by proclamation, declaring sovereignty obtained by cession over the North Island and simply asserting it over the South Island and Stewart's Island.[20] These steps were sufficient for the Crown. Sovereignty was based on treaty and/or proclamations.[21] Concerned to acquire title from Māori, the New Zealand Company initially also took the view that Māori were independent sovereigns with the capacity to transfer land to third parties. Later, they moved to endorsing the doctrine of discovery.[22] The company then took the stance that lands that were not subject to Māori proprietorship could be transferred by Crown grant to settlers in its proposed settlements.[23] In 1839 the company began the acquisition of land in the lower part of the North Island and the upper portion of the South Island by purchase from the Māori.[24] For Chapman, therefore, one of the key issues was the timing of the acquisition of sovereignty, and the consequent status of land titles acquired prior to the Treaty of Waitangi in 1840. It was no coincidence that Chapman published a number of works on the acquisition of Crown sovereignty in the critical year of 1840.

Chapman agreed that sovereignty had been effectively established over New Zealand. Despite acknowledging the capacity of native nations to contract, Chapman denied that sovereignty followed from either of the instruments accepted by the Crown: the Treaty or Proclamation. Rather, he based the Crown's sovereign rights on the doctrine of discovery and subsequent possession/occupation, prior to the signing of the Treaty of Waitangi. He thus stated repeatedly that "it is a well-known principle of international law that discovery and occupation give to the discovering nation a right of sovereignty *as against all civilized powers*. The relations which the discovering country may establish with the native tribes do not in any way affect this right of sovereignty."[25] In "Is Killing No Murder in New Zealand?—A Dilemma" he reiterated that that "we have already expressed our opinion that her Majesty has possessed a right of sovereignty over New Zealand from the period of Cook's discovery. This right has been repeatedly exercised; and, until recently, was never disputed."[26]

As an advocate for the New Zealand Company, Chapman found it certainly suited to argue that sovereignty had already been acquired by the late 1830s: "the expedient of repudiating the sovereignty of New Zealand, seems to have been hit upon for the purpose of deterring people from joining in, or in any way seconding, any plan of colonization which might be put forward."[27] Chapman recited what he perceived as a number of anomalies flowing from the Colonial Office's repudiation of sovereignty before 1840, suggesting that "the inconsistencies into which government must necessarily be involved by the foolish jealousies of the colonial-office would fill one number, and therefore tire our readers"[28] Unsurprisingly, the Land Claims Commission was seen as a major anomaly.[29] If there was no sovereignty prior to1840 then the commission could not have had jurisdiction to consider land titles from the earlier period. If jurisdiction did exist prior to 1840 then Hobson's proclamation on titles in 1840 was "a dead letter." Either way, the company's pre-1840 interests could be maintained. He concluded, "The Treaty of cession and the [Land Claims] commission are like buckets in a well—both cannot appear on the stage together."[30]

Chapman, therefore, viewed the process of acquisition of sovereignty by the Crown as simply an attempt to "embarrass the New Zealand Company,"[31] labeling Hobson's commission as consul, later lieutenant governor, as a "farce."[32] It was, he said,

> extremely difficult to understand the principle on which a part of the executive government of this country can treat as *alien* a country over which we have certainly constantly exercised sovereign functions.... It has been exercised in many ways. Magistrates have been appointed; criminals have been taken up, have been carried to Sydney, and there been tried and punished. Yet in 1839 her Majesty was advised to declare that the crown had no jurisdiction over those islands... and that if we accredited any representative of the crown to make his appearance in New Zealand, it must be in the character of a *consul* only that he could enter into preliminary negotiations with the chiefs, to barter sovereignty for a blanket.[33]

Chapman thus viewed the Colonial Office as actively obstructionist regarding the New Zealand Company's acquisitive activities, commenting in 1836 (albeit in a slightly different context) on "the hatred of all official personages to the proposal of a colony to pay its own expenses."[34] At that time, he could be almost dismissive of the place of Māori in the affairs of colonial administration. In his entry on "Zealand, new," for example, Chapman discussed the Māori largely in order to point out the advantages to them of colonization by the company and their limited needs for land as cultivators.[35] He noted in August 1840 that "some time since, it suited the Government to treat with a few of the chiefs as independent sovereigns. There was nothing in this, as the Americans do so every day: but after it had been nearly forgotten, as any other amusing farce would have been, it was laid hold of, among other events, as a reason for renouncing the sovereignty of New Zealand."[36]

By 1845, Chapman remained unequivocal in his rejection of treaty-based sovereignty: "The Waitangi Treaty [is] considered (erroneously) as the *foundation* of the Queen's sovereignty."[37] Discovery was a surer ground than the treaty , as it obviated the "legal difficulty noticed" that the treaty was not binding on those who had not signed it.[38] However, although Chapman may not have seen the treaty as the foundation of sovereignty, that did not mean it was null. It clearly was binding on those who signed it, and in any case it was a sufficient mechanism by which *iwi* could divest themselves of the limited sovereignty that they retained post-discovery: "It is [their] modified sovereignty which the natives of New Zealand part with by the Treaty of Waitangi."[39] Thus, although Māori might be admitted to the *ius gentium* as treaty sovereigns, it was for a limited purpose only—to contract away rights—making their "sovereignty" quite different to that of Britain.[40] This was a cautious, but not complete, admittance to the *ius gentium*.

In his writings prior to his appointment to the New Zealand Supreme Court, Chapman's attention was thus focused primarily on the Crown's acquisition of sovereignty, principally to assert the Crown's claims over the Māori, but also against the French.[41] At that time sovereignty served the purpose of bolstering the goal of systematic colonization and the plans of the company. As a matter of governance, the doctrine of discovery provided Chapman with a means of arguing for the acquisition of sovereignty prior to 1840 and hence for the prior title rights of the company. However, the doctrine of discovery is a configuration of sovereignty with consequences, if for no other reason than that its result is divided sovereignty. This is clear from Chapman's own formulations. According to Marshall CJ's decisions in *Johnson v M'Intosh* and *Cherokee Nation*, cases with which Chapman was familiar, sovereignty via discovery was acquired principally against other European nations, while the Indian nations retained a domestic dependent version of sovereignty, subordinate to that of the United States and tied to a territorial base.[42] Unless and until they parted with that sovereignty or it was extinguished by conquest, the tribes retained their residual sovereignty.[43] Each party (federal, state, and tribal) has different spheres of ordering in which they have competence and responsibility, although the boundaries between these competences are fluid and subject to reinterpretation.

Thus, the American constitutionalism of the 1840s stood in stark contrast to that of Britain, both internally and as emerging within the order of British Empire in the nineteenth century.

II. Crown and Empire

In turning to the writings of George Cornewall Lewis, we move to a different intellectual genre—that of the "science of politics"—to consider a construction of sovereignty that differs significantly from those discussed so far. Paul McHugh has written of the emergence of a particular version of sovereignty that came to dominate British constitutionalism in the mid-nineteenth century and beyond, particularly in relation to its dependencies. McHugh refers to this as "Leviathan sovereignty."[44] It is, of course, Leviathan only in so far as its nineteenth-century architects, Austin and Bentham, and later Dicey, made use of Hobbes, albeit a Hobbes transformed by his reception in the common law domain.

By the time of the colonization of New Zealand, the British Empire was "conceived increasingly in terms of hierarchy and subordination, rather than, as the American colonists had originally viewed it, as an 'empire of liberty.' "[45] Since the 1770s, Britain had survived a series of colonial crises including the loss of the American colonies and upheavals in Canada. These forced thinking about the ordering of empire. What was required was a united empire, controlled effectively from London, through the medium of the British Parliament. This in turn led to an emphasis on the sovereignty of the imperial Parliament, with a concurrent downplaying of the liberties of colonists and the requirements of representative government in the colonies.[46] This new authoritarian atmosphere was mirrored at home, a response to concerns over order and licentiousness in the mid to late eighteenth century. The position is summed up by Thomas Erskine May in 1841: "The authority of parliament extends over the United Kingdom and all its colonies and foreign possessions. There are no other limits to its power of making laws for the whole empire."[47] Here, therefore, the task of sovereignty was to organize and structure a certain relationship within Empire between England and the colonies.

At the time of New Zealand's colonization a number of tracts began to appear on Britain, the empire, and Britain's relationship to her dependencies. Perhaps the best known was by Herman Merivale, although his contemporaries probably saw Cornewall Lewis's *Government of Dependencies* as intellectually superior.[48] These tracts were joined by a raft of other publications between 1840 and 1860, by John Roebuck, Macaulay, J.S. Mill,

Thomas Erskine May, Jerrod and Clark, to name a few.[49] These were largely works of political economy and of constitutional law. George Cornewall Lewis was a classicist, lawyer, government servant, and self-proclaimed disciple of the English legal philosopher John Austin (1790–1859).[50] Lewis was a prolific writer, publishing in linguistics, classics, political theory, and law. He also held a number of government posts, including chancellor of the exchequer, home secretary, and secretary of state for war. Lewis was never secretary of state for the colonies, but he influenced Herman Merivale, who did hold that post. His *Government of Dependencies* (1841) is frequently referred to and infrequently read, while his *Use and Abuse of Political Terms* (1832) is even less well known.[51]

Use and Abuse was described by its editor, Thomas Raleigh, as "the first fruits of John Austin's lectures."[52] It was one of the first works by a student of Austin. Like Austin, Lewis took great pride in delineating his field of study. Also like Austin, Cornewall Lewis held a perspective that was juridical. He was interested in juridical rather than political sovereignty—that is, in the constitutional or public-law powers of the Crown. What makes Lewis interesting for our present concerns is his willingness to grapple with the contemporary nature of sovereignty, both conceptually and within the British colonial order, at the moment of New Zealand's founding as a Crown colony. In this he relied on Austin's conception of sovereignty (if not his methodology) as the basis for understanding the nature and form of a sovereign government, and of the relations of a dominant and dependent community.[53] Late in the nineteenth century, the philosopher John Dewey credited Hobbes and Lewis, rather than Austin himself, with the main version of "Austinian sovereignty" that circulated during that century: "A careful study of Austin's *Jurisprudence* has convinced me that the theory that is ordinarily put forward under his name is not his at all. If it belongs to anyone, Hobbes and Cornewall Lewis deserve that it be credited to them."[54] As Walter Bagehot put it in the 1881, "Mr Austin seized hold of several strong minds, and by the help of these he greatly influenced his time. You will find thoughts distinctly traceable to him far away among people who have never heard of him."[55]

Cornewall Lewis intended to be precise in his understanding and use of the word "sovereignty." As he wrote in 1832 in his *Use and Abuse of Political Terms,* the book was "intended to assist in assuring the results or detecting the fallacies of political reasoning by putting the reader on his guard against unconsciously passing from one signification of a word to another."[56] His method was to determine the province of words from "agreed vocabularies," specifically including the works of those authors with whom he disagreed, such as Blackstone.[57] As such this method appears more Benthamite than Austinian, although it may, in fact, have owed more to Whatley.[58] Austin generally proceeded by analytic taxonomy, not agreed usage. Nevertheless, in the particular context of "sovereignty" Cornewall Lewis noted that certain "words owe a divided allegiance to politics and law—there is an imperfect separation of their provinces so they lie on debatable ground. In these, such as right, sovereignty &c, I have followed the definitions laid down by Mr Austin in the outline of his lectures on General Jurisprudence."[59] Unsurprisingly, he also used the same sources as Austin, for example, Paley, Bentham, and Blackstone. In effect, what results is a genealogy of key terms, perhaps not unexpected from one trained as a common lawyer. Lewis noted that he had also the "advantage of hearing filled up by Mr Austin, in his oral lectures,"[60] an advantage enjoyed by Chapman as well. Along with others of the Bentham circle, including Cornewall Lewis, Chapman attended Austin's lectures in the early 1830s at University College London, labeling him "a great writer on jurisprudence."[61]

Cornewall Lewis's view of the nature of sovereignty is placed within the context of the British constitutional structure. Like Austin, Cornewall Lewis was of the opinion that juridical sovereignty was vested in the King-in-Parliament, rather than in parliamentary electors or, still less, in a rights-bearing Lockean "people."[62] Britain was a "constitutional" (aristocratic) monarchy. Sovereignty was, therefore, located in the King, House of Commons, and the House of Lords. On this doctrine, the political authority of the King-in-Parliament is constitutionally absolute in the sense of being subject to no higher agency or law: "There is no law which it has not power to alter, repeal or enact."[63] Thus, "it is an error to suppose that sovereign government is subject to any other than moral restraints, and that it does not possess an absolute and despotic power. All attempts to limit legally the power of a sovereign government by positive laws, promises, compacts, and constitutional checks or balances, are nugatory."[64]

It is not possible to devote significant space to Austin's views on law and sovereignty here. In brief, Lewis chiefly based his understanding of sovereignty on Austin's distinction between rights and obligations and powers. According to Lewis, a sovereign has powers but cannot be subject to legal (as opposed to moral) rights or duties, as these are the product of positive law, and positive law is the creature of the sovereign.[65] "Law properly signifies a general command of the sovereign, whether conveyed by way of *direct* legislation, as in the case of statutes, or of *permissive* legislation, as in the case of legal rules established by courts of justice."[66] All laws, therefore, are positive laws and, as a result of this distinction between rights and powers of the sovereign, "as long as a government exists, the power of the person or persons in whom the sovereignty resides, over the whole community, is absolute and unlimited."[67] A civil government is, in turn, a body of persons yielding obedience to no superior and issuing commands to do or forbear from certain acts.[68]

This is the conception of sovereignty that underpins Lewis's *Government of Dependencies. Dependencies,* however, has a more specific purpose: to explain the nature of the relationship between Britain and her dependencies. Lewis prefixes an essay, "Preliminary Inquiry," to *Dependencies.* This is an "inquiry into the powers of a sovereign Government," viewed as a necessary precursor to any discussion of the relationship between dominant and subordinate communities. The section on sovereign power derives directly from the definitions in *Use and Abuse.* For Lewis then "a dependency is part of an independent political community which is immediately subject to a subordinate government."[69] This included colonies such as New Zealand.[70] Whatever the type of dependency, according to Lewis, the sovereign government of United Kingdom—consisting of the Crown and the two Houses of Parliament—is supreme in every British dependency.[71] This, of course, is not to preclude subordinate governments residing conjointly with the Crown, such as the East India Company or certain elected bodies, but in all cases these derive their existence and powers from the sovereign.

While early colonies or plantations were practically independent, later colonies were generally placed under subordinate government; since the American War, policy had changed.[72] Cornewall Lewis noted that "since the close of the American war, it has not been the policy of England to vest any portion of the legislative power of the subordinate government of a dependency in a body elected by the inhabitants."[73] Lewis's understanding of sovereignty, as hierarchical and vested in Parliament, sits in opposition to (Lockean) concepts of birthright and liberties of colonists, as invoked, for example, in the many American colonies.[74] This meant that although Lewis was in favor of representative government for colonies, he regarded this as something granted by the imperial sovereign government, rather than as arising from the inalienable rights of the colonists. He declares that what are called *inalienable rights,* such as birthright and liberty, "in most cases never have been rights."[75] This is because the "theory of the state of nature and the social contract," from where they originate, is "an absurd and mischievous doctrine."[76] "All rights must be subsequent to the establishment of government, and are the creatures of the sovereign power."[77] The supremacy of Parliament in the colonies and the subordination of the Crown, which exercises a delegated power over dependencies, to Parliament, were, according to Lewis, confirmed by *Campbell v Hall.* As a result, "in those colonies which are a dominion of the King in right of his Crown, the Crown can give no rights which are contrary to fundamental principles: that is, those laws or rules of law sanctioned by Parliament."[78]

Dependencies owes much to mixed traditions. In part filtering through Austin and Bentham, Lewis draws on political theory concerning the origins and legitimacy of governments and uses this in the task of institutional design. It is perhaps not surprising that this should be the case in the period following the loss of the American colonies, when the issue of legitimate sovereignty had become enmeshed with that of representative government. This is in part the eclecticism of the common lawyer, reliant on materials drawn from an array of sources.

Much of *Dependencies* is taken up with the practice and history of empires, including that of the British Empire. For Lewis, if practice was not theory, then there was at least a high degree of coincidence between them. Lewis's empirical descriptions of the British Empire reveal an external structure that had come to more closely reflect the internal constitutional structure of Britain post 1688.[79] Whatever its intellectual origins, the sovereignty of *Dependencies* is singular and absolute, vested in the Imperial parliament.

III. Sovereignty and Order

If Cornewall Lewis offered a view of colonial sovereignty from the heights of metropolitan jurisprudence, then Chapman's viewpoint was that of a jurist directly engaged in the New Zealand colonial enterprise. We thus return to Chapman in order to consider his views on the legal ordering of colonial relations through the genre of judicial judgment. Here we are interested in the way in which legal science could be put to work as a mode of governance: a pragmatic response to the conditions of the colony—including its violence and "unacceptable" practices—and a means of ordering legal relations between settlers and Māori.

With Chapman as the second judge appointed to the New Zealand Supreme Court, the concept of sovereignty was called on to perform a new set of tasks. Chapman, along with the chief justice, William Martin, played a key role in the organization of relations between Crown, settlers, and Māori. However, in his new office it is not only the task of sovereignty that changes, so too does Chapman's relation to its enunciation. No longer a critic or supplicant of sovereignty, Chapman as Supreme Court judge speaks as an instrument or agent of sovereignty. Seen this way, we are reminded that the courts are one strand of an internally pluralized Crown.[80] From this vantage, the understanding of New Zealand sovereignty appears as an accretion of a number of not necessarily consistent views, not just views held *contra* the Crown but also those held within and by the different strands of the Crown itself.[81] Nonetheless, Crown sovereignty remained the "central principle of constitutional organization" within the colony.[82]

By the mid-1840s, the position of Māori had become increasingly central to Chapman's views on sovereignty. In his 1845 report "The status of the native races considered in relation to the sovereignty," he directly considers the legal relations between Māori and the Crown, in particular the relative characters of Māori and Crown sovereignty. One of the central concerns of this text is with what Chapman saw as the failure of the Crown to deal with Māori disorder and violence. He decried as unacceptable the "toleration" by the Crown of various practices: war, murder, rape, cannibalism. It was the policy of the Crown that laws against the "universal rules of humanity" should not be tolerated, yet the Crown failed either to determine which specific customs should be abrogated or to take action in this regard.[83] In Chapman's opinion, in New Zealand "some Crown officers" had similarly taken the view that no customs of the native tribes, however barbarous, savage, or repugnant to the laws of God, were to be interfered with or put down. This was also the view of many settlers.[84]

In "The status of native races," Chapman remained committed to discovery as the mode of acquisition of sovereignty over New Zealand. His remarks suggest that, like Marshall, he continued to think that where acquisition was by discovery some residual sovereignty may still continue in Māori and that consequently sovereignty was divided. Certainly at the point of discovery some "limited" Māori sovereignty at least was maintained "inter se until they have parted with it by treaty."[85] What, however, was the status of Māori absent the Treaty? Following Marshall's line of argument, did they retain subordinate or domestic sovereignty? His initial comments on this point suggested that the answer was in the affirmative: "I apprehend that the Queen's authority as sovereign by discovery and occupation gives her the clear right...to suppress murder and cannibalism—without interfering with the sovereignty of the tribes."[86] If this were the case, Chapman would not have been the first Australasian judge to argue this position.[87] Not content with this justification for superordinate British sovereignty, however, Chapman immediately adds another: "there is another principle, which ought to have restrained any subjects of the Queen from disputing the propriety of an exercise of sovereign power," namely, the principle of de facto possession. Thus "the mere declaration of the Queen's sovereignty over these Islands is binding and conclusive on all persons who owe her allegiance and even supposing there had been any previous sovereignty in the Islands it would not be entitled to obedience while out of possession." The result is that "the practical application of the rule in New Zealand is that no sovereignty of native chiefs (putting the

Treaty of Waitangi out of the qn) can be legally set up against the authority of the Queen."[88]

Chapman was not the only one to express doubts as to whether absent the Treaty all Māori sovereignties had been effectively "parted with." In 1842 and again in 1843 Swainson, the second attorney-general, suggested that as some *iwi* had not given their consent to the Treaty, they retained their sovereignty and their members were not British subjects. These arguments received short shrift from the Colonial Office. Its stance was that Britain had effectively established sovereignty over all of New Zealand,[89] despite the fact that residual dependant-nation sovereignties had been adopted in other parts of the Empire.

The language of sovereignty based on discovery had been convenient for Chapman when he was an advocate for the New Zealand Company. Once the internal legal ordering of the colony became focal for his official role as Supreme Court judge, though, the consequences of residual Māori sovereignty became problematic. As a result, Chapman goes to some length to confirm that ultimate (singular) authority is vested in the Crown. Subordinate, or residual, sovereignty could ultimately lead to territorial enclaves, areas where "intolerable" customs would be beyond the reach of the sovereign. Confirming Crown sovereignty confirmed the power of the Crown to abrogate such customs. Chapman was not only in favor of this, as might be expected, but went so far as to suggest categories, or lists, of customs to be abrogated and customs that could be tolerated, if not actively enforced, by the courts.[90]

It was not until 1847 that Chapman finally articulated his understanding of the nature of Crown and Māori sovereignty and the relationship between them. Whether acquired through the Treaty of Waitangi, or because of the Crown's de facto possession, he confirmed that the Crown was the only sovereign entity. In the cases of *Rangitapiripiri* (1847) and *Ratea* (1849), Chapman was called upon to determine whether British law applied to the crime of murder *inter se* (between Māori).[91] Here he argued that although Britain held sovereignty, "native law" remained in force between themselves, except where those laws were "contrary to humanity or the Christian religion."[92] He further explained that "in small matters of custom the Court would not interfere;...but in so grave an offence as that of murder, those laws would cease the moment the superior power came into the sovereignty."[93]

Sovereignty, therefore, had two tasks. It provided both the power to judge and the form of judgment. But the shape of that sovereignty is important. Singular sovereignty gives the power to abrogate unpalatable customs. Chapman arrogates to himself as agent of the colony's highest court a power that other Crown officers will not exercise. Although discovery was a useful tool to Chapman as colonial advocate, as judge he required sovereignty to do another task: to enforce fundamental legal norms of conduct for a colonized territory. Chapman may also well have been aware that "small matters of custom" were not always being left to Māori themselves: they were being heard by the courts. But it did not matter, as his concern was not the smaller everyday matters of colonial life and law, but the larger problem of the legal ordering of the colony and the ability of the Crown to effectively manage internal colonial relations.

In affirming singular sovereignty, however, Chapman goes only as far as he needs to. Within empire sovereignty could still take other shapes. Chapman does not, for example, firmly tie sovereignty to territory, as had begun to increasingly characterize the judgments of his Australasian counterparts. Sovereignty gave the right to legislate throughout the territory and to abrogate customs, but it did not necessarily lead to territorial jurisdiction over all inhabitants of the colony in all legal matters. Chapman is well aware that the Crown was not in a position to enforce law and order throughout the colony and that Māori continued to live in many areas under their traditional customs. The precise configuration of sovereignty at any time or location is in part a pragmatic decision of the dictates and capacities of governance. It would be impossible to assert jurisdiction over every "small matter."

Unlike Cornewall Lewis, therefore, but in common with his judicial colleagues in other Australasian colonies, Chapman was engaged in formulating a legal settlement suitable to local circumstances. His judgments thus display an increasing convergence of theory with practice. In New Zealand, New South Wales, South Australia, and Western Australia judges struggled with the same issues, each instituting a slightly different legal understanding of a potential plurality of sovereignties. Nevertheless, Chapman's "pluralism" is located within an increasingly singular and absolute understanding of sovereignty developed within the context of colonial governance. Pluralism can be tolerated, but only under the auspices of the superior normative and coercive power of the Crown.

IV. Concluding Comments

For both Chapman and Cornewall Lewis, judicial sovereignty could be deployed for particular juridical and political purposes. Their legal ordering of empire and colony is a shuttling between the practical dictates of governance and systematic logic or knowledge: constitutionalism as norm and as practice. For Chapman, the legal settlement of the colony was unfolded in the space between pragmatic dictates of governance and the available "scientific" and common-law vocabularies of sovereignty. For Cornewall Lewis, empire and colony took shape between bureaucratic policy and the early nineteenth-century discourse of positive law and singular sovereignty. Both Chapman and Cornewall Lewis had absorbed the new legal science of the early nineteenth century. Their writings offer revealing insights into the manner in which conceptions of sovereignty were deployed in the context of imperial governance during this period. They also indicate profound shifts in the way sovereignty was conceived within the empire during the first half of the nineteenth century.

Notes

1. My particular thanks to Ian Hunter and Shaun McVeigh for comments and suggestions, as well as generally to all the participants of the "Transpositions of Empire" Symposium, Prato, Italy, 2009.
2. On "Victorian International Law" see the essays in *Victorian Visions of Global Order: Empire and International Relations in Nineteenth-Century International Thought*, ed. Duncan Bell (Cambridge: Cambridge University Press, 2007). Like several other recent works this one begins its discussions with the 1860s and thus tends to overlook the vital contributions of the early part of the nineteenth century to resulting formations of sovereignty.
3. Shaunnagh Dorsett, "'Sworn on the Dirt of Graves': Sovereignty, Jurisdiction and the Judicial Abrogation of 'Barbarous' Customs in New Zealand in the 1840s," *The Journal of Legal History*, 30 (2009), 175–97.
4. J.G.A. Pocock, *Political Thought and History: Essays on Theory and Method* (Cambridge: Cambridge University Press, 2009), particularly pp. 4–6.
5. P.G. McHugh, *Aboriginal Societies and the Common Law* (Oxford: Oxford University Press, 2005).
6. J.G.A. Pocock, "The Treaty between Histories" in *Histories: Power and Loss*, ed. Andrew Sharp and P.G. McHugh (Wellington: Bridget Williams Books, 2001), pp. 75–96 (p. 77).
7. See Ian Hunter, "Natural Law, Historiography and Aboriginal Sovereignty," *Legal History*, 11 (2007), 137–68.
8. Peter Spiller, *The Chapman Legal Family* (Wellington: Victoria University Press, 1992), p. 23.
9. [Sir Frederick Revans Chapman] "Memo [to the Department of Internal Affairs] on Presenting His Father's Copy of Jeremy Bentham's Works to the Alexander Turnbull Library," Alexander Turnbull Library (ATL), MS Chapman Papers 1835–1929, Folder 19, Reel 6.

10. On utility ("greatest happiness" etc.) see H.S. Chapman, "Preliminary Reforms: Being a Summary of the Principles Advocated in these Pamphlets," in *Pamphlets for the People*, ed. John Arthur Roebuck (London: Charles Ely, 1835–?), I, No. 22 (1835), 10–16. As to his political bent, see, for example, "Toryphobia," II, No. 9 (1836), 12–16.
11. On the views of Smith, Bentham and others see Donald Winch, *Classical Political Economy and Colonies* (London: Bell & Sons, 1965).
12. H.S. Chapman, "The Colonies," in *Pamphlets for the People*, ed. John Arthur Roebuck, II, No. 8 (1836), 8–12 (pp. 11–12).
13. H.S. Chapman, "Zealand, New," *Encyclopaedia Britannica*, ed. Macvey Napier, 7th edn., 21 vols. (Edinburgh: A & C Black, 1842), XXI, 975–83.
14. See [H.S. Chapman] "The English, the French and the New Zealanders," *The New Zealand Journal*, 1 (1840), 1–2; "Is Killing No Murder in New Zealand?–A Dilemma," *The New Zealand Journal*, 1 (1840), 173–74; and [untitled], *Dublin Review*, 9 (1840), 189–210.
15. H.S. Chapman, "Legal Notes," c1858, ATL, MS-Papers-8670–047. This is a collection of materials which has been collated and designated "1858." By content, this document was written around early 1845.
16. The 1845 document was eventually delivered as a lecture in property law to the Melbourne University Law students in the early 1860s: John Waugh, *First Principles: The Melbourne Law School 1857–2007* (Melbourne: Miegunyah Press, 2007), p. 27.
17. On the clear recognition by both the Colonial Office and the Company that Māori were at a different place on the scale of civilization see Mark Hickford, "Making 'Territorial Rights of the Natives': Britain and New Zealand, 1830–1847" (unpublished doctoral thesis, University of Oxford, 1999)
18. For a detailed legal history of this see P.G. McHugh, "The Aboriginal Rights of the New Zealand Maori at Common Law" (unpublished doctoral thesis, Cambridge University, 1988), p. 83ff; Hobson read two proclamations, the first declaring the boundaries of New South Wales to include New Zealand; the second stating the Crown's intention to only recognize titles derived from the Crown itself: Issued January 30, 1840, Hobson to Gipps, The National Archives, London (TNA), CO 209/7, fols. 23–24.
19. McHugh, *Aboriginal Societies*.
20. Issued May 21, 1840, TNA, CO209/6, fols. 156–58; Hobson to Russell, TNA, CO 209/7, fols. 61–62; *London Gazette*, October 2, 1840; McHugh "Aboriginal Rights of the New Zealand Maori."
21. Stanley to Shortland June 21, 1843, GBPP 1844 xii (556) Appendices, p. 475; Stephen to Hope, minute, December 28, 1842, TNA, CO 209/18, fol. 416.
22. Hickford, "Decidedly the Most Interesting Savages," p. 153.
23. Ibid., p. 136.
24. Ibid., pp. 136–37.
25. Chapman, "Zealand, new," p. 981; "Legal Notes"; "The English, the French and the New Zealanders."
26. Chapman, "Is Killing No Murder," p. 173; and Chapman, "Zealand, new," p. 981.

27. Chapman, *Dublin Review*, p. 208.
28. Chapman, *Dublin Review*, p. 210; Chapman, "Is Killing No Murder," p. 173.
29. *New Zealand Land Claims Act* (1840), 4 Vic. No. 7 (NSW); *Land Claims Ordinance* (1841), 4 Vic. No. 2 (NZ). The Commission was established to examine pre-1840 land transactions. Titles were confirmed or overturned after investigation of the surrounding circumstances of the transaction.
30. Chapman, "Is Killing No Murder," p. 173.
31. H.S. Chapman, "What Law does a New Colony Take?" Chapman Papers Relating to Cases and Land Sales, ATL, MS-Papers-8670–046 (original in MS-Papers-8670–06) (document is unpaginated). From content, it was written post-1854, based primarily on the earlier work in the *Encyclopaedia Britannica* and the *Dublin Review*.
32. Chapman, *Dublin Review*, p. 207.
33. Ibid., p. 207; and Chapman, "Zealand, new," pp. 980–81.
34. H.S. Chapman, "Lord Glenelg and The Australian Colonies," in *Pamphlets for the People*, ed. John Arthur Roebuck, II, No. 10 (1836), 10–12 (p. 12).
35. Chapman, "Zealand, new," p. 979.
36. Chapman "Is Killing No Murder," p. 173.
37. Chapman, "Legal Notes," p. 25.
38. Ibid.
39. Ibid., p. 16.
40. J.G.A Pocock "The Treaty between Histories," p. 76.
41. As to the French see Chapman, "The English, the French and the New Zealanders"; and "Zealand, new."
42. *Johnson v M'Intosh* 8 Wheat. 543 (1823), 21 US 543; *Cherokee Nation v. Georgia*, 30 U.S. (5 Pet.) 1 (1831); *Worcester v. Georgia*, 31 U.S. (6 Pet.) 515 (1832); and Chapman, "Zealand, new."
43. On Marshall and divided sovereignty see McHugh, "Aboriginal Rights," p. 109; see also *The State v Foreman* 16 Tenn 256 (1835) (SC Tenn) Catron CJ.
44. See, for example, P.G. McHugh, "A History of Crown Sovereignty in New Zealand" in *Histories: Power and Loss*, ed. Sharp and McHugh, pp. 189–211.
45. Christopher Bayly, "The First Age of Global Imperialism, c.1760–830," *Journal of Imperial and Commonwealth History*, 26 (1998), 28–47 (p. 28) qtd. in Duncan Bell, "Dissolving Distance: Technology, Space, and Empire in British Political Thought, 1770–1900," *Journal of Modern History*, 77 (2005), 523–63 (pp. 523, 541).
46. P.D. Marshall, "Empire and Authority in the Eighteenth Century," *Journal of Imperial and Cth Hist*, 15 (1987), 105–22 (pp. 106–9).
47. Thomas Erskine May, "The Imperial Parliament," in *Knight's Store of Knowledge for all Readers*, ed. Charles Knight (London: Knight, 1841), p. 101.
48. George Cornewall Lewis, *Government of Dependencies*, rev. edn. (New York: Walter Dunne, 1901) (first published 1841).
49. Herman Merivale, *Lectures on Colonization and Colonies* (London, 1841); J.S. Mill "Considerations on Representative Government" in *The Collected*

Works of John Stuart Mill, ed. John Robson, 33 vols. (Toronto: University of Toronto Press, 1963–1991), vol. 19; James Mill, "Colony," in *Supplement to the Encyclopedia Britannica* ed. Archibald Constable (London: J. Innes, 1825); John Roebuck, *The Colonies of England, a Plan for the Government of Some Portion of Our Colonial Possessions* (London: Parker, 1849); Thomas Erskine May, "The Imperial Parliament."

50. According to Bagehot "Sir George Lewis was deeply penetrated by this abstract teaching. . . . Once a jurist, always a jurist." See Walter Bagehot, *Biographical Studies,* ed. Richard Hold Hutton (London: Longmans, 1881), p. 236. Lewis later agreed to the Commission to Malta to "serve" Austin: *Letters of the Right Hon. Sir George Cornewall Lewis, Bart., to Various Friends,* ed. Gilbert Franklin Lewis (London, 1870), p. 56.
51. George Cornewall Lewis, *Remarks on the Use and Abuse of Some Political Terms,* ed. Thomas Raleigh, new edn. (Oxford: Clarendon Press, 1898) (originally published 1832). Both works receive only a passing mention in R.W.D. Fenn (in association with Sir Andrew Duff Gordon, Bart.), *The Life and Times of Sir George Cornewall Lewis, Bart.* (Almeley: Logaston Press, 2005). One of the only works to consider *Dependencies* in any detail is Mark Francis, *Governors and Settlers* (London: Macmillan, 1992).
52. Lewis, *Use and Abuse,* p. xi.
53. According to Lewis, these questions are *the* subjects of the science of politics: Lewis, *Dependencies,* Author's Preface, p. B2.
54. John Dewey, "Austin's Theory of Sovereignty," *Political Science Quarterly,* 9 (1894), 31–52 (p. 31).
55. Bagehot, *Biographies,* p. 235.
56. Lewis, *Use and Abuse,* p. 2.
57. Ibid.
58. In 1829 Lewis published *An Examination of some Passages in Dr Whatley's Elements of Logic* (Oxford: Parker and Murray, 1829), a work also concerned with language and the meaning of words.
59. Lewis, *Use and Abuse,* p. 12; John Austin, "Outline of a Course of Lectures on General Jurisprudence or the Philosophy of Positive Law," in *The Province of Jurisprudence Determined* (London: John Murray, 1832), pp. i–lxxii.
60. Lewis, *Use and Abuse,* p. 12.
61. Chapman, "The English, the French and the New Zealanders." Enrolments in the lectures were apparently dismal, although the first of his lecture series, November 1829–July 1830, was attended by a number of the Benthamite circle: Edwin Chadwick, Edwin Strutt, Charles Buller, J.S. Mill (who reportedly took the class twice), John Romilly and Charles Villiers. Cornewall Lewis attended in 1831.
62. Lewis, *Use and Abuse,* p. 43.
63. Ibid., p. 41.
64. Lewis, *Dependencies,* p. 2
65. Lewis, *Use and Abuse,* p. 41, fn 1, directly citing Austin.
66. Ibid., p. 39.
67. Ibid., p. 41.

68. Ibid., pp. 18–19.
69. Lewis, *Dependencies*, p. 41.
70. For an extended essay on the meaning (and advantages) of colony at the time see James Mill, "Colonies": "Colony denotes an egress of people from the Mother Country to a new and permanent abode, a territory which is an outlying possession" (pp. 3–4).
71. Lewis, *Dependencies*, p. 89.
72. Ibid., p. 91.
73. Ibid. Although a number of colonies gained limited constitutions and representative bodies from the 1850s onward, Miles Taylor mounts the case that these were less independent than some historiographic traditions might suggest—that the British Parliament always retained the "upper hand": Miles Taylor "Colonial Representation at Westminster; c. 1800–1865," in *Parliaments, Nations and Identities in Britain and Ireland, 1600–1850*, ed. Julian Hoppit (Manchester: Manchester University Press, 2008), pp. 206–20.
74. Francis, *Governors and Settlers*, ch 2; and Miles, "Colonial Representation at Westminster."
75. Lewis, *Use and Abuse.* While the weaving of Locke into common law historiography is beyond the confines of this paper, for the marriage of Locke's timeless rights and liberties with the language of the "ancient constitution" see Hunter, "Natural Law," p. 139.
76. Lewis, *Use and Abuse*, p. 33.
77. Ibid., p. 7.
78. Lewis, *Dependencies.*
79. As argued by P.G. McHugh in "The Lawyer's Concept of Sovereignty, the Treaty of Waitangi, and a Legal History of New Zealand," in *Sovereignty and Indigenous Rights: The Treaty of Waitangi in International Contexts*, ed. William Renwick (Wellington: Victoria University Press, 1991), pp. 170–89.
80. See P.G. McHugh "Sovereignty in Australasia: Comparatively Different Histories," *Legal History*, 13 (2009), 57–92. For a work exploring some other aspects of this pluralized Crown see Mark Hickford "Strands from the Afterlife of Confiscation: Property Rights, Constitutional Histories and the Political Incorporation of Māori, 1920s" in *Raupatu: The Confiscation of Maori Land*, ed. Richard P. Boast and Richard Hill (Wellington: Victoria University Press, 2009).
81. For Colonial Office policy see Damen Ward, "A Means and Measure of Civilisation: Colonial Authorities and Indigenous Law in Australasia," *History Compass*, 1 (2003), 1–24.
82. McHugh, "A History of Crown Sovereignty," pp. 191–92.
83. Chapman, "Legal Notes."
84. Dorsett, "'Sworn on the Dirt of Graves.'"
85. Chapman, "Legal Notes," p. 26.
86. Ibid.
87. See *R v Bonjon*, published in *Australian Indigenous Law Reporter*, 3 (1998), p. 417; Damen Ward, "Constructing British Authority in Australasia: Charles Cooper and the Legal Status of Aborigines in the South Australian Supreme

Court, c. 1840–60," *Journal of Imperial and Commonwealth History*, 38 (2006), 483–504; and Lisa Ford, *Settler Sovereignty: Jurisdiction and Aboriginal People in America and Australia, 1788–1836* (Cambridge, MA: Harvard University Press, 2010). For New Zealand reports of *Bonjon* see *New Zealand Gazette and Wellington Spectator*, March 15, 1843, p. 3; *Nelson Examiner and New Zealand Chronicle*, March 18, 1843, p. 216. These were published prior to Chapman's arrival.

88. Chapman, "Legal Notes," p. 29.
89. Ward, "Constructing British Authority," p. 490.
90. Chapman, "Legal Notes," p. 22. See Dorsett "'Sworn on the Dirt of Graves.'"
91. *R v Rangitapiripiri (alias Kopitipita)*, [HS Chapman], Notebook entitled "Criminal Trials," No. 5 (1847–49), Hocken Library, Dunedin (HL), MS-0411/013, entry for December 1, 1847, pp. 23–36, reported in *The New Zealand Spectator and Cook's Strait Guardian*, December 4, 1847, pp. 2–3; *The Queen v Native*, Chapman "Notebook," entry for Monday, September 3, 1849, pp. 205–219, reported in *The New Zealand Spectator and Cook's Strait Guardian*, September 5, 1849, pp. 2–3.
92. *New Zealand Spectator and Cook's Strait Guardian*, December 4, 1847, p. 3.
93. Ibid., September 5, 1849, p. 3. See Dorsett "'Sworn on the Dirt of Graves.'"

Chapter 12

Imperial Policy, Colonial Government, and Indigenous Testimony in South Australia and New Zealand in the 1840s

Damen Ward

I

In the 1830s and 1840s proposals to allow indigenous testimony in colonial courts were part of broader disputes about the shape of colonial government and attempts to use courts to "civilize" indigenous peoples. In 1840, the English law officers concluded that any potential witness in a common law court had to perceive future moral or religious consequences to giving false testimony. Where an appropriate oath or other ceremony related to this belief could be identified, the witness might be sworn. If not, the witness lacked the legal capacity to give evidence.[1] The law officers considered these rules to be fundamental elements of "British jurisprudence" that colonial legislatures could not amend. On this basis, a New South Wales ordinance allowing "unsworn" Aboriginal testimony was disallowed.[2] In 1843, however, the imperial Parliament authorized colonial legislatures to pass their own ordinances on unsworn indigenous testimony. South Australia and New Zealand passed legislation allowing indigenous testimony as part of assimilationist policies, but the significance of the respective ordinances in each colony was markedly different. The shifting political significance of the admissibility of indigenous testimony across time and place suggests the importance of considering particular institutional configurations of colonial law and government. Indigenous testimony issues point to the importance of legislation to colonial legal systems, and to the significance of the administration of law in creating patterns of colonial government.

In the 1830s and 1840s, a range of proposals for British colonization in Australia and New Zealand sought extensive grants of self-government to either the colonization promoters as a board or commission, or to the settler community itself through elected seats in a legislature. The promoters argued that their social and moral character deserved institutional recognition within the constitution. Promoters' political and social agendas were deployed with a particular sense of history, in which generous interpretations of previous North American colonization mixed with a variety of vague claims about the advances supposedly provided by new economic theories.[3]

These proposals were often aimed at generating commercial and, particularly, political interest and support. To build political coalitions and to present a "respectable" face to government and the public, promoters stressed the moral and economic independence offered by emigration as well as the greater freedom of action offered by colonial settings. In the case of South Australia and New Zealand, many promoters of colonization were loosely connected through support for various ideas of "colonial reform" and "systematic colonization."[4] Such proposals were not without their critics, particularly given the questionable credentials of prominent promoters such as Edward Gibbon Wakefield. In British debates colonies could be presented as being socially fragile, bereft of the stability that long-standing institutions of law, religion, and property might be seen as giving a society. To try to counter such perceptions, systematic colonization proposals often involved detailed proposals for institutional structures and constitutional relationships. Such proposals were designed to show respectable authorship and provide assurances of colonial stability.[5]

Across the 1830s, British colonization lobbyists increasingly referred to the use of courts (and legislation about courts) in their schemes, particularly in relation to indigenous peoples. An interest in litigation, one author suggested, was "a valuable quality with which to work in attaining civilization."[6] Participation in law and legal institutions was to be a means and measure of civilization, and an expression of a particular type of colonial subjecthood.[7]

Legal historians have considered the treatment of indigenous land rights and court jurisdiction in these schemes.[8] One neglected element of many of these colonization proposals is the attention given to the law on indigenous testimonial capacity. The extent to which non-Christian indigenes could give evidence in court and the measures necessary to secure admissible testimony were contested in courts across the empire. The common law threshold was often summarized as belief in the spiritual or ethical consequences of giving false evidence under oath; the conscience of the witness had to be bound.[9] With indigenes, a religious or supernatural perception of the weight of an oath was often looked for. Admitting evidence might, therefore, involve acknowledging the general capacity of indigenes to perceive right and wrong, and (implicitly) to participate in proceedings based on a common sense of "truth" and falsehood. It was open to a judge to assess the legal capacity to give evidence on a witness-by-witness basis. However, where admissibility became an issue of public debate, those debates were often about indigenous religion or cosmology, and the testimonial capacity of indigenous people in general. The ability to meet the criteria for being a witness was often presented as an element of culture or race, rather than a function of individual character.[10]

Debate about legal capacity, therefore, raised questions about the assessment of indigenous "civilization," and about indigenous peoples' incorporation or differentiation within colonial institutions.[11] There was ongoing political debate about such issues in Australasian colonies and across the empire in the early- to mid-nineteenth century. It is worth distinguishing between particular elements of this broader debate. Importantly, the assessments of indigenous society involved in evidence issues could be presented as being independent of assessments involved in identifying native title. For Saxe Bannister, the former New South Wales law officer and colonial lobbyist, denying Aborigines the capacity to testify stopped civilization "at the threshold."[12] The ability to give evidence was repeatedly described by commentators on British colonization as a basic step in the "civilization" of indigenous peoples.[13] For Edward Eyre, the ability to give evidence was the most pressing issue of South Australian race relations by 1843. Eyre insisted, "no permanent improvement of [Aboriginal] character or conduct can ever be expected" without being able to draw Aborigines into juridical networks of interaction with whites. The provision of courts to adjudicate disputes was central to this, and allowing Aboriginal evidence a necessary part of such a court system.[14] If Aborigines could not give evidence, the legal system was not a viable alternative way of resolving disputes and expressing authority; the violence of customary law, as Eyre saw it, would remain unchecked.[15] As importantly, indigenous evidence might be the only evidence available to convict settlers for crimes against Aborigines. Such issues were starkly illustrated by the Myall Creek controversy in New South Wales in 1838. In 1845 the Aborigines Protection Society (APS) ranked issues of evidence law second in importance only to indigenous land rights.[16]

Altering the law on oaths and evidence had been a recurrent issue among lobbyists and commentators on imperial affairs in the early nineteenth century. Issues of slave and indigenous evidence were often of concern to the Colonial Office. A series of contentious reforms in 1809 and again in 1828 allowed limited categories of unsworn testimony in the Cape Colony, as part of attempts to assert control over and anglicize Cape institutions and social structures.[17] As Russell Smandych has explored, following the abolition of slavery the office sought to prevent colonial assemblies, restricting the admissibility of evidence by ex-slaves.[18]

Ostensibly "philanthropist" groups set up in association with the South Australian colonization scheme advocated allowing unsworn indigenous testimony.[19] However, the testimonial capacity of Aborigines was of limited concern to the South Australian lobbyists before the colony's founding legislation was passed in 1834. Colonization plans reflected intellectual currents, but they also reflected political pressures and preoccupations. The metropolitan promoters of South Australia focused on convicts and irregular settlers as the colonial challenges facing their schemes. Aboriginal rights emerged as a late and hurriedly addressed issue.[20] However, a number of systematic colonization lobbyists from the South Australian scheme moved on to formulate proposals for New Zealand settlements.[21] The volume of information available in Britain about New Zealand and the level of interest in Māori society encouraged promoters to theorize how Māori society might interact with colonial government and society, and to use such theorizing as part of political lobbying. Admitting Māori testimony became a stock means of claiming an informed and "enlightened" approach to colonization.[22] Nonetheless, references to evidentiary capacity in colonization proposals had limited impact on government. In 1838 Lord Glenelg deflected New Zealand Company proposals for the admission of Māori evidence in any new colonial system, saying the issue was too sensitive to be resolved in the abstract.[23] Imperial legislation was predominately reactive. In the absence of a particular political controversy there was limited political will to respond to abstract appeals to principle from London observers, particularly given the self-interest of promoters seeking to purchase land directly from Māori.[24]

Admitting evidence without an assurance by oath that the witness was conscious of the legal and moral gravity of giving testimony seemed to raise, in the minds of some British colonial observers, the prospect of corruption and widespread perjury.[25] However, sensitivity over evidence reform reflected not just concern over permitting individuals to a particular status of competency and civic status; it also reflected British governments' more general caution about the speed and nature of locally directed legal reform of superior courts and the colonial common law. Having introduced the issue of testimonial capacity, I want to put it in a broader context as a question of colonial legal structure.

II

As late as 1840, within some British government departments at least, access to a court system containing certain distinctive elements of "British" law could be seen as raising "fundamental" matters that only the imperial legislature could alter.[26] For example, New Zealand legislation abolishing grand juries was rejected as repugnant to the laws of England. The Colonial Office expressed alarm at similar steps in South Australia.[27] As noted, in 1840 the British law officers had viewed elements of the law of evidentiary capacity as fundamental parts of "British jurisprudence." They rejected a New South Wales ordinance designed to alter the common law, because the ordinance recited that Aborigines did not perceive the significance of an oath or the importance of truthful testimony and were, therefore, outside the common law test. For the law officers, such elements of "British jurisprudence" could be seen as a thread linking colony and metropole, a link that could be altered only by the imperial Parliament.[28] Such approaches stressed particular elements of court procedure and access to courts as fundamental elements of imperial law.

Settler colonization groups certainly saw court structures as significant, but this significance was often framed in terms of attempting to constrain independent gubernatorial power and to extend settler control or checks on gubernatorial discretionary authority. Disputes over the operation of courts in relation to indigenes were, therefore, of wider importance in colonial politics.[29] By the late 1830s, colonial governors were increasingly asserting a general territorial political authority and the general (statutory) territorial jurisdiction of the Supreme Court. The notion that indigenous peoples within colonies were not fully subject to the authority of the Crown's courts was increasingly unacceptable to governments.[30] This could create tensions where sections of settler communities expected that government and courts would conform to their social attitudes or expectations when making, interpreting, or enforcing the law.

Such tensions contributed to colonial debates about unsworn evidence. However, some caution is needed when discussing the interaction between social attitudes and the operation of legal arguments. Identifying a norm that regulated social or political practice does not necessarily indicate what the law was perceived to be. Not all established social practices constituted "common law," and not all social norms were presumed to have or deserve legal effect or consequences. People might easily act according to choices and judgments that diverged from the relevant law.[31] However, particularly in young colonies, it was not always clear which of the various settlers' social norms and practices would be given particular legal notice or effect. The extent to which indigenous custom might or could be given legal recognition was, of course, also a matter of dispute and contest.[32] Legal arguments were often attempts to translate perceived or preferred social, political, or economic claims into a particular legal form or result.[33] Metropolitan influences were never reproduced unaltered in colonial settings as if colonial societies were merely alternative venues for Westminster politics.[34] Nor should intellectual or jurisprudential concepts be presented as *simply* being resources to be deployed for immediate colonial political ends. A more complex interplay was at work.[35]

Such observations may seem unremarkable in light of the scholarship in the other chapters in this book. However, there is value in considering the interplay between legal rights or processes and particular social or political practices in the construction of colonial government. I would suggest that no single analytical concept or category of legal authority or right, whether property, territory, jurisdiction, or sovereignty, holds the key to the historical construction of British colonial government. The concept of "the Crown" and Crown prerogative authority complicated the relationship between such notions.[36] More importantly, legal and political notions were interconnected. Political debate and disputes generated *configurations* of definitions, institutions, and authorities, in which particular sorts of authority closely interacted in some settings and operated with a degree of autonomy in others. Different parts of these configurations had different significance across time and place.[37] Let me develop these points in relation to jurisdiction and territory; by doing so, we can see how questions of evidentiary capacity related to broader configurations of law and government.

A series of colonial controversies led to British and colonial governments stating their views on jurisdictional matters in the late 1830s and 1840s. In the approach that emerged from London (supported by colonial governors), Supreme Courts had formal jurisdiction over defined territorial areas, set by statute or other legal instruments, regardless of the tenure on which land was held or whether it had been purchased from indigenous owners. Such determinations, therefore, distinguished between geographic territory, jurisdiction, and property in delineating the Crown's prerogative authority and the authority of colonial courts. Of course, these legal distinctions were not always adhered to with such starkness or with consistency in various colonial political debates. Alternative legal viewpoints persisted; as is well known, some judges and officials took different views to the Colonial Office well into the 1840s. Further, the Crown's claim to an underlying interest in land could blur notions of sovereignty, property, and territory. Nonetheless, the distinctions outlined above were drawn with clarity by colonial secretaries in London in the early- to mid-1840s.[38]

In colonies, the tension between formal legal right and substantive practice remained significant. In New Zealand, for instance, governors advocated the general territorial authority of the Crown and superior courts as a primary function of formal sovereignty. Simultaneously, they urged discretion in the actual exercise of authority by the courts.[39] Such an approach preserved the formal ability of the colonial courts to adjudicate on any cognizable dispute but often left difficult issues about the practical operation of courts, and substantive questions of what rights might be claimed in court, for ongoing debate in the political sphere.[40] Further, local statutes gave New Zealand governors administrative powers to set the territorial jurisdiction of inferior courts. This illustrates an important distinction between sovereignty and jurisdiction in the formal legal frameworks of the colony. Structuring specific geographic jurisdictions for lower courts was one potential way to manage practical limitations to Crown power and resources, while still insisting on a particular formal authority for government and superior courts.[41]

Such techniques were tools in the political arrangement of the colonial legal order. The details of such techniques mattered to historical actors. Certainly, distinctions between the formal legal categories and the practice "on the ground" might be stark. Some settlers saw that distinction as embarrassing and undesirable. But that tension could be also seen by politicians as something to be managed across time and place, by both legal and political means. Nineteenth-century British imperial systems were based on a "politically managed empire and not simply a creation of 'jurisdictional imperialism'."[42] Decisions about institutional practice and decision-makers' discretion could mediate legal and social expectations. Critical struggles in colonial politics were often about who was entitled to control the nature of such practices, and how legal discretions relating to them were exercised in practice.[43]

This meant that questions about court structure and court practice could be highly controversial. The law on testimonial capacity is a useful example of a legal rule that had the potential to disrupt or illuminate social practice in ways that might have immediate social and political consequences. Indigenous testimony, reported by the press, might reveal violence that had previously been obscured. Such testimony might encourage courts or governments to give specific social or legal norms/expectations institutional status or support. Indigenous testimony could, potentially, lead to the imprisonment or execution of settlers.[44] These implications went beyond questions of specific crimes. In New South Wales, evidence law became part of political debate, in part, because governors sought to enforce the criminal law against settlers. Evidence law reform became an important part of that policy, both as practical matter (often only Aboriginal evidence was available) and as an indication of the government's commitment to implementing its policy aims in rural districts.[45] It should be noted, however, that political disputes about the admissibility of Aboriginal testimony were generated in a number of colonies in the 1830s and 1840s. The APS highlighted South Australian confusion over Aboriginal testimony in the late 1830s, drawing on Quaker correspondence networks that included Thomas Hodgkin, the APS secretary.[46] Further, it was a Western Australian law, discussed below, that eventually led to an imperial statute.

Questions of testimonial capacity seem to have been disputed most in criminal contexts. Issues of criminal jurisdiction over indigenes caused considerable transcolonial and imperial correspondence. Disputes over the criminal law highlighted the Crown's claims to be the only legitimate coercive authority and could also bring questions of substantive power to the fore. Criminal law jurisdictional policies toward indigenous peoples were debated in House of Commons' select committees on South Australia and New Zealand in 1841 and 1844. The New Zealand select committee in particular produced significant volumes of material. By 1844 a number of settlements had been established in New Zealand by the New Zealand Company. The company and its supporters had a well-organized campaign for gathering information and lobbying British parliamentarians. They presented the government's perceived willingness to modify or avoid the application of colonial criminal law to Māori as indicative of a failure to sufficiently assert the benefits of British rule and settlement. Certainly, issues of jurisdiction were secondary to issues of land title in the select committee debates. However, New Zealand Company lobbyists stressed perceived failures in enforcing British criminal law, and gubernatorial attempts to modify colonial criminal law, as indicative of a general failure in government.[47] An earlier select committee on South Australia had treated criminal jurisdiction in a similar way.[48]

Criminal jurisdiction issues had a greater political impact in New Zealand than in South Australia. Disputes over criminal law and its application played a role in the recall of Robert FitzRoy and formed an important part of the Colonial Office's instructions to FitzRoy's successor Sir George Grey. In New Zealand Grey developed a system of using resident magistrates to oversee arbitration courts and encourage Māori engagement with colonial institutions. Grey avoided a range of technical issues by giving the courts freedom to act on "equity and good conscience," rather than applying common law rules of evidence or procedure. Grey's scheme was derived from other colonial models. However, he paid considerable attention to promoting his scheme in his despatches to London. He presented it as a highly successful adaptation of English law principles and metropolitan theorizing to colonial circumstances. In this he stressed civil litigation more than criminal jurisdiction.[49] This obscured the politically fraught issue of Māori amenability to criminal law by stressing the promotion of "civilization" through settling disputes by civil adjudication. Grey had many motives for such an approach. His stress on civil disputes was a pragmatic response to Māori desire to use civil courts in the townships. It probably also reflected the fact that the application of colonial law to indigenes was a topic that could animate imperial correspondence networks. Discussion over a single case could easily generate broader controversies over gubernatorial policy and powers. Gubernatorial despatches to London and the governor's role as the conduit for official communication with the British government gave Grey a powerful medium of political communication.[50] Grey stressed his resident magistrate's policy in correspondence to Britain partly because he knew such issues were important to the government's perceptions of his administration, and to his reputation among relevant interest groups.[51]

The operation of such information networks has been of much recent historiographical interest. Active and extensive networks across colonies have been seen as an important part of the construction of British patterns of colonial governance.[52] However, the evidentiary capacity issue indicates another manifestation of imperial and colonial interactions. While imperial communication networks could be powerful processes in shaping ideas of empire and colonial governance, evidentiary capacity issues show how the impact and role of such networks varied. The Colonial Office ministers and staff had been surprised by the 1840 rejection of the New South Wales ordinance. James Stephen had opposed evidence law reform early in his career at the Colonial Office, but by 1840 he thought the common law flawed and in need of reform. Further, both officials and ministers seem to have favored a narrow definition of repugnancy.[53] Indeed, the law officers' views seem to have slipped quickly from officials' recollection. In 1841, the Colonial Office reviewed a Western Australian ordinance that allowed unsworn Aboriginal evidence in certain circumstances. The ordinance was disallowed, mainly because of concerns about the summary powers it gave to local magistrates. The governor was instructed to pass a replacement reform ordinance. Significantly, the 1840 opinion does not appear to have been considered.[54] It may have been thought that the wording of the new ordinance would avoid the characterization of Aborigines that had invalidated the New South Wales law. The law officers, however, returned a similar analysis to 1840.[55] The colonial secretary, Lord Stanley, instructed officials to prepare imperial legislation. The resulting bill quickly became the Colonial Evidence Act 1843.[56] The legislation attracted little opposition in Parliament, or in the English press.[57] The statute authorized colonial legislatures to pass ordinances altering the law relating to indigenous evidence.

Two colonies to quickly respond to the imperial act were New Zealand (July 1844) and South Australia (August 1844).[58] Attempts to pass local ordinances in New South Wales caused considerable controversy.[59] However, it is worth noting that the imperial act did not achieve a lasting reputation in the empire. The New South Wales governor Charles FitzRoy raised the issue of the status of Aboriginal evidence anew with the Colonial Office in 1846. (The Colonial Office sent a further copy of the 1843 Act). In the mid-1860s the status of indigenous unsworn testimony emerged as a significant issue in Vancouver Island. With few copies of imperial or British statutes available, local authorities were unaware of the Colonial Evidence Act. The purchase of a set of South Australian statutes may have contributed to the passage of a Native Exemption Ordinance in British Columbia in 1865.[60]

In New Zealand and South Australia, adoption of the imperial act reflected the position of governors who pursued broadly assimilationist policies. Although the political style and acumen of the two men was very different, both Robert FitzRoy (in New Zealand) and George Grey (in South Australia) looked to indigenous involvement with colonial judicial bodies or magistrates as a critical means of assimilation. Both saw indigenous evidence as an important part of indigenous engagement with courts. In New Zealand, FitzRoy's evidence ordinance was part of a set of "exceptional laws" that modified the way colonial law applied to Māori. George Grey had advocated the admission of all indigenous evidence in an 1840 memorandum to the Colonial Office on the application of English law to Aboriginal peoples. It should be noted, however, that Aboriginal policy was far less of a priority for Grey in South Australia. Edward Eyre, then a resident magistrate at Moorundie, appears to have played a role in urging Grey to pass an ordinance following the imperial act.[61]

How Māori evidence was treated by courts and juries requires further detailed research by historians. Interestingly, however, the admission of unsworn Māori evidence per se does not appear to have posed the same political challenges or implications to New Zealand or South Australian settlers as those it may have in New South Wales. In New South Wales and Western Australia evidence law reform was bound up with attempts to assert government authority and policies over rural districts, and opposition to indigenous evidence was part of settler opposition to such government policies. In South Australia, there was no similar dispute at the time of the testimony ordinance. In New Zealand, proponents of competing particular interpretations of native title or Māori rights all deployed Māori evidence in their political lobbying. Early commissions to review pre-1840 land sales were statutorily authorized to hear all Māori evidence.[62] Māori testimony had been received in lower courts prior to 1844; Chapman J.'s enforcement of the common law rules at the first sitting of the Supreme Court in Wellington took some local lawyers by surprise.[63] The use of Māori witnesses in the Supreme Court after 1844 seems to have been relatively common.[64] The very significance of Māori testimony to local litigation and politics limited the relevance of admissibility of Māori evidence per se as an issue in colonial or imperial debate. There were disputes over the content and weight to be given to Māori evidence in relation to property rights. These were arguments about the operation of the law in practice. Few New Zealand settlers after 1844 seem to have felt that indigenous evidence should be inadmissible as such, even where firm doubts about the ability of Māori to give truthful or accurate testimony remained. British perceptions of Māori society as semi-civilized were no doubt important in shaping Pākehā views, in particular, the visible level of Māori Christianity and literacy, and the degree and manner of political engagement between Pākehā officials and Māori leaders in the settlements.[65]

This chapter has explored one small part of the history of indigenous legal status in South Australia and New Zealand. In each colony, the complex relationships between the formal law, the practice of legal actors and institutions, and the social practices of those who brought actions and gave evidence, or declined to do so, requires more detailed examination by historians. The history of the Colonial Evidence Act shows that colonial legal systems can be seen in an imperial context; it also shows that an imperial context can highlight the need to better appreciate local contexts. A brief outline of the subsequent history of the New Zealand and South Australian legislation illustrates this point further.

III

The South Australian ordinance contained a proviso that limited the probative force of Aboriginal evidence. This proviso became the focus of repeated amendment because of confusion over its application, and ongoing debate about the reliability of Aboriginal evidence. In 1846, amendments to allow some convictions based on solely Aboriginal evidence were justified by the advocate-general on the basis of "keeping up order": the existing law preventing such convictions hindered prosecutions in *inter se* cases and caused confusion in cases involving whites.[66] However, the protector of Aborigines warned that Aboriginal witnesses were generally biased, confused, and easily led when giving evidence.[67] Although the ordinance was amended, Aboriginal evidence remained insufficient by itself to convict where the penalty was death or transportation. The emphasis in debate was on the amendment being an allowance for Aboriginal incivility, rather than a means to advance "civilization." The lack of any wider European economic or political imperative to utilize ideas of civilization and assimilation reinforced this shift from the uses of law apparent in the 1830s. Difficulties in securing translators for the range of Aboriginal languages hindered the use of Aboriginal evidence and probably discredited such evidence as a category.[68] Further, the South Australian example reinforces what British advocates of courts as forums for civility came to appreciate across the mid-nineteenth century: the results of formal mechanisms depended on social attitudes that influenced their administration and implementation. By 1849, Aboriginal witnesses from rural districts often appear to have been arrested and held in custody to secure their appearance; cross-examination during Aboriginal evidence in chief was standard practice (there was a widespread view that Aboriginal languages lacked a word for truth).[69]

In New Zealand, the criminal and civil jurisdiction of courts in relation to Māori retained real significance as a constitutional issue across the mid-nineteenth century. In such a context, testimonial capacity was a procedural element of the legal system that was unlikely to be the focus of particular legal or political attention. Indeed, Governor Grey sought to promote the use of inferior colonial courts with more flexible procedural rules than those of the common law courts. The focus of New Zealand controversies in the late 1840s and 1850s was on more substantive issues: the application of particular laws to Māori (including, often, concern about Māori reaction to such application), and settler attempts to use disputes over legal structures to limit both the scope of governors' political discretion over Māori policy and the de facto autonomy of Māori *runanga* (councils).[70]

It was these larger issues that were more likely to generate concern in London. Importantly, by the mid-1850s, the status of indigenous evidence did not appear to pose the same difficulties within British government as those it had in the 1830s.[71] The declining sense of evidence capacity as a problem of imperial policy may reflect a number of factors. Events in Jamaica, South Africa, and elsewhere during the 1830s and 1840s had dulled the faith of evangelical movements in the effectiveness of law and legal institutions to achieve social and moral change.[72] Evidence law had been of real interest to humanitarian lobbyists, but once addressed in 1843 the issue seldom manifested itself in a way that directly required imperial concern or expenditure.

An underlying jurisprudential or constitutional shift may be identified here. Increasingly, access to political representative forums was the center of political debate in colonies. The development of representative and responsible government affected the ways particular configurations of property, authority, and status might attract colonial and imperial political attention. The British concern with domestic stabilization after 1848 and the colonial transformation of representative government into responsible government combined to widen the permissible scope for colonial legislative innovation.[73] This was by no means a smooth, preordained transition. Nonetheless, the political significance of courtroom status and legal procedure was altered by the constitutional changes of the 1840s and 1850s.[74] In 1840, the law officers had expressed "British jurisprudence" as setting constitutional benchmarks that colonial legislatures could not exceed. The rise of responsible government in Australia and New Zealand made ideas of "British jurisprudence" more abstract and generalized. The authority to decide what "British jurisprudence" meant, and how it should be manifested in colonial institutions, shifted over time to the local legislature and government.[75]

Proposals for colonial law reform could be used as part of wider political proposals for colonization. However, Lord Stanley proposed imperial legislation on unsworn testimony in 1843 in response to what had emerged as a specific political issue in several Australasian colonies, and to address the apparent oversight of the previous 1840 legal opinion by his department in relation to a Western Australian ordinance. If testimonial capacity highlights the need to consider the "web" of empire rather than the "radial" relationship between Britain and specific colonies,[76] it also shows that some significant issues might not resonate clearly across empire. Particular colonies could form discrete sites of policy and politics, in which imperial networks might have partial and contingent significance on certain issues.[77] Thus, the Colonial Evidence Act was quickly utilized by some colonies and quickly forgotten elsewhere. The Colonial Evidence Act illustrates the contingent, largely reactive, character of British imperial government in the mid-nineteenth century. The issue of indigenous capacity also offers an alternative angle from which to approach the definitions and structures used by colonial legal systems. It shows the way technical legal definitions could impact significantly on substantive issues. It highlights the centrality of legislation to colonial legal systems. A concern with procedure or process, such as the rules on testimonial capacity, can, therefore, highlight or clarify the role of other legal concepts. As such, issues of testimonial capacity offer new points of engagement for historians to better understand the processes of empire.

Notes

1. Henry Roscoe, *A Digest of the Law of Evidence*, 4th edn. (London: Saunders and Benning, 1846), pp. 98–99; *New Zealand Gazette and Wellington Spectator*, May 1, 1844, p. 2.
2. Law Officers to Colonial Office, July 27, 1840, The National Archives, London (TNA), CO201/303, fol. 43.
3. Edwin Hodder, *The Founding of South Australia* (London: Sampson Low Marston & Co., 1898), p. 96; Douglas Pike, *Paradise of Dissent: South Australia 1829–1857,* 2nd edn. (Melbourne: Melbourne University Press, 1967), pp. 65–67; Sir Charles Napier, *Colonization: Particularly in Southern Australia* (London: T & W Boone, 1835), pp. 1–5; Edward Gibbon Wakefield, *A View of the Art of Colonization* (London: John W. Parker, 1849), letter 36; Torrens to Goderich, July 9, 1832, TNA, CO13/1, fols. 171, 218; Stephen, memorandum, TNA, CO13/1, fols. 265–283; Hill to Napier, May 22, 1835, TNA, CO13/3, fol. 54.
4. Damen Ward, "The Politics of Jurisdiction. 'British' Law, Indigenous Peoples and Colonial Government in South Australia and New Zealand, c. 1834–60" (unpublished doctoral thesis, University of Oxford, 2003). See note 3.
5. South Australia Literary Association, minutes, October 3, 1834, August 7, 1835, Adelaide, State Records Office of South Australia (SROSA), GRG44/83; *Prospectus of the Society for the Benefit and Protection of the Aborigines of the British Colonies,* undated, Wellington, Alexander Turnbell Library (ATL), MS-89–096; Ward, "Politics of Jurisdiction," pp. 54–83; cf. Whitmore to Goderich, June 18, 1832, TNA, CO13/1, fol. 126; Robert Gouger, Journal, December 13, 1835, in Hodder, *Founding of South Australia,* pp. 65–66; "Memorial," August 25, 1831, TNA, CO13/1, fol. 55; South Australian Association to Colonial Office, December 15, 1831, TNA, CO13/1, fol. 76.
6. Saxe Bannister, *Humane Policy: Or Justice to the Aborigines of New Settlements* (London: T & G Underwood, 1830), p. 41.
7. Damen Ward, "A Means and Measure of Civilisation: Colonial Authorities and Indigenous Law in Australasia," *History Compass*, 1 AU 409 (2003), 1–23 <doi: 10.1111/1478–0542.049> [Accessed August 1, 2008].
8. P.G. McHugh, *Aboriginal Societies and the Common Law* (Oxford: Oxford University Press, 2005), pp. 4–58, 166–206; Damen Ward "Constructing British Authority in Australasia. Charles Cooper and the Legal Status of Aborigines in the South Australian Supreme Court, c. 1840–60," *Journal of Commonwealth and Imperial* History, 34 (2006), 483–504; Lisa Ford, "Empire and Order on the Colonial Frontiers of Georgia and New South Wales," *Itinerario: Geographies of Empire,* 30 (2006), 95–113.
9. Chapman J, "Address to the Grand Jury," April 12, 1844, *New Zealand Gazette and Wellington Spectator*, May 1, 1844, p. 2.
10. R.H.W. Reece, *Aborigines and Colonists. Aborigines and Colonial Society in New South Wales in the 1830s and 1840s* (Sydney: University of Sydney Press, 1974),

pp. 180–81; Matthew Moorhouse, "Report respecting the value of native evidence in a court of justice," July 14, 18, 46 SROSA, GRG24/6/1846/879.

11. Frederick Cooper, *Colonialism in Question: Theory, Knowledge, History* (Berkeley: University of California Press, 2005), pp. 23, 77, 172–73.
12. Saxe Bannister, evidence to select committee on Aborigines, August 31, 1835, *Great Britain Parliamentary Papers (GBPP)*, VII (1836), 538 (p. 176).
13. *Prospectus*, ATL MS-89–0962, p. 3; George Grey, "Report upon the Best Means of Promoting the Civilization of the Aboriginal Inhabitants of Australia," June 4, 1840, in Lord John Russell to Hobson, December 9, 1840, *GBPP*, XXVII (1841), 311 (p. 43); Timothy Keegan, *Colonial South Africa and the Origins of the Racial Order* (London: Leicester University Press, 1996), p. 54; Eyre to colonial secretary, February 1, 1843, SROSA, GRG24/6/1843/170; and Aborigines Protection Society (APS) to Stanley, March 27, 1845, in APS, *Extracts from the Proceedings of the Aborigines Protection Society* (London: William Ball, 1845), II, p. 3; see also note 3.
14. Eyre to colonial secretary, February 1, 1843, SROSA, GRG24/6/1843/170.
15. Edward Eyre, *Journals of Expeditions of Discovery into Central Australia* (London: T & W Boone, 1845), pp. 6–9, 147.
16. APS to Stanley, March 27, 1845, in APS, *Extracts*, II, p. 3; APS to Colonial Office, July 30, 1839, in *Historical Records of Victoria*, ed. Ian MacFarlane, 8 vols. (Melbourne: Victorian GPO, 1983), ii(b), p. 578.
17. Lauren Benton, *Law and Colonial Cultures. Legal Regimes in World History, 1400–1900* (Cambridge: Cambridge University Press, 2002), pp. 167–209; Keegan, "Colonial South Africa," p. 84.
18. David B. Swinfen, *Imperial Control of Colonial Legislation 1813–1865* (Oxford: Oxford University Press, 1970), pp. 125, 157; Russell Smandych, "'To Soften the Extreme Rigor of their Bondage': James Stephen's Attempt to Reform the Criminal Slave Laws of the West Indies, 1813–1833," *Law and History Review*, 23 (2005), 538–86.
19. *Prospectus,* ATL, MS-89–096.
20. Ward, "Politics of Jurisdiction," pp. 62–70.
21. Peter Adams, *Fatal Necessity: British Intervention in New Zealand 1830–1847* (Auckland: University of Auckland Press, 1977), pp. 253–54; Pike, *Paradise of Dissent*, pp. 197; Gawler to Angas, June 23, 1842, Adelaide, State Library of South Australia, Mortlock Collection (SLSA), PRG174/21.
22. "Abstract of an Act of Parliament...," enclosed in Baring to Melbourne, November 11, 1837, TNA, CO209/2, fol. 402; Bannister, *Humane Policy*, pp. 197, 243; Montague Hawtrey, *An Earnest Address to the New Zealand Colonists* (London: John W. Parker, 1840), pp. 82–85, 94–96; Standish Motte, *Outline of a System of Legislation for Securing Protection to the Aboriginal Inhabitants of all Countries Colonized by Great Britain* (London: John Murray, 1840), pp. 7, 8, 10, 19–20.
23. Glenelg, memorandum, December 15, 1837, TNA, CO209/2, fol. 409; APS, *Extracts*, i, p. 67.
24. Glenelg, memorandum, December 15, 1837, TNA, CO209/2, fol. 409; Glenelg to Durham, December 29, 1837, TNA, CO209/2, fol. 410; A.G.L.

Shaw, "British Policy towards Australian Aborigines, 1830–50," *Australian Historical Studies*, 25 (1986), 265–85 (pp. 278–79).

25. Somes to Lord Stanley, January 24, 1843, TNA, CO209/26, fol. 85; *Observer*, July 4, 1846, p. 4; Hutt to Russell, January 24, 1842 (extracts) TNA, CO18/33, fol. 67, pp. 78–79.
26. Law Officers to Colonial Office, July 27, 1840, TNA, CO201/303, fol. 43.
27. Stanley to Hobson, January 31, 1843, TNA, CO209/14, fols. 421–22; R.M. Hague, *History of the Law in South Australia* (Adelaide: Barr Smith Press, 2005), pp. 557–58; Alex C. Castles and Michael C. Harris, *Lawmakers and Wayward Whigs: Government and Law in South Australia, 1936–1986* (Adelaide: Wakefield Press, 1987), pp. 49–51.
28. Law Officers to Colonial Office, July 27, 1840, TNA, CO201/303, fol. 43; Roger Milliss, *Waterloo Creek: The Australia Day massacre of 1838, George Gipps and the British Conquest of Australia* (Sydney: University of New South Wales Press, 1994).
29. Ward, "Civil Jurisdiction, Settler Politics, and the Colonial Constitution, 1840–58," *Victoria University of Wellington Law Review* 39 (2008), 497–532.
30. Ward, "Constructing British Authority," pp. 491–98.
31. This distinction does not cease simply because the law itself may have been ambiguous: Gerald J. Postema, "Classical Common Law Jurisprudence (Part 1)," *Oxford University Commonwealth Law Journal*, 2 (2003), 155–80; Hendrik Hartog, "Pigs and Positivism" *Wisconsin Law Review* (1985), 899–935; Ward, "Politics of Jurisdiction," pp. 118–23.
32. Shaunnagh Dorsett, "'Sworn on the Dirt of Graves': Sovereignty, Jurisdiction and the Judicial Abrogation of 'Barbarous' Customs in New Zealand in the 1840s," *Legal History*, 30 (2009), 175–97; cf. Jeremy Webber, "Relations of Force and Relations of Justice: The Emergence of Normative Community Between Colonists and Aboriginal Peoples," *Osgoode Hall Law Journal*, 1 (1995), 623–60; see also, George Grey to John Grey, January 16, 1845, SLSA, D7063.
33. Litigation and legislation were often strategic maneuvers within a political context, but these politics were part of wider social and intellectual contexts. See notes 27, 32, 35, 38; David Ibettson, "What Is Legal History a History of?" in *Law and History*, ed. Michael Lobban and Andrew Lewis (Oxford: Oxford University Press, 2003), pp. 33–40.
34. Memorial to Governor FitzRoy, *GBPP*, XXXIII (1845), 247 (p. 25); *Nelson Examiner*, February 10, 1844, p. 2; McHugh, *Aboriginal Societies*, pp. 7–12, 26–29.
35. Ann Laura Stoler and Frederick Cooper, "Between Metropole and Colony: Rethinking a Research Agenda" in *Tensions of Empire: Colonial Cultures in a Bourgeois World*, ed. Ann Laura Stoler and Frederick Cooper (Berkeley: University of California Press, 1997), pp. 1–58; see also notes 23, 31, 33, 55.
36. Stephen, memorandum, July 14, 1832, TNA, CO13/1, fol. 276. *The Nature of the Crown. A Legal and Political Analysis*. ed. Maurice Sunkin and Sebastian Payne (Oxford: Oxford University Press, 2003).
37. Ward, "Civil Jurisdiction," pp. 497–532; Cooper, *Colonialism in Question*, p. 179; Hobson to Shortland, May 23, 1840, Hocken Library, Dunedin (HL),

MS0052/4; Stanley to Hobson, January 9, 1843, TNA, CO209/14, fols. 414, 418–20; Mark Hickford "Settling Some Important Principles of Colonial Law: Three 'Forgotten' Cases of the 1840s," 35 (2004), VUWLR, 1–31 (pp. 1, 2–11, 19–31).

38. Ward, "Constructing British Authority," p. 490; *R v Bonjon*, September 16, 1841 (Supreme Court of New South Wales) at <http://www.law.mq.edu.au/scnsw/> [accessed October 29, 2009]; McHugh, *Aboriginal Societies*, pp. 104–8; see also, Mark Hickford, "'Decidedly the Most Interesting Savages on the Globe': An Approach to the Intellectual History of Māori ori Property Rights, 1837–53," *History of Political Thought*, 27 (2006), 122–67.
39. Stanley to W. Shortland, June 21, 1843, *GBPP*, XIII (1844), 556 (appendices, p. 475); Stephen to Hope, May 19, 1843, TNA, CO209/16, fols. 455–57.
40. Ibid. *R v Rangihaiata* [Rangihaeata], January 28, 1843, *New Zealand Colonist*, March 10, 1843, p. 3; *Graham v Tye*, February 16, 1848, *New Zealander*, February 19, 1848, p. 2; Hobson to W. Shortland, July 24, 1840, HL, MS0052/9.
41. See, for instance, *Court of Requests Ordinance* (1841), 4 Vic. No. 6 (NZ); *County Courts Ordinance* (1841), 5 Vic. No. 2 (NZ); *Resident Magistrates Court Ordinance* (1845), 10 Vic. No. 16 (NZ); *Native Districts Regulations Act* 1858 (NZ). This technique was not without its own difficulties. Poor communication might create confusion over whether particular laws applied in certain districts. Wyatt to colonial secretary, April 3, 1848, May 2, 1848, September 28, 1850, ATL, MS-179. Note that was this method was not always used to reconcile formal authority and substantive power; see Thomas Beckham, evidence to select committee on Native Offenders Bill, July 28, 1856, *Appendices to the Journal of the House of Representatives* [NZ] (Wellington: Government Printers, 1860), E5A.
42. Colin Newbury, *Patrons, Clients and Empire* (Oxford: Oxford University Press, 2003), pp. 256–57.
43. Ward, "Constructing British Authority," pp. 491–98; Ward, "Civil Jurisdiction," pp. 519–27; Sally Engle Merry, *Colonizing Hawaii. The Cultural Power of Law* (Princeton: Princeton University Press, 2000), pp. 49, 118.
44. *Register*, October 16, 1844, p. 3; Moorhouse, memorandum, December 6, 1844, SROSA, GRG24/6/1844/1446.
45. Milliss, *Waterloo Creek*. Reece, *Colonists and Aborigines*.
46. Hack to Hodgkin, undated [1835], Oxford, Rhodes House Library, Mss Brit Emp 18, c122/40; APS to colonial secretary, July 30, 1839, *Historical Records of Victoria*, ii(b), p. 758.
47. Report of Select Committee on New Zealand, *GBPP*, XIII (1844), 556 (pp. xvi–xix); Mark Hickford, "Making 'Territorial Rights of the Natives': Britain and New Zealand, 1830–1847" (unpublished doctoral thesis, University of Oxford, 1999), pp. 238–41; Ward, "Politics of Jurisdiction," pp. 118–29.
48. Select Committee on South Australia, *GBPP*, IV (1841), 119 (p. 394).
49. Grey to Earl Grey, December 15, 1847, *GBPP* XLIII (1847–48), 1002 (pp. 55–56); Earl Grey to Grey, July 7, 1848, *GBPP*, XLIII (1847–48), 1002; Grey to Earl Grey, March 15, 1849, *GBPP*, XXXV (1849), 1120] (p. 56); Grey

to Earl Grey, September 15, 1851, *GBPP*, XLV (1854), 1779 (p. 43); Speech to the Legislative Council, *Nelson Examiner*, November 21, 1846, p. 3.

50. On despatches, see Zoë Laidlaw, *Colonial Connections, 1815–45. Patronage, the Information Revolution and Colonial Government* (Manchester: Manchester University Press, 2005).
51. Grey to Earl Grey, December 15, 1847, *GBPP*, XLIII (1847–8), 1002 (pp. 55–56); Grey to Colonial Office, March 23, 1848, CO209/59, fols. 430–41.
52. *Colonial Lives across the British Empire: Imperial Careering across the Long Nineteenth Century*, ed. David Lambert and Alan Lester (Cambridge: Cambridge University Press, 2006).
53. Stephen minute on Gipps to Normanby, October 14, 1839, cited in *Historical Records of Victoria*, ii(b), p. 761; Smith to Russell, [October 1840], TNA, CO201/304, fol. 267; Stephen, September 8, 1840, minute, TNA, CO201/304, fol. 264.
54. Hutt to Russell, January 24, 1842, TNA, CO18/33, 67, fols. 78–79. Russell Smandych, "Contemplating the Testimony of 'Others': James Stephen, The Colonial Office, and the Fate of the Australian Aboriginal Evidence Acts, circa 1839–1849," *Legal History*, 10 (2006), 97–143; Stephen to Hope, July 27, 1842, TNA, CO18/33, fol. 107; and Lord John Russell, minute, March 10, 1842, TNA, CO13/16, fol. 102 suggest an awareness of the law officers' 1840 approach.
55. Law Officers to Stanley, October 26, 1842, CO18/33, fol. 55 and December 24, 1842, TNA, CO18/33, fol. 165; Smandych, "Contemplating the Testimony," pp. 129–31. It may have been thought that a different repugnancy approach would have applied: Gardiner, minute on Law Officers to Colonial Office, October 28, 1842, TNA, CO18/33, fol. 55; Leferve to Stephen, July 24, 1842, TNA, CO18/33, fol. 106.
56. 6 Vic. c. 22; Stanley to attorney-general, March 9, 1843, TNA, CO18/33, fols. 106–7; Smandych, "Contemplating the Testimony," pp. 270–72.
57. Jane Samson, "British Voices and indigenous rights: Debating Aboriginal legal status in nineteenth-century Australia and Canada," *Cultures of the Commonwealth: Essays and Studies* (1996–97), 5–16 (p. 10).
58. (1844) 7 Vic. No. 16 (NZ); (1844) 7 Vic. No. 8 (SA). Smandych, "Testimony," pp. 132–43. In Western Australia an August 1843 ordinance re-enacted the 1841 ordinance, although confirmation of the passage of the imperial legislation had not yet reached the colony: Ann Hunter, "The Origin and Debate Surrounding the Development of Aboriginal Evidence Acts in Western Australia in the Early 1840s," *University of Notre Dame Australia Law Review*, 9 (2007), 115–45.
59. Smandych, "Contemplating the Testimony," pp. 259–63.
60. Samson, "Aboriginal Legal Status," pp. 10–13.
61. Grey, "Report." Eyre to colonial secretary, February 1, 1843, SROSA, GRG24/6/1842/170; advocate-general to colonial secretary, May 14, 1844, SROSA, GRG24/6/1844/477; Also see *Register*, July 17, 1844, p. 2; August 10, 1844, p. 3.
62. (1841) 4 Vic. No. 2 (NZ), s 9. My thanks to Shaunnagh Dorsett for pointing out this section.

63. *New Zealand Gazette and Wellington Spectator*, May 1, 1844, p. 3.
64. See the various cases compiled in the New Zealand's Lost Cases database: <http://www.victoria.ac.nz/law/nzlostcases/cases.aspx> [accessed October 29, 2009].
65. *Southern Cross*, July 13, 1844, pp. 2–3; July 20, 1844, pp. 2–3; Bishop Selwyn, memorandum, [November 1845], Wellington, Archives New Zealand (ANZ), G19/1, 72–73, 80–81.
66. *Observer*, July 4, 1846, p. 4.
67. Moorhouse, "Report," July 14, 1846, SROSA, GRG24/6/1846/879; *Observer*, July 18, 1846, p. 4.
68. *Observer*, July 4, 1846, p. 4; April 7, 1846, p. 4.
69. *South Australian*, September 11, 1849, pp. 3, 4; *Observer*, July 28, 1849, p. 4; Cooper to Robe, February 27, 1847, SROSA, GRG24/6/1851/1564; Amanda Nettelbeck and Robert Foster, "Reading the Elusive Letter of the Law: Policing the South Australian Frontier," *Australian Historical Studies*, 38 (2009), 296–311.
70. Alan Ward, *Show of Justice. Racial Amalgamation in Nineteenth-Century New Zealand*, rev. edn. (Auckland: Auckland University Press, 1995); Gore Browne to Labouchere, April 19, 1856, ANZ, G25/6; Ward, "Civil Jurisdiction," pp. 521–24.
71. Reginald Good, "Admissibility of Testimony from Non-Christian Indians in the Colonial Municipal Courts of Upper Canada/Canada West" *Windsor Yearbook Access to Justice*, 23 (2005), 55–94 (pp. 73–74).
72. Catherine Hall, *Civilising Subjects: Colony and Metropole in the English Imagination, 1839–1867* (Chicago: University of Chicago Press, 2002), pp. 250–57, 290–380; Andrew Bank, "Losing Faith in the Civilizing Mission: the Premature Decline of Humanitarian Liberalism at the Cape, 1840–1860," in *Empire and Others: British Encounters with Indigenous Peoples, 1600–1850*, ed. Martin Daunton and Rick Halpern (Philadelphia: University of Pennsylvania Press, 1999), pp. 364–83.
73. Miles Taylor, "The 1848 Revolutions and the British Empire," *Past & Present*, 166 (2000), 146–80; Peter Burroughs, "Liberal, Paternalist or Cassandra? Earl Grey as a Critic of Colonial Self-government," *Journal of Imperial and Commonwealth History*, 18 (1990), 33–60.
74. Ward, "Civil Jurisdiction," pp. 521–32; In 1873, the New Zealand Court of Appeal reviewed the law on admitting non-Christian evidence. Neither the colonial nor imperial legislation was mentioned (*R v T.H. Barclay* (1873) 2 NZCA 251).
75. Swinfen, "Imperial Control," pp. 62–63, 168–83; Good, "Admissibility," pp. 73–74; Ward, "Civil Jurisdiction," pp. 521–32.
76. Tony Ballantyne, *Orientalism and Race: Aryanism in the British Empire* (Basingstoke: Palgrave, 2003).
77. Simon Potter, "Webs, Networks and Systems: Globalization and the Mass Media in the Nineteenth- and Twentieth-Century British Empire," *Journal of British Studies*, 46 (2007), 621–46.

Chapter 13

Law and Politics in the Constitutional Delineation of Indigenous Property Rights in 1840s New Zealand

Mark Hickford

This chapter discusses the deployment of European legal vocabularies, drawn from the common law and *ius gentium*, as means of framing indigenous forms of land-holding and tribal authority for the purposes of the colonization of New Zealand.[1] I contend that policymakers and officials saw common law sources and those of *ius gentium* as inadequate insofar as incorporating Māori narratives as to the content and substance of indigenous customary property rights within New Zealand in a way that assuaged intra-European politics. These transposed genres were perceived as less than adept at formulating Māori land tenure and political authority within their own terms, with this sense of incommensurability being recognized by some among the colonizers as requiring adaptations of policy. How formulators of policy responded to others who said otherwise in the later 1840s reasserted the preeminence of local colonial administration, rather than nongovernmental actors, in commanding the material and intellectual resources for political negotiation at a number of points with ongoing Māori political autonomy. Deeds of purchase were used to neutralize not only the proprietary interests in territory that Māori polities might claim but also the normative indigenous authority or jurisdiction to determine how such resources might be allocated and to whom. The *residuum* of indigenous authority regarding the allocation of resources was to be addressed and silenced.[2] A place was cleared for the making of untroubled Crown grants under royal prerogative to others. So the aspirations of theory and at least the look of practice went.

These ranging, intra-Anglophone disputes tended to engage two principal questions: first, the extent to which transposed legal sources were capable of embracing the translation of diverse indigenous voices regarding claims to property and natural resources (the extent to which they afforded portals of commensurability and communicability); and, second, whether such sources introduced with settlement were reshaped at all or remained relatively insulated and untouched. Distinct preferences for sorting out the nature of Māori tenure in land and natural resources politically—rather than working through the juridical and philosophical underpinnings of legally binding recognition of such tenure—were in evidence from time to time.

New Zealand supplies a rich profusion of debated material on this subject. Neither the New Zealand Company nor the Colonial Office saw transposed legal norms as sufficiently accommodating to incorporate Māori determinations as to what custom said about the nature and extent of Māori tenure in land. Yet each assumed this view for different reasons. The New Zealand Company and a number of its political allies within Westminster and New Zealand claimed that the common law and law of nations (*ius gentium*)[3] were omnicompetent in sorting out the proper nature and scope of Māori property rights in natural resources (land principally) and the interactions between Māori tenure, political autonomy, and the introduced legal regime from 1840. The Colonial Office generally disagreed with this claim for much of the 1840s, arguing that neither the common law nor *ius gentium* had much to offer by way of concrete policy development. It did not necessarily accept that common law was sufficiently flexible to assist in coordinating the coexistence of customary property interests of Māori communities (howsoever conceived), and the adjustments wrought by an introduced system of English tenure (in the limited areas where that tenure was effective).[4] A third and less unified group of participants in the debate—the Aborigines' Protection Society in London, the chief justice (William Martin) at times, and various missionaries on the ground within New Zealand, as well as their parent societies in Britain—had their own views and interpretations of the common law and *ius gentium* with regard to Māori land-holding.

The central issue was what role, if any, could vocabularies of common law and the law of nations play in mediating the interaction and intersections between indigenous cultural forms and an alien legal regime that traveled with the voyaging Crown and its settlers. Law was one of the languages in which a usable sense of the past and the present could be united for Europeans.[5] But the languages of European jurisprudence proved to be less than adept at accommodating Māori conceptions of property and authority that belonged, in fact, to a different historical and cultural universe. Crucial disputes concerning such conceptions arose in the context of establishing and acquiring space for enclave or bridgehead settlements.[6] They were thus fundamentally disputes between European stakeholders vying for such acquisition or seeking to impose a governmental order on it from a distant colonial office. Different understandings of these important architectural features of colonial New Zealand—the role of the incoming Crown, the occupation of land, the disciplining effect of preexisting property rights of Māori and Māori political autonomy upon both the introduced Crown and its immigrant subjects—churned the political waters of both colony and imperial metropole. Formulating these differences in the vocabularies of European jurisdiction and sovereignty represented a form of constitutionalism. They reflected efforts of the various participants in those debates to explain the form and substance of the Crown—as sovereign political and juridical authority—introduced to New Zealand, as well as the legitimacy and scope of its authority to sort out proprietary rights within the colony. In what follows I look at some examples of how the arguments over the constitutional form of land appropriation and distribution played out in practice, with a view to clarifying the political use of the languages of the common law and European *ius gentium*.

The Law and Politics of "Occupation"

Intra-European contestation over the construction of property rights during the 1840s and 1850s in New Zealand demonstrates something of the sinuosities of common law opinion and argument, as well as its limitations. The disputes also reveal the plurality and dynamism of the factions contributing to imperial policy formation on the property rights of Māori and settlers both in New Zealand and in Britain. Various vocabularies drawn from common law sources or texts concerning *ius gentium* were used, often divergently, by contending parties seeking to formulate their political and economic agendas within the norms of European law.[7] Such vocabularies proved to be powerful currencies of political argument and colonial debate. The Colonial Office certainly neither inhabited nor exhibited a homogeneous "common law mind." Rather, political officials regulated the flow of legal recognition to various parties in accordance with certain governmental practices and values, as opposed to others. This proved to be particularly important in circumstances where the material resources of government—revenue and personnel—were relatively meager. The threat of the withholding of recognition proved to be a potent one, particularly as secure and legally unchallenged Crown-granted titles had failed to materialize in key settlements, such as Wellington, even by the mid-1840s. As such, the imperial administration and its representatives within colonial New Zealand used claims to property rights recognized at law as a means of ordering the distribution of land to settlers and, therefore, as conducive to state formation. In the event, it preferred relatively free-floating politics and policy to doctrinaire positions nourished by texts on the common law or the law of nations, although these sources might be of use from time to time.[8] The recognition of ill-defined "territorial rights of the natives" was less an attempt to represent indigenous rights than it was a floating means for disciplining settler conduct with regards to the pace, spatial extent, and distribution of settlement.[9]

From 1840, the New Zealand Company and its political allies in Britain were the principal drivers in using northern American jurisprudence on relations between Amerindians and increasingly intrusive colonial polities.[10] In effect, the company claimed an entitlement to influence policy outcomes at Westminster and in New Zealand, largely through the networks of its directors and members in the House of Commons and in commercial enterprise. A cluster of northern American sources was gathered up and deployed, specifically James Kent's *Commentaries on American Law* and Joseph Story's *Commentaries on the Constitution of the United States*, as well as reports containing the judgments of the Supreme Court of the United States during the period of John Marshall's tenure as chief justice (from 1801 until 1835). In his *Commentaries on the Constitution of the United States*, the American jurist and justice of the United States Supreme Court, Joseph Story, observed in a chapter on the "origin of the title to [the] territory of the colonies" that the "aboriginal inhabitants" or "natives" populating the eastern seaboard of northern America were "admitted to possess a present right of occupancy, or use in the soil, which was subordinate to the ultimate dominion of the [European] discoverer."[11] Numbered amongst the fragile idiosyncrasies of the Native American "right of occupancy" was that, "notwithstanding this occupancy, the European discoverers claimed and exercised the right to grant the soil, while yet in the possession of the natives." In this, Story certainly echoed the language of Marshall in *Johnson v M'Intosh*, and a view expressed in that decision that certain commentators have since considered controversial.[12] Yet again he contributed an interesting gloss in adding that the "title so granted was universally admitted to convey a sufficient title in the soil to the grantees in perfect dominion, or, as it is sometimes expressed in treaties of public law, it was a transfer of *plenum et utile dominium* [by which he meant the passing of the full right of property in the space, including an entitlement to complete enjoyment of the fruits of such property]."[13] Elsewhere, Story cited *Worcester v Georgia*, James Kent's *Commentaries on American Law*, and Thomas Jefferson's correspondence as the bases for the view that "the title of the Indians was not treated as a right of propriety and dominion; but as a mere right of occupancy."[14]

The New Zealand Company and its affiliates used these sorts of sources for different purposes at manifold points on a case-by-case basis. Initially in 1840, the company sought to privilege James Cook's landfall upon New Zealand shores in 1769 and 1770 as a "discovery" of New Zealand. On this analysis, following the decisions of the Supreme Court of the United States in *Cherokee Nation v Georgia* (1831) and *Johnson* (1823), such "discovery" was imbued with legal effect. It was treated as establishing the preeminence of the sovereign rights of the United Kingdom as against other European polities. Henry Chapman, the editor of New Zealand Company-sponsored periodical *The New Zealand Journal* (until 1842), was sufficiently circumspect in April 1840 when claiming that U.S. jurisprudence on such relations was relevant to New Zealand in leaving the question of the substance of territorial rights of Māori relatively moot. He stated that it "must be clear that the rights reserved to the native tribes could only be of a modified character, but whether those rights were abridged or extensive—whether they were confined to a mere right of occupation, or amounted to something deserving the name of sovereignty, was a question which did not affect the relation between the discovering nation and other civilised powers."[15]

Such understandings of common law and *ius gentium* brought with them their own senses of regional (European) customary usage but not in a manner that opened them to comparable Māori customs and understandings. In December 1842, protectors of Aborigines within New Zealand were directed to furnish reports on "the nature of the holding of landed property among the aborigines of New Zealand, settling the more particularly whether they have an individual right or a common right or interest in the soil and what is the right or interest of the chief."[16] Yet, there was no sense of the information to be so obtained as acting to transform notions of, say, English customary usages endemic within the common law that was brought to New Zealand. That is, the imported common law would not accommodate such officially mustered information and render it juridical—something that could be unraveled and tested in the ordinary courts. There was to be no casual convergence between a pragmatic anthropology and the edifice of European property law.

In the main, these policy disputes wrestled with the problematic of "occupancy" (*occupatio*)[17] and its apparent stress upon the significance of physically tangible forms of interaction with a landscape, such as cultivating crops and constructing fortifications or dwelling places. The New Zealand Company and its political fellow-travelers preferred to focus upon this sort of evidence of a material footprint upon the landscape rather than more intangible signs of connection to place: memorialized narratives of genealogical connections to certain sites or resources; accounts of remembered warring or of voyaging across territories; or recitations of battles for prestige. Indeed, many of these subtleties were rubbed out, assessed as capriciously driven or motivated, as unduly complex, or as irrelevant or unhelpful archaisms; although that is not to say that these sorts of accounts would not claim places of relevance in the future. We see this complex process in action throughout the decade starting in 1840, the year in which the Crown formally asserted British authority within New Zealand. Profoundly tied to questions of "occupancy" were issues about locating the identity or identities of those who had authority to speak for certain areas and resources: to whom should officers of the intrusive Crown speak? These were as much questions of political authority and jurisdiction concerning space as they were of property.

Whilst technical meanings of "occupancy" and "occupation" in international law and the common law doctrine of tenure could be expounded in textbooks, their impact on preexisting indigenous communities and cultures was by no means straightforward. The conceptual complexities of initial and ongoing "occupancy," and what it might look like in terms of observable conduct or habits, were well appreciated by those versed in the main legal idioms. There was, however, no necessary concurrence on these matters. In such circumstances of interest-driven disagreement, the realm of politics became preeminent in working through what was to be done, even if the vocabularies of common law and *ius gentium* were themselves used (in various ways) by political actors to formulate their competing interests. In this context, New Zealand offers insights on how a conception of "occupancy" fared in a particular field for British settlement in the early nineteenth century. Philosophical niceties were left abstractly indeterminate and unresolved while the colonial office, the New Zealand Company, and its assorted critics used legalistic sources and arguments in largely political, non-juridical sites, rather than in the courts. They did so with a view to obtaining leverage in political settlements about what to do at least for a time, without resolving abstract questions about the nature and extent of Māori tenure in land.

Legal sources feeding into the politics of Crown decision-making thus remained disparate, discursive, and unsettled. These sources materialized in letters, in the correspondence of the commissioner appointed to inquire into the New Zealand Company's claims to land in New Zealand, and in debates in the House of Commons in 1840 and 1845.[18] While these legalistic genres undoubtedly presented as important ways of seeing and talking about property rights, the Supreme Court in New Zealand was seldom resorted to in settling questions of land tenure, except in relation to particular intra-European disputes. Even then, however, courts were not the preeminent sites for constitutional discussions of the sort this chapter is focusing on. To express it another way, the formalistic judicial or adjudicative dimension of the Crown—in the form of the monarch's oath-bound judges of the Supreme Court—was not as regularly called upon in litigation. Furthermore, much of what the executive arm of the Crown did (or omitted to do) was not the subject of formal judicial scrutiny. In leaving the prerogatives of the Crown in granting land to others within New Zealand largely unconstrained, the Supreme Court in Wellington and Auckland allowed crucial issues of land distribution to be settled in the space of political negotiation rather than formal legal proceedings. Whether based in London or in Wellington and Auckland, those who participated in these political negotiations were well aware that Māori populations were in a state of flux, had warred amongst each other, and had displaced prior populations. In spite of Jeremy Waldron's suggestive essay on "first occupancy," therefore, the intellectual vocabularies drawn from common law sources or texts regarding *ius gentium* and European political practices were deployed as instruments for shaping localized juridical and political orders regardless of the philosophical niceties or precise a priori foundations of these sources (or absence of them).[19] Participants in the politics of negotiability, whether Māori-settler interrelations or intra-Māori and intra-European interaction, lived with theoretical indeterminacy. As Sunstein has pointed out, incompletely theorized agreements on a general principle to be adopted, or on a particular approach or an outcome to be pursued, if only for a time, tend to assist in concealing significant or considerable disagreement about particular cases or even the details of the general principle.[20] Localized and temporally specific or bound practices of claiming and negotiating property rights suffused the early constitutional orders of colonial New Zealand and subsequently.[21] Understandably, the practices of politics tended to yield temporary fixity or provisional agreements on such matters as property rights, rather than substantive intellectual consensus or closure.[22] Such points of agreement about what was to be done for the time being were never stable.

Land Claims as Instruments of Political Negotiation and Contestation

Despite this de facto malleability, what was still seen as vexed and challenging, however, was sorting out the role of indigenous narratives in providing "occupancy" with practical legal and policy content. This issue ignited a broad-ranging political controversy in Westminster and in New Zealand in 1845 and again in 1847–1848. In 1845 the "New Zealand question," as it was called, emerged out of the New Zealand Company agitation concerning the insecurity of land titles within its settlements. In a personal memorandum presented to George Grey dating from June 1847, the Anglican missionary Octavius Hadfield displayed access to a host of sources on U.S. jurisprudence, political philosophy, the English common law, and the government of colonies.[23] Retained within Grey's personal papers, Hadfield's script claimed that

> by . . . [the] cession ["acquired by Treaty with the native tribes"] (through a fiction of law derived from feudal usages, but now prevalent in all European countries, and in the United States of America) the Crown acquires a *paramount* title to all *waste lands* [and] not to wild lands (as her been ignorantly asserted), but lands without owners.[24]

The immediate purpose of Hadfield's statement was to contest statements concerning Māori territorial rights within the third Earl Grey's instructions as secretary of state for colonies to George Grey of December 23, 1846.[25] These instructions suggested that the appropriate theory underpinning native title was that which restricted their "occupancy" to that which they used by way of cultivation. Earl Grey proposed institutions for ascertaining what land was subject to Māori proprietorship and what was not. To this end, the proposed charter for the colony of New Zealand, which accompanied the instructions, proposed "land courts" to establish finally, in a domesday fashion, the proprietorship of all such territories within the colony, with the results of that investigation precisely registered and any land not owned or sufficiently occupied to be declared royal demesne.[26] Although this proposal came to naught on account of considerable political pressure exerted within New Zealand and in the United Kingdom, it is revealing for the particularity of inquiry into continuity of occupation that it envisaged for the determination of native title.

What we begin to see in the New Zealand setting from the 1840s is the emergence of a distinct language of "claiming" or "claims." This language was used to characterize the interests in territory that certain Māori communities asserted and that required neutralizing through purchase or the payment of compensation.[27] On this basis, political engagement with indigenous communities could occur principally through the diplomatic mechanics of purchase, without engaging in forensic inquiries vis-à-vis the quality or substance of Māori interests. In other words it was a language that opened onto a non-judicial strategy for dealing with land-appropriation and distribution. In practice, this language of purchasing or compensating "claims" began to suffuse official communications on the ground within New Zealand, as well as those in London. By 1846 a special committee of the New Zealand Company was also expressing an awareness of the problem of "claims" and "claiming" in stating, "We have only to leave the natives undisturbed in the northern and middle parts of the northern island, and to form our settlements in the neighbourhood of New Plymouth, or of Wellington, or in the middle and Stewart's islands, the whole extent of which is unencumbered by the presence or claims of native tribes."[28] In March of that year, Stanley's successor as secretary of state for the colonies, William Ewart Gladstone, prepared a draft note for George Grey, lieutenant governor of New Zealand, in the wake of the recall of Robert FitzRoy, stating, "I deem it probable that the middle island [the South Island] may be regarded as in no respect subject to the native claim of property in the gross."[29]

"Claim" and "claiming" were conventionally used as terms that could apply to broader areas of space than those that were physically "occupied" in the form of cultivated sites, villages, or fortified emplacements. It proved to be a persistent way of talking. The concept apparently converged, relatively neatly if not completely, with the Māori term *take* or an underlying "cause," "basis," or "foundation," which had already surfaced in a number of Anglophone sources by the late 1840s.[30] In 1840, Robert Maunsell, a Church Missionary Society representative, introduced the term *take* in relation to aboriginal title, denoting a "root" or foundation to an assertion of interest in a territorial tract.[31] In this assessment, the difficulties of negotiating territorial transfers with Māori were evident: "The land does not, generally speaking, belong to one individual, but chiefly to the tribe."[32] Maunsell admitted that a single *take* might be embodied in a multiplicity of persons, stressing the significance of intra-Māori political relations and diplomacy. Nonetheless, the language of "claim" in relation to *take* might be viewed in terms of the emergence of an improvisational bridgehead between the discrepant cultures, indicating the appearance of piecemeal, often bespoke "windows" of mutual intelligibility outside of the universalistic languages of law and philosophy.

Other approaches to characterizing indigenous narratives about natural resources were evident in other regions. Edward Shortland, an itinerant assistant protector of aborigines, endeavored to nuance his views on aboriginal tenure at Banks Peninsula in the South Island by predicating these perceptions on classes of Māori claims possessing ranked priorities. These priorities ranged from *i a ratou te turuturu o te kaika* or "those [claims] of persons who have especially a right to the place," to *nga piringa* or "those persons allied to the former."[33] He advised it was necessary to obtain the names of individuals entitled to an individual right or *i a ratou te turuturu o te kaika* before completing any purchase of land. Shortland's precise, localized, treatment of intelligence on Māori descent-groupings and aboriginal tenure in the Bay of Plenty or southern island conveyed tales of complexity to an administration at Auckland. In general, however, both the notion of *take* and other descriptions of the bases of Māori tenure implied a historical narrative as to how particular claims had emerged. Shortland, for instance, realized that genealogical trails were linked to claims to territories and resources. Such a conclusion accentuated the significance of identifying, if at all possible, the complicated intersections of historical, familial, and political relations amongst and between Māori descent-groupings. The concept of "claims" was soon deployed by William Spain, appointed as commissioner on January 20, 1841, and who investigated and reported upon the putative purchases of the New Zealand Company from various Māori (under deeds in 1839 and early 1840) through convening hearings at Port Nicholson (Wellington), New Plymouth in the Taranaki, Wanganui, and Nelson.[34]

In the event, an untidy melding of concepts of "occupancy" and "claiming" was adapted and deployed within colonial New Zealand.[35] In this space of political negotiation and governmental improvisation, European legal conceptions were partially adapted to Māori forms of land-holding and land-claiming, even as the latter took shape within the imported legal and governmental landscape. These localized inflections, occasioned by negotiated practices in the field, reflected political practices specifically adapted to the exigencies and complexities of negotiating multiple engagements with assorted Māori descent-groups. Bespoke or customized forms of interaction with certain Māori groupings on issues relative to the occupation of territorial space occurred in areas set around the nodes of Pākehā settlement at places such as New Plymouth, Wanganui (Petre), and Port Nicholson (Wellington). Imperial administration assumed and insisted upon its primacy in attributing the rationale and meanings to such activity as opposed to simply imposing legalistic genres in some abstract or a priori fashion. Nevertheless, the degree to which the meanings attributed to these specific sets of negotiations might have been shared or mutually understood on the part of a variety of Māori audiences remains in the shadows, obscured. Various agendas and calculations relevant to the positioning of intra-Māori concerns and politics were being played out.

Appreciating the fluidity of indigenous relations and the considerable difficulties in precisely assessing the quality of physically tangible interaction with particular landscapes, resources, and environments came to suffuse Anglophone materials and debates. But these forms of appreciation were interpreted in various ways. Complexity proved to be unwelcome even though some adapted and readapted practices and an intellectual vocabulary—a rationale—to address this very complexity. Far from assisting the process of acquiring secure titles for settlements, these critics of imperial policy maintained that the collection of intelligence about "custom" simply encouraged tactical play and capriciousness amongst Māori informants. Joseph Somes, the governor of the New Zealand Company, responded to intelligence reports and retellings of detailed Māori conceptions of tenure with incredulity. In a despatch of January 24, 1843, to the secretary of state for colonies, he argued that "it requires little discernment to conceive what a mass of perjuries the boundless mendacity of savages will produce, under the direction of white advisers; [...] what strange notions of right will be advanced on the strength of unknown and incomprehensible customs of a savage state."[36]

Others responded in a manner contrary to the New Zealand Company, arguing that by prying territory for settlement away from Māori politics and customary authority, purchase would prove to be a practical and conceptual panacea for colonial New Zealand. Processes of negotiation and purchase would broker and pacify Māori politics to an extent, as settlements were placed as buffers within disputed areas. In a putatively anonymous pamphlet of 1847, intended for limited circulation within the United Kingdom, the chief justice of the Supreme Court of New Zealand, Martin, contended that what he characterized as the "territorial rights" of the "New Zealanders" (used in the sense of Māori) were, in the main, areas that descent-groupings were disposed to defend by force of arms.[37] In other words, the language of claiming and the competing intra-European political strategies driving this language created a space of intelligibility for particular ways of understanding Māori land-holding, and a space for Māori themselves to engage in land competition under the aegis of this understanding.

The Law and Politics of "Native Title"

What impact did these localized negotiations and contestations have upon the legal sources that were introduced to New Zealand? Are we able to discern an approach that is specific to colonial New Zealand and the manner in which imperial government imagined such a New Zealand? Māori were to be treated as "British subjects," so the third article of the treaty initially signed at Waitangi on February 6, 1840 claimed. Yet, when it came to delineating customary property rights or "native title," Māori were partly catapulted into the universe of *ius gentium* and other European legal and intellectual cultures that were quite alien to them. Thus, paradoxically, they were other or less than "British subjects," at least concerning the holding of tenure in land for the purposes of municipal law in the new and rudimentary coastal municipalities of Auckland, New Plymouth, Port Nicholson (Wellington), and Nelson. In such places, the sway of English legal norms could be registered, interpreted, and acted upon in specific cases in the Supreme Court at Wellington or Auckland. In other areas, certain missionaries had begun to develop the practice of instituting particular forms of dispute resolution amongst Māori associated with their ministries, such as *whakawā* or *kōti whakawā*, as Ballara has touched upon.[38] At these sites, negotiated forms of engagement were very much in evidence.

In spite of limits on the practical reach of such courts and resident magistrates, as well as protectors of aborigines, certain commentators, such as Hadfield and Henry Chapman—who assumed the role of first puisne judge of the Supreme Court of New Zealand from December 26, 1843—thought that British curial and legal jurisdiction extended throughout the New Zealand archipelago.[39] Chapman's and Hadfield's commentaries on "native title"—framed as advice for others in the later 1840s in the context of political negotiations to secure spaces for settlement—attest to the attempts to adapt imported intellectual vocabularies to dynamic, localized political environments. For Hadfield, unlike Chapman, "sovereignty is acquired by *Treaty* [and not through discovery or otherwise] with the native tribes,—who cede the sovereignty formerly possessed by themselves."[40] The "right of discovery," claimed Hadfield, "is merely a *right* to colonise—*as against all other civilised nations*:—it confers no actual right to the country discovered."[41] That is, it did not, properly speaking, entitle the discovering polity to assert untrammeled sovereignty over the New Zealand archipelago and its inhabitants. A secondary transaction was required in the form of a treaty of cession. As previously noted, however, Hadfield had advised Grey in this memorandum that it was by virtue of the specific event of cession that the Crown obtained a "*paramount title* to all *waste lands*—not to wild lands (as has been ignorantly asserted), but land without owners."[42] Hadfield's reference to "land without owners" spoke to the need to develop a methodology for identifying such proprietors, that is, locating those who could speak for a particular space and its natural resources on behalf of others.

Chapman's personal notes dating from approximately 1845 or 1846 on the "status of native races considered in relation to the sovereignty" averred that "savage nations … retain a sort of modified sovereignty until abrogated by treaty."[43] There are reasons for dating his memorandum on native title as having been written at this time. These notes, uncirculated as far as we know, were intended for the "purpose of informing the inferior magistrates and protectors as of warning and instructing the native population."[44] The protectorate department was remodeled and effectively abolished in 1846. In Chapman's account of the mid-1840s, inspired by his readings of the jurisprudence of the U.S. Supreme Court in *Johnson v M'Intosh* (1823) and *Cherokee Nation v State of Georgia* (1831) and since adapted to the New Zealand context, the discoverer acquired "the sovereignty" of the islands. In his legal notes of 1845 or 1846, Chapman said that, until a compact expressly cleared the vestiges of the "modified" or residual sovereignty away, the entitlements of the discovering polity were effective against all other European jurisdictions. On this legal analysis, the "native inhabitants retain their sovereignty and national character in relation to each other and to the discovering nation except in so far as such sovereignty impairs the sovereignty of the discovering nation in relation to its own subjects and other European powers."[45] In the various treaties within his personal collection, Chapman noted that "in such documents [the tribes] ... are called '*nations*' and are held capable of maintaining the relations of war & peace and in case of the former are deemed 'enemies' not 'rebels.'" He concluded it was "this modified sovereignty which the natives of New Zealand parted with by the treaty of Waitangi [in 1840]."[46] Chapman cautioned that, in "considering the question of what laws prevail in a newly settled country where a civilized people come into contact with a rude people, the idea of sovereignty must not be confounded with that of laws either generally or in relation to the title to the land."[47] In this manner, he was able to subtly address the material actuality of the territorial autonomy of Māori communities and the aspiring theory of British jurisdiction. This permitted him to argue that the Crown's overarching claims to "sovereignty" within New Zealand and the legal jurisdiction throughout the territory were not compromised or rendered problematic in spite of certain legitimate de facto exceptions in particular cases.

Yet this reasoning also allowed Chapman to criticize the "views taken by some of the officers of the governments of New Zealand" in a fashion noticeably distinguishable from Hadfield's in 1846. According to Chapman, these views of elements within the executive arm of colonial government muted and undermined assertions of the Crown's preeminence as the ultimate authority and sovereign in the New Zealand islands. He adverted to "private wars" between Māori polities that ought to have been quashed but had not. This observation attested to the practical persistence of both intra-Māori and inter-hapū politics beyond the ken of introduced officialdom. In this part of his discussion, a noticeable sense of discomfort and frustration intruded. As Chapman lamented, "the judges cannot constitutionally act until the case is before them" and he suspected that "the executive [would] abstain from bringing any case before the courts."[48] Here we see an acknowledgment, properly given, of the significance of official activity in contributing to the practical ways in which the constitutional order associated with the executive dimensions of the Crown within the colonial New Zealand were understood.

Nevertheless, Chapman confused the situation in his own account by analyzing the "legal difficulty," as he called it, occasioned by the Treaty of Waitangi. He argued that the "Waitangi treaty considered (erroneously) as the *foundation* of the Queen's sovereignty [had] led to this difficulty," evidenced by the emergence of certain imprudent official views and conduct. Furthermore, argued Chapman, the "treaty can of course only be binding on such independent tribes as are parties thereto and doubts have therefore been expressed as to whether the Queen had any authority at all in districts occupied by tribes, the chiefs whereof had not become parties to the treaty."[49] Yet, Chapman continued, the rights of sovereign authority resided with the incoming Crown by virtue of "discovery [and subsequent] occupation." Accordingly, the "limited sovereignty, which the clients of savage tribes retain[ed] *inter se*" was consistent with the "clear right" in the Crown "(a right founded in humanity and sanctioned by the comity of nations) to suppress murder [and] cannibalism."[50] The practice of Crown officials might be seen in this context, with purchase deeds purporting to neutralize Māori territorial claims together with the claimed political authority to speak for such territories and their resources.

The negotiating spaces for these secondary compacts or deeds of purchase were preeminently a place for politics, for negotiations with the localized practicalities of Māori political and territorial autonomy. Chapman's sense of the limits of native title coalesced with this sort of approach but also, paradoxically, made it possible to register something of the local nuances of Māori political autonomy on questions of land tenure. Chapman regarded native title as non-justiciable, that is, as not legally enforceable at the suit of Māori against the Crown or grantees of the Crown. He argued that the "rights and dominion which native tribes exercise over land are not such as come within the cognizance of the tribunals."[51] He also stated by way of conclusion that "no grant can be disputed to the subject on the ground that the Crown has not extinguished the native title."[52] In Chapman's notes, Māori had a "mere right of occupancy," not translatable into English law: "All that the courts could recognize as vesting in the [Māori as] the vendor [of land] would be an estate of occupancy in common with the conveying tribe and not the right to reduce any piece of land into personal possession."[53] In mid-1847, after writing these notes and following the decision of the Supreme Court of New Zealand in *Regina v Symonds*, Chapman disclosed in private correspondence that his interpretation of the substance of Māori rights in property accorded with that of the third Earl Grey in the despatch of December 23, 1846.[54]

In certain key senses, then, Māori remained nonconsensual and uncomprehending subjects of particular interpretations of *ius gentium*, particularly regarding any proprietary interests in natural resources or land. Something of the sense of caution amongst certain Anglophone settlers with access to officialdom that such treatment occasioned can be garnered from the commentary in 1844 of John Whiteley. Whiteley was a missionary of the Wesleyan Missionary Society at Taranaki who witnessed the negotiations to settle the New Zealand Company's purported acquisition of space for the precarious New Plymouth settlement. Characterizing the negotiations as "this intricate question," Whiteley went on to comment that

> the Law of England and the Laws of Nations may hopefully bear the comparison [between occupants and absentee Māori] out in the award which [William Spain, the commissioner] has given, but I submit that in such a case as this, the Natives ought on the strict principles of justice to be dealt with in accordance with their own usages and laws and not according to laws of which they never heard.[55]

In London, a periodical publication of the Aborigines' Protection Society, *The Colonial Intelligencer or Aborigines' Friend*, would sound a similar note of caution in late 1847, in the midst of a still-intense dispute about the nature of Māori property rights that had arisen out of Earl Grey's despatch of December 23, 1846. It reported that "the important point to remember is this, that the New Zealanders will not stop to ask us to define territorial rights for them, nor will they defer to the authority of writers on the *Jus Gentium*."[56] Such views were buttressed by the Crown's limited ability to influence the outcomes of intra-Māori politics, regardless of Chapman's reflections on questions of "modified sovereignty" and native title. In 1846, Hadfield, appointed by George Selwyn as the Church Missionary Society rural dean for the western districts of Wellington and Taranaki in 1844, casually remarked in a memorandum to lieutenant governor George Grey that "each tribe possesses absolute sovereign rights within the boundaries of its own territory."[57]

Deploying English common law and European *ius gentium* as genres for intra-European argument on land appropriation and distribution had the effect of detaching the cultural practices and pathways of Māori communities from the New Zealand landscapes that were analyzed and examined through those imported sources. Claims to property in land were inevitably formulated through the grammar of European legal genres, hence remaining alien to the web-like interconnectedness between communities and the territories and resources they claimed. The cultural specificities of relations between a Māori community and its resources, let alone amongst Māori polities themselves, were often missed or occluded in these accounts.[58] Reasoning extracted from either the common law or *ius gentium* did not necessarily pry open a portal of recognition for the incorporation of intelligence regarding these narratives or what they might have suggested about the relationships of various Māori populations to particular landscapes or questions of autonomy to influence the relations of strangers to those landscapes. Intra-European debates concerning the property rights claims of indigenous populations thus served to reveal the relative imperviousness of common law sources to often complicated customary information provided from diverse Māori sources.[59] Neither the common law nor the law of nations proved as receptively porous as some have claimed, whether in the 1840s or subsequently. What was in play, therefore, was a series of principally intra-European negotiations and enactments seeking to implement the terms of imperial policies with regard to colonial land tenure, the security of titles, the production of public revenue through the control of land transactions, and the acquisition of space for pākehā settlements. Allowing the politics of negotiation to address information concerning customary usages and norms permitted Anglophone parties to these disputes to hold to their preferred intellectual views irrespective of practices within the field. Colonial and imperial politics would see the continuation of these sorts of dispute into the 1850s. In reflecting on recent warring in the Taranaki in June 1861, once matters had deteriorated further, the fifth duke of Newcastle observed as secretary of state for the colonies that the relevant indigenous participants could "scarcely be looked upon as subjects in rebellion."[60]

The frailties of customary property rights or "native title" as a form of tenure within transposed legalistic genres and the placing of such rights-claims beyond the municipal reach of English common law on tenurial estates had consequences for the location of Māori groups within constitutional arguments. In the 1850s, for instance, the predominant (albeit not uncontested) view of "native title" was that it was neither intelligible to conceptions of English real property nor sufficient to qualify Māori for the electoral franchise under the *New Zealand Constitution Act 1852*.[61] In November 1863 against the background of legislation contemplating the confiscation of Māori land, Martin observed, "The case stands thus: no native can in any way enforce any right of ownership or occupation of land, held by the native tenure in the courts of the Colony."[62] He added, "The native land is excluded from the political franchise, even in cases where there is in fact, a right of individual occupation, on the ground that his right, whatever it might be, is not in the technical sense a 'tenement'."[63] This was a class of proprietary interest referred to in section 7 of the

New Zealand Constitution Act 1852—imperial legislation enacted by the legislature at Westminster.[64]

Conclusion

While the genres of English common law and European *ius gentium* were indeed deployed to assist in formulating the relative rights and entitlements of Pākehā and Māori during the 1840s and 1850s, the limited efficacy of these legal instruments was determined in the predominantly non-judicial spaces of intra-European political negotiations. The practical reception of such sources was inflected by the obtaining of intelligence from Māori sources themselves, but this occurred in a way that did not necessarily effect a profound reshaping of the legal sources that had traveled across the seas, at least for the purposes of conversations internal to Anglophone audiences. Despite the theoretical pretensions of claims about the curial jurisdiction of the Anglophone courts extending throughout colonial New Zealand, Māori populations were practicably treated as subjects dwelling within the universe of *ius gentium* but in a space where political negotiation and diplomacy predominated, a point with significance for their incorporation within a form of political rather than juridically driven constitutionalism. It was in the space of such negotiation (the politics of negotiability), where discrepant conceptions of land-holding and political authority were jostled together by political exigency, that circumscribed windows of mutual intelligibility were ventured between colonial administration and indigenous polities.

Notes

1. The essay is based upon research conducted for my doctoral thesis at the University of Oxford (completed in 1999).
2. Cf. Jeremy Webber, "Relations of Force and Relations of Justice: The Emergence of Normative Community between Colonists and Aboriginal Peoples," *Osgoode Hall Law Journal*, 33 (1995), 623–60 (pp. 625, 628–29).
3. On *ius gentium*, law shared by all peoples, and *ius inter gentes*, the norms governing the relations between one people and another: David Armitage, "Hobbes and the Foundations of Modern International Thought," in *Rethinking the Foundations of Modern Political Thought*, ed. *Annabel Brett, James Tully and Holly Hamilton-Bleakley* (Cambridge: Cambridge University Press, 2006), 219–35 (pp. 228–29).

4. Mark Hickford, "'Decidedly the Most Interesting Savages on the Globe': An Approach to the Intellectual History of Māori Property Rights, 1837–1853," *History of Political Thought*, 27 (2006), 122–67 (pp. 151–55).
5. Gordon Schochet, "The 'Ancient Constitution' as Necessary Interpretative Trope," in *The Political Imagination in History: Essays Concerning J.G.A. Pocock*, ed. D.N. DeLuna (Baltimore: Owlworks, 2006), pp. 11–25 (p. 20).
6. On the significance of the "bridgehead" to territorial expansion: John Darwin, "Imperialism and the Victorians: The Dynamics of Territorial Expansion," *English Historical Review*, 112 (1997), 614–42.
7. Mark Hickford, "Making 'Territorial Rights of the Natives': Britain and New Zealand, 1830–1847" (unpublished doctoral thesis, University of Oxford, 1999).
8. Hickford, "'Decidedly the Most Interesting Savages.'"
9. Hickford, "Making 'Territorial Rights.'"
10. Hickford, "'Decidedly the Most Interesting Savages'"; Hickford, "Making 'Territorial Rights'"; Mark Hickford, "'Settling Some Very Important Principles of Colonial Law': Three 'Forgotten' Cases of the 1840s," *Victoria University of Wellington Law Review*, 35 (2004), 1–71.
11. Joseph Story, *Commentaries on the Constitution of the United States; With a Preliminary Review of the Constitutional History of the Colonies and States, before the Adoption of the Constitution*, 3 vols. (Boston: Hilliard, Gray, & Co. and Cambridge: Brown, Shattuck & Co., 1833), I, p. 7. Story dedicated this text to the then United States Supreme Court Chief Justice, John Marshall (I, pp. iii–iv).
12. Stuart Banner, *How the Indians Lost Their Land: Law and Power on the Frontier* (Cambridge: Harvard University Press, 2005), pp. 168–90. But see Hickford, "'Decidedly the Most Interesting Savages,'" p. 152, referring to a 1765 legal opinion by John Kempe, then the attorney-general for the colony of New York.
13. Story, *Commentaries on the Constitution*, I, p. 8.
14. Story, *Commentaries on the Constitution*, I, p. 135.
15. [H.S. Chapman], "The English, the French and the New Zealanders," *New Zealand Journal*, 1.5 (1840), 1–2.
16. Colonial secretary's office (Auckland) to Clarke senior, December 15, 1842, Archives New Zealand, Wellington (ANZ), IA4/271, fols. 90–91.
17. I have addressed this conception previously albeit from the perspective of the entwining of stadial histories and *ius gentium* in debates concerning the proprietary rights of Māori populations: Hickford, "'Decidedly the Most Interesting Savages.'"
18. Hickford, "Making 'Territorial Rights.'"
19. Jeremy Waldron, "Indigeneity? First Peoples and Last Occupancy," *New Zealand Journal of Public and International Law*, 1 (2003), 55–82.
20. Cass Sunstein, "Incompletely Theorized Agreements," *Harvard Law Review*, 108 (1995), 1733–72.
21. Mark Hickford, "Strands from the Afterlife of Confiscation: Property Rights, Constitutional Histories and the Political Incorporation of Māori, 1920s,"

in *Raupatu: The Confiscation of Maori Land*, ed. Richard Boast and Richard Hill (Wellington: Victoria University Press, 2009). Also, Richard P. Boast "Recognising Multi-Textualism: Rethinking New Zealand Legal History," *Victoria University of Wellington Law Review*, 37 (2006), 547–82.

22. Hickford, "'Decidedly the Most Interesting Savages,'" p. 166.
23. The cited sources included an unidentified edition of William Blackstone, *Commentaries on the Laws of England*, 1st edn., 4 vols. (Oxford: printed at the Clarendon Press, 1765–1769); Thomas Arnold, *Miscellaneous Works of Thomas Arnold, D.D.*, ed. A.P. Stanley (London: B. Fellowes, 1845); George Cornewall Lewis, *An Essay on the Government of Dependencies* (London: John Murray, 1841).
24. Hadfield to Grey, June 15, 1847, Auckland Public Library [APL], GLNZ H1(2) (emphasis in original).
25. Ibid.
26. Earl Grey to Grey, December 23, 1846, National Archives, London [TNA], CO209/47, fol. 277. The charter was produced under the enabling authority of 9 & 10 Vic. c.103.
27. Hickford, "Making 'Territorial Rights,'" pp. 224–31.
28. April 1, 1846, TNA, CO209/48, fol. 158.
29. Gladstone to Grey, [March 1846], British Library, London [BL], Add Mss44363, fol. 294.
30. In the early part of his appointment as an assistant protector of aborigines, Edward Shortland, referred to "taki" (*sic*) in his journal entry for October 12, 1842 in relation to a dispute in the Tauranga district: APL, NZMs15/3.
31. Alexander McKay, *Appendix to the Journals of the House of Representatives* 1890, G-1, p. 6; Robert Maunsell (October 24, 1810?–1894) was a member of the Church Missionary Society and ordained as a priest in 1834. He arrived in New Zealand on November 26, 1835.
32. McKay, *Appendix*.
33. Shortland to Clarke, March 14, 1844, APL, NZMs998/4.
34. Spain was appointed a Commissioner "for investigating and determining Titles and Claims to Land in Our said Colony" under a warrant dated January 20, 1841 issued in London under the royal prerogative: TNA, CO380/122, fols. 291–295.
35. Hickford, "Making 'Territorial Rights'"; Hickford, "'Decidedly the Most Interesting Savages,'" pp. 164–66.
36. Somes to Stanley, January 24, 1843, TNA, CO209/26, fols. 85–85a. Also [Anon.], "New Zealand," *Fisher's Colonial Magazine and Journal of Trade, Commerce and Banking*, 1 (1844), pp. 204–5.
37. [William Martin], *England and the New Zealanders: Part I. Remarks upon a Despatch from the Right Hon. Earl Grey to Governor Grey dated Dec[ember] 23. 1846* (Auckland: Bishop's Auckland, 1847), p. 51.
38. Angela Ballara, *Taua: "Musket wars," "Land wars" or Tikanga? Warfare in Māori Society in the Early Nineteenth Century* (Auckland: Penguin, 2003), pp. 436–43.
39. Chapman, notes, undated [1845–1846?], ATL, Ms-Papers–860–047.

40. Hadfield to Grey, June 15, 1847, APL, GLNZ H1(2) (emphasis in original).
41. Ibid.
42. Ibid (emphasis in original).
43. Chapman, ATL, Ms-Papers–860–047, p. 15.
44. Ibid., pp. 24–25.
45. Ibid., pp. 15–16.
46. Ibid (emphasis in original).
47. Ibid., pp. 16–17.
48. Ibid., pp. 25.
49. Ibid., pp. 25 (emphasis in original).
50. Ibid., pp. 26.
51. Ibid., pp. 31. On the question of the justiciability of native title at common law: Hickford, "Strands from the Afterlife," pp. 176–77.
52. Chapman, ATL, Ms-Papers–860–047, p. 33.
53. Ibid., pp. 32.
54. Chapman to Chapman senior, June 15, 1847, ATL, qMs-0419, fols. 437–438.
55. Whiteley to George Clarke senior, July 10, 1844, ATL, Ms Papers 4647.
56. *The Colonial Intelligencer or Aborigines' Friend,* 1.10 (1847), 152.
57. Hadfield to Grey, memorandum, 1846, APL, GNZ Mss 17, fols. 73–96.
58. Lyndsay Head, "Land, Authority and the Forgetting of Being in Colonial Māori History" (unpublished doctoral thesis, University of Canterbury, 2006), pp. 191–92.
59. Cf. Duncan Ivison, "The Nature of Rights and the History of Empire," in *British Political Thought in History, Literature and Theory, 1500–1800,* ed. David Armitage (Cambridge: Cambridge University Press, 2006), pp. 191–211 (p. 201).
60. Newcastle to Grey, June 5, 1861, TNA, CO209/156, fol. 244.
61. 15 & 16 Vic. c. 72 (Imp).
62. Martin to Fox, November 16, 1863, TNA, CO209/178, fol. 163.
63. Ibid. I address this issue more fully in Hickford, "Strands from the Afterlife."
64. Section 7, 15 & 16 Vict c. 72.

Index

Note: Individual races of non-European people will be found under their own names e.g. Māori. Reference to non-Europeans generally will be found under Aboriginal People—being the term used by The Colonial Office and various Evangelical movements.